THE LIVES OF THE GREAT COMPOSERS

Volume Two

D0313654

F

Also by Harold C Schonberg

THE GREAT CONDUCTORS
THE GREAT PIANISTS

Harold C Schonberg

The Lives of
The Great Composers

VOLUME TWO

Futura Publications Limited

An Omega Book

First Omega edition published in Great
Britain in 1975 by Futura Publications Limited
Warner Road, London SE5

Publisher's Note

The two volumes of THE LIVES OF THE
GREAT COMPOSERS published by Futura
Publications Ltd were originally one volume
entitled THE LIVES OF THE GREAT
COMPOSERS, published by Davis-Poynter Limited

ISBN 0 8600 7723 3
Printed in Great Britain by
Hazell Watson & Viney Ltd
Aylesbury, Bucks

Futura Publications Limited
Warner Road, London SE5

Again, to Rosalyn

Contents

Preface

I have written this book for the intelligent layman, and have tried to organize it so that the consecutive line from Johann Sebastian Bach to Arnold Schoenberg has been traced. Music is a continually evolving process, and there has been no genius, however great, who has not taken from his predecessors.

Also, in the process of writing this book, I have tried to humanize the great composers, to give an idea of what they felt and thought. This approach is somewhat unfashionable today. Many musical scholars insist that the work rather than the man is the thing; that a piece of music can best be explained *as music*; that thorough harmonic and structural analysis is the only valid "explanation." The rest is sentimental program-note writing and has no real application to the music. I happen to disagree. I firmly believe that music can be explained by the man; indeed, *must* be explained by the man and his times. For a man's music is a function of himself, and is a reflection of his mind and his reaction to the world in which he lives. Just as we see the world through the eyes and mind of a Rembrandt, Cézanne, or Picasso when we look at their paintings, so we experience the world through the ears and mind of a Beethoven, Brahms, or Stravinsky when we hear their music. We are in contact with a mind, and we must attempt an identification with that mind. The closer the identification, the closer it is possible to come to understanding the creator's work. That is why the French pianist Alfred Cortot insisted that his pupils, while studying a piece of music, also read biographies of the composer, his letters, and the letters of his contemporaries. Then the pupil had to relate the piece of music to the composer's entire life and work.

Hence this book is greatly concerned with the biographical aspects of the great composers. There is little on form and analysis. Technical terminology is kept to a minimum, though sometimes it is unavoidable, especially in a discussion of twentieth-century dodecaphonic and serial music. It is easy to make a mystique out of form and analysis; but are not these topics best left to the student and the professional? I have always been amused by books supposedly for the layman which are full of complicated musical examples. Some of those examples—score reductions and the like—Vladimir Horowitz himself would find difficult to play. A reader who is an able enough musician to play them does not need them, while a reader who has trouble following a single line in C major on a G clef—and that includes the majority —cannot use them.

A glance at the Table of Contents will reveal that most of the greatest composers receive a complete chapter devoted to themselves. Other great composers whose contributions to the history of music are better understood when compared with one or more contemporaries are bracketed with them within a single chapter. And, finally, there is a third kind of chapter devoted to an entire period or a specific time and place, offering general material to supplement the succession of biograhical chapters.

I have started with Bach in volume one, not because there were no great composers before Bach, but because Bach is where the active repertoire really begins. The book ends in volume two with the Second Viennese School. It had to cut off *somewhere*, and the trinity of Schoenberg, Berg, and Webern seemed the logical place. A postlude briefly discusses major trends since 1945. This may be a cowardly evasion, but the development of serial, postserial, electronic, stochastic, aleatoric, and mixed-media music is so complicated and so lengthy a subject that it demands a book in itself.

Orthographical problems always arise in books on music. I have followed normal American professional usage in spelling and terminology. Some British writers have accused my previous books of being too "American" in style. Did they think I was Mongolian? American usage, for example, dictates "twelve-tone music" instead of the British "twelve-note," for reasons explained in the chapter on Schoenberg. American usage dictates, to give two examples, *Harold in Italy* yet, inconsistently, *Symphonie fantastique*. Never have I heard the former work referred to as *Harold en Italie,* just as one rarely if ever hears reference to the Berlioz *Fantastic Symphony*. Generally it is just *Fantastique:* "Bernstein conducted the Berlioz *Fantastique* last night."

Russian and other foreign names pose their familiar problems. The "v" endings are used for Prokofiev, Balakirev, and the others. Yet Rachmaninoff is spelled with the double "f" because that is how he himself signed his name, just as Schoenberg insisted on that spelling and not Schönberg. Similarly, Handel rather than Händel. If there are inconsistencies throughout the book, I apologize.

Some of the material in the following pages originally appeared as Sunday articles in my weekly New York *Times* column, and several appeared as

Times magazine pieces. All have been revised and amplified. I wish to thank the New York Times Company for permission to use that material. A substantial portion of the chapter on Charles Ives originally appeared in the December, 1958, issue of *Esquire*, and is reprinted by permission of Esquire Magazine, Inc. I would like to thank my wife for her constant help and encouragement. Eric Schaal was kind enough to supply several rare photographs of composers from his famous collection, and Rosemary Andersen was extremely helpful in gathering others. And Robert E. Farlow, my editor at W. W. Norton, gave the manuscript a stupendously thorough scrutiny, one unparalleled in my fairly wide experience. In more than one respect it is "our" book.

❦ I ❧

Waltz, Polka, and Satire

STRAUSS, OFFENBACH, SULLIVAN

If a measure of a composer's music is its longevity, at least three creators of light music in the nineteenth century have survived time and fashion so triumphantly that they legitimately can be called immortals. The waltz and Viennese operetta of Johann Strauss, Jr., the opéra-bouffe of Jacques Offenbach, and the operetta of Sir Arthur Sullivan remain with us, as charming, pert, and inventive as they ever were. Meyerbeer is all but forgotten; Gounod lives primarily through one opera; such formerly great names as Goldmark, Rubinstein, Heller, and Raff are only names in the history books. But the world continues to be entertained and even enchanted by Strauss, Offenbach, and Sullivan.

The waltz came first. It stemmed from the Ländler, an Austro-German dance in three-quarter time. Between 1770 and 1780 the waltz first appeared. Almost immediately it became the craze of Europe, and not only in Vienna, though that city was its headquarters. Michael Kelly, the Irish tenor who sang in the world premiere of Mozart's *Le Nozze di Figaro,* remarked on the craze when he came to write his memoirs in 1826. "The people of Vienna," he noted, "were in my time [the 1780's] dancing mad; as the Carnival approached, gaiety began to display itself on all sides. . . . The propensity of the Viennese ladies for dancing and going to carnival masquerades was so determined, that nothing was permitted to interfere with their enjoyment of their favorite amusement." Kelly cited a Viennese arrangement to clinch his point. So overwhelming was the craze, he said, that "for the sake of ladies in the family way, who would not be persuaded to stay at home, there were apartments prepared, with every convenience, for their accouchement, should they be unfortunately required." Kelly, a connoisseur, thought the Viennese ladies graceful; but, "for my own part, I thought waltzing from ten at night until seven in the morning, a continual whirligig, most tiresome to the eye and ear."

13

Naturally the waltz became a commodity, and throughout the entire nineteenth century even the greatest composers were not too proud to help supply the demand. There had been a precedent. Haydn and Mozart had written quantities of dance music. Schubert wrote several volumes of waltzes to supply the demand for the new craze. Weber's *Invitation to the Dance* for piano solo (later it was orchestrated by Berlioz) established the concert waltz. Chopin wrote idealized waltzes, not for dancing. Brahms contributed a set for piano and two sets for vocal quartet. Dvořák wrote some pretty waltzes. Richard Strauss's *Der Rosenkavalier* makes much use of the waltz. Ravel wrote a great waltz for orchestra, and a piano set called *Valses nobles et sentimentales*. Debussy composed several waltzes. There even is a waltz in the grim *Wozzeck* of Berg.

There were cries of immorality soon after the waltz appeared. Its first great exponent was Johann Strauss the elder, and Puritan nations knew where to put the blame. "This fiend of German birth, destitute of grace, delicacy, and propriety, a disgusting practice," bellowed an English publication, referring not to the Austrian-born Strauss but to the waltz form itself. But the tide was irreversible. "In every house, on every piano in Vienna," wrote a French journalist in 1852, "lie Strauss waltzes." This time the reference is to the younger Strauss. "He has written over 200, all are favorites, all are sung and trilled, and played throughout Europe. Plebeian and aristocrat hum and pipe them; orchestra and barrel organ play them. We hear them on the street, at the ball, in the garden, and at the theater. The dancing Viennese carry him in triumph on their shoulders and shout 'Strauss forever!' The rest of Europe re-echoes the sound and cries 'Strauss forever!' "

But there was more to the waltz than entertainment, and the better musicians were tremendously impressed with what the elder Strauss was doing. Berlioz visited Vienna in 1845 and had a good deal to say about the technical innovations brought in by the waltz and other dance music. In his *Memoirs* he devoted a long paragraph to the subject:

The Redoutensaal takes its name from the great balls frequently held in the hall during the winter season. There the youth of Vienna gives rein to its passion for dancing. . . . I spent whole nights watching these incomparable waltzers whirling around in great clouds, and in admiring the choreographic precision of the quadrilles—two hundred people at a time, drawn up in two long lines—and the vivid character dances, which for originality and polished execution I have not seen surpassed anywhere except in Hungary. And there stands Strauss directing his splendid orchestra; and sometimes, when one of the new waltzes he writes for every society ball makes a special hit, the dancers stop to applaud and the ladies go over to his rostrum and throw him their bouquets, and they all shout "bis" and make him come back at the end of the quadrille (since dancing feels no jealousy and allows music its share in the triumph and the fun). This is no more than justice; for Strauss is an artist. It is not sufficiently recognized what an influence he has already had on the musical taste of Europe as a whole by introducing cross-rhythms into the waltz. (Their effect on the dancers themselves has been so stimulating that they have devised the two-step waltz in an attempt to imitate it, though the music keeps the triple rhythm.) If the public outside Germany is ever brought to appreciate the extraordinary charm that can on occasion result from combined and constrasting rhythms, it will be owing to him. Beethoven's marvels in this line are too exalted to have affected more than a small minority of listeners. Strauss, on the other hand, deliberately appeals to a popular audience; and by copying him, his numerous imitators are perforce helping to spread his influence.

Even Henry Fothergill Chorley, that ponderous Tory, that Colonel Blimp of music criticism, grudgingly admitted that there was some value in the music. He heard the Strauss orchestra in 1844 and decided that the waltz, as conducted by the Viennese master, contained "a truth for all musicians to ponder." Never had Chorley heard such variety and subtlety of orchestral playing. And never had he heard a type of music that lent itself to such niceties of interpretation. "The manner in which silences, breathing-spaces and like piquancies, can throw life into a movement, without its becoming fragmentary, might be studied advantageously by the symphonic composer." Chorley was referring to the orchestra of the senior Strauss, and he had a cogent point. Orchestral playing as it is understood today was still in its infancy in the early 1840's. At that date the phenomenon of the autocratic conductor, the father-figure who by the force of his personality bends the wills of individual musicians into an integrated whole, was just coming on the scene. Previously there had been divided leadership, in which the first violinist and the musician at the clavier shared the conducting responsibilities. Early conductors like Weber, Spohr, Spontini, Mendelssohn, Wagner, Berlioz, and François Habeneck (who had founded the Concerts du Conservatoire in 1828) had started to break the system of divided leadership, but even as late as the 1840's most orchestras in Europe were hit-and-miss affairs that gave relatively few concerts a season. The best orchestra in France during the 1840's, the Conservatoire orchestra, could be heard only six times a year. In all of Europe there might have been a half-dozen orchestras that were well drilled. The others exhibited a kind of discipline, intonation, ensemble, and interpretation of an order that would not be tolerated today. The 1850's were to see the growth and development of the symphony orchestra into powerful and efficient groups; but in the 1840's, it is safe to say, the dance orchestras of Paris and Vienna supplied a kind of virtuosity that was unique at the time. Men like the two Strausses in Vienna and Napoléon

Musard in Paris took a carefully selected group of players, trained them, and set them to work night after night. No wonder they were superior to symphony orchestras. In addition, they were conducted by despots who would stand for no nonsense. Adam Carse, the British student of orchestral life and manners in the early years of the nineteenth century, has pointed out that Musard and the elder Strauss were the first modern conductors in the sense that when Habeneck or Mendelssohn conducted an orchestra, the audience would come to hear the music; but when Musard or Strauss conducted, the audience would come to hear and see *them*.

Johann Strauss, Sr., was born in Vienna on March 14, 1804. He took up the violin as a child, and at the age of fifteen he was a professional, playing in various orchestras. In 1826 Strauss and one of his friends, the violinist Josef Lanner, formed a small group. It was a success, and soon the orchestra numbered twelve players. Strauss did the conducting, leading (as was customary in the day) with the bow. Lanner did the composing. Josef Lanner (1801–1843) was an unusually skillful composer, and some of his music, especially the *Hofballtänze*, with its insinuating melodies, its grace and, in one episode, sudden bursts of febrile energy (anticipating in a way the restlessness of Ravel's *La Valse*), is on a par with any work later composed by any of the Strausses. Stravinsky did Lanner the honor of inserting one of his waltzes into *Petrushka*. In the early 1820's, Strauss too felt the urge to compose, and that was where trouble developed between him and Lanner. The gossip in Vienna was that Lanner appropriated some Strauss music, introducing it under his own name. The two men actually came to blows at a concert in the *Zum Bock* ballroom. Strauss went off and formed his own orchestra, taking with him some of his best men, while Lanner celebrated the event with a waltz that he entitled *Trennung* ("separation"). Now Vienna had two fine dance orchestras, and sides were taken. As Eduard Hanslick wrote:

> One cannot imagine the wild enthusiasm which the two created. . . . Over each new waltz the journals used to fly into raptures. There appeared innumerable articles about Lanner and Strauss, enthusiastic, frivolous and serious ones, and longer, to be sure, than those devoted to Beethoven and Mozart. That the sweetly intoxicating three-four rhythm, which took hold of hand and foot, necessarily eclipsed great and serious music, and made the audience unfit for any intellectual effort, goes without saying.

Lanner's kind of music differed from Strauss's. It was more lyric, while Strauss's had fire, temperament, and showmanship. The Viennese had a saying: "With Lanner, it's 'Pray, dance, I beg you.' With Strauss, it's 'You must dance, I command you.'" Strauss never forgot that he was composing dance music, even when he expanded the form into the concert waltz. He also made the Viennese waltz a big business. Lanner's competition spurred him on. Much to Strauss's disgust, it was Lanner who in 1829 received the commission to supply music for the Redoutensaal. Strauss, however, came up with a contract for something almost as important, the Sperlsaal. Soon he was employing some 200 musicians, and he was able to supply music for as many as six balls a night. He composed steadily, producing such lovely and still-popular pieces as the *Donaulieder* and the *Radetzky* March. It was not only waltzes that the Viennese demanded. They also expected galops, polkas, quadrilles, and marches. Strauss gave them what they wanted.

Everybody in Vienna visited the Sperl, the large beer garden and dance hall where Strauss mostly held forth. The writer Heinrich Laube observed the scene and has left a picturesque pen portrait of Strauss in action:

Under the illuminated trees and in open arcades people are seated at innumerable tables, eating and drinking, chatting, laughing and listening. In their midst is the orchestra, from which come the new waltzes, the bugbear of our learned musicians, the new waltzes that stir the blood like the bite of a tarantula. In the middle of the garden on the orchestral platform there stands the modern hero of Austria, the Austrian Napoleon, the musical director Johann Strauss. The man looks as black as a Moor; his hair is curly, his mouth energetic, his lips sneer, he has a snub nose. If his face were not so white he would be the veritable King of the Moors. . . . Typically African, too, is the way he conducts his dances. His own limbs no longer belong to him when the desert-storm of his waltz is let loose. His fiddle-bow dances with his arms; the tempo animates his feet . . . and the Viennese accept this passionate behaviour with unparalleled enthusiasm. . . . And now begin the preparations for the real dancing. To keep the unruly crowds back, a long rope is put up, and all who remain in the center of the hall are separated from the actual dancers. . . These orgies last until the early morning; and then Austria's musical hero packs up his violin and goes home to sleep a few hours and dream of new battle stratagems and waltz themes for the next afternoon.

In the middle 1830's Strauss took his orchestra on tour: Hungary and Germany in 1834; Paris in 1837 and 1838, where he shared programs with Musard; London in 1838. Everywhere it was the same story. Strauss conquered. Everybody loved his music; everybody was awed by the brilliance, finish, precision, and power of his orchestra. Musicians were fascinated with Strauss's rhythmic subtlety, and Berlioz wrote a long article about Strauss and rhythm in the *Journal des Débats*. The schedule of the Strauss orchestra was killing. In France, Strauss and his men gave eighty-six concerts in ninety-one days. In England, seventy-two in a hundred and twenty. Strauss worked himself to collapse and dragged himself back to Vienna more dead than alive.

He had a home life, of sorts. His wife, Anna Streim, bore him a large family—Johann II (born on October 25, 1825), Josef, Nelli, Therese, Ferdinand, and Eduard. He was as despotic a parent as he was a conductor. The only things he lived for were his orchestra and to make money. He was not very much interested in his wife and family. But on one thing he was firm. He did not want any of his children to become a professional musician. Johann, Jr., his eldest son, was talented, but such was his father's antipathy to the life of a professional musician for any of his children that he had to take lessons on the sly. Then something happened that made it easier for young Johann's training, however hard it may have been on his mother. The elder Strauss moved out and took up with another woman, who bore him four children. It was a great scandal in Vienna. Strauss died on September 25, 1849, but not before he had seen his son established in his footsteps. There was nothing he could do about it. Though he raged and raved, in the end he had to give his grudging consent.

Johann II was nineteen years old when he decided to compete against his father. Vienna was agog. There were few secrets in the city, and everybody knew about the tensions in the Strauss household. Johann II got an engagement at Dommayer's Garden Restaurant and at his first concert tactfully ended the evening with his father's *Lorelei-Rheinklängen*. The debut was a complete success. "Good night, Lanner. Good evening, Father Strauss. Good morning, Son Strauss." So ran a review in a Viennese paper. Johann II and his father became reconciled, and when the older man died, Johann II took over his father's orchestra and combined it with his own. He eventually had six orchestras, running from one to the other every night, making a short appearance at each. Business was business. Strauss had to employ a full crew —musicians for the six orchestras, assistant conductors, a librarian, copyists, publicists, booking agents. Like his father, he took his best orchestra on tour and captivated Europe.

Soon he was in a position to stop his nightly jaunts. He concentrated on composing, leaving the conducting to his brother Eduard except for special occasions. The 1860's saw the beginning of his great series of concert waltzes, marches, and polkas—a series that was to include *Acceleration, Perpetuum mobile, Morning Papers, Tales from the Vienna Woods, Voices of Spring, Vienna Blood, Emperor, Artist's Life*. And, of course, *On The Beautiful Blue Danube*. These are more than dance music. With their elaborate introductions and codas, their melodic inspiration, their delicately adjusted orchestration, their fine and subtle rhythm, they are authentic contributions to the great musical repertory. Small wonder that Brahms autographed Frau Strauss's fan with the opening measures of the *Blue Danube* and signed them: "Alas, not by Johannes Brahms." It also was Brahms who said: "*There* is a master of the orchestra, so great a master that one never fails to hear a single note of any instrument."

In addition to the orchestral music there were the operettas. In 1871 came *Indigo, or The Forty Thieves* (eventually this was reworked as *1001 Nights*). In all, Strauss composed seventeen stage works, of which only two represent him at anywhere near his consistent best. Those were *Die Fledermaus* and *Der Zigeunerbaron*. Most of the others—*Der lustige Krieg, Eine Nacht in Venedig, Cagliostro in Wien, Waldmeister*—have impossible librettos. The music itself may be wonderful (sections of *Waldmeister*, indeed, are ravishing) but the books do not make sense even by the loose standards of operetta. Strauss never worried about librettos. He composed *Eine Nacht in Venedig* without knowing the plot, and was terribly unhappy when he finally got around to reading it. "I never saw the dialogue but only the words of the songs. Consequently I put too much nobility into some parts of it that did not suit the work as a whole. . . . At the final rehearsal, when I learned the complete story in its correct sequence, I was horrified." That was typical of Strauss's happy-go-lucky way of operetta composing. But *Fledermaus*, at least, is a work of genius; and in the second act of *Zigeunerbaron*, where the lovers join voices in *"Und mild sang die Nachtigall, ihr Liedchen in die Nacht: die Liebe, die Liebe, ist eine Himmels Macht,"* it is the essence of nostalgia, of Viennese love and life.

Strauss visited America in 1872, when he was invited to participate in Patrick Sarsfield Gilmore's Peace Jubilee in Boston. Gilmore was a bandmaster who thought big, and he sponsored colossal festivals in Philadelphia and Boston. In line with the size of those undertakings, Gilmore promised Strauss an equally colossal fee—$100,000 for fourteen performances—to conduct his *Blue Danube*. Strauss arrived in New York and newspapermen descended upon him. "Johann Strauss," reported the *World*, "the waltz king, personally, is evidently a good fellow. He talks only German, but he smiles in all languages." Strauss continued on to Boston, went to the great coliseum where the jubilee was being held, and was told what was expected of him while conducting an orchestra of 1,087 musicians. Then he *knew* Americans were crazy. When he returned home he wrote about his experience:

On the musicians' tribune there were 20,000 singers, in front of them the members of the orchestra—and these were the people I was to conduct! Twenty assistant conductors had been placed at my disposal to control those gigantic masses, but I was only able to recognize those nearest to me, and although we had had rehearsals, there was no possibility of giving an artistic performance. . . .

Now, just conceive of my position, face to face with a public of 100,000

Americans. There I stood at the raised desk, high above all others. How would the business start, how would it end? Suddenly a cannon shot rang out, a gentle hint for us 20,000-odd to begin playing the *Blue Danube*. I gave the signal, my twenty assistant conductors followed as quickly and as well as they could, and there broke out an unholy racket such as I shall never forget. As we had begun more or less together, I concentrated on seeing that we should finish together, too. Thank heaven, I managed it! . . .

Strauss collected his $100,000, then made a short tour, doubled his money, and returned to Vienna. By this time, what with his income from Europe, he was a millionaire. Back in Vienna, he continued his series of operettas. He also wanted very much to compose a serious opera, but he never succeeded. On June 4, 1899, he died, the composer of nearly 500 works, as assured of immortality as Beethoven and Brahms. His music has received universal praise—praise from the most naïve and innocent music lover, praise from the most sophisticated of musicians. Strauss's music seems to be beyond criticism, and Richard Strauss's appreciation is typical:

Of all the God-gifted dispensers of joy, Johann Strauss is to me the most endearing. This first, comprehensive statement can serve as a text for everything I feel about this wonderful phenomenon. In particular I respect in Johann Strauss his originality, his innate gift. At a time when the whole world around him was tending towards increased complexity, increased reflectiveness, his natural genius enabled him to create from the *whole*. He seemed to me the last of those who worked from spontaneous inspiration. Yes, the primary, the original, the proto-melody—that's it.

Also I saw him and talked with him in Munich at the *Vier Jahreszeiten*. But I really got to know and love the whole realm of his wisdom in Meiningen, through Hans von Bülow, who had a beautifully-bound copy of all [?] the Strauss waltzes. Once he played them for me an entire evening. For me alone! An unforgettable evening of waltzes. I also willingly admit to having sometimes conducted the *Perpetuum mobile* with far more pleasure than many a four-movement symphony. As for the *Rosenkavalier* waltzes . . . how could I have composed those without thinking of the laughing genius of Vienna?

Where Strauss's music was an evocative bow at almost a fairy-tale Vienna, a Vienna of young hussars and beautiful ladies, a Vienna of sentimentality and charm, a pretty-pretty and never-never Vienna of dance and romance, the music of Jacques Offenbach was much more realistic. It was music of social satire. Strauss was gentle and nostalgic. Offenbach snapped.

Like Strauss, Offenbach came in at the right time. Just as the waltz and carnival were the rage of Vienna, so the polka and the cancan were the rage of Paris. The cancan had probably been introduced by soldiers from Algeria and, as with the waltz, there was a great to-do about its immorality. Ludwig Rellstab, the German counterpart of Chorley, was appalled when he visited Paris and saw the cancan danced at carnival time: "When one sees with what gestures and movements of the body the masked men approach the masked women, press close to them and actually throw them backwards and forwards between themselves to the accompaniment of continued acclamation, laughter and ribald jokes, one can only be filled with disgust—nay, with horror and revulsion at this mass depravity." Napoléon Musard was the hero of polka, quadrille, and cancan. He was an untidy, homely little man, invariably dressed in black, whose promenade concerts were the hit of Paris. Musard while conducting would enliven the proceedings by firing pistols, smashing chairs, and throwing his violin in the air. Berlioz, in 1835, was bemused: "At present we sit dumb over the triumph of Musard who, puffed up by the success of his dancing-den concerts, looks upon himself as a superior Mozart. Mozart never composed anything like the *Pistol Shot Quadrille,* consequently Mozart died of want."

Jacques Offenbach, born Jakob Eberst in Cologne on June 20, 1819, was playing the violin at six, composing at eight, playing the cello at nine. His father, a Jewish cantor and amateur violinist, took him to the Paris Conservatory in 1833, but the boy did not stay long. A year later he left, to play in various orchestras and live a Bohemian life. Even in the reign of the Citizen King who carried an umbrella, and even under the bourgeois rule of the bankers, there was a Bohemian life. The boulevardiers had their own morality, their own set of rules, and Offenbach to the end was a citizen of the boulevards rather than a citizen of Paris. He was at home among the eccentrics and nonconformists, and there was something eccentric about him, too. He was nearsighted (blind without his glasses), skinny, with an enormous nose, and long, wavy hair. He looked like an intelligent scarecrow with the head of a parrot.

As a composer, Offenbach got nowhere at first. He knew he had a flair for the theater, but the Opéra-Comique was not interested. Not until Louis-Napoléon and the Second Empire did Offenbach get started. Despairing of the Opéra-Comique ever staging one of his works, he decided to strike off on his own. "It occurred to me," he wrote in his autobiography, "that comic opera was no longer found at the Opéra-Comique; that really funny, gay, witty music was gradually being forgotten, and that what was being written for the Opéra-Comique was really small-scale grand opera." And, "It was then that I got the idea of starting a musical theater myself, because of the continued impossibility of getting my work produced by anybody else."

Therefore on July 5, 1855, Offenbach opened the Bouffes-Parisiens. The opening program consisted of a pantomime on Rossini themes, and two

21

works composed by himself—a sentimental idyll named *La Nuit Blanche* and a farce, *Les Deux Aveugles*. It was more than a success. It was a sensation, and all Paris tried to crowd itself into the tiny theater on the Champs-Elysées. Within a few months Offenbach had to move to another theater, and this also turned out to be far too small. It was described by the New York *Tribune* in 1863:

There gapes a little cavernous opening which, though dim by day, by night is lighted with superior gas and brilliant promise of good cheer. Over the narrow entrance a modest inscription stands to notify the passers-by that the theater of the Bouffes-Parisiens is within. . . . It is the David of opera houses and, in an indirect way, scatters worse wounds among the Goliaths, its big rivals, than they would care to acknowledge.

The Bouffes-Parisiens is so little as to be almost a joke. You laugh, when you get inside it, at its tiny proportions. Two great muscular jumps would almost clear the stage from wing to wing, and a gentleman in the orchestra stalls might converse in a whisper with his friends in the gallery. There is, in fact, hardly room enough to swing a cat in. People do not, however, go to the Bouffes for the purpose of swinging cats. They go to listen to the brightest and newest music, to witness the best acting, of its order, that the French stage affords. And they are never disappointed. Absolutely never.

Offenbach was joined by two significant figures—Ludovic Halévy, the nephew of the famous composer of *La Juive* and later one of the librettists of *Carmen*, and Hortense Schneider, the singing actress. Schneider was the sex symbol of her day. Buxom, full of personality and *joie de vivre*, she lived as tempestuous a life as any she ever acted on stage. Generous with everything, she gave herself with abandon to a long series of lovers. Generally her lovers were millionaires. Schneider's enthusiasms were always tempered with a good bourgeois sense of the value of money.

Offenbach worked on two levels. He was a skillful composer with a knack for creating lively melodies. But more: he had a streak in him that satirized and parodied everything within sight: Meyerbeer and Wagner, the court, the Emperor himself, the army and politicians, the entire Establishment. So skillfully and wittily were Offenbach's satires put together that Napoléon III himself would laugh when he attended the Bouffes-Parisiens. Offenbach's most popular work, *Orphée aux Enfers* ("Orpheus in the Underworld"), is nominally a satire on the gods and goddesses of Olympus. In reality it is an attack on the French social system. *Orphée* had its premiere on October 21, 1858, and it was moderately successful until Jules Janin attacked it in the *Journal des Débats*. That started a controversy, and everybody rushed to the Bouffes-Parisiens to see for himself. There was a chance for all to attend, for the operetta ran for 228 straight performances. Rossini attended and put the seal of approval on Offenbach. He called him the Mozart of the Champs-Elysées. But one loud dissenting voice was heard. Wagner hated the Bouffes-Parisiens and everything it represented. Offenbach's music, he wrote with his characteristic delicacy, was "a dung heap on which all the swine of Europe wallowed."

Orphée aux Enfers was followed, among other operettas, by *La Belle Hélène* in 1864. It was another satire on the Greek gods and contemporary French life. Then came *Barbe-Bleue* in 1866, *La Vie Parisienne* also in 1866, *La Grande-Duchesse de Gérolstein* in 1867, and *La Périchole* in 1868. The *Grande-Duchesse* was a satire on the military, and ranked with *Orphée* in popularity. For some reason it rubbed the conservatives the wrong way. This was especially true of listeners who had Calvinism and Puritanism in their blood. The conservatives in England and the United States loved Strauss and doted on the Gilbert and Sullivan operettas; but Offenbach made them cough, stutter, and turn red in the face. There was an ever-present suggestion of naughtiness in the Offenbach comic operas. They were not "clean." When the *Grande-Duchesse* was performed in the United States, John S. Dwight of Boston all but got sick. As a moral exhibition, he wrote, the operetta was "the lowest we have ever seen upon the stage. . . . In very shame for the good name of our city that it should even *seem* to forget itself about a thing so shallow, so ambiguous. . . ." All the critical balloons inflated themselves and rose from the ground in wrath. "Offenbach," cried the Philadelpha *Evening Bulletin,* "might be forgiven for his want of genius, but his pruriency is inexcusable. . . . He is the purveyor of bald, bad indecency." Chorley in England was no less shocked, and ended his report on the *Duchesse* in the London *Athenaeum* with: "The vulgarity of some of the words passes all description."

No matter. Offenbach's popularity went up and up, in England and America as well as in France. In 1872 Paris saw three simultaneous Offenbach productions—*Fantasio, La Boule de Neige,* and *Le Corsaire Noir.* Meyerbeer was still dominating the grand opera stage, Offenbach was the king of light opera, and the violently anti-Semitic Vincent d'Indy sneeringly referred to the stranglehold of those two composers as "L'école judaïque." Offenbach was collaborating with the famous playwright Victorien Sardou at the time, and the Paris correspondent of the Augsburg *Allgemeine Zeitung* called the Offenbach-Sardou combination "the Egyptian plague of the last decade." But the plague, if that is what it was, did not last long after that. Offenbach's popularity had virtually run its course by 1873. His German birth had not made him welcome in Paris during the Franco-Prussian war, even though Offenbach considered himself French: "I hope that this William Krupp and his dreadful Bismarck will pay for all this. Alas! What terrible people these Prussians are, and what despair do I feel that I myself was born on the Rhine and am connected by many links to these savages! Alas! My poor France! How much do I thank her for accepting me among her children!" In addition, the public was beginning to tire of the Offenbach operettas and was looking for something new. Something new did turn up in 1873, with Charles Lecocq's *La Fille de Mme. Angot*. Then came Robert Planquette with his *Les Cloches de Corneville;* and, finally, André Messager, with a series of charming light works that could well stand revival today, especially *Véronique* and *Monsieur Beaucaire*. The French had had enough of social satire, and turned to the romantic escapist operetta of Lecocq and Planquette.

Desperately Offenbach tried to hold his own. He took over the Théâtre de la Gaîté and started a series of spectacle productions. Soon he was bankrupt. He summoned his company: "You shall be paid to the last sou, my children. If I have been careless, I shall at least remain honorable." To add to his troubles, Johann Strauss came to Paris and conquered the city with *Die Fledermaus*. Poor Offenbach found himself an anachronism. And so, like Strauss, he went to America where, as every good European knew, one could pick up vast sums of money in any convenient horse trough. Maurice Grau, the impresario, cabled him an offer of $1,000 a night for a minimum of thirty nights. Offenbach was happy to accept. On his arrival in New York he was greeted with an editorial in the New York *Times* of May 8, 1876:

> On Friday last, Europe, to the extent of one person of Hebraic origin but of rather vague nationality, arrived in this City with a view to attending the Centennial celebration [in Boston]. A proud and grateful country seized the opportunity to show how it can welcome a distinguished foreign guest. Two rival clubs sent committees to welcome the steamer which conveyed him to our shores, and it is not yet known which club first succeeded in offering him a complimentary dinner. Reporters swarmed around him before he had yet landed, and one of them, connected with a Tammany evening paper, was actually presented with one of the great man's private cigars, and testified with much feeling that "mortal man never smoked their superior in quality."

The editorial called Offenbach the creator of our "fleshly school of music," and then let its Puritanism peep through. It commented that while *Geneviève de Brabant* (an Offenbach operetta) was "not without musical merit," its melodies "appear to have been written for a Phallic festival. . . . The opéra-bouffe is simply the sexual instinct expressed in melody." Then the *Times* took a stern—one is tempted to say stiff—stand: "What a shame! Such a reception is an insult to every great and honorable artist. . . . Priapism is not on a level with music."

24

Offenbach's first concert, at Gilmore's Garden, turned out to be the greatest event since Jenny Lind had toured under Barnum's auspices in the early 1850's. Speculators were getting as high as $25 for a pair of tickets. It seems that everybody was convinced that the composer would dance the cancan while conducting the score of *Orphée*. This everybody had to see. Offenbach, of course, merely came out and conducted, and there was a general feeling of letdown. About a third of the audience, some disappointed and others insulted, left before the concert was over. Obviously Grau's press agents had promised a great deal more than Offenbach was prepared to deliver. Subsequent concerts were financial losses, and the only events that showed a profit were several staged performances of *La Jolie Parfumeuse*. Offenbach was not happy about his reception, but, then again, some critics were not happy about his appearances in the United States. The *Music Trade Review* of May 18, 1876, prefaced a long article with: "We don't mean, and we do not wish to be, uncourteous to a foreign guest, but we would ask Mr. Offenbach himself: Has he ever made five dollars in Europe as a conductor? What is there in his appearing as a *chef d'orchestre* that should so much interest the American public as to justify the hope that they would flock with eagerness to see him, and pay one dollar admission to a concert which offers nothing worth paying that dollar?" The article continued with an attack on the programs, on the music itself ("He is the outgrowth of the governing demi-monde epoch of the Second Empire, the froth of tisane, neither healthy nor nourishing"), and on the orchestra. Offenbach naturally resented these attacks and could not wait to get home. Back in Paris he announced, all but kissing the street, "I am Offenbach again." He promptly wrote a small and, under the circumstances, thoughtful book about his experiences in America. Among his observations was one about American womanhood. Womanhood was a subject upon which Offenbach could pronounce with decided authority, and he gave the American girls a high rating: "Out of every hundred you meet, ninety are lovely."

The last years of his life were spent in a race against death. He desperately wanted to finish his one opera, *Les Contes d'Hoffmann*, which he had started in 1877. The libretto was written by Barbier and Carré after their play, which Offenbach immensely admired, and was based on stories by E. T. A. Hoffman. Perhaps he identified with the hero, or, one might better say, anti-hero. He spent much more time on *Hoffmann* than on any of his operettas, and he pleaded with Carvalho, director of the Opéra-Comique, to hurry the production. "I have not much time left, and my only wish is to see the first night." But he never lived to see his remarkable opera on stage. He died on October 5, 1880, leaving some of the score unfinished. The recitatives and part of the scoring were finished by Ernest Guiraud, and the premiere took place on February 10, 1881. It would have been Offenbach's

102nd work for the stage. Of all the European critics, Eduard Hanslick struck the correct note in his obituary notice: "Much as he wrote, Offenbach was always original. We recognize his music as Offenbach-ish after only two or three bars, and this fact alone raises him high above his French and German imitators, whose buffo operas would shrivel up miserably were we to confiscate all that is Offenbach-ish in them. He created a new style in which he reigned absolutely alone." Nietzsche, who concurred with Hanslick about Offenbach's talent, actually set him up against—of all composers—Wagner. In *The Will to Power,* Nietzsche, who was at the height of his anti-Wagner frenzy, wrote that "If by artistic genius we understand the most consummate freedom within the law, divine ease and facility in overcoming the greatest difficulties, then Offenbach has more right to the title of genius than Wagner." (That is what happens to people, even great philosophers, when emotion conquers reason.)

Offenbach's music, despite the ethnic background of the man, is as French as Strauss's is Viennese. It is clean, uncluttered, unsentimental, pointed, classic. If it reflects the frivolity of the age, it does so with extreme wit and sophistication. No music has ever lived unless it has originality, and Offenbach, who could be hasty and formula-ridden, could also rise to moments of great melodic invention. As Hanslick said, he was different from all other composers. *The Tales of Hoffmann,* his most famous work today, is exceptional in his output. Its breadth alone would make it so; and it also has a curiously appealing libretto based on the figure of a loser—a poet who cannot win happiness in life or love. There is a strange air of finality about *Hoffmann,* even considering such extroverted excerpts as Olympia's coloratura aria and the Barcarolle. In this opera, man, no matter how hard he tries, is not the master of his fate. Through *Hoffmann* looms the sinister figure of a force of destiny named, variously, Lindorf, Coppélius, Dappertutto, and Dr. Miracle. Against this force Hoffmann is lost. He is continuously skewered by this evil genius; he is a fish continually and compulsively biting at the same baited hook, always with the same dreadful results. Offenbach's music rises to eloquence in the last act; and the final scene, with Hoffmann drunk and helpless while Lindorf steals away to repeat once more the never-ending sequence, leaves a bitter taste in the mouth.

In England the team of Sir Arthur Seymour Sullivan and Sir William Schwenck Gilbert instituted a tradition comparable to those started in Vienna by Strauss and in Paris by Offenbach. The Gilbert and Sullivan operettas are much closer to Offenbach than to Strauss, in that they are often topical and satirical. But as musicians, Sullivan and Offenbach had little in common. Sullivan was a well-trained composer of the Mendelssohn school who by rights should have composed only stuffy oratorios, respectable operas, and strict sonata-form symphonies. Everybody expected him to do so;

and, as a matter of fact, his works do include a symphony, quantities of stuffy and conventional church music ("Onward Christian Soldiers" is his), and a long-forgotten grand opera, *Ivanhoe*. Great things were expected of Sullivan. He was the fairhaired boy of British music, and he did have great talent. The London *Times* in 1866 referred to the young Sullivan as a musician "who, if we are to expect anything lasting from the rising generation of national composers, is the one from whom we may most reasonably and on the fairest grounds expect it."

Born in London on May 13, 1842, Sullivan won the first Mendelssohn Scholarship at the Royal Academy of Music in 1856 and studied for two years at Leipzig. He composed, in addition to the D minor Symphony, two oratorios, much incidental music to plays, and a large number of successful ballads (one of them is *The Lost Chord*). But it was the operettas he composed with Gilbert that brought in the money, and to the Victorians there was something sinful about a composer getting rich with such material. Everybody, from Queen Victoria herself down, assured Sullivan that he was wasting his time composing operettas. After a while Sullivan came to believe it. But he had expensive tastes. He gambled at Monte Carlo, raced two thoroughbreds (Cranmer and Blue Mark), kept a mistress or two, liked to move with royalty and rich people. All that took money, and operetta was an easy way of making money. So Sullivan turned out operettas and went to his grave on November 22, 1900, with guilt feelings. He thought that he had prostituted his art.

His partner, W. S. Gilbert, had no such feelings. Gilbert was a prolific creator who wrote seventy-one works for the stage, of which sixty-nine were produced. There was also prose and poetry. Eighty-one of Gilbert's published verses were collected into the *Bab Ballads*, illustrated with amusing and completely professional pen drawings by the author (some of the *Bab Ballads* were developed into librettos for the Savoy operas). In his early years, Gilbert worked for the Civil Service. Then he was admitted to the bar. Finally he found his true vocation, as humorist and satirist. He became a contributor to the magazine *Fun*, and by 1866 was writing successful farces and plays. From 1871 to 1880 he wrote thirty-three stage works and had thirty-two of them produced. Among the works in that prolific period were four operettas to music by Sullivan.

The fame of Gilbert and Sullivan primarily rests on their collaboration. It is true that each could function without the other, and each did achieve success on his own. But hardly any of their individual efforts have lived, while nearly everything they wrote as a team is as popular as ever. Never in the history of music has there been such a symbiotic relationship. And that even though the two men did not even particularly like each other. Gilbert, a touchy and irascible man, quarreled mightily with Sullivan toward the end; and their relationship, which had started in 1871, broke off with the unsuccessful *The Grand Duke* in 1896. Later Gilbert realized what the rupture had meant. "A Gilbert is no good without a Sullivan, and I can't find one," he wrote in 1903, three years after his partner's death. Sir William lived until 1911, when he died on March 29, trying to save a young lady from drowning.

The producing end of the Gilbert and Sullivan team was Richard D'Oyly Carte, a composer of songs and operettas who became a manager and then an impresario. A genius for publicity, and a man with an instinct for success, he had brought Gilbert and Sullivan together for their first successful collaboration, *Trial by Jury*, in 1875. Previously the two men had been thrown together in an operetta named *Thespis*, an Offenbachian work about the gods growing old. It had run for a month and then was forgotten. Nor was the score ever published. In 1875, D'Oyly Carte, then manager of the Royalty Theater, suggested to Gilbert that he write a one-act trifle to act as a curtain-raiser for Offenbach's *La Périchole*. D'Oyly Carte also suggested Sullivan as the composer. Gilbert quickly worked up a script and visited Sullivan. "He read it through," Sullivan recalled, "as it seemed to me, in a perturbed sort of way, with a gradual crescendo of indignation, in the manner of a man considerably disappointed with what he had written. As soon as he had come to the last word he closed up the manuscript violently, apparently unconscious of the fact that he had achieved his purpose as far as I was concerned, inasmuch as I was screaming with laughter the whole time." *Trial by Jury* was such an immediate hit that D'Oyle Carte moved fast. He secured the services of Gilbert and Sullivan, formed a Comedy Opera Company to stage their works, and presented *The Sorcerer* in 1877. The series was launched, the world kept laughing at the operettas, and the three principals became very rich men.

The Sorcerer ran for 175 performances, but that was nothing against the run of *H.M.S. Pinafore* in 1878, which had a run of 700 consecutive performances. The English-speaking world went mad. In the United States *Pinafore* was enthusiastically pirated and produced everywhere. Remarked *Dwight's Journal of Music:* "Hundreds of companies, professional and amateur, have been acting and singing it. In the great cities, *Pinafore* has held the stage in half a dozen theaters at once. . . . It has been served up in every theater and hall; church choirs go around the country singing it; every child sings and hums it; the tuneful images repeat themselves as in a multiplying mirror, from every wall, through every street and valley." In Chicago, eleven companies staged *Pinafore* in 1879, some of them simultaneously. There were Negro performances of *Pinafore* and, for the German-speaking population in America, *Pinafore* in German. (After World War II there was, briefly, a Yiddish *Pinafore*, staged by a Hadassah group in Brook-

28

lyn.) Some hundred-thousand barrel organs were built to play *Pinafore* selections. As a result, Gilbert and Sullivan themselves came to America to share the wealth. They staged an "authentic" *Pinafore* at the Fifth Avenue Theater in New York. On their return to England they saw to it that their next production, *The Pirates of Penzance*, would have simultaneous openings in London and New York. The London premiere of *Pirates* took place in 1879 at the Savoy Theater, newly built by D'Oyly Carte for the Gilbert and Sullivan operettas. Hence the terms "Savoy Opera" and "Savoyard."

After *The Pirates of Penzance* there followed *Patience* (1881), *Iolanthe* (1882), *Princess Ida* (1884), *The Mikado* (1885), *Ruddigore* (1887), *The Yeomen of the Guard* (1888), *The Gondoliers* (1889), *Utopia Limited* (1893), and *The Grand Duke* (1896).

These operettas are regarded by some as Victorian, in the pejorative sense. In some respects they are. But they are redeemed by a gentle sense of satire and a keen sense of the ridiculous. As Establishment figures, Gilbert and Sullivan were not interested in social reform; there is in their work none of the fierce indignation that so animated writers like Dickens. But the Gilbert and Sullivan operettas are never conventionally moralistic, and they poke fun at some cherished notions of the Victorians. England during Victoria's day was a class-conscious nation, and seldom did anybody ever cross over. "He knows his place" was an approving remark, and there was a famous hymn of the day:

> The rich man in his castle,
> The poor man at his gate,
> God made them high and lowly,
> And ordered their estate.

But *Pinafore* joked with this code of values. Captain's daughters did not, in real life, fall in love with simple sailors. They only did so in sentimental novels. Gilbert in *Pinafore* had his fun with this particular convention; but in the process there are shrewd thrusts at the Admiralty. The libretto is an example of topsyturvydom (a word commonly used with Gilbert and Sullivan) on a grand scale. *Trial by Jury* and *Iolanthe* put Parliament and the legal system through a series of absurd maneuvers; *Patience* took the aesthetic movement of the pre-Raphaelites, Wilde and Swinburne to a sort of *reductio ad absurdum; Princess Ida* poked fun at women's rights and female education; *The Gondoliers* satirized republican government; *Ruddigore,* one of the most parodistic, took off on the barnstorming melodramas so popular in their day.

The basic plots of the Gilbert and Sullivan operettas are in themselves simple and, frequently, farcical. Industrious researchers have pointed out that there is nothing particularly new in any Gilbert and Sullivan situation. Even one of the most famous *Pinafore* passages—"What, never?" "No, never!" "What, never?" "Well, hardly ever."—has a precedent. At least, S. J. Adair Fitzgerald pointed out, with great glee, that the following occurs in Persius: "Quis haec legat?" "Nemo mehercule." "Nemo?" "Vel duo, vel nemo." Which he translates as: "Who will read this?" "Surely nobody." "What, nobody?" "Well, hardly anybody." Persius died in 62 A.D.

From Gilbert and Sullivan came a body of work that has a significant place in the hierarchy of creative effort in Victorian times. Sullivan composed the only English music of his period worth talking about. Except for him it was a terrible age, musically speaking. The shadow of Mendelssohn had obscured England, just as the shadow of Handel had blocked sunlight from the English composers some hundred years previously. Sullivan may have been indebted to Mendelssohn (and to Schumann and Donizetti), but his workmanship was impeccable. He was a much better technician than Strauss or Offenbach. He also was a better musical parodist than Offenbach. Take the wonderfully funny Handelian sequences sung by that precious trio, Arac, Guron, and Scynthius, in *Princess Ida:* they are among the wittiest things in music, as are also the Handelian parodies in *Trial by Jury*. And a waltz like "Poor Wand'ring One" perfectly mocks the bel canto style. But beyond all the fooling around is the writing of a completely equipped, inventive musician. The fact that Sullivan's music flows so easily deceives some listeners, making them think it is second-rate. It is far from that. Sullivan was a supreme technician of the lyric stage, and there is something Mozartean about the effortless grace and purity of his music. And his ability to set the English language was of a transcendental order. Nobody has set English words to music with comparable ease and sheer rightness. But Sullivan needed the proper words to fire him, and those he received from Gilbert. The two men were indispensable to each other. Without Sullivan, no Gilbert. Without Gilbert, no Sullivan.

❧ 2 ❧

Faust and French Opera

FROM GOUNOD TO SAINT-SAËNS

The Paris Opéra, which had taken the lead in the 1830's, suddenly became an anachronism in the 1850's. Indeed, most French music seemed to stagnate. It was a bad period, and nothing seemed to be coming up. At the Opéra-Comique, works by Boieldieu, Adam, and Auber, all composers of the 1830's and before, made up most of the repertory. Between 1852 and 1870, only five—*five!*—new French operas were added to the repertory of the Opéra. The management was not taking any chances on new works. Thus the new school of French composers had to turn elsewhere. Fortunately for them, Léon Carvalho, director of the Théâtre-Lyrique, was hospitable to new music. So was Jules Pasdeloup, who founded the Concerts Populaires in 1860 and saw to it that French music—and Wagner, too—got a hearing. It was ironic that the new French opera which turned out to be the most popular of its time, the opera that springs to most people's mind when French opera is mentioned—Charles Gounod's *Faust*—had its premiere not at the Opéra but at the Théâtre-Lyrique.

Faust was a triumph of bourgeois music applied to bourgeois taste. Its libretto by Jules Barbier and Michel Carré was adapted, in a milk-and-water fashion, from Goethe. Its music was nowhere so advanced as Berlioz'. It had the stagiest of stage devils, and a heroine who ascended to heaven accompanied by the proper noises of the celestial choir. But it swept Europe and the United States. Between Verdi's Big Three of 1851–1853 and the Wagner craze that came after the first Bayreuth season of 1876, it was one of the very few operas to take Europe by storm. "*Faust, Faust, Faust,*" complained a British critic in 1863, "nothing but *Faust. Faust* on Saturday, Wednesday and Thursday; to be repeated tonight, on Tuesday, and 'every night until further notice,' as they say at the theaters."

Charles Gounod, who composed thirteen operas, is still represented in the international repertory by two other works, *Roméo et Juliette* and *Mireille*.

31

But neither has come near the popularity of the one work by which his name is known to most people. Born in Paris on June 18, 1818, Charles François Gounod was an interesting figure. His father was a talented though unsuccessful painter who died when Charles was four years old. His mother, a skillful artist herself, took over her late husband's classes and in addition gave music lessons. Charles picked up both arts with facility. He was a good draftsman, and at the age of twelve he also was starting to compose. He decided to leave art in favor of music when he was thirteen; the impetus was a performance of Rossini's *Otello* that he heard. "If they had attempted to prevent me from learning music," Gounod later stated, "I should have run away to America and hidden in some corner where I could have studied undisturbed." In 1836 he entered the Conservatory, winning the Prix de Rome three years later. Rome fascinated Gounod. He discovered a great deal of sixteenth-century ecclesiastical music there, and started to make a serious study of it. And, close to the fount of the Church, he became very religious. In fact, for a time he could not make up his mind whether or not to go on with music or to enter the Church.

He returned to Paris in 1843 by way of Vienna and Leipzig. In Vienna he arranged for performances of several of his religious works, thus launching his career; and in Leipzig, where he spent four days with Mendelssohn, he heard the choral music of Bach for the first time. It left an overwhelming impression. His first position in Paris was as musical director of the Chapel for Foreign Missions, and he immediately brought Bach, Palestrina, and other early composers into the services, over great objections.

At the Chapel for Foreign Missions he wore semiclerical dress, signed himself "Abbé Gounod," and then, in 1847, entered the Carmelite monastery as a novitiate. Like Liszt, he was torn between flesh and the devil, and in some quarters he was called "the philandering monk." He also was an outgoing kind of person who liked to be liked; and with his overpowering charm, there were few who could resist him. Those who could resist him found his behavior excessive, and they looked askance at his habit of kissing people indiscriminately. Edmund Got, the actor, wrote in his diary that Gounod was "as talented musically as he is exuberant and shamelessly pushy as a man. He actually kissed me on both cheeks the first time I ever met him!" Henri Meilhac, the writer and one of the *Carmen* librettists, told a friend: "Gounod spent all day Wednesday and Thursday with us. Never have I been kissed so often in so short a time."

The only way to fortune in the French musical establishment was through opera, and Gounod turned his hand to it starting in 1850 with *Sapho,* which was produced the following year. Several more operas followed and made no impression. He supported himself through his position as conductor of the Orphéon, a union of choral societies, for which he held a grand title: Superintendant of Instruction in Singing to the Communal Schools of the City of Paris. His father-in-law was instrumental in steering Gounod to the post. In 1852 Gounod married Anna Zimmerman, the daughter of a famous piano teacher in the Conservatory. Pierre Zimmerman trained many of the best pianists of the period, and has achieved an extra footnote in history from one pianist he did not train. He turned down Louis Moreau Gottschalk, the prodigy from New Orleans, in 1842 with the comment that no pianist could possibly come from America, a land of savages and steam engines.

Gounod started work on *Faust* in 1856, but broke it off to work on another opera, *Le Médecin malgré lui*. It was produced in 1858 and was a success. On March 19, 1859, *Faust* had its premiere at the Théâtre-Lyrique. From then on, Gounod was the most famous composer in France. The opera contained many of the elements that Massenet was to refine—spicy chromatic harmonies, sweetness of melody, sentimentalism, graceful orchestration, completely idiomatic writing for the voice. French opera of the latter half of the nineteenth century is an art of delicate adjustment, no matter how imposing the forces involved. A large orchestra may be used, but the scoring is much slighter than in a corresponding German work, where the pages are black with notes. *Faust* is grand opera, but a kind of grand opera that makes its best effect only when presented with style, rightness of proportion, and delicacy of sound.

Gounod spent the rest of his life trying to write another *Faust*. He never did, though he composed a great deal of music. His own favorite opera, *La Reine de Saba* (1862), made little headway. *Mireille* (1863) and *Roméo et Juliette* (1864) did better, but neither came anywhere near *Faust* in popularity. A relatively unexplored area of Gounod's *oeuvre* involves his songs. *Venise* and the *Biondina* cycle are characteristic—elegant, charming, sweet. They constitute an important part of the international song repertory and have been unjustly neglected outside of France. They also influenced the development of French song through Debussy, and Ravel in 1922 pointed out their significance: "The real founder of song writing in France was Charles Gounod. It was the composer of *Venise,* of *Philémon et Baucis,* and of the Shepherd's song in *Sapho* who rediscovered the secret of harmonic sensuality that had been lost since the French harpsichordists of the seventeenth and eighteenth centuries."

In the last part of his life, Gounod turned to religious music and achieved a great deal of success, especially in England, with such works as *Mors e Vita, La Rédemption,* and the *Messe à Sainte-Cécile.* Listeners responded enthusiastically to the disguised eroticism of the music. It was not for nothing that Gounod wanted to be known as the Musician of Love; and he was referring to things other than love in the Christian sense. "If a good

Catholic were to dissect me," Gounod once said in a candid moment, "he would be much surprised at what he would find inside."

The Franco-Prussian War sent Gounod to England, where he remained from 1870 to 1875, and it was there that he had his affair with Mrs. Georgina Weldon. She was born Georgina Traherne, married a Captain George Weldon, and lived in London at Tavistock House, which had once been the residence of Charles Dickens. It was a situation out of *Vanity Fair.* She was a sort of Becky Sharp and her husband the equivalent of Colonel Crawley. Georgina became Gounod's business manager, and Tavistock House became the scene of an amiable *ménage à trois* after Gounod's wife packed up and indignantly went back to Paris. Later she sent her son, Jean, to look into the matter. He promptly tried to seduce Georgina and she threw him out of the house. But Gounod finally tired of her and left England. Safely in Paris, he asked her for his scores, effects, and money he had loaned. Instead, the Weldons instituted a countersuit, including a large bill for room and board for three years. Eventually Gounod did get his music back, after settling for $50,000, but for years he lived in mortal fear that Georgina would descend upon Paris and claim him. That did not happen, and he died peacefully on October 18, 1893.

It was conceded that Gounod was an immortal, and that his great religious works would survive eternity itself. Saint-Saëns was impelled to write: "In the dim distant future when inexorable time has done its work and the operas of Gounod are forever at rest in the dusty sanctuaries of libraries, the *Messe à Sainte-Cécile,* the *Rédemption* and the oratorio *Mors e Vita* will still have life in them. They will show the coming generations what a splendid musician lent lustre and renown to France in the nineteenth century." Posterity has not endorsed Saint-Saëns's flattering estimate. Occasionally the *Sainte-Cécile* is heard, and it plods along in a saccharine, platitudinous manner, full of plagal cadences, full of choruses with harps sounding prominently in the accompaniment. As Martin Cooper has written, Gounod after 1870 "might as well have echoed Tennyson's despairing cry that he was the greatest master of English living and had nothing to say."

After *Faust,* the next great French opera was *Carmen.* The brilliantly gifted Georges Bizet, who died at the age of thirty-seven, is almost a one-work man—but what a work! *Carmen* was the only piece he wrote that represented him in full maturity. Had he lived, he might have revolutionized opera in France. As it was, *Carmen* soon became recognized as a work of genius, and some saw in it a corrective against Wagner. Nietzsche was one. "My favorite among the contemporary Frenchmen are Bizet and Delibes," he wrote. Léo Delibes (1836–1891) composed two of the most exquisite of all ballet scores, *Coppélia* and *Sylvia;* and his opera *Lakmé,* as well as that lovely song, *Les Filles de Cadiz,* still remains in the repertory. "Bizet's opera

Carmen," continued Nietzsche, "I know well. It is music that makes no pretensions to depth, but it is delightful in its simplicity, so lively, so unaffected and sincere, that I learned it all practically by heart, from beginning to end."

Nietzsche underestimated *Carmen*. It is a far deeper work than his rather condescending remarks would indicate, and its last act has something of the terror and inevitability of the last act of *Don Giovanni*. Carmen in a way is a female Don Giovanni. She would rather die than be false to herself, and that makes her an authentically great figure. The opera does not have a perfect libretto—Micaela is dragged in, and her contribution to the opera is entirely unconvincing—and there are also weak moments in the score; but the work is nevertheless a blazing conception and even to this day a startling one. When the great inspiration of the opera, the Fate theme, is heard in the orchestra, stark and threatening, it takes a most blasé listener not to feel his adrenalin surge.

It was no inspired dilettante who composed *Carmen*. Georges Bizet, born in Paris on October 25, 1838, was one of those children with all the musical gifts—absolute pitch, fast reflexes, everything. He was in the Conservatoire at the age of nine and took every prize in sight—piano, organ, composition, solfège. He easily won the Prix de Rome in 1857. Prior to that he had met Gounod, who exerted a strong influence on Bizet's development. Bizet's early and lovely Symphony in C is virtually a copy of Gounod's Symphony for Wind Instruments. But the melodies are Bizet's own. From the beginning he had a refined, superior melodic sense, and taste to go with it. He never wanted to be a heaven-stormer, and preferred Apollo to Dionysus. "I have the courage to prefer Raphael to Michelangelo, Mozart to Beethoven, Rossini to Meyerbeer," he once wrote. His talents attracted attention, and many professionals felt that he was the coming man. There was nothing in music he could not do—this plump, short-tempered young man, always elegantly dressed, constantly nibbling on sweets, cakes, chocolate, and *petits fours*. (To get on the good side of Bizet one had to cater to his sweet tooth.)

His first opera was *Les Pêcheurs de Perles*, and it had a terrible libretto. Michel Carré and Eugène Cormon (real name, Pierre-Étienne Piestre) supplied the book, and Cormon later said that had he and Carré realized Bizet's talents they would not have saddled him with "that white elephant." It had its premiere at the Lyrique in 1863, and such was the appeal of its music that it never entirely was dropped from the repertory. Even today it enjoys occasional revivals. It should be mentioned that *Les Pêcheurs de Perles*, with its action set in Ceylon, was one of the many operas of the time that reflected the vogue for exoticism. One could include Meyerbeer's *L'Africaine*, Gounod's *Reine de Saba*, Delibes' *Lakmé*, Bizet's *Djamileh*.

35

The French were always fascinated by Near East and Oriental exoticism. In the last quarter of the century a great interest in the exotic music of Spain became manifest, to be represented by *Carmen* and explored by such composers as Chabrier, Debussy, and Ravel.

Bizet's next significant opera was *La Jolie Fille de Perth,* performed at the Lyrique in 1866. This too suffered from a poor libretto and it failed. Bizet was discouraged. He continued to compose operas, starting many he never finished. In 1869 he married Géneviève Halévy, daughter of the composer of *La Juive.* (She was Proust's model for the Princesse de Guermantes.) The Franco-Prussian War found Bizet a soldier in the National Guard. Nearly all of the prominent French composers did their bit. Saint-Saëns also joined the National Guard, while Massenet and Fauré were infantrymen. During the war Bizet composed one of his most delightful pieces, the *Jeux d'Enfants* for piano duet. In 1872 he completed *Djamileh,* an opera that had ten performances, was retired, and did not turn up again until 1938. That same year, 1872, Bizet composed the incidental music to Daudet's *L'Arlésienne* and started to think about *Carmen.* Henri Meilhac and Ludovic Halévy prepared the libretto, taken from the story by Prosper Mérimée. The Opéra-Comique was unhappy about the idea. "Mérimée's *Carmen?* Isn't she killed by her lover? And that background of thieves, gypsies, cigar-makers!" Or, "Death on the stage of the Opéra-Comique! Such a thing has never been seen. Never!" Camille du Locle, head of the Comique, had no faith in the work. He considered it too daring, risqué, unconventional. As it had spoken dialogue rather than recitative, it belonged to the Opéra-Comique, but du Locle was worried about the subject matter and its impact on audiences. France had the reputation abroad of being a naughty country, but the French middle class always has been sturdily moral and even Puritanical. Du Locle had visions of his entire clientele boycotting his house.

But du Locle had committed himself, and *Carmen* received its first performance at the Opéra-Comique on March 3, 1875. Bizet pronounced it "a definite and a hopeless flop," and became ill. Bizet always had a tendency to become discouraged when things did not go his way, and he would develop all kinds of psychosomatic ailments. It so happened that *Carmen* was not "a definite and hopeless flop." Neither was it a great success. The opera had forty-eight performances, but it played to smaller and smaller houses. Three months after the premiere, on June 3, 1875, Bizet died of cardiac complications. Not much later, Ernest Guiraud transformed the spoken dialogue into recitatives for the Viennese premiere, and it is in that form which *Carmen* is customarily heard. It took only a few years for *Carmen* to be played all over Europe. Even Wagner was impressed: "Here, thank God, at last for a change is somebody with ideas in his head." Tchaikovsky adored the opera, and Brahms said that he would have gone to the ends of the earth to embrace the composer of *Carmen*.

In a way, *Carmen* started the verismo school. It contained contemporary characters true to life and traced the disintegration of an honorable soldier. Carmen herself is a more subtle character than the usual leering, hip-swinging, soprano or mezzo-soprano (both sing the role) would suggest. Carmen, indeed, is moral rather than immoral because she is always honest with herself. She never violates her own code of conduct. If she does not follow bourgeois sexual codes, neither is she promiscuous. She belongs to only one man at a time. She knows her powers and does not hesitate to use them, but sexual power is not the most important element in her makeup. Indeed, a well-acted Carmen should suggest her contempt for most men, and for humanity in general.

Technically the score is full of original ideas. The orchestra is not a mere support for singing. It has its own life. *Carmen* is an opera of passion, power, and truth, and is infinitely superior to the carefully arranged, prettily served canapés of Gounod and Massenet. They were skilled professionals, but Bizet was a genius. He sought the kind of honesty that Mussorgsky sought in *Boris Godunov*. Art had to reflect life—not idealized life, but life as it actually was lived.

Jules Massenet, the most popular French opera composer of the last quarter of the nineteenth century, was a businessman musician who knew what the public wanted and decided to give it to them. He was an opportunist not very popular with his colleagues. He was too successful, too cynical, too preoccupied in pandering to public taste, too smug about his success. Bizet could see what was coming. "That little fellow is about to walk all over us," he said. Massenet's special mixture was a kind of sugared eroticism—an *"érotisme discret et quasi-religieux,"* as Vincent d'Indy described it—and the international public could not seem to get enough of it. It was also strongly prevalent in Massenet's religious music, about which he was as cynical as he was about his operas. "I don't believe in all that creeping Jesus stuff," Massenet told d'Indy, "but the public likes it, and we must always agree with the public." No wonder Rimsky-Korsakov called him "a crafty fox"; no wonder that most of his colleagues considered him a jealous, ambitious, and hypocritical flatterer. Yet for some thirty years Massenet dominated French opera to a point where his kind of melody could be heard even in the music of such iconoclasts as Debussy. Romain Rolland was to say that in the heart of every French composer was a slumbering Massenet.

Massenet was born on May 12, 1842, and died on August 13, 1912. At the age of eleven he was in the Conservatoire, and he won the Prix de Rome in 1863. Four years later his first opera was produced—the first in a series of twenty-six. At the turn of the twentieth century such Massenet works as *Hérodiade, Le Cid, Thaïs, Sapho, Cendrillon, Le Jongleur de Notre-Dame, Don Quichotte, Werther,* and *Manon* were given everywhere. Not until the 1920's did their popularity begin to recede. Today, outside of France, it is primarily *Manon* on which Massenet's fame rests. His other operas are as dated as Meyerbeer's. In *Manon* everything coalesced. Massenet, a skillful musician, here used leitmotifs *à la* Wagner, sentimental melodies *à la* Gounod, an orchestra that produced soothing and sensuous sounds, a libretto that could titillate the tired businessman and yet send him out of the theater morally uplifted (Manon comes to a bad end).

It is curiously feminine music, and *Manon* has a great deal of feminine charm about it. "Massenet," wrote Debussy, "seems to have been the victim of the fluttering fans of his fair hearers, who flirted them so long to his glory; he yearned to reserve for himself the beating of those perfumed wings; unfortunately he might as well have tried to tame a cloud of butterflies." Debussy pointed out that music to Massenet was a delightful avocation rather than the cruel god who controlled Bach and Beethoven. Slim, courtly, elegant-looking, romantic, Massenet turned ladies' heads. He liked and understood women, and they reciprocated. Bessie Abbott, the opera singer, remembered how "he could make women so happy with his adroit verbal petting that one could listen to him forever. He had a pretty trick of telling his fair companions that she suggested a melody, and he would go to the piano and improvise some honey-sweet strain that really did suit the personality of the one so highly complimented." (Bessie's grammar is as vivid as her writing.) And so Massenet prospered. He made enormous amounts of money, invested wisely, and remained the perpetual charmer both in his music and in his life.

The obituary notice in the *Musical Courier* made a special point of trying to explain Massenet's extraordinary popularity: "It is pretty sure that if Massenet had not lived just when he did, when the world was thirsting for a little melody, and when few composers were attempting to write melody, that Massenet would have been a failure. But it just so happens that Massenet wrote melody, combined with a little modernism and just a touch of Wagnerism, at a time when most composers were trying to get beyond the old school. Therefore Massenet was appreciated. We welcome his poor melodies because we have no others."

No opera composer in France could compete with Massenet. Alfred Bruneau's *Le Rêve* (1891) had a run but was dropped and never returned. Camille Saint-Saëns wrote many operas but had only one success, and that an early one, with *Samson et Dalila* in 1877. Gustave Charpentier wrote several operas, and did create a furor with one, *Louise* (1900). This followed the lead of *Carmen* as a verismo work, and took it one step further into socialism and free love.

38

In advanced musical circles, *Louise* was hated as much as any Massenet opera. It was considered eclectic and cynical. Debussy all but became wild when discussing it, and the general attitude of musicians is summed up in the 1955 edition of *Grove's Dictionary of Music and Musicians*, where the writer calls *Louise* "superficial and spurious . . . depending for its appreciation on a mere passing curiosity." That may be, but the curiosity has had a long time to exhaust itself. *Louise*, composed in 1890 and not produced until 1900, is still in the repertory and has many admirers, which is not bad for a mere passing curiosity. It has its faults. It is sentimental (its verismo aspects nothwithstanding), it has too many touches of Massenet, and it is heavily Wagnerian (the influence of *Die Meistersinger* is strongly pronounced in *Louise*). Yet it has strength, and above all it has Paris.

Nominally the opera is about two lovers and the breakaway of a girl from her bourgeois background. In reality the opera is an evocation of Paris. "*Cité de force et de lumière! Splendeur première! Paris, ô Paris! cité d'amour.*" So sing the lovers (to Charpentier's own words; he wrote the libretto himself). And the very last word in the opera is "*Paris!*" Louise runs away for good and her father knows very well where the blame lies. It is not Louise's mother. It is not Julien the lover. It is Paris, and he shakes his fist at the great city.

Charpentier lives by this one work. He was an unusual type. Born in Dieuze on June 25, 1860, he went to Paris at the age of twenty-one as a music student from the provinces. His love affair with the city was spectacular, and he was never happy outside of Montmartre. He even lived his part, looking like something out of *La Bohème* with his flowing pantaloons, his long, black artist's tie and slouch hat. He was a socialist, and some of his own background went into the opera. Louise works in a dressmaking shop, while Charpentier himself had worked in a textile factory. He had taken up with a seamstress named Louise Jehan, who was employed in a dressmaking shop in the Rue Lepic. Charpentier even took her first name for his opera. *Louise* was a shocker in its day. Here was an opera that took place in the present, that contained working girls and a dressmaking shop, that made a plea for free love and the dignity of the individual, that castigated parents for holding too tightly to their children. Charpentier threw a rock through the glass window of French middle-class morality. Yet *Louise* became one of the most popular of French operas, and it does have some beautiful things in it. The Noctambulist scene is evocative of the city loved by all the civilized world; and when Julien and Louise sing their apostrophe to Paris, something very French and genuine comes through. There is, of course, *Depuis le jour*, that haunting, high-floating aria; and the twittering seamstress scene; and the rapturous first-act duet. None of this, to be sure, has the integrity of Bizet's one great opera. Charpentier was basically a sentimentalist; and while he based his opera on one or two episodes from his own life, he created a world that existed only in his own imagination and went no further. But *Louise* still has authentic period charm and something more.

Charpentier lived until 1956, when he died on February 18 at the age of ninety-six. To the end he wore his nineteenth-century costume and was one of the sights of Paris. He was not one of the most polished of men. When he went to Vienna in 1903 to superintend the *Louise* premiere, the first thing he tried to do was make love to the beautiful Alma Mahler, wife of the composer-conductor who was the head of the opera house and in charge of the premiere. The Montmartre exponent of free love was so clumsy about it that the Mahlers were vastly amused and not at all angry. Alma Mahler wrote about him in her diary: "Spits under the table, chews his nails, draws your attention by a pressure of his knee or a nudge of his elbow. Trod on my foot last night to call attention to the beauty of *Tristan*. . . . He's a socialist and wants to convert me." Eventually Charpentier wrote a sequel to *Louise* and called it *Julien*. It was as still-born as an opera could be, and after a few performances it disappeared for good.

A much greater composer—though his operas are not in the repertory—was Emmanuel Chabrier, one of the true originals of music. Among the oddities of his career is the fact that all of it was compressed into a ten-year period. Chabrier, born in Ambert on January 18, 1841, was playing the piano at the age of six, but his father opposed music as a profession. Therefore Chabrier took a law degree in 1862 and for the next eighteen years worked in the Ministry of the Interior. He moved in musical and artistic circles; was friendly with Manet and Verlaine, but for a long time did not compose. He collected paintings, and owned works by Manet, Renoir, Fantin-Latour, Sisley, Forain, and Monet. After his death, forty-eight paintings from his collection were sold at auction, on March 26, 1896. They brought a fair sum then. Today . . .

Not until the late 1870's did he appear as a composer. *L'Étoile,* an operetta, came out in 1877, and the one-act *Une Éducation Manquée* in 1879. Then he heard *Tristan* and was so impressed he decided to devote the rest of his life to music. He resigned from the Ministry in 1880. There followed, in rapid succession, a remarkable group of piano works named *Dix pièces pittoresques;* the orchestral rhapsody, *España;* a long opera, *Gwendoline;* a comic opera, *Le Roi malgré lui,* more piano music, and a group of songs. All of these were composed in the 1880's. Toward the end of the decade he had a mental breakdown and was incapable of writing. He died in Paris on September 13, 1894.

No composer in France at the time was more original. *Gwendoline,* which hardly anybody has ever heard, is supposed to be Wagnerian, and in some respects it is, though a study of the score shows music of unusual harmonic and melodic originality. But that is not what Chabrier stands for. He

brought, in his other works, something new to music—the notion of frivolity as an end in itself. Even in the early *L'Étoile* there are all the marks of
what he was to represent—a breakaway from the Offenbachian kind of operetta into something much more sophisticated. There is in *L'Étoile* something of the music hall, something of the circus. It is Toulouse-Lautrec in
tone. There are bubbling duets; there is one duet, between tenor and baritone, that is the funniest satire of a bel canto aria ever written; there are
harmonies so sophisticated and even "bluesy" that they could have come
from Gershwin; there is something that leaps the years and lands on Satie
and the French group of the 1920's known as *Les Six*. Chabrier, not Satie, is
the spiritual father of *Les Six*, both in his deliberate use of froth and his
equally deliberate flight from Wagnerism. Though Chabrier had been influenced by Wagner, he soon tried to avoid all traces of German music. He
even began to have the same approach as Debussy, *musicien français*. While
working on his *Briséis*, an opera he never completed, he wrote to a friend,
"I do not know whether the music will be French, but of one thing I am
certain—it will not be German. For better or worse I must be of my country. It is my first duty!"

Chabrier never was one to go in for development or classic form. He had
his own kind of unity, one that adhered to its own built-in logic, the kind
represented by the later music of Berlioz. Chabrier greatly admired his famous predecessor. "Did Berlioz, a Frenchman above all (he wasn't old-hat in
his time), put variety, color, rhythm into *La Damnation de Faust, Roméo et
Juliette* and *L'Enfance du Christ*? But they lack unity, people say. I answer, *merde!* If in order to be *one* I am fated to be boring, I prefer to be 2,
3, 4, 10, 20—in short, I prefer to have ten colors on my palette and to break
up all the lines. And to do that I don't necessarily want to do over and over
again the devastating (1) act for the exposition, (2) act with silly women and
vocal exercises by the queen, (3) act with a ballet, and the interminable ballet that reshuffles the cards, (4) the indispensable love duet, (5) the drunken
orgy at twenty minutes before midnight, firing of muskets, Jews' cauldron,
death of the leading characters." Chabrier clearly did not like Meyerbeerian
grand opera.

His ideas are basically melodic. They appear and then disappear for good
without the Germanic kind of development. In a way, Chabrier was an inspired amateur. "I am virtually self-taught," he wrote. "I belong to no
school. I have more temperament than talent. There are many things that
one must learn in youth which I shall never attain; but I live and breathe
in music, I write as I feel, with more temperament than technique. But
what's the difference? I think I am an honest and sincere man." Amateur or
not, his piano music is very difficult to play. The figurations can be so unconventional that conservatory-trained hands have to learn different pat-

41

terns and reflexes. It is wonderful piano music, with verve and wit; and the harmonies, with their constant ninth chords, anticipate Debussy. The *Trois valses romantiques* are masterpieces in miniature, and the last of the three waltzes is disquieting in its harmonic fluctuations. This is music that approaches decadence. *España,* on the other hand, is all brightness and ebullience, and leads directly into Ravel. Chabrier's masterpiece is *Le Roi malgré lui,* a lighthearted work of extraordinary sophistication. It should be revived. George Balanchine made use of some of the waltzes for his ballet *Bourrée fantasque* and they give an idea of the brilliance of the scoring and the vivacity of the melodic invention. But the public is still unfamiliar with the lovely vocal writing in *Le Roi malgré lui.* Many previous composers could be light and amusing, but Chabrier was the first to be *serious* about being light and amusing, He raised his concept to the level of an aesthetic. Except for *Gwendoline* and the unfinished *Briséis,* he never aimed for big things. He was the apostle of spontaneity, of the short, elegant idea set forth in jewel-like manner. This he achieved perfectly, and within his restricted frame was one of the most remarkable composers of the period.

Quite different was Camille Saint-Saëns, the most perfect of technicians. A good deal of Saint-Saëns's music is still in the repertory, but his reputation outside of France is low. The common charge against Saint-Saëns's music is that it is all technique and no ideas, that it is empty form, that it is elegant but superficial. In a way he was the French Mendelssohn. His career is worth examining, for in his long life—October 9, 1835 to December 16, 1921—he spanned many of the musical revolutions of two centuries and he had his own contribution to make.

It is not generally realized that Saint-Saëns was probably the most awesome child prodigy in the history of music. His I.Q. must have soared far beyond any means of measurement. Consider: at $2\frac{1}{2}$ he was picking out tunes on the piano. Naturally he had absolute pitch. He also could read and write before he was three. At three he composed his first piece. The autograph, dated March 22, 1839, is in the Paris Conservatoire. At five he was deep in analysis of *Don Giovanni,* using not the piano reduction but the full score. At that age he also gave a few public performances as a pianist. At seven he was reading Latin and interesting himself in science, especially botany and lepidoptery. He also collected geological specimens. His formal musical training started at seven, and he made his official debut at ten. As an encore at his debut recital he offered to play any of Beethoven's thirty-two sonatas from memory. His fame reached as far as the United States, and an item in the Boston *Musical Gazette* of August 3, 1846, states that "there is a boy in Paris, named St. Saëns, only ten and a half years old, who plays the music of Handel, Sebastian Bach, Mozart, Beethoven and the more modern masters, without any book before him." Saint-Saëns had total recall.

If he read a book or heard a piece of music it was forever in his memory.

He grew up to be one of the important pianists and organists of his day, a fine conductor, a brilliant score reader, a composer who worked prolifically in all forms, a sound musicologist, and a lively critic. Outside of music he dabbled in astronomy (he was a member of the Astronomical Society of France) and archaeology, looked into the occult sciences, published a volume of poetry, and tried his hand at playwriting. At the beginning of his career he was considered one of France's musical revolutionaries. As he grew older he was known as an archconservative. He admitted to being an eclectic, and said of his music: "I ran after the chimera of purity of style and perfection of form." He was a small, dandified, peppery man, and a dangerous one to cross despite his foppish looks. Pierre Lalo described him: "He was short, and always strangely resembled a parrot: the same, sharply-curved profile; a beaklike hooked nose; lively, restless, piercing eyes. . . . He strutted like a bird and talked rapidly, precipitately, with a curiously affected lisp."

For many years he was organist at the Madeleine (Liszt called him the greatest organist in the world). He took up the cause of Wagner and fought for *Tannhäuser* and *Lohengrin*. He also allied himself with the other progressives, Liszt and Schumann. In 1861 he became a teacher at the École Niedermeyer. Fauré was his most prominent pupil. He toured as a pianist, and in an age of flamboyant virtuosos, Saint-Saëns was an exponent of purity, clarity, refinement, and classicism. He gave a cycle of the Mozart piano concertos, probably the first pianist in history to do so. In the meantime his own music did not make much headway. Some were secretly pleased that this phenomenal but somewhat arrogant musical mind was having so little success. Berlioz, witty as ever, quipped of Saint-Saëns that "He knows everything but he lacks inexperience." Saint-Saëns began to make enemies. He could not stand Franck's music, and he feuded with Massenet. Massenet was elected a member of the *Institut*, an honor avidly desired by Saint-Saëns. Ever the flatterer, Massenet sent Saint-Saëns a telegram: "My dear colleague, the *Institut* has made a terrible mistake." Furious, Saint-Saëns wired back: "I entirely agree with you." A few years later Saint-Saëns was elected and became an Immortal. But, years later, he saw to it that Debussy was kept out of the *Institut*. He despised Debussy's music. "I've thtayed in Parith to thpeak ill of 'Pelléath and Mélithande,'" he told a friend. He also had bad things to thpeak about the music of d'Indy and Strauss.

The evil that he did lives after him. Many seem to have forgotten the good he did. He not only was a progressive force in his day. In addition he founded, with Romain Bussine (a voice professor at the Conservatoire), the Société Nationale de Musique in 1871. This organization stood godfather to the entire new generation of French composers. The purpose of the Société was to give new French music a hearing, and it did, for many years, introducing works by Franck, d'Indy, Chabrier, Bruneau, Chausson, Dukas, Lekeu, Magnard, and Ravel. Romain Rolland called the Société the "cradle and sanctuary of French art. . . . All that has been great in French music from 1870 to 1900 has come by way of it. Without it the greater part of the works that are the honor of our music not only would have been unperformed but perhaps would not even have been written." Nor was it only French music that interested Saint-Saëns. Aside from his propaganda for Liszt and Wagner, it was he who introduced the music of *Boris Godunov* to French musicians, bringing back the vocal score after a trip to Russia. He kept doing what he thought was best for music. But by 1890 he was a bitter reactionary—sour, ill-tempered, restless, with a compulsion to travel. Perhaps he secretly realized he had never lived up to his glorious potential. In addition his personal life collapsed. In 1878 he lost both of his children within a few months. André fell out of a window and Jean died of an infantile disease. Three years later Saint-Saëns walked out on his wife. There was no divorce or separation, but they never met again. (She died in 1950 at the age of ninety-four.) Brooding, Saint-Saëns wrote a philosophical book entitled *Problèmes et Mystères*. It was a study in pessimism that advocated atheism. Art and science, Saint-Saëns maintained, will take the place of religion. Life has no purpose. "People have always been disappointed in their search for final causes. It may simply be that there are no such things." Existentialism in France had a spokesman in Saint-Saëns long before Sartre.

Like any ambitious French composer of his day, he composed operas. After two tries he succeeded with *Samson et Dalila* in 1877. It had its premiere not in Paris but in Weimar. None of Saint-Saëns's twelve other operas came within remote distance of its popularity, though experts say that *Ascanio* (1890) is a better work. But it is *Samson* that has remained in the repertory. Indeed, considering the generally low repute of his music, it is amazing how much of his work does remain in the repertory. There are the G minor and C minor Piano Concertos, with No. 5 in F sometimes performed; there is the Symphony No. 3 (*Organ*) in C minor; there are the Violin Concerto in B minor and the Cello Concerto in A minor; there is the *Carnival of the Animals,* from which comes *The Swan.* The Introduction and Rondo Capriccio for violin and orchestra is heard very often. Of the symphonic poems, the *Danse Macabre* is famous, and once in a while *Le Rouet d'Omphale* gets a hearing.

This is not a bad representation. It suggests that Saint-Saëns is a better composer than he is reputed to be. There must be some vitality in the music to have kept it alive so long. There also is something aesthetically satisfactory about the logic of his music, its neatness, finish, clear outlines, sheer professionalism. It is a music rooted in the classic tradition, whatever

44

its departures from orthodox form. A case can be made for Saint-Saëns as the first of the neoclassicists. Above all his music has classic elegance. Of all French composers of his time he was the most chaste, and his music completely avoids the supersensuous sounds of Franck and his school. The G minor Piano Concerto or the *Organ Symphony* may not probe very deeply, but at least they avoid the banality and bad taste of so much music of the period. His piano music, almost never played, verges on the salon but escapes triteness because of its brilliance and objectivity. It is very effective music. A good example is the C minor Toccata (the solo version of the last movement of the Fifth Concerto). It has the kind of glitter that bridges Liszt and Ravel. It may be that Saint-Saëns is due for a reassessment. A turn of the wheel might find his kind of consummate craft, and his lightweight but elegant and clear-cut musical ideas, worthy of revival. The trouble is that Saint-Saëns is best known by his worst music—*Samson et Dalila, The Swan,* the *Danse Macabre*—and not by the Septet for Piano, Trumpet and Strings, the D minor Violin Sonata, and the Piano Quartet in B flat.

From *Saint-Saëns and His Circle* by James Harding, Chatto and Windus Ltd., London

SAINT-SAËNS, CARICATURE BY "HIS RESPECTFUL PUPIL" GABRIEL FAURÉ.

❧ 3 ❧

Russian Nationalism and the Mighty Five

FROM GLINKA TO RIMSKY-KORSAKOV

The idea of a country's aspirations being consciously reflected in its music was a nineteenth-century development and was most strongly pronounced in those countries a little outside the mainstream of European thought. Russia, Poland, Hungary, Bohemia, and Spain all produced at least one nationalistic composer of stature. The people in most of those countries had the most to aspire to. Rich countries with satisfied citizens do not normally produce nationalistic music, which in a way is propaganda—a spiritual call to arms. A country with a people under the domination of a foreign power, such as the Kingdom of Bohemia under Austrian rule, or a country where the people groaned under the iron fist of a czar and his entrenched, grasping aristocracy, was not capable of much in the way of social protest. But protests could be made in literature and music; and they were. Where the hands of the activists were tied, the musician at least could express his country's longing for freedom, or his country's pride in its traditions. And all this was helped by the romantic identification with "the folk."

Nationalism in music is the conscious use of a body of folk music, appearing even in such extended forms as symphony and opera. Wagner is the most Teutonic of all composers, but he is not a nationalist composer because he never drew upon the heritage of German folk music. Even if a composer occasionally does write a piece in which folk elements are used, that does not necessarily make him a nationalist. Brahms wrote a set of *Deutsche Volkslieder*, but that did not make him a national composer, no more than Schubert was when he composed his *Divertisement à la Hongroise*. Those pieces were outside the main body of their work, as were Liszt's *Hungarian Rhapsodies*. Nationalism in music is not a superficially applied patina of folk music. Rather it is an evocation of the folk spirit, of

46

the songs, dances, and religious music of a people. The true nationalist does not have to quote that material directly. He is so impregnated by the *melos* that all of his music evokes, as a specific response, the music of his homeland. The *melos* of the composer's country is an essential part of his actual mental and aural processes, as much as the air he breathes, the food he eats, and the language he speaks.

Though neither Chopin nor Liszt were true nationalists, Chopin had shown the way in his mazurkas and polonaises, and Liszt in his rhapsodies. (The nineteenth century had a much higher opinion of the Liszt rhapsodies than later ages did.) When Russia began to stir, it was to Chopin and Liszt rather than the academic composers to whom most of her musicians looked. Chopin and Liszt represented freedom as opposed to the "rules" of the German and Austrian conservatories. And the Russian nationalists hated rules. Russian composers were the first ones in Europe to make an aesthetic out of nationalism. Mikhail Glinka (1804–1857) started it off with his opera *A Life for the Czar*, in 1836. It took only fifty years after that for Russia to produce a handful of nationalist composers who turned out to be among the most original and powerful in the history of music.

Russian music until Glinka had been dominated by the Italians. Such important eighteenth-century composers as Manfredini, Galuppi, Paisiello, and Cimarosa had worked in Russia. Opera in Moscow and St. Petersburg—as, indeed, in other European cities—meant Italian opera. The music of the few native-born Russian composers active before Glinka is known only to specialists. Russia was a mysterious nation at the turn of the nineteenth century—an immensely powerful one, as Napoleon found out, but just emerging from a medieval condition. The entire Western tradition of philosophical thought, culture, and science was largely unknown there except to a few enlightened members of the aristocracy. Musically the country had a rich heritage of folk song, but there was nothing in the way of a musical establishment. As late as 1850 there was no conservatory of music in all of Russia. There were very few teachers, very few music books and publications. In St. Petersburg there was an organization known as the Russian Philharmonic Society. It gave two concerts a year.

Musicians were second-class citizens. As Anton Rubinstein wrote before setting up the St. Petersburg Conservatory in 1862, "Russia has almost no artist-musicians in the exact sense of this term. This is so because our government has not given the same privileges to the art of music that are enjoyed by the other arts, such as painting, sculpture, etc.—that is, he who practices music is not given the rank of an artist." This is important. What Rubinstein is saying is that musicians literally had no social status. A painter could be recognized by the government and given the title of "artist of the state." Not a musician.

The history of Russian music as it is known today starts with Glinka, who wrote a large quantity of inferior, Western-influenced music before his two great operas, *A Life for the Czar* and *Russlan and Ludmilla*. Tchaikovsky, for one, could never get over Glinka's transformation. "A dilettante who played now on the violin, now on the piano, who composed colorless quadrilles and fantasies on stylish themes, who tried his hand at serious forms (quartet, sextet) and songs, but composed nothing but banalities in the taste of the '30's—who suddenly in the thirty-fourth year of his life produces an opera which by its genius, breadth, originality and flawless technique stands on a level with the greatest and most profound music!" Glinka, as the founder of the Russian national school, was deified by his successors. Tchaikovsky's remark is typical. All Russian composers, then and now, regarded Glinka much the way a disciple gazes upon the face of the Master. Tchaikovsky again: "The present Russian school is all in *Kamarinskaya,* just as the whole oak is in the acorn. . . . From *Kamarinskaya* all Russian composers (including myself) draw contrapuntal and harmonic combinations whenever they have to deal with a Russian dance tune."

Mikhail Glinka was born on June 1, 1804, into a wealthy landowning family. He had violin and piano lessons, including several piano lessons from the celebrated John Field, the Irish pianist-composer who had settled in Russia in 1803. At best, however, Glinka's musical education was sketchy. He became a civil servant in 1824, in the Ministry of Ways and Communication in St. Petersburg. In 1828 he resigned and traveled in Europe, spending nearly three years in Milan, where he met Bellini and Donizetti, and then spent a year in Berlin, studying theory under Siegfried Dehn. The music he composed through this period is primarily cosmopolitan, and the Russian touches are not much more pronounced than Beethoven's use of Russian themes in his *Razumovsky* quartets. Glinka's Sextet for Piano and Strings, for instance, is strongly Mendelssohnian. Considering that it was composed in 1832, it has a strikingly romantic, idiomatic piano part, and it does quote a Russian folk song in an unadorned manner. But the musical materials can under no circumstances be called original.

Back in Russia in 1834, friendly with Pushkin and Gogol, Glinka decided to compose an opera on a Russian subject. He settled on a national hero, Ivan Sussanin (in Russia the opera is called *Ivan Sussanin* to this day, rather than *A Life for the Czar*), and he spent two years on the score. The opera is about the peasant Ivan Sussanin, who misdirected a body of the Polish army, thus saving the life of the first Romanov at the expense of his own. Glinka said that he was inspired by the story: "As if by magic, both the plan of the whole opera and the idea of the antithesis of Russian and Polish music, as well as many of the themes and even details of the working-out—all this flashed into my head at one stroke." The opera had its premiere on December 9, 1836, in the presence of the Imperial family, and was a great success. There is no reason why it should not have been. The Court was habituated to Italian opera, and *A Life for the Czar* is strongly Italianate. Harmonically it poses no problems, and melodically it is attractive. To twentieth-century ears, it is a pleasant work but scarcely revolutionary, and it is hard to understand Tchaikovsky's all but hysterical eulogy. But the twentieth century is too far removed. To Russians in 1836 and for many years thereafter, *A Life for the Czar* stood alone—the first opera on a Russian subject, the first with a libretto that concerned peasants instead of nobles, the first to quote Russian folk song.

Glinka never had an equivalent popular success, though *Russlan and Ludmilla* is a much more interesting and important opera. Composed in 1842, it was strongly nationalistic, with Orientalisms, a use of the whole-tone scale, some rugged dissonances, and with much more personality than *A Life for the Czar*. But it was a failure. At least one major European musician liked it. Liszt, on a tour of Russia, read the full score at the piano and went around trumpeting its worth. Always alert to new talent and new sounds, Liszt was one of the few musicians outside Russia to keep a constant eye on that country's development. In later years he described exactly what Russian music represented. Having developed independently far from any foreign-born influence, the Russians (said Liszt) brought something new into music that delighted him in its rhythmic and fresh taste. One of the fresh concepts that the experienced ear of Liszt relished was the exotic quality of the Russian folk song that played so large a part in Glinka's late music and in the music of his successors. Rhythmically, Russian folk music is highly irregular, frequently in five-four or seven-four time, meters used relatively little by Western composers until Stravinsky popularized them in the twentieth century. It was no accident that Stravinsky's rhythmic irregularity was so marked; as a pupil of Rimsky-Korsakov, he knew a great deal about Russian folk song.

Depressed by the lack of interest in *Russlan and Ludmilla*—a work too advanced for the Russians of his day—Glinka left in 1844 for an extended visit to France and Spain. The latter country entranced him, and he even tried to learn Spanish dancing. "My feet were all right, but I couldn't manage the castanets." The *Jota Aragonesa*, one of the first attempts of any European composer to use Spanish melodies and rhythms, was the result, as was an overture named *A Night in Madrid*. Nor did Glinka neglect his Russian-derived music, and in 1848 came the symphonic poem *Kamarinskaya*, the progenitor of an entire half-century of orchestral music based on Russian folk themes. But on the whole he did little composing. He traveled, he took up with a series of agreeable young ladies (his own marriage in 1835 had ended with separation in 1839 and divorce in 1846), he met and entertained his colleagues all over the continent. He was bored. Finally he found a new interest—church music. He went to Berlin to study Bach and the church modes. There he caught a cold, and on February 15, 1857, he died. Immediately he became a national hero. "Beethoven and Glinka!" exclaimed Anton Rubinstein. Rubinstein's Russian contemporaries saw nothing exaggerated in the coupling.

The next development in Russian music came when a group of inspired amateurs gathered around a father-figure named Mili Balakirev, a short, squat, Asiatic-looking, largely self-taught composer. What resulted was one of the strangest things in musical history, and it could not have taken place anywhere else in the world.

Balakirev was born in Nizhny-Novgorod on January 2, 1837. At the age of ten he was taken by his mother to Moscow, where he studied piano and was more or less adopted by Alexander Ulibischev, an enthusiast who wrote books on Mozart and Beethoven. Ulibischev encouraged young Balakirev, who started composing before he knew anything about the rules of music. His friend and fellow student, the violinist Peter Dmitrievitch Baborikin, attested to the fact that Balakirev owned not a single book on harmony, orchestration, or theory. But Balakirev, who had determination, who had a good musical mind and a good ear (including absolute pitch), persisted; and when he heard the Glinka operas, he decided to devote himself permanently to music. In 1855 he set himself up in St. Petersburg. There, encouraged by Glinka, he became active as a pianist and composer.

He was a man of strong opinions who expected to be obeyed, and he became the leader of Russian music after Glinka died in 1857. Not only the leader; he became the czar. Around him gathered a group of young musicians who were to be known as The Russian Five—a group of self-taught dilettantes active in other fields. Several of them remained part-time composers all their lives. César Cui, in 1856, was the first to be attracted to the Balakirev orbit. Cui (1835–1918) was an army officer and remained one to the end of his life. He was an engineer, and his specialty was fortifications. As a composer he was the least talented of The Five, and although he wrote a good deal none of his music has remained in the repertory except a salon piece named *Orientale*. He was more valuable to the group as a critic. His articles appeared in France as well as in Russia, and he was constantly explaining the nationalistic principles of The Five.

Modest Mussorgsky (1839–1881) was the next to enter the circle. He appeared to be an unlikely candidate for immortality. At that time, 1857, he was an eighteen-year-old ensign in the crack Preobrajensky Regiment, and had been taught what every good regimental officer of the Preobrajensky had to know—how to drink, how to wench, how to wear clothes, how to gamble, how to flog a serf, how to sit a horse. Of this set of accomplishments, Mussorgsky found drinking the most congenial. His other big accomplishment was an ability to play the piano. His mother had taught him, and his repertory consisted of fashionable potpourris of the day. Alexander Borodin, then an army medical officer, met him in 1856, while both were duty officers at the same hospital. In a letter to the critic Vladimir Stassov, many years later, Borodin wrote of his first impression of Mussorgsky:

I had just been appointed an army doctor and Mussorgsky was a newly hatched officer. Being on hospital duty, we met in the common room; and feeling bored and in need of companionship, we started talking and forthwith found one another congenial. The same evening we were invited to the army doctor's house. Having a grown-up daughter, he often gave parties to which the officers on duty were asked. Mussorgsky was at that time a very callow, most elegant, perfectly contrived little officer: brand-new, close-fitting uniform, toes well turned out, hair well oiled and carefully smoothed-out, hands shapely and well cared for. His manners were polished and aristocratic. He spoke through his teeth, and his carefully-chosen words were interspersed with French phrases and rather labored. He showed, in fact, signs of a slight pretentiousness; but also, quite unmistakably, of perfect breeding and education. He sat down at the piano and, coquettishly raising his hands, started playing delicately and gracefully, bits of *Trovatore* and *Traviata*, the circle around him rapturously murmuring "*Charmant! Délicieux!*"

Music was what Mussorgsky loved above all. So overwhelming was the impact of Balakirev upon him that he resigned his commission in 1857 and plunged madly into the study of music. There was money in the family, and thus Mussorgsky had no financial problems. Borodin ran into him two years later and was more impressed: "Nothing in his aspect recalled the quondam officer. His attire, his manners, were as dainty as ever, but no trace of foppishness remained." It was not until 1861, when the serfs were emancipated, that Mussorgsky began to have problems. Many landowning families, Mussorgsky's among them, were hard hit. Mussorgsky had to go it alone, without financial help from his family, and was forced to take a civil service job.

Into the Balakirev circle next came a young naval officer named Nicolai Rimsky-Korsakov (1844–1908). Like Mussorgsky, he came from an aristocratic family. Unlike Mussorgsky, he was not even a capable pianist, though he dabbled with that instrument and also the cello. He wanted to compose, but he did not know where to turn until he met Balakirev. They came together through Rimsky's piano teacher, one Feodor Canille. "Last Sunday," Rimsky wrote to his parents early in December, 1861, "Canille introduced me to M. A. Balakirev, a well-known musician and composer, and also to Cui, who has written an opera, *The Prisoner of the Caucasus.*" Rimsky-Korsakov was overwhelmed, and didn't know how to thank Canille enough "for such a magnificent acquaintance." Balakirev saw something in Rimsky and clutched him to his heart. In a letter to Stassov, Balakirev wrote that Cui was "a talent but not a human being in the social sense," and that Mussorgsky was "practically an idiot." But Rimsky-Korsakov! "I put my trust in you," he told the young naval officer, "like an old aunt in a young lawyer nephew." Rimsky had already brought him sketches for a symphony in E flat minor. Balakirev urged the eighteen-year-old composer to finish it.

Alexander Borodin joined the Balakirev circle in 1862. Borodin (1833–1887), the illegitimate child of Prince Luka Gedeonoshvili, was trained as a scientist and remained one all his life. He went to the Academy of Medicine, graduated with honors, and went on to study at Heidelberg. Chemistry was his specialty. His doctoral thesis was entitled "On the Analogy of Arsenical with Phosphoric Acid." In the meantime, there was his music. Like Mussorgsky, he was an amateur pianist with an urge to compose, and his teachers at the medical school would upbraid him for devoting so much of his time to music.

So there they were—the army engineer, the ex-ensign, the naval cadet, and the chemist. There were also peripheral members of the circle, such as the art historian and music critic Vladimir Stassov; or the two talented Purgold daughters, one a singer and one a pianist. There was Alexander Dargomijsky (1813–1869), not a member of The Five but a composer with some original ideas who was closely associated with the circle. They were constantly meeting at his house, and he could have been the leader instead of Balakirev, but he was of frail health, without Balakirev's ability to command and inspire. There was Alexander Serov, the first important music critic in Russia and himself a composer. But the active workers were Cui, Mussorgsky, Rimsky-Korsakov, and Borodin. They sat directly at Balakirev's feet. Their curriculum and method of study would have brought tears to the eyes of a good German professor. Lacking books, lacking basic knowledge, they simply leaned on each other and against Balakirev. They would get whatever scores they could, from Bach through Berlioz and Liszt, playing through them, analyzing their form, taking the pieces apart and putting them together again. Perhaps that is not a bad way to study music. They criticized one another's works, helped one another compose, advanced in tiny steps. They were a close-knit group, and two of them, Mussorgsky and Rimsky-Korsakov, actually roomed together for a while. As Borodin wrote, "In the relations within our circle, there is not a shadow of envy, conceit or selfishness. Each is made sincerely happy by the smallest success of another."

Self-taught and proud of it, they defiantly made a virtue of their liabilities, and raised the flag of their doctrine in an uncompromising manner. As a group they preached spontaneity, "truth in music," nationalism, opposition to academism and Wagnerism. To them the villains of Russian music were the Rubinstein brothers and their conservatories, for they were the Enemy, representing the Western academic tradition. Anton Rubinstein (1830–1894), Russia's first great pianist, was a prolific composer who turned out piece after piece in the Mendelssohn-Schumann-Chopin tradition of early romanticism. His *Ocean Symphony* was probably the most popular orchestral work in Europe during the last half of the nineteenth century. As in his other music, there is not a trace of nationalism in the *Ocean Symphony*. Only recently has Rubinstein's music virtually disappeared, though the Melody in F is still known, the D minor Piano Concerto and a few solo piano pieces are still occasionally heard, and his opera, *The Demon*, is still performed in Russia. In 1862 Rubinstein founded the St. Petersburg Conservatory. Two years later his brother, Nicholas, founded the Moscow Conservatory. Nicholas Rubinstein (1835–1881) was also a fine pianist. Tchaikovsky considered him superior even to his more famous brother.

Both of the Rubinsteins were anathema to The Five. "It would be a serious error to consider Rubinstein a Russian composer," Cui wrote. "He is merely a Russian who composes." To The Five, the two conservatories represented the sterile, dead weight of the German conventions. Balakirev considered the St. Petersburg Conservatory a plot "to bring all Russian music under the yoke of the German generals." The Five were looking for something else. Their interest was primarily in dramatic music for the voice, or in orchestral music representing the traditions of their own country. Their idea of "truth" differed considerably from the Rubinstein idea of truth. As Cui explained their doctrine, "Dramatic music must have an intrinsic worth, as absolute music, independent of the text." And: "Vocal music must be in perfect agreement with the sense of the words. . . . The structure of the scenes must depend entirely on the relation of the characters and on the general movement of the play." Away with coloratura roulades, away with those calling cards named "leit motifs," away with the "immutable stereotyped forms." Inspiration was the important thing, much more important than "rules" or sonata form.

The dislike of The Five toward the academicians was fully reciprocated. To the conservatory-trained musicians, the Balakirev circle consisted of amateurs. Tchaikovsky, for one, was constantly ridiculing the (to him) outrageous and self-satisfied claims of The Five. "One must always *work*, and a self-respecting artist must not fold his hands on the pretext that he isn't in the mood. . . . I have learned to master myself and am glad I've not followed in the footsteps of those Russian colleagues who have no self-confidence and no patience, and who throw in the sponge at the slightest difficulty. That is why, in spite of their great gifts, they produce so little and in such a desultory way." In a long, famous letter to Nadejda von Meck, his

53

patroness, Tchaikovsky wrote exactly what he thought of The Five. The letter, dated January 5, 1878, is an important document, illustrative of what the "educated" Russian musicians of the day were thinking:

> . . . All the newest Petersburg composers are very gifted persons, but they are all afflicted to the marrow with the worst sort of conceit and with a purely dilettantish confidence in their superiority over all the rest of the musical world. Rimsky-Korsakov has been the recent exception. He too was self-taught like the others, but a radical change has occurred in him [Rimsky had recently been appointed professor of composition at the St. Petersburg Conservatory] . . . As a very young man he fell in with a group of people who first assured him he was a genius, then told him it was not necessary to *study*, that schooling kills inspiration, dries up creativity, and so on. At first he believed this. His first compositions reveal a very great talent devoid of any theoretical training. In the circle to which he belonged, every one was in love with himself and with one another. . . . Cui is a gifted dilettante. His music is devoid of originality, but is elegant and graceful. . . . Borodin is a 50-year-old professor of chemistry at the Academy of Medicine. Again a talent—even an impressive one— . . . he has less taste than Cui and his technique is so weak that he cannot write a line without outside help. Mussorgsky you very correctly call a has-been. In talent he perhaps exceeds all the others; but he has a narrow stature and lacks the need for self-perfection. . . . The most outstanding person of this circle is Balakirev. But he has grown silent after accomplishing very little. He has immense gifts; and they are lost because of some fateful circumstances that have made a saintly prig of him. . . . This, then, is my honest opinion of these gentlemen. What a sad thing! With the exception of Rimsky-Korsakov, how many talents from whom it is futile to await anything serious! And is not this generally the way in Russia? Tremendous powers fatally hindered by a sort of Plevna from taking the field and enjoining battle as they should. Nevertheless these powers exist. Even a Mussorgsky, by his very lack of discipline, speaks a new language. It is ugly, but it is fresh. . . .

Tchaikovsky was trying hard to be fair, but his distaste and prejudices show through. He was, however, honest enough and musician enough to see the elemental power of Mussorgsky. About Balakirev he was, on the whole, correct. Balakirev was more a catalyst than a composer, and very little of his music has survived. The only work that still has any currency is his tremendous piano piece, *Islamey*. Sir Thomas Beecham used to conduct Balakirev's First Symphony, and Serge Koussevitzky had a liking for the symphonic poem *Thamar*. Neither work has been much heard in the West since those two champions died.

The 1860's was the decade during which The Five worked together as a unit. Balakirev in addition kept busy as the head of the Free School of Music, which he set up in opposition to the St. Petersburg Conservatory. The Free School sponsored concerts, and Balakirev conducted about twenty a year, introducing many new Russian scores (including several by Tchaikovsky). He continued to ride herd over his young friends, and Rimsky-Korsakov referred time and again to his "iron-grip." Balakirev on the one hand was sincerely interested in their development. On the other hand he was a despot who had to have things his own way, and he resented it when the members of his circle started going off on their own, maturing, ignoring his advice. As he felt his influence decrease, his attitude became sharper and more domineering than ever. "I particularly dislike the one-sidedness of his musical opinions and the acerbity of his tone," Tchaikovsky, who had dealings with him, complained. Rather than take a secondary position, Balakirev began to avoid the circle, a fact that Borodin noted in 1871:

I don't understand why Balakirev turns away so stubbornly . . . Perhaps it's only his conceit gnawing at him. He is so despotic by nature that he demands complete subordination to his wishes, even in the most trifling matters. It doesn't seem possible for him to acknowledge freedom and equality. He cannot endure the slightest opposition to his tastes or even to his whims. He wants to impose his yoke on everyone and everything. And yet he is quite aware that we all have already grown up, that we stand firmly on our feet and no longer require braces. This evidently irks him. More than once he has said to Ludma: "Why should I hear their things; they are all so mature now that I've become unnecessary to them, they can do without me," etc. His nature is such that it positively requires minors around whom he can fuss like a nurse around a child. . . . Meanwhile the alienation of Mili, his obvious turning away from the circle, his sharp remarks about many, especially about Modest, have considerably cooled those sympathetic to him. If he goes on like this he may easily isolate himself and, this, in his situation, would amount to spiritual death.

Borodin was an accurate prophet. Balakirev soon broke entirely from the circle. In 1872 he left music completely to take a job with a railroad company. He felt rejected and useless, and he became a religious fanatic. That lasted several years, and then he returned to the musical wars, resuming the directorship of the Free School and taking a new group of pupils, among them the talented Serge Liapunov. He also started to compose again, eventually finishing two symphonies and a huge piano sonata. (Balakirev previously had been notorious for starting but never finishing his compositions.) He became friendly with Tchaikovsky, bombarding him with suggestions and advice. But he no longer was the symbol he had been. He

55

was respected, but his word no longer was law. The founding father of The Five was the last but one of the group to die (Cui outlived him by eight years). At his death in 1910 he was little more than a name to the younger generation of Russian composers. But without him the course of Russian music would have taken a completely different turn.

Mussorgsky was the first of The Five to come to fulfillment. Of the group, he was the most original and the most uncompromising. He lived only for music, and perhaps he drank so much because he never could achieve his vision. Certainly nothing but alcohol interfered with his quest. He paid next to no attention to his civil service position, he seems to have had no love affairs (suggestions that he was a homosexual are unsupported), he had no money, and he lived only to get on paper the sounds that were in his mind. He believed that an artist had to hew his own path and not follow the crowd. There is a revealing sentence in a letter he wrote to Rimsky in 1867. He was writing about Wagner, a composer he did not like very much, but he felt "Wagner is powerful, powerful, in that he lays hands on art and yanks it around." Little by little Mussorgsky worked out his philosophy. Basic to his ideas was the concept of the reproduction of human speech in musical terms, and he tried to achieve it in a setting of Gogol's *The Marriage,* of which he completed only one act. He called that act his Rubicon. "This is living prose in music . . . this is reverence for the language of humanity, this is a reproduction of simple human speech."

He became fixated on the subject. Time and again he referred to it, and he was obsessed with the problem. "I want to say that if the expression in sound of human thought and feeling is truly produced by me *in music,* and this reproduction is musical and artistic, then the thing is in the bag." Or: "If it is possible to tug at the heartstrings by the simplest of means, merely by obeying an artistic instinct to catch the intonations of the human voice —why not look into this matter?" Or: "I should like to make my characters speak on the stage exactly as people do in real life, without exaggeration or distortion, and just write music that will be thoroughly artistic. . . . What I project is the melody of life, not of classicism." Mussorgsky decided that he had a mission "unexampled in the history of the art: that of setting to music prose straight out of life, of turning out musical prose." He had not pulled these ideas from the empty air; they previously had been promulgated by Dargomijsky, whose opera *The Stone Guest* stood as a concrete example of sung speech in its pure state. Dargomijsky in 1857 had written: "I do not intend to debase music to the level of mere amusement . . . I want the notes to express exactly what the words express. I want truth." *The Stone Guest* was derided as "a recitative opera," and Dargomijsky never finished it. (Cui completed the final scene, and Rimsky-Korsakov scored it.) But the work, and Dargomijsky's theories, made an enormous impression on

Mussorgsky. The entire concept was new. No composer previously had thought of opera in that fashion, Wagner least of all. Wagner's *Stabreim* was a literary device, far removed from natural speech.

Allied to the Mussorgsky concept of sung speech was a strong nationalism. He wanted to express the Russian people. "When I sleep I see them, when I eat I think of them, when I drink—I can visualize them, integral, big, unpainted, and without any tinsel." To achieve his ideal, Mussorgsky was prepared to break any rule, go to any length. He despised anybody— Saint-Saëns, for instance—who in his opinion took the easy way out by pandering to public taste, and his comments on Cui and Rimsky-Korsakov after the circle began to break up have an indignation that curiously anticipates the writings of Charles Ives: "When I think of certain artists who dare not cross the barrier, I feel not merely distressed but sickened. All their ambition is to detail, one by one, carefully-measured drops of prettiness. A real man would be ashamed of doing so. Devoid of wisdom and will power, they entangle themselves in the bonds of tradition."

Mussorgsky started working on his masterpiece, *Boris Godounov,* in 1868. The great score has a peculiar history. Mussorgsky adapted his text (he wrote the libretto himself) from a Pushkin play. It is a libretto that is more a series of pageants than anything else, but it is held together by the tremendous figure of Boris and, more, by an inexorable sweep that passes from the intrigue of the court to the life of the people. The opera may be named *Boris Godounov,* but it far transcends any one figure. It is Russia: the Russia of king and boyar, priest and intriguer, common man, field, city, and forest. The score was finished in December, 1869, after fifteen months of work. Mussorgsky submitted it to the theater and it was rejected on the grounds that it lacked a major female role. There were other reasons for the rejection, and it is a matter of record that the committee was shocked by the novelty of the opera and its bleakness—it's "truth." Stassov and other friends urged Mussorgsky to revise *Boris Godounov,* and he reluctantly set about it. He dropped a scene in St. Basil Square, cut sections from other scenes, inserted new arias of an almost orthodox nature, and composed an entirely new third act, the Polish act, which has a prominent part for soprano. Now the opera ended with the Peasant Revolt and the song of the Simpleton. The revision was completed in 1874. Some Mussorgsky experts, including his biographer, M. D. Calvocoressi, believe the second version to be weaker than the first.

In 1873, three scenes from *Boris* were staged at the Maryinsky Theater. The following year the vocal score was published by Bessel. Finally, on January 27, 1874, the entire opera was staged, though with a few cuts. It had a decided success with the public, and less of a success with the critics. Among the dissenting critics was Cui, who attacked *Boris* for its "feeble" libretto, its "Wagnerism," its "crude tone painting," its "immaturity," its "lack of technique." Mussorgsky was crushed. Then he became furious at Cui. *Boris God-ounov* remained in the repertory for several years, disappearing in 1879. In five years it received twenty-one performances. After Mussorgsky's death the opera received five more performances and then, in 1882, was withdrawn.

The history of *Boris Godounov* does not end there. As a tribute to the memory of his friend, Rimsky-Korsakov undertook the preparation of all Mussorgsky manuscripts for publication. *Boris* came under his editorial supervision. Rimsky-Korsakov was a skilled composer, a devoted and honest musician, and a loyal friend; but he also had a conventional mind and certain things about the opera appalled him: "I worship *Boris Godounov* and hate it. I worship it for its originality, power, boldness, independence and beauty. I hate it for its shortcomings, the roughness of its harmonies, the incoherencies in the music." He knew there would be opposition: "Although I know I shall be cursed for so doing, I will revise *Boris*. There are countless absurdities in its harmonies, and at time in its melodies. Unfortunately, Stassov and his followers will never understand."

And so, Rimsky took it upon himself to edit, change, reharmonize, and reorchestrate *Boris Godounov*. It is the Rimsky-Korsakov edition that was promptly used in opera houses the world over, and is still generally in use, despite protests by musicologists and critics. Not until 1928 was the original full score published. There have been several attempts to present the "original" *Boris*, but most musicians believe that the original score has to be touched up to make it "sound." Thus when the Metropolitan Opera staged what purported to be the original, it was in a heavily touched-up version by Karol Rathaus. At least Rathaus left the original harmonies unchanged. Other adaptations have been made, including a version by Dmitri Shostakovich that out-Rimskys Rimsky. The fact seems to be that the original version of *Boris* has so many instances of inept scoring that some editorial work has to be done. The controversy about how much to do is still raging.

After *Boris Godounov*, Mussorgsky turned his attention to another opera, *Khovantchina*. He also went through a profound psychic upheaval. His private life became a mess, and his friends were frightened by his compulsive drinking. Mussorgsky had turned into a dipsomaniac. Borodin lamented. "This is horribly sad! Such a talented man and sinking so low morally. Now he periodically disappears, then reappears, morose, untalkative, which is contrary to his usual habit. After a while he comes to himself again—sweet, gay, amiable and as witty as ever. Devil knows what a pity!" Mussorgsky's friend, the artist Ilya Repin (whose frightening, unforgettable portrait of Mussorgsky in his last days is one of the masterpieces of nineteenth-century portraiture), has recorded the disintegration:

It was really incredible how that well-bred Guards officer, with his beautiful and polished manners, that witty conversationalist with the ladies, that inexhaustible punster . . . quickly sank, sold his belongings, even his elegant clothes, and soon descended to some cheap saloons where he personified the familiar type of has-been, where this childishly happy child, with a red potato-shaped nose, was already unrecognizable. . . . Was it really he? The once impeccably-dressed, heel-clicking society man, scented, dainty, fastidious? Oh, how many times V.V. [Stassov] on his return from abroad was hardly able to get him out of some basement dive, nearly in rags, swollen with alcohol.

Nevertheless Mussorgsky continued to compose and to work at his government position, though haphazardly. He managed to hold on to his job in the Forestry Department of the Ministry of State Property. Then he was transferred to Government Control, where he had an indulgent superior who turned his head aside when Mussorgsky showed up drunk. The piano score of *Khovantchina* was finished in 1874 (he never scored the opera, which was brought to completion by Rimsky-Korsakov), and from 1875 to 1877 Mussorgsky worked on, among other things, his opera *The Fair at Soro-chintzi* and the cycle *Songs and Dances of Death*. He even pulled himself together to make a tour of Russia as piano accompanist for a singer. But his heavy drinking continued. In 1880 and 1881 he had fits of delirium tremens. Finally he had a stroke and died at the age of forty-two on March 16, 1881. At the unveiling of a monument to him in 1885, the other members of The Five lifted the four corners of the veil.

Mussorgsky's total output was small, and he lives today only by a handful of works. There is *Boris Godounov*, of course, with its epic sweep, real-life characters, and spirit of the Russian people. There are the four songs of the *Songs and Dances of Death*, one of the most powerful and terrifying cycles ever written. With its jarring harmonies, its mixture of recitative and melody, its poignancy, and its brooding atmosphere, it stands next to *Boris* as one of Mussorgsky's sublime achievements of "truth" in music. The specter of death throws a black shadow across every measure, and the *Lullaby* of the *Songs and Dances* is searing in its bleakness and pity—a pity that never descends to sentimentalism. There is the *Pictures at an Exhibition* for piano solo, a permanent concert-hall favorite (and also a favorite with conductors in the Ravel orchestration). There is a group of remarkable songs, including two cycles, *Sunless* and *The Nursery*. The two last operas, *Khovantchina* and *The Fair at Sorochintzi*, were completed by other composers. How much of Mussorgsky remains in them, and how much of Rimsky-Korsakov and Vissarion Shebalin respectively, is impossible to say. The Prelude to *Khovantchina*, a beautiful tone picture, occasionally appears on a symphony program, as does the early symphonic sketch *A Night on Bald Mountain*.

Mussorgsky did not live entirely unrecognized outside of Russia. Liszt was interested in his music, and in 1874 *Boris Godounov* created much talk in professional French circles when Saint-Saëns returned from Russia with the score. There were those then, as there are today, who came to the conclusion that Mussorgsky was an inspired dilettante. What many academically trained musicians failed to see was that while Mussorgsky's music could be awkward and even full of errors in relation to the rules, it was often *purposely* rough and awkward. The rules often were deliberately broken. Naturally, Mussorgsky's music would be of greatest interest to those composers who themselves broke the rules. Debussy, who knew the score of *Boris* and heard other music by Mussorgsky when he was Nadejda von Meck's pianist in Russia, was fascinated. Above all Western musicians, Debussy responded to Mussorgsky's modalism, irregular scales and rhythms, and asymmetrical patterns. Yet even Debussy implied that Mussorgsky was a kind of untutored savage: "He is unique and will remain so because his art is spontaneous and free from arid formula. Never has a more refined sensibility been conveyed by such simple means; it is like the art of an inquiring savage discovering music step by step through his emotions." Today it is recognized that Mussorgsky was by far the most original and modern of nineteenth-century Russian composers. He was of the future, and he probably knew it. "The artist believes in the future because he lives in the future," he wrote in his dedication of *Boris Godounov*.

As for Borodin and Rimsky-Korsakov, their destinies took different paths. Borodin never left science, and he composed even less than Mussorgsky. After his return from Heidelberg in 1862—he came back to St. Petersburg with a wife, a Russian pianist he had met in Germany—he was appointed to the faculty of chemistry in the Academy of Medicine. He moved into an apartment on the grounds. There he lived for the rest of his life with his wife, innumerable cats, and equally innumerable relatives, in a state of happy and maniacal disorder. He was an easy-going, kind-hearted man. Professor Borodin, one of the most respected chemists in Europe, was loved by his pupils. How he found time to compose *anything* remains a mystery. Students, friends, scientists, musicians, and in-laws were constantly wandering through the rooms of the Borodin apartment. The samovar was at a perpetual boil. Borodin never had any privacy. Often he found a relative or visitor in his own bed, and with a resigned shrug he would camp on the sofa for the night. He described himself as a Sunday composer. "Science is my work and music is my fun." A levelheaded man, he was not as disturbed as the others when The Five started to break up. "So far as I see, this is nothing but a natural situation. As long as we were in the position of eggs under a setting hen (thinking of Balakirev as the latter) we were all more or less alike. As soon as the fledgelings broke out of their shells, they grew feathers. Each of them had to grow different feathers; and when their wings grew, each flew to wherever his nature drew him." Borodin said that eventually everybody came to understand this but Balakirev.

Borodin's major work was the opera *Prince Igor*, which occupied him for some twenty years. But he never found the time to finish it. Rimsky-Korsakov and Alexander Glazunov had to reconstruct it from a mass of sketches and what they remembered when Borodin himself played and sang excerpts. There was not even an overture in notation, though Borodin had composed one, and Glazunov had to notate it from memory. The feat is not as difficult as it sounds. Glazunov had a remarkable ear and memory, watery as his own music is. *Prince Igor* is a beautiful work with the emphasis on folklore, and is more akin to the Rimsky-Korsakov operas than to *Boris Godounov*. Or is that because Rimsky edited *Prince Igor* as extensively as he had edited the Mussorgsky opera? There are, however, a handful of works that presumably are Borodin's own. One never really knows, for The Five were constantly tinkering with one another's scores, and Borodin was a very complaisant man. In any case, the Symphony No. 2 in B minor is a masterpiece. Borodin had a refined ear for orchestral sound and, working as closely with Rimsky-Korsakov as he did, knew the potentiality of each instrument in the orchestra as well as any composer in Europe. Rimsky would arrive at the Borodin house lugging three or four instruments, and the two men would spend a weekend experimenting with, and trying to play, the tuba, the English horn, the bassoon, or whatever instruments were at hand. Between the two of them, they worked their way through every instrument of the orchestra. In the B minor Symphony there is, besides the gorgeous, resilient, exotic-sounding melodies, a kind of bright orchestral sound of unusual personality. Rimsky-Korsakov is supposed to be one of the great masters of the orchestra, and he is, but his scores sound thick next to the wonderfully articulated sounds and mixtures of the Borodin B minor. There are those who, like Debussy and his friends at the conservatory, put that work at the top of all Russian symphonies, including the last three by Tchaikovsky.

Borodin's music achieved a sizable reputation outside of Russia. Often he would travel to scientific conferences, and at those times he would take the opportunity of meeting Europe's foremost musicians. He showed the manuscript of the B minor Symphony to Liszt, who was impressed enough to put it on a program. In Belgium the Countess de Mercy-Argenteau, a patroness who was greatly interested in Russian music, sponsored performances of Borodin's First Symphony. In Paris, his String Quartet in A major was played. Such success might have spurred other men, but Borodin continued to remain a Sunday composer, full of musical ideas and projects without the time to accomplish them. On February 2, 1887, he was at a party, had a heart attack, and died instantly.

Today he is remembered primarily by four works—*Prince Igor*, the

String Quartet No. 2 in D, the B minor Symphony, and a tone picture called *In the Steppes of Central Asia*. The opera, which has a static libretto, is a musical evocation of early Russia, with its heroes, boyars, and Asiatic tribes. The *Polovetsian Dances* occur in the second act, and at the turn of the century were considered an authentic representation of barbaric Russia. Time, and Stravinsky's *Sacre du Printemps*, have relegated the *Polovetsian Dances* to a form of light music, but the dances nevertheless remain effective, and the opera as a whole has some of the grandeur, if not the truth, of *Boris*. Of Borodin's two string quartets, No. 1 in A is long and rambling, but the D major is a jewel. Less nationalistic than much of Borodin's music, verging on the salon, it is a sweet, gentle, and attractive work, beautifully composed, and by far the single most popular piece of chamber music that has come out of Russia.

Nicolai Rimsky-Korsakov, born in the Novgorod district on March 18, 1844, became The Grand Old Man of Russian music. As a young man he had, while still a naval officer, worked under Balakirev's guidance and produced such interesting and individual works as the *Antar* Symphony, the symphonic poem *Sadko* (later to be the subject of one of his most famous operas), and the opera *The Maid of Pskov*. In the 1860's The Five would often gather at the house of Nicolai Purgold, a wealthy connoisseur. Of Purgold's ten children, two were talented musically. Alexandra was the singer and Nadejda the pianist. Those two girls were the first to see much of the new music produced by The Five, and they performed it at the many soirées held by the hospitable Purgold. Between Nadejda and Rimsky-Korsakov a romance sprang up, and they were married in 1873.

That was two years after he became associated with the St. Petersburg Conservatory. Rimsky-Korsakov had been invited to become Professor of Practical Composition and Instrumentation. He spent sleepless nights worrying about the invitation, as well he might. He already had a great reputation as a composer, but only he knew how little he knew. Balakirev's teaching had not included even the most elementary aspects of the art of music. As Rimsky-Korsakov wrote in his autobiography:

It was not merely that I couldn't at that time have harmonized a chorale properly, had never written a single contrapuntal exercise in my life, and had only the haziest understanding of strict fugue, but I didn't even know the names of the augmented and diminished intervals or of the chords, other than the tonic triad and the dominant and diminished sevenths. Though I could sing anything at sight and *distinguish* any conceivable chord, the terms "chord of the sixth" and "six-four chord" were unknown to me. In my compositions I strove after correct part writing and achieved it by instinct and by ear. My grasp of the musical forms (particularly of the rondo) was equally hazy. Although I scored my own compositions colorfully enough, I had no real knowledge of string technique or of the practical possibilities of horns, trumpets and trombones. As for conducting, I had never led an orchestra in my life.

This was the new professor. He was allowed to remain in the navy, and he taught in uniform. What ensued was comedy on a grand scale. Rimsky started to study furiously, keeping just one step ahead of his classes. He went deep into counterpoint, harmony, and analysis. In a few years he became a fine teacher. But some of The Five, especially Mussorgsky, were furious. Rimsky-Korsakov had sold out; was considered a renegade who had joined the enemy, who was throwing over his Russian heritage to compose fugues and sonatas. "The Mighty Five have hatched into a horde of soulless traitors," snarled Mussorgsky.

And The Five did break up. But Rimsky-Korsakov, far from being a renegade, turned into the most national of all Russians except Mussorgsky himself. He composed a series of operas—*Snow Maiden* (1881), *Christmas Eve* (1895), *Sadko* (1896), *The Czar's Bride* (1898), *The Story of the Czar Saltan* (1898), *The Legend of the Invisible City of Kitezh* (1905), *The Golden Cockerel* (1907)—that were the essence of the Russian folk heritage. They are not as deep as *Boris Godounov*, they do not probe character, and their harmonies are very polite. But they open up a delightful new world, the world of the Russian East, the world of supernaturalism and the exotic, the world of Slavic pantheism and vanished races. Genuine poetry suffuses them, and they are scored with brilliance and resource. Rimsky was a master of orchestral color, and also of picture painting in music. Nobody has described his orchestral sound better than Serge Rachmaninoff, himself no mean orchestrator:

> In Rimsky-Korsakov's scores there is never the slightest doubt about the "meteorological picture" the music is meant to convey. When there is a snowstorm the flakes seem to dance and drift from the woodwinds and the sound holes of the violins; when the sun is high, all instruments shine with an almost fiery glare; when there is water, the waves ripple and dance audibly through the orchestra, and this effect is not achieved by the comparatively cheap means of a harp glissando. The sound is cool and glassy when he describes a calm winter night with a glittering starlit sky. He was a great master of orchestral sound-painting and one can still learn from him.

On the whole, the Rimsky-Korsakov operas are underrated works. A score with the devastating power of *Boris Godounov* can make an overwhelming impact sung in any language. But the more delicate Rimsky-Korsakov operas are so bound up with the Russian folk tradition that they wither in translation. Those who have seen *Sadko*, *Kitezh*, and other Rimsky operas in Russia can attest to a kind of vitality and charm that productions else-where are not able to muster.

In addition to the operas, Rimsky-Korsakov wrote much orchestral music. The *Capriccio Espagnol* was finished in 1887, *Schéhérazade* and the *Russian Easter* Overture in 1888. There was a one-movement, Lisztian, Piano Concerto (1883) based on Russian themes. There was a Symphony in E flat minor (1865) and also a Symphony in C (1873) that are no longer played. He also composed songs, piano pieces, choral works, and church music. When he was not composing, he was conducting, or traveling around the country as inspector of naval bands (although he had left the navy in 1873). He was assistant director of the court chapel (1883–1884), he contin-ued to teach at the Conservatory, wrote a famous book on orchestration, fought off periodic bouts of Dostoievskian depression, made trips to France and Belgium as conductor and exponent of Russian music. From all ac-counts, he was not a very good conductor. Igor Stravinsky, who was his pupil from 1906–1908, offers a little picture:

> Rimsky-Korsakov was a tall man, like Berg or Aldous Huxley, and, like Huxley, too, he suffered from poor eyesight. He wore blue-tinted spectacles, sometimes keeping an extra pair on his forehead, a habit of his I have caught. When conducting an orchestra he would bend over the score and, hardly ever looking up, wave his baton in the direction of his knees. His difficulty in seeing the score was so great, and he was so absorbed in listening, that he gave almost no directions to the orchestra at all.

In the early 1880's there arose a new circle, this one gathered at the feet of Mitrofan Petrovich Belaiev. Belaiev (1836–1904) was the son of a wealthy timber merchant and a lover of chamber music. In 1885 he founded a pub-lishing house, setting it up in Leipzig to secure international copyright, and in the same year he also sponsored the Russian Symphony Concerts in St. Petersburg. All of these activities were aimed at helping Russian composers. A new school was rising, and its members gathered in Belaiev's house, with Rimsky-Korsakov as adviser and old master. There were Anatol Liadov, Al-exander Glazunov, Mikhail Ippolitov-Ivanov, Anton Arensky. All were pu-pils of Rimsky-Korsakov, as were, in his last days, Prokofiev and Stravinsky. The St. Petersburg Conservatory represented, and still does, the Russian na-tional school, as opposed to the Moscow Conservatory, which stands for a more international, European style from Tchaikovsky through Sergei Ta-neiev and Sergei Rachmaninoff. In a way, the old Rimsky-Korsakov became the new Balakirev. When he died, on June 21, 1908, the great age of Rus-sian music died with him—and a new one was to begin two years later, when Stravinsky's *Firebird* received its first performance.

Surcharged Emotionalism

PETER ILYICH TCHAIKOVSKY

The Mighty Five never knew exactly what to make of Peter Ilyich Tchaikovsky. He was a conservatory graduate and he composed symphonies more or less in the classic style with orthodox developments. That was enough to make one suspicious. On the other hand, he liberally quoted folk songs, and his music was undeniably Russian. That was good. So where did he stand? At first there was hostility between Tchaikovsky and The Five. Later Balakirev became interested in his music and introduced some of it to the Free School audiences. There was a truce. But Tchaikovsky never had a high opinion of Balakirev and his circle. Basically Tchaikovsky was a conservative and could not subscribe to the "truth" of Mussorgsky or to the loose organization of much of the music composed by the members of the circle.

It was not that Tchaikovsky himself was a complete master of form. But he was much more in the European tradition. And he had what many of The Five lacked—a sweet, inexhaustible, supersensuous fund of melody. It was this melody that was to make him famous, first in Russia, then internationally. It was a peculiarly Russian kind of melody, plangent, introspective, often modal-sounding, touched with neuroticism, as emotional as a scream from a window on a dark night. The music reflected the man. He was a nervous, hypochondriacal, unhappy man—unhappy at home, unhappy away from home, nervous in the presence of other people, terrified lest his homosexuality become open knowledge. He was largely successful at hiding his emotions, his fears and neuroses, from most of the persons with whom he came into contact. But to a few close friends and to his diary he confided everything. He could converse in an urbane way with people, and little did they know they repelled him. Thus he notes in his diary that he carried on "an unbelievably amiable and incredibly animated conversation. . . . But in my soul there was despair and a desire to flee from them to the ends of the world." When he arrived in New York in 1891 he went to his hotel. "I

65

made myself at home. First of all, I wept rather long." Then he bathed, dined, walked along Broadway and returned to his room, where he "took to whimpering again several times." In Paris he avoided, as much as possible, his colleagues. "Every new acquaintance, every fresh meeting with somebody unknown, has always been for me a source of suffering . . . springing possibly from a shyness that has increased to a mania, possibly from a complete lack of any need for human society, possibly also from inability, without an effort, to say things about oneself that one doesn't think (which is unavoidable in social intercourse)—in short, I don't know what it is."

This surcharged emotionalism, implicit in almost every note he wrote, acted upon audiences in several ways. From the beginning, most listeners enjoyed the emotional bath in which they were immersed by the composer. Others, more inhibited, either rejected Tchaikovsky's message out of hand or despised themselves for responding to it. A composer is supposed to be more "manly." There is something embarrassing, even immoral, about such hysteria in music. For a long time Tchaikovsky, so loved by the public, was discounted by many connoisseurs and musicians as nothing but a weeping machine. In recent years there has been a new estimate, and musicians tend to find much more to admire in Tchaikovsky's music than they previously did. His orchestration is a subject of admiring comment—that dark-colored yet brilliant-sounding and perfectly calculated scoring. The structure of the last three symphonies is studied as a successful compromise between the demands of the classical symphony and the new forms imposed by the demands of a postromantic age. In any case, Tchaikovsky did as well without the approval of the learned musicians as he did with it. Of the late romantics, only Brahms has established himself so securely in the repertory. Tchaikovsky's last three symphonies, his three ballets (*Swan Lake, Sleeping Beauty, Nutcracker*), his Piano Concerto in B flat minor and Violin Concerto in D, his *Romeo and Juliet Overture* and two of his operas, *Eugene Onegin* and *The Queen of Spades,* are played everywhere. Almost as popular are such works as the *Manfred* Symphony (a program work based on the Byron drama and not listed among the six symphonies), *Francesca da Rimini,* the *Capriccio Italien,* the *Hamlet Overture-Fantasy,* and the Serenade for Strings. Each of his three string quartets and the Piano Trio in A minor has beautiful things in it. Recitalists still program his songs. And there are always the *Marche Slave* and the *1812* Overture . . .

As a creator Tchaikovsky developed slowly. Born in Kamsko-Votinsk of a well-to-do middle-class family on May 7, 1840, he was a precocious child, but the precocity showed itself in things other than music. At the age of six he could read French and German; at seven he was writing verses in French. He was very sensitive, and his governess called him "a porcelain child." Had his parents subjected him to intensive training he could have been a Wunderkind, for he was ultrasensitive to music and had a delicate ear. When he heard music—he was taking piano lessons at the age of seven—it stuck in his mind and kept resounding. "This music! This music! Take it away! It's here in my head and won't let me sleep!"

His family moved to St. Petersburg in 1850, and he went to school there. He had a mild interest in music and, though relatively untrained, was trying to compose when he was fourteen. In school he did not study music at all. After graduating from the School of Jurisprudence, in 1859, he entered the Ministry of Justice as a clerk first-class. Then in 1861 he went abroad, spending much more than he could afford. At this time there was little money in the family; his father had lost almost everything in a series of bad investments. "If ever I started on a colossal piece of folly," he wrote to his sister, "it was this journey. . . . You know, I have a weakness. As soon as I get any money, I squander it on pleasure. It's vulgar and stupid, I know, but it seems to be part of my nature." (Tchaikovsky never was able to hold on to money. He made a good deal during his life, but gave away much and spent the rest. He was once asked where he invested his money. Tchaikovsky laughed. "In the Kokorev Hotel when I stayed in Moscow." When he received an advance from New York for his trip to the United States in 1891, he sent out a note to friends and creditors: "I have just received good money. Come and get your share while it lasts.")

Not until he was twenty-one years old did he start to study music seriously. He worked with Nicolai Zaremba until the St. Petersburg Conservatory opened in 1862. Zaremba enrolled there, and Tchaikovsky followed him. Tchaikovsky joked about his studies, but secretly dreamed of being another Glinka, and in 1863 he resigned from the Ministry to devote his life to music. Anton Rubinstein, the director of the Conservatory, decided that Tchaikovsky had talent, and took a personal interest in him. Tchaikovsky went through the curriculum and even studied conducting. He was terrified when he stood in front of an orchestra, and he was terrified all his life, even when he was in constant demand as a guest conductor for his own music. He got the idea that his head was going to fall from his shoulders, and he actually would put his left hand under his chin to keep it attached. It is not surprising that he was not exactly a conductor who could inspire his players. But, aside from this, Tchaikovsky was one of the best Conservatory students, and in 1866 Anton Rubinstein recommended him to his brother Nicholas, who was looking for a harmony teacher for the Moscow Conservatory. The pay was small but Tchaikovsky had nowhere else to turn. He moved to Moscow and for six years lived with Nicholas, who swamped the wretched, homesick young man with kindness.

His life was quiet. He taught, composed, made friends. Within three years he had completed a Symphony in G minor (*Winter Daydreams*, 1866), some other orchestral music, and an opera, *The Voyevode* (1868). On a visit to St. Petersburg in 1868 he spent some time with the members of The Five. They liked his symphony, which he played to them from the manuscript. It had enough nationalism in it to interest them. As Rimsky-Korsakov wrote, "Our former opinion of him changed to a more favorable one, though his Conservatory education still placed a considerable barrier between him and us." Tchaikovsky meanwhile privately referred to The Five as "The Jacobin Club." Back in Moscow later that year, he had a flirtation with the Belgian soprano Désirée Artôt. But she married a Spanish baritone, ending whatever hopes Tchaikovsky may have had for a more permanent relationship. They remained close friends, and Tchaikovsky always looked her up whenever he was in her vicinity on his travels.

Compositions steadily came forth. *Romeo and Juliet* was finished in 1869 and Tchaikovsky sent it to Balakirev, who rubbed his hands and proceeded to tear it to pieces. By 1875 Tchaikovsky had finished the Second Symphony (*Little Russian*) on Ukrainian themes, the symphonic poem *Fatum*, three operas, the Third Symphony (*Polish*), and the B flat minor Piano Concerto. He intended to dedicate the concerto to Nicholas Rubinstein, but that worthy criticized it in so devastating a manner that Tchaikovsky instead dedicated it to Hans von Bülow (whom he had never met), and Bülow gave the world premiere in Boston on October 25, 1875. John Dwight, Boston's leading critic, was predictably horrified. He could not understand "the extremely difficult, strange, wild, ultra-Russian concerto." He conceded that it was brilliant and exciting, but his review ended with a rhetorical question: "Could we ever learn to love such music?" Dwight never could but others did, and Tchaikovsky's work began to be heard in Europe. While there were pockets of opposition, especially from Hanslick in Vienna, Tchaikovsky's reputation steadily grew.

In 1877, there occurred two epochal events in Tchaikovsky's life. He married, and he entered into his curious relationship with Nadejda von Meck. His wife was a pretty girl named Antonina Ivanova Miliukova. They had met at the Moscow Conservatory. She had a hero-worshiping crush on him, and presumably he married her thinking it would make him respectable. He also felt sorry for the girl. Undoubtedly he must have thought they could arrive at some kind of working relationship. Things not only did not work out; the marriage was a positive disaster. Antonina turned out to be a stupid woman, and in addition she appears to have been a nymphomaniac —not the mate for a sensitive terrified homosexual. It took Tchaikovsky only a short time to realize he had made a colossal blunder. "A few more days and I should have gone mad." As it was, he attempted suicide by immersing himself in a river, intending to catch pneumonia. Instead he caught only a monumental cold. His brother Modest, also a homosexual, rescued him and they fled to St. Petersburg, where Tchaikovsky promptly had a complete nervous breakdown. The marriage lasted nine weeks—that is, it broke up after nine weeks. He supported her, and she took up with a series of lovers. Finally in 1896 she was placed in an insane asylum where she died in 1917.

Nadejda von Meck, when she and Tchaikovsky first began to exchange letters, was a fabulously wealthy, music-loving widow of forty-six with eleven children. She loved Tchaikovsky's music and offered to subsidize him with the proviso that they were never to meet. Tchaikovsky accepted and for fourteen years received a generous allowance. They corresponded voluminously, and Tchaikovsky's letters to her provide a picture of a composer and his way of thinking and working unparalleled in the literature except for Mozart's letters. Why was she afraid of meeting him? Did she think she would be disillusioned? In one of the early letters in the correspondence, she writes: "There was a time when I was very anxious to make your acquaintance; but now, the more you fascinate me, the more I fear your acquaintanceship. I prefer to think of you from afar, to hear you speak in your music and share your feelings through it." Tchaikovsky was, of course, relieved. In his answer he wrote about misanthropy and his own problems: "There was a time when I was so possessed by this fear of mankind that I became almost insane." He said that he fully understood her position. "I'm not at all surprised that, in spite of your love for my music, you don't want to make my acquaintance. You are afraid you will fail to find in my personality all those qualities with which your idealizing imagination has endowed me. And in that you are quite right." They stuck to their pledge and never met, though they attended the same concerts and looked at each other out of the corner of their eyes. Once they came face to face. Both turned crimson with embarrassment. Tchaikovsky raised his hat, and she fluttered around and didn't know what to do. They fled from each other.

Psychiatrists can best discuss the relationship between the two. But from it came fourteen years of financial independence for Tchaikovsky. He was able to indulge himself and, as additional money from commissions and performances came in, to resign from the Conservatory in 1878 and buy himself a country home at Maidanovo. He was a rather striking figure— over average height, handsome, prematurely grey, with blue eyes and a neatly trimmed beard. He wore elegant clothes and his manners were exquisite. But his emotional problems did not cease with financial security. He suffered from incessant headaches, still wept easily, had constant doubts about himself and his music, and drank far too much. Liquor was one of his escapes. "It is said," he wrote in his diary, "that to abuse one's self with alcohol is harmful. I readily agree to that. But nevertheless I, a sick person, full of neuroses, absolutely cannot do without the alcoholic poison." He also was addicted to cards and had to have his nightly game of whist. Lacking that, he would lay out hands of solitaire.

In his diary and letters he wrote about his musical likes and dislikes. Wagner bored him, and he detested the music of Brahms. "It angers me that that presumptuous mediocrity is recognized as a *genius*. Indeed, in comparison with him, Raff is a giant, not to mention Rubinstein, who is still a big and vital personality." He had reservations about Beethoven: "I bow before the greatness of some of his works but I do not *love* Beethoven." The composer he adored above all others—and that was rare not only in the Russia of his time but also in the Europe of his time—was Mozart. He called Mozart "a musical Christ." The baroque period left him cold. "I play Bach gladly . . . but I do not recognize in him (as some do) a great genius. Handel has for me an entirely fourth-rate significance and he is not even entertaining." Of two other great composers before Beethoven, "Gluck, despite the relative poverty of his creation, is attractive to me. I also like certain things of Haydn."

As a student of the music of Mozart and the classical composers, and as a creator who tried to clothe his music in appropriate forms, Tchaikovsky throughout his life struggled with architectural problems. Unlike The Five, he was greatly concerned with form. But his mind did not have the kind of logic and imagination that could weld various elements into an organic whole. In his early symphonies his developments are patchwork, full of uninventive padding in a desperate effort to keep things moving. Not until the Fourth Symphony did he develop a kind of form that would fit the rapturous, dancelike, essentially spontaneous and lyric nature of his music. Tchaikovsky was well aware of the problem, and he wrote about it to Nadejda in 1878:

. . . What has been written with passion must now be looked upon critically, corrected, extended and, most important of all, condensed to fit the required needs of the form. One must sometimes go against the grain in this, be merciless, and destroy things that were written with love and inspiration. Although I cannot complain of poor inventive powers or imagination, I have always suffered from lack of skill in the management of form. Only persistent labor has at last permitted me to achieve a form that in some degree corresponds to the content. In the past I was careless. I did not realize the extreme importance of this critical examination of the preliminary sketch. For some reason the succeeding episodes were loosely held together and the seams were always showing. That was a serious defect, and it was years before I began to correct it. Yet my compositions will never be good examples of form because I can only correct what is wrong with my musical nature—I cannot change it intrinsically.

Analysts who use as a criterion the German symphonic form as laid down by Mozart and Beethoven have been citing "defects" in the Tchaikovsky symphonies ever since they were written. But strict application of formalistic criteria misses the point. Tchaikovsky's symphonies, even the first three, have such personality and such melodic appeal that they continue to sound eternally fresh. Despite the frequent naïveté of such works as the *Polish* and *Little Russian* symphonies, they are full of color, originality, and a very personal kind of speech. The last three Tchaikovsky symphonies break all of the rules as laid down by the textbooks, but here Tchaikovsky achieved a kind of synthesis that makes them as convincing structurally as any Brahms symphony—waltzes, march movements, and free forms notwithstanding. For they have a consistent emotional line and a consistency of workmanship, and the ideas progress surely and naturally. In his struggles with symphonic form, Tchaikovsky wrote three other symphonies and dodged the problem by calling them "suites." (The Suite No. 4, *Mozartiana*, is merely an orchestration of some piano pieces by Mozart.) The first three suites are generally neglected, but they have some gorgeous music in them, and they are permeated with the dance spirit—or, more specifically, the ballet spirit.

Ballet is implicit in a very large number of Tchaikovsky scores, even though he composed only three ballets proper. Much ballet music up to Tchaikovsky had been um-pah-pah music. A breakaway was made by Léo Delibes, who showed what a really skillful composer could do. Tchaikovsky admired Delibes's music a great deal, and in sections of *Swan Lake* the debt is apparent. Tchaikovsky's three ballets are close to opera, except that the "voice" parts are scored for dancers instead of singers. Each score has the equivalent of arias, duets, and ensembles. Tchaikovsky worked very closely with Marius Petipa, the choreographer for his ballets. During the creation of *Sleeping Beauty*, Petipa would write such instructions as: "Suddenly Aurora notices the old woman who beats on her knitting needles two-four measure. Gradually she changes to a very melodious waltz in three-four but then, suddenly, a rest. Aurora pricks her finger. Screams pain. Blood streams. Give eight measures in four-four, wide." For *Nutcracker* in 1891, Petipa's instructions were even more detailed. Tchaikovsky finished the score and looked at it with his usual pessimism. "No," he wrote, "the old man"—meaning himself—"is breaking up. Not only does his hair drop out or turn as white as snow; not only does he lose his teeth, which refuse their service; not only do his eyes weaken and tire easily; not only do his feet walk badly or drag themselves along; but he loses bit by bit the capacity to do anything at all. The ballet is infinitely worse than *Sleeping Beauty*—so much is certain."

Classic ballet is an idealized form of dance in which the ballerina, *en pointe,* tries to escape from the earth and its gravitational pull. The balle-

71

rina herself is idealized; she floats in the air; she is worshiped by the cavalier; she is young, radiant, and beautiful. There is no such thing as an old, ugly, or stout ballerina. Tchaikovsky identified himself with the idealistic qualities of ballet. There is a certain kind of homosexual who derides women; there is another, more feminine type, who loves women (except physically) and thinks like a woman. Tchaikovsky was one of the latter, and that helps explain the feeling of identification conveyed by the long-arched, proud, and sensuous melodies given to the ballerina—the *Rose Adagio* of *Sleeping Beauty* or the great *pas de deux* in *Nutcracker*. Tchaikovsky and the ballerina were one. The world of the ballet—the romantic, fairy-tale world of the ballet and its plush and gold surroundings, its beautiful women, its glamour, its homosexual ambience, its feeling of pomp and wealth, its intrigues, its association with royalty, its backstage gossip, its supple rhythms—this world comes up again and again in Tchaikovsky's music.

A good part of Tchaikovsky's career was spent in writing operas. When he could find a libretto that had a heroine with which he could identify, the result was excruciatingly beautiful music. In *Eugene Onegin* he found such a woman, and he composed his operatic masterpiece. Some consider the *Queen of Spades* a greater work, and it does have more intensity, a greater sweep, a mounting feeling of horror and inevitability. But the melodic materials are inferior to those found in the eternally lyric and elegiac *Onegin*, and the reason lies in the fact that Tchaikovsky was so attracted to Tatiana. *Eugene Onegin* is a quiet opera with a true-life ending—an ending that would have shocked every theatrical instinct of Verdi or the verismists. For the lover, who previously has spurned Tatiana, is simply sent away, and the curtain falls to quiet memories and nostalgia rather than a chorus shrieking vengeance or everybody in sight slaughtered.

Tchaikovsky's attitude toward opera was something like that of a Victorian's attitude toward sex. He loved it but at the same time had guilt feelings, thinking there was something sinful about it. Reflections about opera occupy a good deal of space in his letters. He could call opera "a false type of art" and in the same breath admit that there was in the form "something irrepressible that attracts all composers." Never a revolutionary, Tchaikovsky was content to accept the operatic conventions as they were. "The style of theater music must correspond to the style of scene painting: simple, clear, colorful." But unlike many composers of the time, Tchaikovsky was primarily interested in character rather than vocal effect or, indeed, any kind of effect. What he wanted was a libretto featuring strong human emotions, around which he could supply illustrative music. "I cannot write music with love and enthusiasm for any subject, however effective, if the characters do not compel my lively sympathy. If I do not love them, *pity* them, as living people love and *pity* . . ." Love and pity pervade *Onegin*, which has scarcely an inexpressive note in it, which has a piercing sadness and sweetness, and which is much more a singing opera than the *Queen of Spades*.

It may be this quiet sadness, this lack of sharp contour, that has held back the full success of *Onegin*. Tchaikovsky could write effectively for the voice, but he almost never supplied his singers with bravura work. Song is used to express character and mood, not to exploit the vocal cords. Verdi knew how to drive an audience to a frenzy, but Tchaikovsky constantly understates. Verdi and Wagner were musically tough; Tchaikovsky in his operas was uniformly gentle and yielding. Naturally Tchaikovsky's operas make less of an impression. But Tchaikovsky did not have to defer to anybody in his fund of melody and his knowledge of the orchestra; and, in its quiet way, *Eugene Onegin* can have an extraordinary impact. It has a continuous melodic wash, and idea follows idea: the exquisite opening duet (which grows into a quartet); the rapturous duet of Lensky and Olga followed by what surely is one of the great love arias in all opera, Lensky's *"Ya lyublu vas, Olga"*—"I love you, Olga." Tatiana's letter scene is the most familiar part of the opera (aside from the orchestral dances), and as one studies it there comes greater and greater respect for Tchaikovsky's powers as a craftsman. How surely he builds to the climax—Tatiana's outburst "Now I am alone!" with the orchestra welling up to one of those unforgettable, Tchaikovskian inspirations. Then there are the quarrel sequences, especially the bleak duel scene, with Lensky's great aria to his youth. At the end of the opera there is the muted but desperate confrontation between Tatiana and Onegin. All this is in a style that owed little to any composer. Tchaikovsky, who had analyzed the Wagner operas, did use a few leitmotifs, but in an elementary way. There is nothing the least Wagnerian about *Eugene Onegin*, and there certainly is nothing Verdian. The opera, which is based on Pushkin's poem, is in addition an altogether realistic picture of a certain stratum of Russian society. *Eugene Onegin* is to opera what *The Cherry Orchard* is to the legitimate stage.

As Tchaikovsky's music became well known throughout Europe, he traveled more and more. A blow came in 1890, when his annuity from Nadejda von Meck ceased. She thought she was going bankrupt, which did not happen to be the case. But she abruptly terminated the arrangement and refused to answer any of Tchaikovsky's letters. He was shattered. It was not the money; it was the fact that he felt soiled—the plaything of a capricious woman who could so bluntly sever so many years of emotional intimacy. He remained bitter for the rest of his life. "All my conceptions of mankind, my faith in the best of it, have been overturned." Later his brother, Modest, wrote: "Neither the triumph of the *Queen of Spades* nor the profound sorrow caused by the death of his beloved sister in April, 1891, nor even his American triumph served to soften the blow she had inflicted." What Tchaikovsky did not know was that Nadejda was going through a period of mental instability. Her relations with everybody had changed. Some writers hint that she severed relations with Tchaikovsky because she had learned of his sexual perversion. There is nothing to support such an assertion.

Tchaikovsky fled to the West. In 1891 he was invited to New York to share in the opening-week dedication of the Music Hall (renamed Carnegie Hall a few years later). The fee, $2,500 for four concerts, was handsome enough, and Tchaikovsky arrived toward the end of April. He was homesick, but the natives fascinated him. He was especially struck by the frankness and openhandedness of the people:

> Amazing people, these Americans! Compared with Paris, where at every approach, in every stranger's kindness, one feels an attempt at exploitation, the frankness, sincerity and generosity of this city, its hospitality without hidden motives and its eagerness to oblige and win approval, are simply astonishing and, at the same time, touching. This, and indeed American customs, American manners and manners generally, are very attractive to me—but I enjoy all this like a person sitting at a table set with marvels of gastronomy, devoid of appetite. Only the prospect of returning to Russia can awaken an appetite within me.

He admired the skyscrapers, though he could not see how anybody could live on such a dizzy height as the thirteenth floor of a building. He described a dinner given for him by Morris Reno, the president of Music Hall. What struck him was that at the service of each lady was his portrait in a graceful frame; and, in the middle of the dinner, which lasted from 7:30 until 11, "an ice was served in some kind of small boxes to which were attached small slates, with pencils and sponges, on which excerpts from my works were finely written in pencil. Then I had to write my autograph on these slates." He visited Niagara Falls and Washington, conducted concerts in Philadelphia and Baltimore in addition to his four Music Hall appearances, and hastened back to Russia.

His last great work was the Symphony No. 6 in B minor, the *Pathétique*. He was going to make a mystery of it. "This time a program-symphony, but with a program that shall remain an enigma for everybody. Let them puzzle their heads over it. The work will be called simply *Program* Symphony (No. 6). The program is subjective through and through, and during my journey I often wept bitterly while composing it in my head." (At least one person thought he knew the secret program of the Sixth Symphony. Havelock Ellis called the work a "homosexual tragedy.") Tchaikovsky was happy at the speed and authority with which the symphony progressed. "You can't think of what a delight it is to feel that my time is not yet over." He claimed that he had "put his soul" into the work. It had its premiere in St. Petersburg on

74

October 28, 1893. After the premiere, at which the new work was received rather icily, Tchaikovsky gave up the idea of calling the score the *Program Symphony*. Modest Tchaikovsky suggested *Tragique* and then *Pathétique,* and Tchaikovsky decided on the latter. The next day he changed his mind again, but it was too late. "*Pathétique*" held. It is the greatest of his symphonies, and its last movement, which starts with a cry and ends with a moan, is the most unusual and pessimistic he ever wrote. Less than a week later he was dead. He had drunk a glass of unboiled water and contracted cholera. After a few days of suffering he died, on November 6, 1893.

Whether or not he is the greatest of all Russian composers, he has proved to be by far the most popular. No label fits him. He passed from nationalistic music to music of a more cosmopolitan kind, but nevertheless all of his music could have been written only by a Russian. Many music histories give the idea that Tchaikovsky was not a nationalistic composer. That is really a half-truth. As Stravinsky has written, "Tchaikovsky's music, which does not appear specifically Russian to everybody, is often more profoundly Russian than music which has long since been awarded the facile label of Muscovite picturesqueness. This music is quite as Russian as Pushkin's verse or Glinka's song. While not specifically cultivating in his art 'the soul of the Russian peasant,' Tchaikovsky drew *unconsciously* from the true, popular sources of our race." Tchaikovsky was strongly conscious of his folk heritage, and was constantly using it. In a letter to Nadejda in 1878 he expressed his attitude:

> As regards the Russian element in my works, I may tell you that not infrequently I begin a composition with the intention of introducing some folk melodies into it. Sometimes it comes of its own accord (as in the finale of our symphony [No. 4]). As to this national element in my work, its affinity with the folk songs in some of my melodies and harmonies comes from my having spent my childhood in the country and, from my earliest years, having been impregnated with the characteristic beauty of our Russian folk music. I am passionately fond of the national element in all its varied expressions. In a word, I am Russian in the fullest sense of the word.

Later in life he was not so consciously nationalistic. From the beginning, of course, his music was slanted more to the West than to the music of The Five. But it would be a mistake to eliminate Tchaikovsky entirely from the School of Russian nationalistic composers, different as was his approach from that of Mussorgsky and Rimsky-Korsakov. Where Rimsky-Korsakov spread out his arms to embrace Russian antiquity and folklore, where Mussorgsky spread out his arms to embrace the entire Russian people, Tchaikovsky spread out his arms to embrace—himself.

❧ 5 ❧

From Bohemia to Spain

EUROPEAN NATIONALISTS

After the Russians it was the Kingdom of Bohemia that, in Bedřich Smetana and Antonin Dvořák, turned out the most significant nationalistic composers in Europe. But unlike Russia, Bohemia (now part of Czechoslovakia) had a distinguished musical tradition. It had produced, at the turn of the nineteenth century, some internationally known composers and performers; and in 1811 it had opened one of the first musical conservatories in northern Europe. It was also the country that encouraged Mozart when he most needed encouragement.

Many of the early Czech composers, it is true, had left Bohemia to make their fortunes elsewhere. Austria dominated the Kingdom of Bohemia until concessions were made midway in the nineteenth century, and it was natural that many Bohemian musicians should settle in Vienna. Others went to Germany. Jiři Benda (1722–1795), who won praise from Mozart, was an émigré. So was Jan Ladislav Dussek (1761–1812), a fascinating composer, one of the most important pianists of his day and one of the first touring virtuosos, as much at home in St. Petersburg as he was in London. He lived a glamorous and even reckless life. In his youth he was extremely handsome (he was known as *le beau Dussek*) and his amours were the talk of Europe. Later in life he grew monstrously fat. It was Dussek (or Dusik, as his name sometimes is spelled) who contributed at least one immortal idea to the history of piano playing. He was the first to place his instrument sideways on the stage so that the public could admire his profile. As a composer, especially of piano music, he was prophetic. His ideas about piano technique were in advance of anybody at the time. More important was his preromanticism, and it is a romanticism that at times is not only "pre." His music, as in the Concerto for Two Pianos in B flat, can sound in part as though it had been composed by Schumann or even Brahms. *Grove's Dictionary* gives several startling examples of Dussek's advanced harmonies. Among other

Bohemian composers, Vaclav Tomášek (1774–1850) and Jan Voríšek (1791–1825) are mentioned in any Schubert biography as composers who strongly influenced the Viennese master's piano music.

But none of those composers were nationalists. Bedřich Smetana was the first to go to Bohemian folk song and use it as the basis for art music. Born on March 2, 1824, Smetana started out as a formidable prodigy. At the age of five he was a good enough violinist to take part in a Haydn quartet, and at six he played in public as a pianist. At eight he was composing. "I wanted to become a Mozart in composition and a Liszt in technique," he later said. But while he was a brilliant pianist, he did not go to the conservatory and was musically unlettered. As he wrote to Liszt, in 1848, "When I was 17 years old I did not know C sharp from D flat. The theory of harmony was a closed book to me. Though ignorant of this, yet I wrote music." His early music, mostly for piano, is a watery distillation of Liszt. Smetana was in Prague when the abortive revolution of 1848 was quashed. As he had sided with the patriots, he was under suspicion for many years. He could find no advancement at home and was glad to migrate to Sweden, where he was active from 1856 to 1861 as a teacher and as conductor of the Göteborg orchestra. In addition to conducting, he composed a great deal of piano music and three symphonic poems.

Smetana returned to Prague in 1862. There was a feeling of resurgence in the air. Austria's hold was weakening. The Provisional Theater was opened that year—it had been built specifically as a Bohemian home for the Bohemians—and Smetana conceived the idea of composing a national opera as a patriotic instrument. He had heard the Glinka operas, with their librettos on Russian subjects and their use of Russian-derived melodies, and they strongly impressed him. Smetana determined to write an equivalent kind of music for his own country. For the Provisional Theater in 1863 he composed his first opera, *The Brandenburgers in Bohemia*. This was followed three years later by *Prodaná nevěsta—The Bartered Bride*.

The Bartered Bride is a flawless work of comic art—spirited, jolly, sparkling. In it Smetana fell back upon the reservoir of Bohemian polkas and other dance music, though he did not quote directly. He invented all of the melodies. The opera is so spiced with the very spirit of the country that many find this hard to believe, but Smetana was proud of his ability to avoid direct quotation, and there is none of it in *The Bartered Bride*. Ralph Vaughan Williams, the British composer, tried to analyze Smetana's method of work and came to the conclusion that "Smetana's debt to his own national music was of the best kind, unconscious. He did not, indeed, 'borrow', he carried on an age-long tradition, not of set purpose, but because he could no more avoid speaking his own musical language than he could help breathing his native air." But strongly national though *The Bartered Bride* is, it is much more Westernized than the operas by Mussorgsky and Rimsky-Korsakov that were to come out of Russia. Prague, after all, was in the Western orbit. The exoticisms of the Bohemian musical language, however, were not in the Western musical consciousness until Smetana appeared. His language is, on the whole, a happy language. When Bohemian composers express melancholy, it is in a delicately elegiac way, without the crushing world-weariness and pessimism of the Russians. More often, Bohemian music expresses joy, happiness, dancing, festivals.

Smetana completed eight operas, of which *The Bartered Bride* is the only one in the international repertory. Most of his others are still performed regularly in Prague—*Dalibor, Libuše, Hubička (The Kiss), Dve vdovy (The Two Widows)* among them. In Czechoslovakia today Smetana is a national hero, much more so than Dvořák. For Smetana, more than any one man, made Czech music what it is, and not only by composing it. As pianist, conductor, teacher, and propagandist, he inspired his people and left a heritage of which they could be proud. Among his compositions still popular internationally are *Vlatava (The Moldau)* from the cycle of six symphonic poems, *Ma Vlast (My Country)*, and his ever-fresh, autobiographical E minor String Quartet *(From My Life)*. Occasionally his piano music is heard. Some of it is bombastic virtuoso rhetoric derived from Liszt and highly dated. The best piano pieces are the *Czech Dances,* inventive and charming sketches, often of considerable difficulty. There is also a Piano Trio in G minor that is of unusual loveliness.

In 1874, toward the end of his life, Smetana, like Beethoven, went deaf; and, like Schumann, mad. He wrote bravely but pathetically about his aural affliction to a friend in 1875: "The ear is quite healthy externally. But the inner apparatus—that admirable keyboard of our inner organ—is damaged, out of tune. The hammers have got stuck, and no tuner has so far succeeded in repairing the damage." He lost his memory and his speech, and was put in an asylum, where he died on May 12, 1884.

Smetana was the one who founded Czech music, but Antonin Dvořák, born on September 8, 1841, was the one who popularized it. His music has been played all over the world ever since Simrock published the *Moravian Duets* in the late 1870's. Since then Dvořák has not slipped from the repertory or showed any signs of doing so. And yet many music lovers accept him on sufferance. Only too often he is regarded as a minor nationalist, one of the better second-rank composers. It was not so in his own day, when he was the idol of Prague, when all Europe waited anxiously for his next work, when Hans von Bülow called him "next to Brahms the most God-gifted composer of the present day." (Bülow also described him as "a genius who looks like a tinker.") Brahms was not too proud to read proofs for Dvořák, whose fame was such that he was invited to New York in 1892 as head of the National Conservatory of Music.

He wrote prolifically in all forms, and his was a unique voice. Those who call him a rustic second-rate severely underestimate him, possibly misled by the innocence and transparency of his music. Of course he was a rustic, a country boy from Bohemia who was apprenticed to a butcher. He was born of peasant stock and his music has a strong peasant strain. That is at once its strength and its weakness. Dvořák was far from the most subtle or intellectual composer of his day, nor was he in any sense a revolutionary. He respected classic forms, he thought in primary emotional colors, and life was a very wonderful, uncomplicated thing to him. He remained throughout his entire creative span the happiest and least neurotic of the late romantics. "God, love, motherland" was his motto. Brahms had his moments of black gloom; Tchaikovsky's neuroses were monumental; Mahler, whose neuroses made Tchaikovsky's neuroses look healthy, beat his chest and rent his hair (looking meanwhile at posterity out of the corner of his eye); Bruckner sat trembling, waiting for Revelation, a mystic and a natural (in the Elizabethan sense of the word); Wagner was a twisted egoist; Liszt was a complicated, paradoxical, Jesuitical poseur of genius. Only Dvořák pursued his simple, uncomplicated way. With Handel and Haydn, he is the healthiest of all composers.

Simplicity and emotional health, of course, are no guarantee of great music. They must be backed by something. In Dvořák's case they were backed by an inexhaustible melodic wealth and a feeling for modulation that are very close to Schubert. But Dvořák differs from Schubert in that nearly all of his best melodies are nationalistic. He was at his best when Bohemia took over; when, un-selfconsciously, he wrote music that expressed his native land and his love for it. He, like Smetana, seldom used actual folk themes, but his nationalism runs just as deep as Smetana's, and perhaps deeper. An absolute composer who happened to be a nationalist, he did not produce copies but created originals.

It is this un-selfconscious nationalism—broadly melodic, original, exotic, full of unexpected twists, enchanting in its harmony—that gives Dvořák's music its great charm and beauty. His nonnationalistic music, what there is of it, is relatively unimportant. That goes even for his Seventh Symphony in D minor (Op. 70). Many critics, especially the British ones (Dvořák and the British had a long association; the British were looking for somebody after Mendelssohn to admire, and they came up with Dvořák), seem to think that because the Seventh Symphony is Brahmsian and the most classically constructed of his works, it has to be the best. The academic mind is always with us. As a matter of fact, the Seventh Symphony up to the third movement is nothing but a façade, despite some lovely moments. Not until the third movement does Dvořák forget about Brahms and symphonic form,

79

and then he composes the most delightful individual movement of any of his symphonies. Here the classic formalities are off, and Dvořák breathes once more, singing forth one of those Bohemian-sounding melodies to which countermelodies cling in the most natural and unaffected polyphony. The D minor Symphony on the whole is nowhere near as good as the Eighth Symphony in G major, or even the early No. 3 in E flat major.

A musician and nothing but a musician, Dvořák was not widely read and, indeed, barely more than literate. In later life he would sporadically try to "improve" himself by reading a primer of some sort, but those efforts never went very far. The only passion he had outside of music was trains. The locomotive engine was to him one of the highest achievements of the human mind, and he often expressed the wish that he had invented it. He used to pay daily visits to the Franz-Josef Station in Prague, had all the timetables memorized, and was never so happy as when he could make friends with a locomotive engineer. He would send his pupils to the station to find out what engine was going on what train, or, when a pupil returned from a trip, would want to know what kind of train he had traveled on, and the name and model number of the locomotive. (Freudians have some things to say about the symbolism of the locomotive and its pistons.) Dvořák's pupils loved him, trains or no, though he could have a temper. They loved his sweetness, his gentleness, his dedication. When he launched on a subject he was oblivious to the world around him. One of his pupils has written about the time he, Dvořák, and several pupils were walking along the street and it started to pour. Dvořák, talking about his experiences in America, did not notice the rain. Everybody got soaked to the skin. Dvořák suddenly stopped, noticed water running from his hat, and said, "Now, children, run along home at once. I think it has started to rain."

Dvořák's talent was apparent from the beginning, and he started taking serious lessons at the age of twelve. His father was an innkeeper and kept a butcher shop, and for a while Dvořák worked in the family shop, but an uncle financed the boy's music studies and when he was sixteen he was sent to Prague. After graduating from the Prague Organ School in 1859 he took pupils and played the viola in various orchestras. As a player at the Provisionial Theater from 1862 to 1871 he participated in the first performances of several Smetana operas. He developed an enthusiasm for Wagner, he composed prolifically, and his music began to be played. His first public success came in 1873 with a strongly nationalistic choral work, *Hymnus*. In 1875 he won the Austrian State Prize for a symphony and came to the attention of two of the jurors, Brahms and Hanslick. Brahms wrote a letter to his publisher, Simrock: "On the recent occasion of allocating a state grant . . . I took much pleasure in the works of Dvořák of Prague. I have recommended him to send you his *Moravian Duets*. If you play them through, you will enjoy them as much as I have done. . . . Decidedly he is a very talented man. Besides, he is poor. Please take this into consideration." Simrock published the duets and had a hit on his hands. The infectious music swept Europe, as did the *Slavonic Dances* for piano duet that shortly followed.

Dvořák was launched. The German critic Louis Ehlert in 1878 wrote an enthusiastic review that was widely quoted: "Here at last is a hundred per cent talent; and, what is new, a completely natural talent." Ehlert went on to rave about the *Slavonic Dances*. Brahms was happy, and Dvořák was ecstatic about his new friend. Brahms could be prickly, but never was there the least hint of tension between the two. Dvořák to Simrock: "Brahms seems to be pleased by his connection with me; and as an artist and a man I am so overcome by his kindness that I cannot help but love him. What a warm heart and great spirit there is in that man! You know how detached he is from even his closest friends, at least where his compositions are concerned, and yet he has not been like that to me." When Brahms corrected proofs for Dvořák while he was away in the United States, Dvořák was overwhelmed: "In the whole world I do not think I could find another musician who would do the same." Dvořák may have been right; proofreading is a nasty, unrewarding job. As for Brahms, he felt very close to Dvořák. There was something in the younger man's personality that attracted him, aside from Dvořák's hero-worship. Brahms once wrote to a friend inviting Dvořák along: "We will eat from the same plate and drink from the same glass." It makes a pretty picture.

A steady series of works came from Dvořák: the *Slavonic Rhapsodies,* symphonies, choral music, considerable chamber music, operas, some piano music (the weakest part of his work), concertos. European audiences became familiar through Dvořák with Bohemian dance forms: the polka, the furiant (which Dvořák often used as a third movement instead of a scherzo), and the dumka, a slow and melancholy folk song. There was a great deal of talk in Europe about nationalism, and when Dvořák came to the United States the American newspapers picked up the subject.

He came to New York at the invitation of Mrs. Jeannette Thurber, the wife of a wealthy grocer. Mrs. Thurber had been instrumental in founding the National Conservatory of Music, and she wanted the famous Dvořák to head the institution. She was prepared to pay handsomely for his services. The terms of the contract specified an annual salary of $15,000, the equivalent of 30,000 gulden. (In Prague, his yearly salary had been 1,200 gulden.) For this, Dvořák was to teach three hours a day, prepare four students' concerts, conduct six concerts of his own music, and be granted a four-month vacation.

Dvořák arrived in New York in September, 1892. The reporters were on hand, and one of them left the following description:

He is not an awesome personality at all. He is much taller than his pictures would imply, and possesses not a tithe of the bulldog ferocity to be encountered in some of them. A man about 5 ft. 10 or 11 inches, of great natural dignity, a man of character, Dvořák impresses me as an original, natural and—as Rossini would say, to be natural is greater than to be original. . . . He is not beautiful in the forms of face, but the lines of his brow are so finely modeled, and there is so much emotional life in the fiery eyes and lined face, that when he lightens up in conversation, his face is not easily forgotten.

Mrs. Thurber helped spread the talk about nationalism. She was greatly interested in fostering a national American school of composition, and one of the reasons she had decided upon Dvořák as the head of the National Conservatory was the fact that he represented nationalism in his own music. She could point him out as an illustration of what American composers could aspire to. In the 1890's serious music in the United States was dominated by the German school, and there was very little that could be classified as "American" aside from some piano pieces by Louis Moreau Gottschalk. (There was a large amount of nationalistic popular music, but the serious composers paid no attention to it. The one breakaway came from Charles Ives, but he worked in a vacuum and his music was unknown.)

Dvořák, as Mrs. Thurber hoped, had strong things to say about the lack of an American nationalistic movement, and he pointed out what in his opinion could be done. "In the Negro songs I have found a secure basis for a new national music school. . . . America can have her own music, a fine music growing up from her own soil and having its own special character— the natural voice of a free and great nation," he told a New York *Herald* reporter. Stimulated by some of the native music he heard, Dvořák practiced what he preached. In his three years in the United States he produced several works that are known as "American," including the F major String Quartet, the E flat String Quintet, and the Symphony No. 9 in E minor, subtitled "From the New World." Most of the *New World* Symphony was composed in the five-room apartment that Dvořák and his family occupied at 327 East 17th Street. The scoring was completed in Spillville, Iowa, where Dvořák spent his summers. Spillville was a Czech settlement.

The *New World* Symphony started a controversy that was not clarified by Dvořák's own contradictory remarks about the score. At first he said that American music had played a part in his symphony: "It is the spirit of the Negro and Indian melodies which I have endeavored to reproduce in my new symphony. I have not used a single one of those melodies. I simply wrote characteristic themes incorporating in them the quality of Indian music." The first movement of the New World did use a Negro spiritual, "Swing Low, Sweet Chariot," and Dvořák also made use of the spiritual

"Goin' Home." Everybody took it for granted that the work was not only an evocation of the American spirit, but that it was full of actual folk tunes or spirituals that Dvořák had encountered. There were those who saw the story of Hiawatha in the *New World*, and one of Dvořák's American pupils, Harry Rowe Shelley, said that he had it from the composer's own lips that a certain passage in the symphony represented the Indian girl's sobbing as she bade Hiawatha farewell. Soon Dvořák became rather annoyed with the fuss that the *New World* Symphony had created, and he flatly denied that there was anything specifically American in it. He described as "nonsense" the claim that the *New World* Symphony was the beginning of an American school, and decided that the music he had composed in America was "genuine Bohemian music," completely contradicting his initial exuberant remarks about Negro and Indian influences. His second thoughts were correct. There are traces of American thematic material and rhythms in the F major Quartet and the *New World* Symphony, but the music nevertheless is as American as St. Wenceslas. Dvořák could not have composed American national music had he tried. But despite his disclaimer, for years there was a controversy in the American press as to whether or not the *New World* was "American."

Among the works Dvořák composed in his last period, many of them written in America, were the dark-colored *Biblical Songs* (so different from his light-hearted *Gypsy Songs* of 1880), the radiant Cello Concerto in B minor, and the *Humoresques* for piano. The latter is worth mention if only for the G flat *Humoresque*, the one whose catchy tune was promptly whistled by everybody and arranged for every instrument and combination of instruments. Dvořák's last two string quartets, in A flat and G major, are his broadest and most serious pieces of chamber music, and possibly his greatest. These too he composed in the United States. On his return to Prague, he taught at the Conservatory and was appointed director in 1901. When he died, on May 1, 1904, it was an occasion for national mourning.

Although a great deal of Dvořák's music remains in the repertory, a great deal more remains to be investigated. The last three of the nine symphonies are frequently played, but No. 6 in D major is less familiar, and No. 5 in F is a total stranger to concert halls outside of Czechoslovakia, while the first four might not have been composed at all judging from their total neglect. Yet the F major Symphony is a gorgeous work; and of the early symphonies, No. 3 in E flat comes close to being a masterpiece. Its first movement is particularly striking. The work was composed in 1873, but already the full power of Dvořák's orchestration is in evidence—that buoyant sound, the golden horns, the instinct for putting each note in the right place. The English conductor Julius Harrison maintained that it is a rare thing to hear a lukewarm performance of any orchestral piece by Dvořák because "each in-

83

strumental part is instinct with life. Nothing stagnates, for Dvořák's ear was fully alive to every voice in the harmony." There is much orchestral music by Dvořák that should be heard with greater frequency—the *Scherzo Capriccioso*, the various serenades and the *Legends*, the Symphonic Variations. His symphonic poems are somewhat weaker, but *The Golden Spinning Wheel* is charming enough to warrant occasional performances.

His concertos remain alive. He wrote an attractive Piano Concerto in G minor with a rather ineffective piano part, a beautiful Violin Concerto in A minor, and a supreme Cello Concerto in B minor. Of his chamber music, the sunny Piano Quintet in A major, the String Quartets in F and E flat, and the *Dumky* Trio are familiar. Less known are the two massive last quartets, the propulsive E flat Piano Quartet, and the equally powerful F minor Piano Trio. Each ranks with the best chamber music of the late romantic period. Dvořák's operas are not in the repertory outside of Czechoslovakia, though *Rusalka* contains such lovely music, Wagnerisms and all, that one wonders why it is not in the steady repertory of an enterprising opera house. *The Devil and Kate* is a lusty comedy with some fine music in it. And, of the choral pieces, the *Stabat Mater* and the Requiem are among the grandest and most expressive works of their kind in the literature.

Last in the trilogy of great Czech composers is Leoš Janáček, born on July 3, 1854. He is a rather puzzling figure. For many years he was known outside of his homeland only by his one international success, the opera *Jenufa*. But after World War II his music, especially his operas, began to be heard in the capitals of the world, and slowly came the realization that Janáček was an original and important composer.

There were only thirteen years between him and Dvořák. But whereas Dvořák was purely an exponent of the late romantic tradition, Janáček, who died on August 12, 1928, reached well into the twentieth century, and his late music shows it. Even in his early years he exhibited a much more modern mind than Dvořák. He was not so great a composer and did not have Dvořák's pristine melodic sense, but he definitely was more powerful and biting, and in a way he was to Dvořák what Mussorgsky was to Tchaikovsky. Dvořák looked for beauty, Janáček looked for truth. Imagine the proper, religious, Victorian Dvořák taking a libretto like that of *Jenufa*, which deals with the murder of an illegitimate baby!

Janáček lived a quiet life, most of it in his own country, and most of *that* in Brno, where he directed a music school he had founded in 1881. Composer, theorist, conductor, and teacher, he started late. Not until he was twenty-two did he attempt composition, and he spent his life wrestling with the materials of music. His first significant work was not produced until he was forty. From that point he kept writing steadily until his death, with no falling-off in inspiration. The older he grew, the more terse, bleak, rugged dissonant, and epigrammatic his music became. He was not an atonalist. Whether or not his music has a key signature, it always has a key center. But some of his harmonies are so harsh that they can suggest atonalism.

Janáček was a nationalist and a scholar of national music, which many of the early nationalists were not. Like Bartók and Kodály in Hungary, Vaughan Williams and Holst in England, he and František Bartoš investigated, catalogued, and edited collections of his country's folk songs. His own music, strongly influenced by his researches, has none of the heart-on-sleeve nationalism of Smetana, Dvořák, Rimsky-Korsakov, or Grieg. It is, like Bartók's, a nationalism that runs deeper. In his operas and vocal music it is a nationalism represented by declamatory patterns peculiar to folk song and speech. It is, in short, an elemental nationalism, one that goes to the raw, naked folk impulse rather than to the later, more smoothed-out, developed, and sophisticated material of the popular song. So closely wrapped up with speech patterns is Janáček's music that a listener must know the Czech language to achieve full identification with it.

Janáček worked out a theory of speech-in-music that is very close to Mussorgsky's, though he never heard a note of the latter's music until relatively late in life. "The study I have made of the musical aspects of the spoken language," he wrote, "has led me to the conviction that all of the melodic and rhythmic mysteries of music can be explained in reference to the melody and rhythm of the musical motives of the spoken language." At the beginning of the 1890's he was systematically notating the melodic and rhythmic qualities of the spoken word, and he discovered that with the help of these "speech-melodies" he could "form the motif of any given word." He could then, he maintained, "encompass the whole of every day life or the greatest tragedy" in music. Janáček became something of a mild fanatic on the subject of "speech melody," and wanted courses in it to be given in every conservatory and school of acting.

Allied to speech patterns was his feeling for nature. "I listen to the birds singing. I marvel at the manifestations of rhythm in its million different forms in the world of light, color and shapes, and my music remains young through contact with the eternally young rhythm of Nature." From anybody else this would be conventional and sentimental blathering, but Janáček did not write sentimental music, and a pantheistic strain does run through his music. Bartók had much the same feeling, and Janáček's nature music is echoed in the "night music" found in so many Bartók scores.

Although Janáček used many folklike materials in his work, it is not as a folklorist or melodist that he makes his impact. His music is recognizable more by certain idiosyncratic thrusts: by melismatic patterns evocative of folk song (his piano music is full of it); by a certain arch humor (as in the Capriccio for Piano and Winds); by a tight, pared-down harmony that often sounds bare. In many respects he straddles the postromantic and the modern world. His harmonies, powerful as they are, are not adventurous enough to be fully modern, and yet are too unconventional to be postromantic. But his style is completely original. He worked out a system of composition that owed very little to previous musicians, and of few composers in the history of music can that be said.

Janáček's early works—*Jenufa* (1902) or the two-movement Piano Sonata (1905)—naturally speak a more conventional language than such late operas as *The Makropoulos Affair* (1924) or *From the House of the Dead* (1926). *Katya Kabanova* (1921) is the pivotal work that straddles the philosophies of two centuries. The very opening chord—F, D flat, B flat, B natural—is stark and modern, but it resolves to B flat minor. Juxtaposed to passages of pungent dissonances are sections that are all but Tchaikovskian, such as the C flat major episode on page 27 of the vocal score. (Janáček's system of composition was always getting him into such "impossible" keys as C flat, and his scores are terribly hard to read because of the profuse accidentals.) The dichotomy continues into the libretto itself. The plot, which deals with a married woman who has an affair and is driven to suicide by her conscience, is modern. Yet Janáček has no hesitation using the old-fashioned device of an interpolated song that has nothing to do with the action. Thus in the second act a character enters. "Nobody here yet? Then I'll sing a song while I'm waiting." And off he goes into a folk song—notated in D flat minor (another "impossible" key). None of these creaky devices occur in the late operas, works in which Janáček brought his "speech melody" to a logical conclusion. Characters declaim rather than sing, and it is the orchestra that has whatever melody there is. On the surface this would appear to lead to boredom, to plays with musical background rather than opera, but Janáček's rhythms are so fascinating, his sung speech inflections so precise, his integrity so great, that the operas exert a tremendous pull. So does the crude (purposely so) *Glagolitic Mass* of 1926, which puts the listener into a primitive Slavonic world.

No composer could be more unlike the grim Janáček than Norway's most important nationalist, Edvard Grieg. Where Janáček was carved from solid granite, Grieg was, in Debussy's words, "bonbons wrapped in snow." In his own time (he was born on June 15, 1841, and died on September 4, 1907) Grieg was tremendously popular. He rode on the wave of nationalism that produced the equally popular Dvořák. But whereas Dvořák composed in big forms, Grieg was primarily a miniaturist; and whereas Dvořák is as popular as ever, Grieg's reputation fell almost as rapidly as it had risen. Shortly after his death few musicians would take Grieg seriously. His once piquant chromatic harmonies, which had so titillated music lovers, were accused of being cloying. The new generation looked upon Grieg with the same condescension with which they gazed upon the photographs in great-grandfather's album. Grieg, in short, was as out of fashion as the stovepipe hats and velveteen jackets of his period. Along with Liszt and Mendelssohn, both of whom were also swamped by the antiromanticism of the period after World War I, Grieg was dismissed with a careless wave of the hand. In recent years, Liszt and Mendelssohn have made a comeback. But Grieg still languishes.

It is true that nobody can make a case for Grieg as one of the immortals. But he was one of the band of nationalists who did bring something new to music, and what Grieg had to say he for the most part said gracefully and prettily, with considerable style, and also with a compositional technique perfectly suited to his content. His music does not deserve the scorn with which it is so often received. At its best it is well made and often melodically distinguished. The G minor Ballade for solo piano is a good example. It uses a folk melody and starts with a slow, almost Franckian series of highly chromatic chords, after which it proceeds to a series of variations. The writing is a combination of nationalism with Schumann-inspired piano technique; but not until the glittering fourth variation, with its cadence of the raised sixth (typical of Norwegian folk music), does the nationalism take the upper hand. Throughout the work the writing is in beautiful taste, virtuosic without being vulgar. It is a lovely piece of music, infinitely above the cheap type of salon writing that flooded Europe at the time.

It is not an easy piece to bring to life, however, for the tradition it represents is gone. Pianists like Percy Grainger and Leopold Godowsky (who recorded the Ballade in the late 1920's) could bring freedom and feeling to Grieg's music. Pianists not trained in the romantic idiom are liable to vitiate the music by playing it too literally, destroying its spontaneity and delicacy, not knowing when to relax a tempo, when to use rubato, how to bring out the inner voices. Composers on a supreme level can survive almost any manner of performance, but lesser composers are peculiarly vulnerable to their interpreters.

Grieg, who studied (with great unhappiness) at the Leipzig Conservatory, was a good all-around musician—pianist, conductor, composer of course, a specialist in the music of his country. He had been strongly influenced by the now almost-forgotten Ole Bull (1810–1880). Bull was a Norwegian violinist who was largely self-taught, and who achieved a big reputation in Europe and the United States. Part genius, part charlatan, an eccentric man with strong opinions, he was a father-figure to Grieg. He himself was interested in Norwegian folk song, and in the 1840's composed a *Notturno* for string orchestra that bears all the marks of what Grieg later was to do. It is a lovely, evocative, and even haunting piece. It was Bull who urged that the fifteen-year-old Grieg be sent to Leipzig. In later years Grieg spoke vehemently of his dislike for the Leipzig Conservatory. He said that his piano teachers were mostly inefficient and that his composition teachers gave him elaborate assignments long before he was ready for them.

He returned to Norway in 1862, gave piano recitals, and then went to Copenhagen, where he worked for a short time with Niels Gade, then the most important Danish composer. In Copenhagen he met his cousin, Nina Hagerup. They became engaged in 1864 and were married three years later. She was a singer who gave the premieres of many of his songs. Up to 1864, Grieg's compositions were in the style of Schumann, Mendelssohn, and the early romantic school. But in 1864 he became interested in Ole Bull's plea for a national Norwegian music, and he also became friendly with a young composer named Rikard Nordraak, who was actually writing in an idiom derived from Norwegian folk melodies. Grieg decided to devote the rest of his life to Norwegian nationalism. He returned to his own country, composed steadily, conducted, gave concerts, and within a few years became known as the brightest musical talent in Norway. Liszt heard some of his music and sent a warm letter of recommendation. Included in the letter was an invitation to visit Liszt at Weimar. The two men did meet in 1869, but in Rome, not Weimar. They became close friends. Later there was an evening in Weimar when Grieg showed Liszt the manuscript of his Piano Concerto in A minor. Liszt, with one of his typically flamboyant gestures, waved the composer away and read the concerto at sight, flawlessly.

When Grieg came to maturity, it was as a short, quiet, exquisite man who specialized in short, quiet, exquisite pieces of music. He had a busy life. In addition to his own creative work, he was active in Norway as a conductor and critic. He gave annual European tours as a pianist, playing his own music; and there were few more popular pianists or composers. Grieg was welcome wherever he went. He was a man with a levelheaded view of life, and he had a quiet wit that endeared him to his friends. There was the time he was made Knight of the Order of Orange-Nassau; he accepted with alacrity, because, as he wrote to a friend, "Orders and medals are most useful to me in the top layer of my trunk. The customs officials are always so kind to me at the sight of them." Always a delicate man, he suffered constantly from pulmonary trouble, but he had been too long before the public as a performer, liked the life and the people he met, and continued his tours almost to the day of his death. Indeed, he was all set to go to England when he was ordered to a hospital on September 3, 1907. He died the following day.

One of Grieg's troubles, as it was Saint-Saëns's trouble, is that he is known mostly by his worst pieces of music—*Peer Gynt,* say, or some of the more sticky *Lyric Pieces,* or several of his *Norwegian Dances.* There is much more to Grieg than those. One of his collections of national dances, the *Slåtter* (Op. 72), comprises bleak and unprettified pieces, amazingly close to what

Bartók was to do in his piano transcriptions of Hungarian melodies. Many of the *Lyric Pieces,* of which he composed ten books, are as good as some of Mendelssohn's *Songs Without Words,* and better than most. The G minor String Quartet served as a model for Debussy's String Quartet, as Gerald Abraham has so convincingly demonstrated. The three violin sonatas are beautifully laid out, appealing in content, graceful to play and hear. And the Grieg songs are of great beauty. He was an authentically distinguished song composer; in the *Haugtussa* cycle, or in such songs as *A Swan,* he achieved perfection in a small package.

Grieg never struck very deep and his range is admittedly narrow. Even the Piano Concerto in A minor, probably his most popular concert piece (*Peer Gynt* seldom turns up any more except in pop concerts), is closer to the fashionable virtuoso concertos of Rubinstein, Herz, Scharwenka, and Litolff than to the masterpieces of the literature. But it is a notch above Rubinstein and company because of its piquant melodies that reflect Grieg and no other composer, whereas the melodies of Rubinstein and the others could have been written by any composer. Grieg does not represent power or revolution. He represents charm, grace, sweetness, and still has a good deal to offer, bonbons and all. He was a minor master, and one of the finest.

Somewhat allied to Grieg were the two first important Spanish nationalists, Isaác Albéniz and Enrique Granados. Like Grieg, they took native melodies and superimposed upon them cosmopolitan techniques in a highly spiced chromatic idiom. Like Grieg, both composed largely in the smaller forms, with an emphasis on piano music. Like Grieg, their music verged on the salon. Unlike Grieg, each of the two composed a resplendent piano work that actually added something new to the repertory—Albéniz with his *Iberia,* Granados with his *Goyescas.*

Spain in the nineteenth century was one of the most backward and reactionary countries in Europe. Its intellectual life was limited, and it is hard to think of an important creative figure except Goya in the Spain of that period. In the country, however, was a body of vital folk song, and European composers would visit Spain, come away entranced with the native music, and write their *Jota Aragonesa, Caprice Espagnol,* and *España.* There was no serious music in Spain during most of the century, nor was there a place where Spanish musicians could be trained (the conservatory in Madrid had no professional standing). When a major talent turned up, such as Juan Arriaga (1806–1826), he had to go outside the country to study. (Arriaga, who died at the age of twenty, was very gifted, and a potentially great composer was lost at his untimely death.) The most popular form of Spanish music was the operetta, or zarzuela, and zarzuela composers spent most of their time copying Rossini and Bellini.

Not until after the middle of the nineteenth century was an effort made to survey the rich heritage of Spanish folk music. Felipe Pedrell (1841–1922) was the moving spirit. He was a composer, musicologist (he edited the works of the great sixteenth-century Spanish contrapuntist, Victoria), and a folklorist whose *Cancionero musical popular español* was for many years the basic guide to the field. Pedrell lived under the shadow of his scholarly work. "They have never done me justice," he told Manuel de Falla, "either in Catalonia or the rest of Spain. They have constantly tried to belittle me, saying I was a great critic or a great historian but not a good composer. It's not true. I *am* a good composer." But whatever reputation he has as a composer resides in Spain, for his music is unknown elsewhere. Throughout most of the century the best Spanish music continued to be composed by non-Spaniards. Glinka may have been the first to come under the spell of Spanish folk music, and he was followed by a battalion of others who became excited by the color, rhythmic snap, and exotic melodic appeal of Iberia. One of the composers most in love with the country was Chabrier: "We make the rounds of the café concerts, where they sing the *malagueñas,* the *soledas,* the *zapatéados* and the *pateneras;* then the dances, which are positively Arabian, that sums it up. If you could see them wriggling their behinds, twisting and squirming, I don't think you'd care to leave." Everybody was taking advantage of Spanish music except the Spaniards.

It was in this period that Isaac Albéniz was born on May 29, 1860, and, a few years later, Enrique Granados, on July 27, 1867. There was a good deal in common between the two composers. Both were concert pianists of international reputation. Both were nationalistic composers who tried to create an authentic Spanish serious music. Neither was completely successful in that both *Iberia* and *Goyescas* remain influenced by Chopin, Liszt, the French turn-of-the-century school, and, possibly, the piano music of Leopold Godowsky. Godowsky (1870–1938) was a pianist's pianist who composed a great deal of keyboard music in which complexity and the movement of inner voices were almost an end in themselves.

Even if they were not originals, Albéniz and Granados did much to break new ground, and they worked on their masterpieces at much the same time, though without contact with each other. *Iberia* was composed between 1906 and 1909, *Goyescas,* 1909 to 1910. Both works are large-scale suites for large-scale virtuosos, full of the scent—there is no other word for it—of Spanish rhythms, Spanish melodies, Spanish life that nobody but a native-born composer could have evoked. Chabrier, Rimsky-Korsakov, and the others were merely tourists. *Iberia* and *Goyescas* were written by men who were at home. Technically the two pieces have much in common. They are extremely difficult, full of countermelodies, and the writing is characterized by exuberant rhythms, wide stretches, delicate pedal effects, textures so rich and thick they are quasi-orchestral, and elaborate ornamentation. Of the two, *Iberia* is the more direct, *Goyescas* the more romantic, dreamier, vaguer in outline, perhaps more haunting.

Albéniz led an interesting life. Exploited as a child prodigy (he was playing in public at the age of four), he was constantly running away from home. At the age of thirteen he made his way to Cuba, New York, and South America before the authorities and his parents caught up with him. His serious studies started at the Leipzig Conservatory in 1874, after which he went to the Brussels Conservatory. Then he had a few lessons with Liszt. In 1890 he studied composition in Paris under d'Indy and Dukas. His life thereafter was that of a touring pianist and composer. For a while he made his headquarters in London, where one of his operas was produced. Then he moved permanently to Paris. He turned out an enormous number of piano pieces, most of which are no longer heard. A few, however—the Tango in D is the most famous example—are known by everybody. Nothing else in his work suggested the scope of *Iberia*. It was of unprecedented difficulty, and the fine French pianist Blanche Selva was appalled when she looked at the music. "It is unplayable!" Albéniz, who was near death, assured her that it could and would be played. He died on May 18, 1909, leaving an unfinished trilogy of operas on the King Arthur legend. One of his operas, *Pepita Jiménez*, had a brief run in the 1890's. It is entirely forgotten.

Iberia is an abstract work based largely on Andalusian folk melody. *Goyescas*, which also uses Andalusian and flamenco elements, is based on etchings and paintings by Goya. Like Albéniz, Granados turned out a large number of pleasant, salonlike piano pieces, and nothing in his previous work would have suggested so grand a piece as *Goyescas*. Granados studied in Barcelona, then in Paris. He returned to Barcelona and settled down to the life of a piano teacher. Soon his compositions began to attract notice, and one of his operas, *María del Carmen*, was a success at its premiere in 1898. He also composed a series of exquisite, fragrant nationalistic songs called *Tonadillas*.

Then came *Goyescas*. Granados had been thinking about the music long before starting to compose it. "I am enamored with the psychology of Goya, with his palette, with him, with his muse the Duchess of Alba, with his quarrels with his models, his loves and flatteries. That whitish pink of the cheeks, contrasting with the blend of black velvet; those subterranean creatures, hands of mother-of-pearl and jasmine resting on jet trinkets, have possessed me." Granados wrote these words from the heart, and it is easy to see why. Those mysterious, beautiful, almost menacing "majas" that Goya painted, those aristocratic women peering behind fans, thinking their secret thoughts, that mixture of cruelty and decadence—all of this has stimulated imaginations much weaker than that of the sensitive Granados.

91

His suite originally had six pieces, to which was added *El Pelele*. By far the most famous, and the most often played in concert divorced from the suite, is *Quejas, o la maja y el ruiseñor*, known in English as *The Maiden and the Nightingale*. It contains one of the loveliest, most plaintive melodies that the period has to show; and, at the end, there are those wispy arabesques and trills of the singing nightingale. But this is far from nature painting; it is poetry in sound, the verses of a man of unusual sensibility.

Granados worked the pieces of *Goyescas* into an opera, to a libretto by Fernando Periquet. He had made a furor in Paris in 1914, playing his own music, and the Opéra commissioned the adaptation. But war came, and the Opéra was unable to stage the work. Giulio Gatti-Casazza at the Metropolitan Opera took it over, and the world premiere was given in New York in 1916. *Goyescas* was politely received, but it did not catch on, nor did it ever. The libretto is supposed to be weak, and it is, though worse librettos are still before the public. It is surprising that the little opera has not been picked up as a curtain raiser. It has authentic flavor.

Had not Granados come to the United States to supervise the production, he would have had many more years to live. As it happened, he was asked by President Wilson to play at the White House. Naturally he was happy to oblige. He canceled his return passage and arranged for a later ship. Finally, on March 24, 1916, he embarked for Dieppe on the S.S. *Sussex*, which was torpedoed in the English Channel. A survivor said that Granados was safe in a lifeboat when he saw his wife struggling in the water. He jumped in to save her, and both went down. The world was deprived of a composer just in the process of finding himself. Granados, after *Goyescas*, knew he was beginning to broaden. "I have a world of ideas," he said shortly before his death. "I am filled with enthusiasm to work more and more." But that was not to be. And so he lives today mainly by *Goyescas*, a few salon pieces, and some piercingly beautiful songs.

The work of Albéniz and Granados was carried on by Manuel de Falla. Falla, who was born in Cadiz on November 23, 1876, studied in Spain, won a national prize for his opera *La Vida Breve* in 1905, and then went off to Paris for seven years. The First World War sent him back to Spain, where he composed such popular pieces as the ballets *El Amor Brujo* and *El Sombrero de Tres Picos*. Also from that period came his *Noches en los jardines de España* (*Nights in the Gardens of Spain*) for piano and orchestra. After the war he composed a puppet opera, *El Retablo de Maese Pedro*, a harpsichord concerto, and a long piano piece named *Fantasia Bética*. After 1926 he composed very little. He moved to Argentina, lived in seclusion, and for the last twenty years of his life worked on a massive project, a sort of opera-oratorio, named *L'Atlántida*. He died on November 14, 1946.

Falla's total output is small, but everything he composed is jewel-like in its workmanship. At first his music resembled the music of previous Spanish nationalists, though it was more sophisticated, with an overlay of impressionistic techniques. It was based on *cante jondo,* Andalusian melodies and rhythms, flamenco, and other aspects of the Spanish *melos,* all filtered through a French-derived workmanship. *Noches en los jardines de España,* composed in 1916, is little more than a counterpart of d'Indy's *Symphony on a French Mountain Air,* composed in 1886. Both scores are for piano and orchestra, both exploit a piano technique abounding in arpeggios and harplike effects, both scores use national elements in a most sophisticated, concert-hall manner. Falla's *Noches,* his *La Vida Breve,* and *Seven Popular Spanish Songs* are none the worse for that, and they have been popular repertory pieces since they appeared. The music is not only charmingly evocative of Spain, but it is also the work of an extremely skilled composer with a subtle ear for color and absolute precision in technique. Falla was not only far above any Spanish composer of his day; he was the *only* Spanish composer of the day who rose above mediocrity.

After World War I there was a pronounced change in his style. The big influence on Falla was Stravinsky, who had composed *L'Histoire du Soldat* in 1918 and was investigating the possibilities of neoclassicism. Falla began to work in the same manner. His *El Retablo de Maese Pedro,* scored for an orchestra of twenty, with such unusual instruments as harpsichord, lute-harp, and xylophone, is a counterpart to Stravinsky's little choreographed tale of the Russian soldier. Similarly, Falla's Harpsichord Concerto, with a small group consisting of flute, oboe, clarinet, violin, and cello, can be described as Hispanic neoclassicism. The music has never achieved the popularity of his earlier works, but it strikes much deeper into Spanish folk song, and in addition evokes the world of Scarlatti (who had spent so many years in Spain). His biggest work, *L'Atlántida,* for chorus, soloists, and orchestra, was left unfinished and seems to have died stillborn. Ernesto Halffter, the Spanish composer who studied with Falla, completed the score. It made very little impression when Ernest Ansermet conducted the American premiere in New York in 1962, and there have been few if any performances since then.

France, Italy, and Germany never had an important nationalistic composer. In England there was Ralph Vaughan Williams and in Hungary Béla Bartók, both to be discussed in later chapters. In Poland, Ignace Jan Paderewski (1860–1941) was turning out a commercial national product—a Chopin kind of nationalism expressed in late-romantic clichés: often graceful, but unimportant. A much stronger Polish nationalist was Karol Szymanowski (1882–1937), who passed from Russian to German to French schools, ending up an internationalist whose music was tinged with Polish folk elements and leaned heavily on late Scriabin. Very little of his work is heard in the West. In Denmark there was Carl Nielsen (1865–1931), a composer who in recent years has been attracting a great deal of attention. Nielsen, unlike Jean Sibelius (1865–1957) in nearby Finland, was not a true nationalist. Brahms and Mahler were stronger influences on his music than Danish folk song. But Nielsen worked out a strong and original style.

His talent showed up at an early age, he became a violinist, and was awarded a state subsidy for study. In all this his career paralleled Sibelius's (though Nielsen's state grant was nothing on the order of the generous one that the Finnish government gave Sibelius). He conducted the Royal Opera until 1914 and became head of the Royal Conservatory in 1915. While conducting a program of his own music in 1926 he had a heart attack and lingered a very sick man until his death in October, 1931.

Where Sibelius was influenced at first by Tchaikovsky and the Russian school, Nielsen looked to the German postromantics. His early works are very much in the postromantic tradition, and never did he entirely discard tonality. He even went so far as to give names to four of his six symphonies: No. 2 is *The Four Temperaments*, No. 3 the *Sinfonia Espansiva*, No. 4 the *Inextinguishable*, and No. 6 the *Sinfonia Semplice*. Actually, these titles did not indicate a Straussian kind of program music. Rather they were a Schumannesque, clue-giving device. Nielsen always was an "absolute" composer, and one whose music shows a steady growth. Like Janáček, he was a composer who had one foot in the nineteenth century, one in the twentieth. In his day he was accused of writing dissonance, of falling in with the atonalists. Today those attacks appear nonsensical. Nielsen was more adventurous than many composers of his day, but basically he was a traditionalist who accepted the classic forms, sometimes surrounding them with more biting harmonies than conventional ears could stand. Even in the Fifth Symphony, with its polytonal clashes, there is never any doubt about the underlying tonality.

While not as determinedly nationalistic as Sibelius's, Nielsen's music does have nationalistic echoes. But the thing that most impresses about it is its breadth. The man thought big. His rhythms are energetic, his melodies are long-breathed, his orchestration is generous. There is a great deal of individuality to his writing. In the 1930's, music lovers were hearing a great deal about the "bardic" qualities of Sibelius. It is ironic to realize that Nielsen, then all but unknown outside of Denmark, had just as much sweep, even more power and a more universal message. Sibelius's reputation fast dissipated after his death in 1957. In 1965, the centenary of his birth arrived with all the force of a feather against an iron anvil. There were a few memorial concerts in the United States, but the public did not seem to care much, one way or the other, and most professional musicians could not have been less interested.

It was different in the 1930's. At that time Sibelius was at the height of his fame, even though he had not composed a note since 1926. His Seventh Symphony of 1924 and *Tapiola* of 1925 were his last two important works. Like Rossini, he then sat back and watched the world go by. But whereas Rossini amused himself by composing jests and *aperçus*, Sibelius never once touched pen to music paper in the last thirty-one years of his life. There were rumors about an Eighth Symphony. Nothing happened. Sibelius clearly had made up his mind that he had nothing important to say any more. But he remained an important name. His music was especially venerated in England and the United States, where Sibelius had such champions as Sir Thomas Beecham, Constant Lambert, Serge Koussevitzky, and Olin Downes. Downes, music critic of the New York *Times*, was constantly reminding his readers about what Sibelius had done to revolutionize symphonic form, and he wrote article after article about the "strength," "masculinity," and "bardic" qualities of Sibelius. In England, Sibelius was taken with equal seriousness. When Lambert published his controversial *Music Ho!* in 1933, a book that looked upon modern music and found it not good, the only contemporary who came out well was Sibelius. "His Fourth Symphony," wrote Lambert, "is as unappreciated now as were the later sonatas and quartets of Beethoven in their day. Nevertheless, just as the later quartets of Beethoven have influenced modern thought far more than the fashionable works of Hummel and Czerny, so will the symphonies of Sibelius have a more profound influence on future generations than the *pièces d'occasion* of his contemporaries—the composers like Hindemith and Stravinsky who have made their compromise with vogue."

It did not work out as Lambert predicted. In the United States the decline of Sibelius started in 1940. Just as Downes had been instrumental in setting Sibelius on his pedestal, so another critic was instrumental in tearing him off. Virgil Thomson, in his first season as music critic of the New York *Herald Tribune,* heard the Sibelius Second Symphony and found it "vulgar, self-indulgent and provincial beyond all description." In a typical Thomsonian burst he wrote that he realized there were sincere Sibelius-lovers in the world, "although I must say I've never met one among educated professional musicians." Thomson was only echoing what many musicians were thinking. To them, Sibelius was little better than an anachronistic relic of postromanticism. In a way that is curious, for starting with the Fourth Symphony of 1911 Sibelius did bring something to music that was new, provocative, and antiromantic. Breaking away from the lush melodies and orchestration of his first three symphonies, breaking away from the long developments of the Mahler and Bruckner symphonic style, Sibelius instead worked with short motifs and a terse kind of development. It has been described as a mosaic style, and it succeeds in avoiding the romantic rhetoric.

95

The last four symphonies are not even specifically nationalistic, though commentators are eager to read into them the trees, snows, and mountains of the icy North.

Yet many professionals after World War II found Sibelius a dated bore. One reason was that music had taken a new departure. Schoenberg and Webern were the heroes; serialism had triumphed. (If Mahler was suddenly popular, it was because the serialists decided that in Mahler lay the seeds of the serial movement.) There may have been still another reason why Sibelius was scorned. Professionals look for consistency in a composer. They distrust a creator who constantly turns out music that is not on a high level, and are apt to regard as freaks those few works that do cause a ripple. How could the composer of *Valse Triste* and the *Romance* in D flat for piano be taken seriously? It cannot be denied that a large quantity of Sibelius's work —and he was a prolific composer—consists of ephemera. His violin works, apart from the D minor Concerto, are salon trifles, and his songs are competent without being striking. Sibelius composed only a handful of works that have any chance of survival. Yet even that is a better average than many composers can show, and in years to come the chances are that the music of Sibelius will occupy a more prominent place than it currently does. At the time of his death he was suffering from a bad name and an aesthetic that ran counter to the age. If a new age does produce a resurgent romanticism or neoromanticism, Sibelius could come back with it. He did, after all, talk with an individual voice when he was at his best, and he deserves to occupy an honorable place among the minor composers.

❧ 6 ❧

Chromaticism and Sensibilité

FROM FRANCK TO FAURÉ

"France! Great in all the arts, supreme in none." So mourned Anatole France. Be that as it may, the last quarter of the nineteenth century saw a large number of important French composers working in Paris, and in the closing decade the music of young Claude Debussy began to be discussed. But now there was a significant shift in their orientation. Through most of the century, France had stood for opera. With the exception of Berlioz— and he too would dearly have wished to be appreciated as a successful composer of operas—most French composers (at least, those of international reputation) had become famous as suppliers of very salable works for the lyric stage. Now appeared a group of composers whose ambition took in other things. Many of them did try their hand at opera, but opera was not the basic reason for their existence. They wrote symphonies, piano works, and chamber music, and they added significantly to the European ferment. Yet they turned out music that did not travel very well. César Franck and Gabriel Fauré, and then their pupils, composed fine works that somehow were for the most part not exportable.

Franck is today out of fashion; the delicate music of Fauré has never been able to secure a foothold outside of France; and the music of their followers —Vincent d'Indy, Ernest Chausson, Édouard Lalo, Paul Dukas, and the others —lies largely neglected, apart from one or two favorites by each composer. To most modern tastes this music is, in the case of Franck, too chromatic, too self-indulgent, too cloying; and, in the case of his followers, too derivative. It is also a music that is curiously ambivalent, in that it is strongly streaked with Wagnerism despite the efforts, sometimes frantic, of French composers to avoid Wagnerism. After the first Bayreuth Festival of 1876, the Wagnerian language swept French music, and every composer dutifully made his pilgrimage to the Festspielhaus, coming back bathed in Wagner's sensuous harmonies. One of Franck's most promising pupils, Guillaume Lekeu, actually fainted after the prelude to *Tristan* and had to be carried out of the theater. Wagner became the god of the symbolist poets, and a magazine, *La Revue Wagnérienne,* was started in Paris to preach the gospel of *Der Meister.*

Superficially there is little Wagner influence in, say, Franck's D minor Symphony or Chausson's *Poème.* Actually there is a great deal. Wagner's fluctuating harmonies, his reluctance to return to a home key, his incessant chromaticism—all that is reflected in French music of the post-Bayreuth period. Franck's chromaticism, indeed, carries Wagner's a notch forward, and a good deal of French opera of the day is a mirror of what Wagner was espousing at Bayreuth. Some French composers, at first enthusiastic Wagnerians, later started to wriggle out of Wagner's embrace. None was completely successful.

Franck was the dominating musical force of the period in France, both as composer and as teacher, and he gathered unto himself a group of pupils who did everything but put a halo over him and worship. There was something in the man that encouraged worship. While he was not the plaster saint d'Indy made him out to be, he was kind to a point of saintliness, serene, otherworldly. Never did a harsh word pass his lips, never a derogatory remark. He was not interested in honors or in money, and a stained-glass aura (reflected in his music) emanated from him. One of his greatest delights was to sit and improvise at the organ of Ste.-Clothilde in a religious ecstasy (in a way, Franck was a French Bruckner). People compared him with Fra Angelico. It was to Franck that the younger generation turned, much to the distress of such members of the Establishment as Saint-Saëns, Ambroise Thomas, and Massenet.

A Belgian who did not become a naturalized Frenchman until 1873, Franck was born in Liège on December 10, 1822. His father tried to exploit him as a child prodigy, and the boy did achieve something of a reputation. In 1835 the family moved to Paris, and at the age of fifteen César was sent to the Paris Conservatoire. He must have been a cocky lad, exultant in his talent. At the finals of the piano competition he was given a difficult piece to read at sight. For some reason he took it into his head to transpose the entire composition, and he played it in C major instead of E flat, transfixing the judges. A special meeting of the jury was held, and the decision, as reported in *La France Musicale* of August 5, 1838, was to give Franck a special prize:

First of all the jury awarded with one voice the first prize to M. Franck. But after that, the jury decided to look into the matter again. After some discussion, M. Cherubini announced with his customary grace: "The jury has now decided that M. Franck stands so incomparably far ahead of his fellow competitors that it is impossible to nominate another to share the prize with him. Accordingly, a second first prize will be given to those who would in ordinary circumstances have deserved the senior award.

A promising beginning; but after leaving the Conservatoire, Franck sank into obscurity. He taught, he concertized, he composed, and his music did come to the attention of Liszt, who praised a set of piano trios. Liszt met Franck and immediately sized him up: "I fancy he is lacking in that convenient social sense that opens all doors." Which, of course, was true. Franck was not an aggressive man. Indeed, his brother Joseph was a much better-known composer at the time. Today Joseph is completely forgotten.

Not until he was thirty years old did Franck switch from piano to organ. He specialized in church work and improvisation, and was considered to be by far the greatest improviser of his time. "Classical" organ playing—the correct performance of baroque organ music—was virtually a lost art in France until Franck and others headed the renaissance in the last half of the century. Jean-Bonaventure Laurens, writing in *La Gazette Musicale* of November 2, 1845, pointed out that whereas the piano music of Bach was well known (note the term "piano music"; nobody at the time would have thought of playing the *Well-Tempered Clavier* and other Bach clavier works on the harpsichord, assuming that a professional harpsichordist could have been found, which in itself is a doubtful assumption), the organ works were unknown, "since they all demand the use of the pedals, a technical feat that practically nobody in this country seems at the moment to have mastered." Not until Adolphe Hesse came to Paris and showed how the Bach organ works should really go was the attention of French musicians and organists turned to this sublime literature.

Franck's investigation into the resources of the organ was naturally accelerated when he became organist of Ste.-Clothilde in 1858. He started composing for the instrument, and his first important series of organ works came out in 1862 as *Six Pièces pour grand orgue*. They were by far the most significant compositions he had produced, and they have remained in the repertoire. But they did not make him famous. Franck at thirty-six was little known as a creative figure. In 1865 he moved with his wife and the four children to 95 Rue de Rennes (now the Boulevard du Montparnasse) and there spent the rest of his life. Mme. Franck was a virago. She was ambitious for her husband, but she did not like his music and she hated his experimentation. She knew just enough about music to be alarmed when Franck broke the rules, and she made no secret of her dislike of the F minor Piano Quintet and the D minor Symphony. She was especially unhappy with the critical reception accorded those works. This was no way for a respectable

French organist to get ahead in the world. She argued and cried, nagged, and pestered. It was not a happy marriage.

Little of Franck's early music is played. He was one of those composers who develops late, and not until the 1880's did he compose most of the music by which he is known. (The *Six Pièces* of 1862 are an exception.) Prior to the 1880's, however, his music had been given occasional hearings. The Société Nationale de Musique, which had as its motto *Ars Gallica,* had put one of his works on its very first program, November 25, 1871. Only a year after that, Franck was appointed professor of organ at the Conservatoire. Very soon he became the most discussed teacher there, with a group of pupils who ran around Paris crying that Franck was the only progressive figure in that conservative institution. Those pupils were called the Franckists and, less politely, Franck's Gang. They included Lekeu (who died at the age of twenty-four), Henri Duparc, d'Indy, Guy Ropartz, Ernest Chausson, Gabriel Pierné, and Alexis de Castillon (another who died young). These young men were different from the general run of Conservatoire students. Many of them had money, one of them (Castillon) was a viscount, another (d'Indy) came from an aristocratic family, and they regarded the rest of the student body as rabble, much as an aviator regards the infantry. This kind of aristocracy and snobbery within the Conservatoire caused a great deal of resentment, all the more in that Franck was supposed to be nothing more than an organ teacher. The secretary of the Conservatoire had some tart words to say: "In this school we have at the present time a professor of organ who makes so bold as to turn his organ class into a composition class." There was grumbling, but nobody did anything about the situation.

As *de jure* teacher of organ and *de facto* teacher of composition, Franck passed to his pupils his ideas on harmony and form. He was uneasy when anybody stayed in the same key for any length of time. "Modulate! Modulate!" he would urge. As one of the pioneers in cyclic form—he had introduced it in his piano trios as early as 1842—Franck preached a kind of musical development in which initial material was subject to manipulation within an entire composition. Liszt, with his ideas of thematic transformation, had been doing much the same thing in the 1840's and '50's. Franck's ideas created strong centers of opposition, and his own music made little headway. When the Piano Quintet had its premiere in 1880 at a Société Nationale concert, Saint-Saëns, who was the pianist, hated every bit of it and stalked off the stage, refusing to return for applause. He even left the manuscript on the piano, although it was dedicated to him, and one of Franck's pupils rescued it. After the premiere of the D minor Symphony in February, 1889, Gounod's famous remark was "An affirmation of incompetence pushed to the length of dogma." Ambroise Thomas wondered why Franck called it a symphony in D minor when it passed through so many keys in so short a time. On the other hand, some important musicians—Chabrier, Théodore Dubois, Ernest Guiraud, and even Massenet—took Franck's side.

Around the mild, genuinely humble and modest Franck was a constant storm. During his lifetime, however, his music had very few performances. His oratorio *Rédemption* was a failure in 1873; his major choral work, *Les Béatitudes* (1869–79), was performed only once while he was alive, and that in his own apartment; his oratorio, *Rébecca* (1881), remains generally unknown to this day; and the D minor Symphony was a failure at its premiere. Critics lit into Franck for his "incomprehensible" way of writing. At his death, on November 8, 1890, he admittedly was the leader of a new French school, but not many observers would have given his music much chance for survival.

As things turned out, Franck became tremendously popular after his death, and it was a popularity that did not recede until the 1930's. Some of his music continues to be heard with regularity—the Symphony, the Symphonic Variations for piano and orchestra (1885), *Les Éolides* (1876), and, probably most famous of all, the A major Violin Sonata (1886). Not long ago his Prelude, Chorale and Fugue for solo piano (1884) and, to a lesser extent, his Prelude, Aria and Finale (1887), would have been included, but they seem to be slipping from the repertory. Organists, however, continue to play the Franck *Chorals* and other works, especially the *Grand Pièce symphonique*.

His music is noble and sincere, but what bothers many listeners is its saccharine quality. That, and a quality described as stained-glass religiosity. The music to them is too thick and its modulations too obvious. And some of the construction is demonstrably weak. When Franck worked in classic forms he was apt to go loosely along, as though improvising at the organ. Indeed his years of improvising strongly conditioned some of the formal elements of his music. The workmanship can be flabby. There is, too, an element of mysticism that repels some listeners. Mysticism is not fashionable any more in an objective, science-dominated age.

Franck had an extremely sensuous style. Pater Seraphicus, as he was called, could evoke some remarkably sophisticated rites in his music. Sections of the symphonic poems *Les Éolides* and *Les Djinns* (1884) have a coloring and sheen that anticipate some of Debussy's orchestral effects. The big Quartet in D (1889) and the Piano Quintet (1879) both aim high, and are broad, beautifully written and very striking works. One would not go wrong calling them masterpieces. Franck's music, basically, is loved by those who respond to the sensuous elements of sheer sound. Only those who have a physiological involvement with sound—a musical sweet tooth, to put it another way—can fully identify with the music of César Franck. Others find it so rich and sweetened that it can actually be sickening.

Of Franck's pupils, the talented Guillaume Lekeu (1870–1894) and Alexis de Castillon (1838–1873) died before they came to maturity. Experts in French music insist that Castillon's music is worth hearing, especially his chamber music. Henri Duparc (1848–1933) was a special case. Franck considered him his best pupil, but in 1885 Duparc had a mental breakdown and never composed another note though he lived for almost another half century. He had written a symphonic poem, *Lénore,* in 1875. That piece is no longer heard, and Duparc's fame rests entirely on thirteen songs (there are three others of less importance), each one unparalleled in France and, indeed, in Europe. Only Hugo Wolf was writing this kind of intense, psychological, rich-sounding and completely realized song.

Franck's two most famous pupils were Chausson and d'Indy. Chausson was the better composer, d'Indy the stronger influence. Those who love Franck's music also love Chausson's, for the music of both is ladled from the same rich, sensuous stream. Chausson was born in Paris on January 20, 1855, the overprotected child of a wealthy building contractor. The boy was given a private tutor and then sent to law school. He received his degree in 1877 but never practiced. All of his inclinations were toward the arts. "Ever since my childhood I have believed that I would write music. Everybody advises me against it. So I try painting and literature. Everybody gives me different advice." It was not until 1879, after exposure to Wagner's music, that Chausson made up his mind to be a composer. At the very late age of twenty-four he enrolled in Massenet's and Franck's classes, then dropped Massenet. In 1883 he left Franck and started to compose. He bought a house at 22 Boulevard des Courcelles and made it one of the artistic centers of Paris —the kind of brilliant salon that the Princess Belgiojoso had run fifty years previously. Painters, musicians, writers, and intellectuals were constantly there, and Chausson was friends with everybody who counted. (At his funeral, such figures as Degas, Rodin, Redon, and Louÿs were in the procession.) Chausson also more or less adopted the young Debussy, and the two men were very close. Chausson would lecture Debussy, and the touchy young fellow would not only take it but come back for more. "You are somewhat like a big, older brother in whom one has complete confidence," Debussy wrote, "and from whom one even accepts an occasional scolding." The generous Chausson befriended many other musicians as well. One was Isaac Albéniz. In fact, Chausson took in Albéniz and his whole family when the Spaniard was hard hit financially. Later Albéniz repaid the debt by privately paying Breitkopf and Härtel to publish Chausson's *Poème* in Germany.

Having no financial problems, Chausson could work when and where he pleased. He was a slow worker who could and did agonize for days over a single measure. His list of compositions is not large, and the important ones can be counted on the fingers of one hand. They are the Symphony in B flat (1891), the Concerto for Piano, Violin and String Quartet (1892), the *Poème de l'amour et de la mer* (1893), the *Poème* for violin and orchestra (1896), and the Piano Quartet (1898). His most ambitious work, the opera *Le Roi Arthus*, was composed between 1886 and 1895, and is not in the repertory. Experts describe it as Wagnerian. Chausson had some big projects in mind when his life was suddenly cut short by a bicycle accident on June 10, 1899. He lost control, crashed into a wall and was killed.

Strongly under Franck's influence, Chausson composed a luscious, opulently chromatic music in which the physiological action of pure sound occupies a major element. Is there anything in music, *Tristan* included, with the sensuous, almost tactile, feeling of the *Poème*? So rich is it that it is all velvet, and it definitely is not music for Puritans. It actually offends some listeners. This, and the Symphony in B flat, are unashamedly erotic, as much as music can be erotic. Chausson did for the symphony what Massenet was doing for the opera, though Chausson's music has more substance. The B flat Symphony is an underestimated work. It has more shape and discipline than the Franck D minor, its phrases are more pointed, its melodic content on an equally high level. The scented allure of Chausson's music is difficult to describe. It has the peculiarly French charm of a Pissarro painting—limited, perhaps oversweet, yet sensitive, purposeful, and powerfully evocative of a specific time and place in history.

All of the pupils of Franck worshiped their teacher, but it was Vincent d'Indy (1851–1931) who raised the worship to a cult. In his writings d'Indy even misrepresented Franck, so anxious was he to preserve the myth. He came to his teacher, like so many Franck pupils, at a surprisingly advanced age. D'Indy had plenty of talent—he had been a child prodigy—but he was essentially a dilettante until the age of eighteen, when he decided to study music seriously. He entered Franck's class in 1872, and his future life was set. It turned out to be one of the busier lives in French music. A man stubborn to the point of fanaticism, d'Indy was the propagandist for "Franck's Gang," and he helped further spread the message when he became director of the Société Nationale de Musique in 1890. In 1894 he founded the Schola Cantorum, along with Charles Bordes and Alexandre Guilmant. The Schola Cantorum originally was intended to be a society for the performance of sacred music, but it soon turned into a school for the study and restoration of old church music in general, and it also busied itself with scholarly work in French folk song. Many important French musicians were trained at the Schola Cantorum, the most prominent being Albert Roussel (1869–1937).

Little of d'Indy's vast output is heard today. The one work that still does make the rounds is the *Symphonie Cévenole* (1886), better known as the

Symphonie sur un chant montagnard français (Symphony on a French Mountain Air). It is a lovely work for piano and orchestra, brilliantly scored, haunting in its second movement, and with an ultrasophisticated use of folk elements. Much more direct than the music of Franck and Chausson, far less persistently chromatic, the *Cévenole* is one of the finest works of French postromanticism. Almost as good is the B flat Symphony (1909), which is seldom heard. French conductors of an older generation—Pierre Monteux was one—would program the B flat Symphony and the *Istar* Variations of 1897 (Koussevitzky was fond of the latter), but the current school of French conductors appears contemptuous of d'Indy's music. It is too bad for there are some beautiful things in the d'Indy *oeuvre*.

Two other French composers highly regarded in their day were Édouard Lalo (1823–1892) and Paul Dukas (1865–1935). Lalo still lives through his *Symphonie Espagnole* (1878) for violin and orchestra; and his opera, *Le Roi d'Ys* (1888), can still be heard in Paris. It is a much more forward-looking work than anything by Massenet and Gounod, and so is Dukas's *Ariane et Barbe-Bleue* (1907), a fascinating amalgam of Wagner and Debussy. Unfortunately Dukas is best-known by a potboiler, *The Sorcerer's Apprentice* (1897), while his fine C major Symphony (1896), his monumental Piano Sonata in E flat minor (1901), and his once-popular "*poème dansé,*" *La Péri* (1910), languish in near total neglect.

The composer who was the antithesis of Franck, and the greatest in France between Berlioz and Debussy, was Gabriel Fauré, and this despite the fact that Fauré worked primarily in small forms. He ranks with the greatest of all song composers, and he also concentrated on piano and chamber music. Because he never wrote a symphony or concerto, and because his one opera, *Pénélope* (1913), has never held the stage, he is apt to be dismissed out of hand. But to dismiss him, as so many outside of France tend to do, as a purveyor of Gallic *Kitsch* is to dismiss one of the most supple, elegant, and refined of all composers.

Fauré was a musician who was constantly developing. At the beginning he wrote charming songs in the style of Gounod and exquisite piano pieces *à la* Chopin and Schumann. As he grew older there came a deepening introspection and a curious harmonic palette. A quality that might be described as austere mysticism—the reverse of the voluptuous mysticism of Franck—entered his music, and some of his final works, sparse and enigmatic, are real puzzlers. Yet as one studies and lives with such music as the Thirteenth Nocturne (1922), or the E minor Violin Sonata (1917), or the song cycle *La Chanson d'Eve* (1907–10), it is with respect that becomes admiration and love. The writing is extremely fastidious, the textures much more transparent than in the early works, the harmonies almost bleak. Fauré, as he neared the end of his long life, was striving for a new kind of expression.

Never was there a more un-German composer. Of all the French composers of his day, Fauré was the most successful in his ability to ignore the siren sounds emanating from Bayreuth. It follows that music lovers whose orientation is to the German classics and to the big sounds of German postromanticism are the ones who like Fauré the least. They think in terms of orthodox structure and developments, and condemn Fauré's music for not being "deeper" or "more profound"—for not being the very thing it tried so hard not to be. This attitude is like condemning Robert Herrick for not being John Donne, and it irritates Fauré's admirers. Norman Suckling, author of the standard biography of Fauré in English, puts it as follows: "His music is, for instance, so transparent that the lovers of the turgid have no option but to accuse him of a lack of profundity. This charge comes with particular readiness from those who in various other connections are desirous of perpetuating the legend of French frivolity and who will therefore assume without further proof that so typical a French thinker as Voltaire was more shallow than, say, Fichte, because his writings are so much more transparent . . ."

Fauré was born in Paniers on May 12, 1845, and died in Paris on November 4, 1924. Mendelssohn, Chopin, and Schumann were alive at his birth, and thus his life spanned early romanticism, the Wagnerian music drama, the postromanticism of Brahms and Mahler, the neoclassicism of Stravinsky, the atonalism and dodecaphony of Schoenberg, and even the emergence of Aaron Copland, whom he conceivably could have heard when the young American was studying with Nadia Boulanger (herself a Fauré pupil). Amid all this, Fauré went his own quiet way. In successive eras of music dramas, bang-bang Straussian tone poems and Stravinsky ballets, he wrote intimate music—quartets, quintets, songs, piano pieces with the nondescriptive titles of Impromptu, Barcarolle, Nocturne, Prélude.

One of the few important French composers not trained at the Conservatoire, Fauré instead studied at the École Niedermeyer. Among his teachers was Saint-Saëns, and Fauré later said that he owed *everything* to his older colleague. In those days, the middle 1850's, Saint-Saëns was one of the progressives, and he introduced his pupils to Wagner and Liszt as well as to Bach and Mozart. Later he supported Fauré with encouragement and help, finding jobs and publishers for him. Fauré probably had a better musical education at the Niedermeyer than he would have received at the Conservatoire, which was largely a factory for producing virtuosos and fashionable composers. Thanks to Saint-Saëns, Fauré was introduced to the whole range of music. It should be remembered that Saint-Saëns, probably the most fabulous musical mind in Europe, was not only a musician who could instantly play anything. He also was a musicologist long before the term came into use. He knew more about old music than any performing musician of the 1850's, and he also was a purist who insisted that the old music be played as written, without romantic interpolations. At the Conservatoire, this kind of musical culture was unknown. As Fauré later wrote, "In 1853 the masterpieces of J. S. Bach, which constituted our daily bread [at the Niedermeyer] had still not found their way into the organ class at the Conservatoire; and in the piano classes at the same Conservatoire, the students still labored at the performance of Herz' concertos, while Adolphe Adam shed his brilliant light upon his composition class."

Fauré left the École Niedermeyer at the age of twenty, with first prizes in piano, organ, harmony, and composition. He had already written a large number of songs and piano pieces. From 1866 to 1870 he was a church organist in Brittany. Then he returned to Paris to become organist at St.-Honoré. He fought in the Franco-Prussian War, returned to the Niedermeyer as professor of composition, became choirmaster and later organist at the Madeleine, and finally, in 1896, entered the Conservatoire as a professor of composition. Fauré had previously been suggested for the post, but it would have been over the dead body of the director, Ambroise Thomas, who considered Fauré a dangerous revolutionary. "If he is nominated, I will resign." When Thomas finally did resign, in 1896, Massenet, who was teaching composition at the Conservatoire, pulled every string he could to get the position. But he would not take it unless it was a lifetime appointment. The Ministry of Public Information, however, decided that in the future no Conservatoire director would receive an appointment for life. Théodore Dubois was appointed, Massenet resigned in disgust, and Fauré was chosen to take over Massenet's class. Through the years, Fauré turned out such distinguished composers as Charles Koechlin, Florent Schmitt, Louis Aubert, Raoul Laparra, Jean Roger-Ducasse, and Maurice Ravel. He became director of the Conservatoire in 1905 and remained its head until 1920.

Fauré ran the Conservatoire with a firm hand. The small, mild, innocuous-looking Fauré proved to be an excellent administrator and a man of firm opinion. As head of the Conservatoire he started to introduce some reforms, and was faced with a revolt. The conservative professors could not see why things should not be done as they had been done in Cherubini's time. Fauré calmly got rid of the dissenters one by one. So numerous were the resignations that it began to be said of Fauré that he "needed his daily cartload of victims, like Robespierre." Théodore Dubois, whom Fauré replaced as head of the Conservatoire, was among those who resigned. Dubois, a hack, had remained on the board of directors as professor emeritus. He sent in his letter of resignation because "M. Fauré was transforming the Conservatoire into a temple for the music of the future." Fauré replaced him with two musicians who knew what it was all about—d'Indy and Debussy.

At the age of sixty-four Fauré received one of France's supreme accolades

—a seat in the *Institut*. It was at this time, too, that he helped organize the Société Musicale Indépendante (S.M.I.), set up in opposition to the Franck-d'Indy-dominated Société Musicale Nationale. Nevertheless Fauré and d'Indy remained friends. Then tragedy. Deafness set in, complicated by distortion of pitch. High frequencies sounded flat, low ones sharp. It must have been agony. Yet Fauré continued to compose, and some of his best music comes from that time. News of his affliction became public, and in 1920 he was asked to resign from the Conservatoire. Almost to the day of his death he continued to compose, finishing his string quartet (the only one he composed) in 1924. He took to his deathbed wondering if he had written anything of value. "What of my music will live?" Pause. "But, then, that is of little importance." Charles Koechlin, in his little monograph on Fauré, claims those were his last words.

One of the major influences on Fauré was Chopin. He had in common with Chopin a delicate sensibility applied to every note, and his music has much the same feeling of melodic inevitability, refinement, taste, unerring judgment, and impeccable workmanship. Heroics had no place in his music. His feeling for delicate applications of tone color was remarkable, and Debussy learned much from him here. Yet Fauré's music is essentially masculine, whereas Debussy leans toward the feminine—or at least epicene—side. Both were masters of the song but worked in different directions. Debussy's songs were influenced as much by Mussorgsky's ideas of language as by earlier French composers. He tried to achieve natural speech patterns, and his vocal lines are often declamatory. Fauré worked much more closely within the traditions of European song, and his vocal lines are singing lines rather than attempts to reproduce speech patterns. From his very first song, *Le papillon et la fleur*, it was clear that Fauré had a genius for setting notes to words. How many composers—even Schubert, even Duparc and Wolf—can boast of so rapturous a song as *Dans les ruines d'une abbaye*, or the intensity and luxuriance of a cycle like *La Bonne chanson?* He composed about a hundred songs, ending with a masterpiece, *L'Horizon chimérique*, written in 1922.

His piano music is lyric and elegant, and difficult to play. There is little in the way of flashy virtuosity (as in Chopin, the ornamentation is functional), but the spread of the writing, its linear complexity and wide range over the keyboard, take it away from the amateur pianist. Fauré sent his Ballade for piano and orchestra to Liszt, and Liszt—Franz Liszt, who could read anything at sight, who was so hospitable to new music—returned the score with a curt note, saying it was too difficult. Fauré's piano music follows the development of his other music. As the composer grew older, the writing became more austere, far removed from the spontaneous lyricism of his youth and early middle age. Some think that Fauré's late music is too intellectual, too bleak to "work" in the concert hall. And it is true that the part of Fauré predominantly in the repertoire consists of those works that predate the problematic later ones. These include the A major Violin Sonata of 1876 (a rapturous work, much finer than Franck's in the same key, and composed ten years earlier); the simple, beautiful Requiem (1887); the C minor Piano Quartet (1879); the *Dolly* Suite for piano duet (1896); the songs; and a handful of early nocturnes, barcaroles, and impromptus. Once in a while the Ballade (1881), turned down by Liszt, is heard. It is a smoothly organized piece, enchantingly lyric, with a neat climax and a good measure of Fauré's delicate poetry. It may or may not have been orchestrated by him. Fauré never made any secret of the fact that he hated to compose orchestral music and that he would assign pupils to do the instrumentation. Charles Koechlin, for example, orchestrated the popular *Pelléas et Mélisande* Suite.

Can there be such a thing as being too sensitive? Fauré was a master whose delicately adjusted music lacks the grand gesture and excitement that could give it mass popularity. The word "Hellenic" is often used to describe his music. "Civilized sensibility" is another description commonly found. It is music that contains the essence of everything Gallic—form, grace, wit, logic, individuality, urbanity. It is music that has attracted a small but fanatic band of admirers; and those who love the music of Fauré love it as a private, cherished gift from one of the gentlest and most subtle of composers.

✸ 7 ✸

Only for the Theater

GIACOMO PUCCINI

Toward the end of his life, Giacomo Antonio Domenico Michele Secondo Maria Puccini wrote to a friend: "Almighty God touched me with his little finger and said 'Write for the theater—mind, only for the theater. And I have obeyed the supreme command." With such compliance and talent did Puccini submit to the inevitable that he composed three of the most popular operas ever written, died worth an estimated four million dollars, had all the opportunity he desired to play poker and to decimate the duck population around his lodge at Torre del Lago, and indulge his passion for fast boats, fast motor cars, and fast women.

That, in essence, is the story of Puccini's life. (He did compose other things than operas, but they are few in number and of supreme unimportance.) He once described himself as "a mighty hunter of wild fowl, opera librettos and attractive women." He also is on record as saying, "Just think of it! If I hadn't hit on music I should never have been able to do anything in the world!" He took no great interest in politics and the world around him. He was not particularly interested in the musical scene or in young composers. Or old ones, for that matter. He was neither a conservative nor a revolutionary. He belonged to no musical clique. He was not representative of the verismo, life-as-it-really-is school that so attracted the Italian composers of the 1890's, though verismo elements appeared in some of his operas. Polytonality, neoclassicism, futurism, impressionism, dodecaphony—to all those calls to battle he was indifferent, though he had looked at the music of such modern classics as Debussy's *Pelléas et Mélisande* and Schoenberg's *Pierrot Lunaire,* and was ready to incorporate what he liked of the new school into his own music. If certain aspects of verismo interested him, he used them in *Tosca* and *Il Tabarro.* If he was struck by Debussy's use of the whole-tone scale, he used it in *La Fanciulla del West.* Normally this kind of plundering would lead to eclecticism, but Puccini was not an eclectic. His own style was too pungent, too much his very own. Whatever he was, he was completely outside the intellectual trend of his time. Musically speaking, Puccini owed little to anybody, and that is one of the miracles about the composer of *La Bohème, Tosca,* and *Madama Butterfly.*

Born in Lucca on December 22, 1858, the last (as it turned out) in the line of five generations of respected musicians, he naturally grew up under the shadow of Verdi, the dominant force of Italian music in the last half of the nineteenth century. It was not that other composers did not compete; there are a few foothills at the base of the Verdian mountain. In the 1870's and thereafter, a few composers did write operas that became repertory pieces. It is amazing how many of those composers became one-work men outside of their native country and even, to a large extent, within Italy. There was Boito, with the revised version of his *Mefistofele* in 1875. Amilcare Ponchielli (1854–1906) came out with *La Gioconda* in 1876, and it was the only one of his nine operas with staying power. Alfredo Catalani (1854–1893) was much talked about in his day, but his two major operas, *Loreley* (1880) and *La Wally* (1892), were swept away by Puccini and the verismists, and are seldom heard outside of Italy.

The new school of verismo composers appeared in the 1890's, and at least two works of stature were the result. The verismists aimed for realism, often putting their characters into contemporary dress, using plots that contained humble people rather than aristocrats, delighting in raw violence on stage, and describing the action and emotional moods in music of stark emotion. Pietro Mascagni (1863–1945) was the first, with *Cavalleria Rusticana* in 1890. Ruggiero Leoncavallo (1858–1945) followed with *I Pagliacci* in 1892. In 1896 came *Andrea Chénier* by Umberto Giordano (1867–1948). Though *Chénier* is set in the French Revolution, it has so many verismo elements in it that it is included in the school.

Verismo opera did not last much more than a decade, and most of the verismo composers are in effect one-work men, much as their predecessors had been. Mascagni never wrote another opera anywhere near as popular as *Cavalleria Rusticana,* though *L'Amico Fritz* (1891) has some lovely things in it, and the "Cherry Duet" from that opera is pure gold from beginning to end. Similarly, Leoncavallo was never able to repeat the success of *Pagliacci,* even if his *Zazà* had a run for some years. Another one-work composer was Francesco Cilèa (1866–1950), whose *Adriana Lecouvreur* had its premiere in 1902. Modern taste tends to dismiss verismo opera as too hysterical and melodramatic, though it must be said that *Cavalleria Rusticana* and *Pagliacci* show no signs of any decrease in popularity.

Puccini grew up in this period but was singularly untouched by it. In his music is relatively little of the verismo blood and thunder. Nor is there any Verdi (except in the *Falstaff*-derived *Gianni Schicchi*), and there is no Wagner at all. Somewhere, somehow, he evolved a personal, inimitable style that stands out among the Italian operas of his time like the song of a nightingale in a flock of starlings. The only composer of the day whose music could faintly be described as comparable was Massenet; and in a way Puccini is an Italian Massenet, though one with a greater feeling for drama and a superior melodic impulse. Most of the Puccini operas have workable librettos, and he was fanatically concerned with the legitimacy of dramatic situation. But that is not what the Puccini operas stand for. Song, tender and sensuous song, is what Puccini offers. Melody came naturally to him, and in this he may be called an instinctive composer, for everything in composition can be taught except how to create an immortal melody. Puccini may have been poor in fugue, but he was rich in expressive melody, the thing that is basic to an opera composer. Rosa Raisa, the great dramatic soprano who created the role of Turandot, said that after decades of singing Puccini and listening to his operas, she invariably came away deeply touched. "At *Bohème* I start crying in the third act."

The Puccini operas may be naïve; and musicians have also accused them of pandering to a listener's baser instincts. There is no denying that many Puccini operas are frank tearjerkers, and those who regard music as an art of spiritual betterment reject them out of hand. Their attitude can be expressed by Arnold Schoenberg's remark that "there are higher and lower means, artistic and inartistic. . . . Realistic, violent incidents—as for example the torture scene in *Tosca*—which are unfailingly effective should not be used by an artist, because they are too cheap, too accessible to everybody." Anybody who so desires can poke holes through any Puccini opera except, perhaps, the perfectly organized *Bohème* or *Gianni Schicchi* (and even there, in *Schicchi*, some critics pick on the pretty aria, *O mio babbino caro*, as a blot on an otherwise tight piece of operatic construction). The last acts of the Puccini operas are likely to be weak, and full of reprise melodies; and all of the operas have tunes so obvious and so sweet that they make some listeners gag. There are those who abominate the Puccini operas, and can cite all kinds of valid reasons why they should be abolished. None of this seems to matter in the least. Puccini hit something that has made audiences strongly react, and he remains one of the most popular of all composers. He achieved his success through melody, plus a compositional technique that was more sophisticated than he is commonly given credit for.

In addition to responding to Puccini's melody, audiences also respond to his characters, especially his heroines. Puccini always was much more convincing in his female characters than in his male ones. Puccini identified with women. Mosco Carner, one of his biographers, puts it perfectly when he writes that "while the ground-bass of Verdi's operas is a battle cry, of Puccini's it is a mating call." Audiences, too, still respond to the Puccini librettos, which are on broad lines and deal with elementals—love, hate, separation, death. The same could be said of the Verdi librettos, but Puccini's do aspire to, and on the whole achieve, a superior literary level (Verdi's *Otello* and *Falstaff* always excepted). Puccini would never get into the tortured complexities of a libretto like *Don Carlo* or *Simon Boccanegra*. His are straightforward, easy to follow, and peopled with characters who face problems that arouse an empathic reaction in all audiences. It may be hokum, but it is *nice* hokum: a dreamworld that never existed, in which emotions are expertly manipulated by composer and librettist. The four young men in *La Bohème* are the archetypes of all creative young men who ever shared a garret and dreamed their great dreams. (Some of this is autobiographical. As a student in Milan, Puccini shared a room with Mascagni. They lived *la vie de bohème*, eating on credit at the *Aïda* Restaurant, and protecting each other from creditors. Puccini even pawned a coat, as Colline does in *Bohème;* only Puccini needed the money to take a ballet girl out for a night on the town.) Cio-Cio-San stands for all women who have loved unselfishly. Mimì, the sweet but not too bright girl who finds herself entangled in a love affair that can only end in unhappiness, is intensely human in her way. And the flamboyant Tosca, that mixture of temperament, passion, and jealousy (she, like Cio-Cio-San and Mimì, is not a very bright girl, either), remains eternally interesting and provocative. Puccini, who knew women so well, seldom created a papier-mâché figure. His women are all too human.

Despite the great care Puccini lavished on detail, and despite his musical craftsmanship and sense of the theater, he was one of the most unintellectual composers who ever lived. Thus it is not astonishing that many learned musicians rail and shake their fingers at the stupid public that continues to support such "trash." A charter member of the Let's-Hate-Puccini Club was Fausto Torrefranca who, in 1912, prophesied that Puccini would be forgotten in a few decades. Puccini, wrote Torrefranca, was "decadent," a "manipulator" rather than a composer. And so on down to Joseph Kerman in 1956, who called *Tosca* a "shabby little shocker" and who insists that *Turandot* is more depraved even than *Tosca,* and that in general the operas of Puccini are "false through and through." The more intellectual the critic, the more he is apt to despise Puccini.

Yet the operas have if anything increased in popularity through the years. A season at a major opera house without the big three Puccini works— *Bohème, Tosca, Butterfly*—is most unusual. *Turandot* and *Manon Lescaut* are coming into their own, and even the once-despised *La Fanciulla del West* (*Girl of the Golden West*) is attracting attention again. *Gianni Schicchi,* one of the funniest operas ever written—what a shame Puccini so seldom exploited his talent for comedy!—is a repertory piece, and the dark-colored *Il Tabarro*, another of the three one-act operas of *Il Trittico* (the others are *Schicchi* and the relatively weak *Suor Angelica*), is a moody, gripping work. It is Puccini's only excursion into out-and-out verismo. Of the other Puccini operas, *Le Villi* and *Edgar* are prentice works, and *La Rondine* is seldom heard. *La Rondine,* commissioned by Vienna, is a bittersweet operetta and probably will be rediscovered. *Turandot* is his last and most massive, ambitious opera and invariably makes a thrilling effect if the soprano and tenor have enough voice.

When Puccini was born, it was expected that he would turn out to be a composer. Puccinis had been musicians and church organists in Lucca since 1712. But young Giacomo was anything but a prodigy. His teachers at the seminary were exasperated by his laziness. "He comes to school only to wear out the seat of his pants," one teacher reported. Anyway, he showed enough talent to be sent to the Milan Conservatory as a scholarship student. There his principal teacher was Ponchielli. Puccini's first success, *Le Villi* (1884), brought him to the attention of Giulio Ricordi, head of the famous publishing firm founded in 1808. Giulio stuck with Puccini through everything, and never made a better investment. After the failure of *Edgar* in 1889 and the moderate success of *Manon Lescaut* in 1893, Puccini came up with *La Bohème* in 1896 and he became rich, Ricordi even richer. Ricordi deserved it, for it was he who had subsidized Puccini through the lean years, and it was he who was always battling away at Puccini's laziness. During the composition of every opera, Giulio (and, after Giulio died, his son Tito) would write desperate letters: "The hunting season has begun. Go easy, Puccini! Don't let your passion for the birds seduce you away from music!"

Puccini married Elvira Gemignani in 1904 after having lived with her for many years. She, a married woman, had eloped with him from Lucca to Milan, and Puccini married her after the death of her husband. They were violently in love at the beginning. Later they had violent quarrels and split up for a time. That was during the Doria Manfredi incident. Doria was a servant at the lodge in Torre del Lago, near Florence, and Elvira got the idea that there was an affair between her and Puccini. She made the matter public, hurled all kinds of accusations at Doria, and hounded the poor girl to death. Doria poisoned herself. An autopsy revealed she was a virgin. Puccini rushed to Rome, locked himself up in a hotel room, and spent days weeping. For having driven Doria to suicide, Elvira was sentenced to five months' imprisonment. "What a theme for an opera!" all Italy said. Eventually Puccini returned to Elvira, but it is doubtful if he ever again was close to her.

From all accounts, Elvira was not an interesting woman. The baritone Titta Ruffo said that her jealousy was "near to lunacy." Musicians who worked with Puccini and were his friends always have been singularly loath to discuss her. One of Puccini's associates described her merely as "not a very literate woman." Another remembered her as "a heavy-set, rather dour sort of person who looked more Teutonic than Latin." She was in every way different from Puccini. As he grew older he became more handsome and urbane, more interesting to women—a fastidious dresser, fairly tall, aristocratic-looking, with an oval face, carefully trimmed moustache, heavily lidded eyes, and sensual lips. The man was a fashion plate, and on his first visit to America in 1907 he made a big impression on reporters used to the leonine thatches of a Paderewski or Gabrilowitsch. Here was a musician who actually had his hair cut. Puccini himself had slighting references to make about musicians "who think they have to have dandruff to be geniuses." Elvira, on the other hand, was dowdy, never a social success, and never helped her husband develop intellectually or emotionally. Had Puccini married the right sort of woman, many believe, he would have developed along more mature lines and perhaps might have lived longer (he died in Brussels on November 29, 1924, while being treated for throat cancer, undoubtedly caused by his excessive smoking, a nervous habit). Certainly he would not have found it so necessary to drift from the arms of one woman to another.

Many also think that it was because of Elvira that Puccini had so few—if any—close friends. Puccini was never close to anybody. Even his love affairs were concerned more with sex than with love. For a while Puccini was on good terms with Arturo Toscanini, who had conducted the *Bohème* premiere in 1896. It was a relationship that blew hot and cold. Giorgio Polacco, the conductor, liked to tell the story about the *pannetone* Puccini sent Toscanini one Christmas during a period of cold war. He suddenly realized that they were not on speaking terms at the moment, and wired Toscanini: PANNETONE SENT BY MISTAKE. PUCCINI. The next day he got an answer: PANNETONE EATEN BY MISTAKE. TOSCANINI.

On the whole, Puccini's life was uneventful. He brought out his operas at regularly spaced intervals, he kept his private life to himself (aside from the Manfredi incident his name never figured in any scandal), and he rarely spoke to reporters. Even in the United States, where reporters were continually besieging him, he had little to say, and desperate newspapermen could come up only with news instead of feature stories about the popular composer. They had fun with him on his departure for Italy on the *Lusitania* in 1910. Giulio Gatti-Casazza, the director of the Metropolitan Opera, and many of the singers saw him off. An army of reporters was present, and this is how the man from the *Telegraph* described the leave-taking. Italian emotionalism always tickled the American press:

> . . . In a body the Met group charged on Puccini. Like a brave man he met them with arms extended and lips pouted.
> A sound like somebody taking off a pair of wet galoshes in a hurry.

That was Gatti-Casazza's double kiss, one for each cheek of Puccini.

A sound like Bossie the Brindle pulling her hind foot out of the mud!

That was Amato's fervent salute.

A sound like somebody stropping a razor rapidly!

That was Scotti the basso putting seven or eight quick ones over .

And so on for many more paragraphs.

Just as there was little for newspapermen to write about Puccini the man, so there was little for them to write about Puccini's music. His operas did not come in on clouds of controversy, as Wagner's did, and as *Salome* did in 1905. Most were immediate, secure successes, and the only failure was the world premiere of *Madama Butterfly* at Milan. Puccini quickly rewrote it, and success followed. Aside from *Il Tabarro* and *Gianni Schicchi*, his operas are pretty much of a piece. There is surprisingly little essential difference between *Bohème* of 1896 and *Turandot* of 1924, even if the latter is broader and somewhat more complex harmonically. Puccini's highly emotional and dramatically transparent works for the stage are in their way as cynical as Massenet's. Puccini knew very well how to stir the emotions of his audience, and he unabashedly did so. At least he was skillful enough to apply the same formulas without falling into self-parody. The operas that break the mold are *Il Tabarro*, with its sounds of the river, its *Cavalleria Rusticana* type of raw emotion and its verismo effects, and above all, the brilliant and scintillating *Gianni Schicchi*. There he composed an opera that is to his output what *Falstaff* is to Verdi's—a comic opera with very few set pieces, completely nonsentimental; an opera in which the orchestra comments on the action; an opera with a bubbling kind of gaiety that pokes affectionate fun at man and his works. It is as Italian as *Die Meistersinger* is German, and it carries its point in a fifth of the time. It is a marvelous work, but Puccini never again attempted anything like it. Instead he turned to grand opera. In *Turandot* he was going to evoke the Orientalisms of *Madama Butterfly*, but on an immense scale.

He died before finishing the last act. At the time of his death Puccini was discouraged. Opera, to him, had taken the wrong turning, and he could see no future. "By now the public for new music has lost its palate," he wrote in 1922. "It loves or puts up with illogical music devoid of all sense. Melody is no longer practiced—or if it is, it is vulgar. People believe the symphonic element must rule, and I, instead, believe this is the end of opera." He may have been right. *Turandot* is the last opera to be a steady repertory piece. The operas of Berg and Janáček are admired, but not by the public at large; the operas of Strauss composed after *Rosenkavalier* in 1911 have only a small following; the operas of Benjamin Britten—and, indeed, of every post-Puccini composer—have not been able to establish themselves.

Turandot is the last of the operas that the public unreservedly loves.

Only the final pages were left incomplete, and the opera was finished by Franco Alfano. At the world premiere at La Scala, on April 25, 1926, Toscanini turned to the audience during the third act and said, "Here the master laid down his pen." There has been some difference of opinion as to whether or not Toscanini continued the performance. Rosa Raisa in 1959 put an end to the controversy by stating that Toscanini did not go on with the opera. Not until the second performance did he conduct Alfano's ending.

Neither a fast nor a prolific composer, Puccini took much time over his operas. Had he found suitable librettos he would have composed more. He considered many librettos and even started work on a few before discarding them. He kept nagging his friends to keep an eye out for suitable material, saying that he could not work if the libretto did not inspire him. While composing an opera, he spent much time on its historical and geographical background. His sense of theater and his passion for exactitude were much admired by singers who worked with him. "With Puccini, it's drama, drama, drama," said Rosa Ponselle. To Raisa, the essence of Puccini was "drama, accompanied by music." To make his dramas authentic, Puccini carefully checked every historic, physical, and psychological point of the libretto. As he wrote to Ricordi in 1899, "You know how scrupulous I am in interpreting the situation or the words and all that is of importance before putting anything down on paper." Working on *Tosca* he wrote to Father Pietro Panchelli, "In order to accentuate the contrast between the filthy desires of Scarpia and the mysterious atmosphere of the place, there should be a great Te Deum. Now, please let me know the exact tone of the church bells in the neighborhood of Castel Sant' Angelo and the exact tone of the big bell at St. Peter's." For *Butterfly* he studied Japanese music, had records made in Japan and sent to him, and did his best "to make B. F. Pinkerton sing like an American," whatever that may mean. For *La Fanciulla del West* he went through much early American popular and folk song "in order to get the atmosphere."

Nothing escaped his notice in his search for realism. Lucrezia Bori has told of the time she was notified by Ricordi that three gentlemen would be coming to Paris to hear her sing, and would she learn a few arias from *Manon Lescaut?* She did, and one day the three gentlemen presented themselves. They were Gatti-Casazza, Toscanini, and Puccini. "They looked at me from head to foot, and then from foot to head," Bori said. "They looked at me thoroughly." They must have been satisfied with what they saw and heard, for presently Bori was rehearsing *Manon Lescaut* with Caruso. She sang the role for the first time as a guest artist with the Metropolitan Opera, then, in 1910, touring Europe.

"I had new costumes made in Paris," Bori said. "They cost me a fortune.

You can imagine. After the dress rehearsal everybody came around to congratulate me. Soon Puccini came up, holding a cup of coffee. 'Bori,' he said, 'everything was perfect. Only in the last act, where Manon is starving and penniless, your costume is too clean.' So he threw the coffee on my gown."

Working with singers, Puccini could be very demanding, but he never really lost his temper. When Edward Johnson sang the leading tenor roles in *Gianni Schicchi* and *Tabarro,* he coached with the composer. "He was worried about me," said Johnson. "After all, I was a foreigner." (Johnson was a Canadian-born singer who eventually became general manager of the Metropolitan Opera.) "When I rehearsed the *Tabarro* duet with the soprano, he couldn't get the quality of sound that suited him. Time after time he would make us change the key, always searching for added intensity." At the Rome premiere of *Il Trittico* the audience screamed for the composer. Johnson remembered the occasion very well. "He came backstage and we artists all rushed up to him. He got us all to line up and then he looked at me and said, '*Tira! Tira!*' meaning that he wanted us to drag him 'reluctantly' from the wings."

Maria Jeritza was his favorite Tosca, and when she worked with him for the Viennese premiere she became worried because she was a blonde. Tosca in the opera is described as a brunette, and blonde sopranos wear wigs to be faithful to the role. Jeritza, proud of her blonde hair, hated to wear a wig. "Madame," Puccini said gallantly, "there are blondes in Italy, and they are the most beautiful women in the world." It was Jeritza, by the way, who started the tradition of singing *Vissi d'arte* flat on the floor. She claimed, in an interview given in 1926, that during the rehearsal the baritone accidentally pushed her off the sofa, and she did not have time to get up. "Never do it any other way!" shouted Puccini from the auditorium. "It was from God!"

Jeritza echoed all singers' remarks about Puccini's patience but firmness. "He would never take no for an answer. If a phrase had to be taken in one breath, he would keep me working on it until he got what he wanted." In Jeritza's opinion, Puccini knew more about the voice than most voice teachers, and while he might ask for difficult things, he never demanded the impossible. "He helped me technically. He also could insult you in the most gentlemanly way. We went over the music step by step, phrase by phrase. He molded me. I was his *creation*. Sometimes he would make me so angry I wanted to cry. Then he would get angry. 'Jeritza,' he would say, 'if I ever wake you at three in the morning and ask you to sing a high C, you *will* sing a high C!'"

Puccini also told Jeritza one thing she never forgot. To her, it summed up his entire musical philosophy.

"*Carissima mia*," he said to her, "you have to walk on clouds of melody."

❧ 8 ❧

Romanticism's Long Coda

RICHARD STRAUSS

From 1888, when *Don Juan* had its premiere, to 1911, when *Der Rosenka-valier* was staged, the most-discussed man of European music was Richard Strauss. His symphonic poems were considered the last word in shocking modernism and his *Salome* in 1905 and *Elektra* in 1909 caused riots and scandals. It was to be expected that the conservatives should dislike Strauss's new music. Saint-Saëns would have disappointed the world had he not waggled his beard and delivered a pronouncement: "The desire to push works of art beyond the realm of art means simply to drive them into the realm of folly. Richard Strauss is in the process of showing us the road." But, it was noted, even those allied to the progressives had nasty things to say. Gian-Francesco Malipiero in Italy, who should have automatically sided with Strauss's new "music of the future," curtly dismissed Strauss as "the Meyer-beer of the twentieth century." Gustav Mahler, on the other hand, called *Salome* a work of genius. Fauré, levelheaded as always, had some perspicacious things to say about the controversial opera. *Salome,* he decided, was a symphonic poem with vocal parts added, but: "Atmosphere and color are portrayed in their finest nuances, all by means of mediocre themes, it is true, but developed, worked, interwoven with such marvellous skill, that their intrinsic interest is exceeded by the magic of an orchestral technique of real genius, until these themes—mediocre, as I say—end by acquiring character, power and almost emotion." Strauss's brilliant orchestration bowled over his contemporaries. Dukas, on hearing *Salome,* said that he thought he knew something about the orchestra but now realized how much he had to learn.

To the public Strauss was The World's Greatest Composer and, incidentally, one of the world's great conductors. Everything he wrote received instant newspaper coverage the world over. What would he come up with next? For every new work was more sensational than the last. *Don Juan* had been succeeded by even more detailed story-telling tone poems, by bigger and bigger effects, by orchestras that grew in size until, in 1904, America heard the *Sinfonia Domestica,* which demanded the mightiest aggregation of players since Berlioz and his ideal orchestra. Sensation: that was the word for Strauss. An aura of sensation surrounded the slim, tall man and his outrageous music. Not only did he use a bigger orchestra than anybody else had used, not only was he the supreme master of that orchestra, he also wrote music that sounded excruciatingly dissonant. He told stories in his music, and you could hear the bleating of sheep or the sound of wind. More: the man undoubtedly was immoral. Who but a man of dubious morality would have set to music a text by Oscar Wilde, that British fellow who . . . you know . . . *Salome* in 1907 received a single performance at the Metropolitan Opera; the public outcry was such that the directors retreated pell-mell, removing it instantly from the boards. The New York reviewers were appalled. Lawrence Gilman, trembling with rage, wrote that he had been bored (an old critical ploy; when a reviewer is shocked to the very base of his fundament he can demonstrate his sophistication by saying he was bored). Henry Krehbiel called *Salome* a "moral stench." There were Letters to the Editor: "Are we to have our women, our children—sons and daughters—witness the spectacle?" In a newspaper headline in New York, *Salome* was called a "Loathsome Opera." The Baptists went on record as registering disapproval, as did the Archbishop of Vienna. Kaiser Wilhelm II of Germany, whose musical tastes ran more to Strauss (Johann) than Strauss (Richard), said he was sorry that Strauss had composed *Salome.* "I really like the fellow, but this will do him a lot of damage." The damage, Strauss noted many years later, "enabled me to build the villa at Garmisch."

Everything he did up until the time of *Der Rosenkavalier* seemed to make newspaper copy. It was not that he was eccentric. He was anything but. He was a good, solid, German bourgeois type, happily married, and never was there the least hint of scandal in his private life. Strauss would not have dared to have an affair. He was afraid of his wife, Pauline. Never was there a more henpecked husband. Perhaps it was this very lack of color that interested the public. It was hard to reconcile the wildness of the music with the sobriety of the man. When he unleashed the storms while conducting his own music he used a tiny beat and few motions; and critics could not get over the flamboyance of the music contrasted with the restraint of his gestures. Or perhaps it was that, like Puccini, he was of the new breed of composers who cut their hair short and dressed conservatively. The man who wrote such "modernistic" music looked like a banker.

Reporters and editors also seemed enchanted by the fact that great sums of money could be made from such music. When Strauss toured America in 1904, the Cleveland *Plain Dealer* ran a long article about Strauss's fees and royalties, figuring out that his income was at least $60,000 a year "and in five years he hopes to double that figure." The American magazine *The Theatre* reported in 1909 that "Richard Strauss is making so much money with his operas that he is likely to become the richest composer who ever lived." It was known that Strauss drove a hard bargain and liked the sound of crisp money as much as the sound of crisp strings. Alma Mahler sat with Strauss at the rehearsal of *Feuersnot* in 1901. "Strauss thought of nothing but money," she wrote in her diary. "The whole time he had a pencil in his hand and was calculating the profits to the last penny." In New York he gave two concerts in Wanamaker's Department Store, and the American press (also such stuffier American colleagues as Walter Damrosch) carried on in such a manner that one would have thought Strauss had given the concerts in a public comfort station. The art of music was forever soiled, they implied.

Strauss was unperturbed. There is nothing wrong for an artist to earn money for his wife and child, he said, pocketing his $1000 fee. It was not that he was mercenary, he told a reporter. He merely wanted to make enough to live comfortably for the rest of his days. The reporter did not ask him what he considered enough. Stories about Strauss's cupidity were constantly making the rounds. Strauss (so went one story) goes to Dresden for a *Salome* rehearsal. On his return to Berlin he is met at the station by his son. "Papa, how much did you get for the rehearsal?" Strauss, weeping tears of joy, enfolds the boy. "Now I know you are a true son of mine."

The more serious, dedicated musicians of the day were disturbed, if not revolted, by Strauss's money-mania, and Fritz Busch, the eminent conductor, who knew Strauss well, hints as much in his autobiography: "The puzzle of Strauss, who in spite of his marvellous talents is not really penetrated and possessed by them like other great artists, but in fact simply wears them like a suit of clothes which can be taken off at will—this puzzle neither I nor anybody else has yet succeeded in solving: his decided inclination towards material things; and with his complete disinclination to any sacrifice, the sworn enemy of social change." Hans Knappertsbusch, another conductor, put it much more bluntly: "He was a pig."

Strauss's shrewd financial manipulations never failed to fascinate the New York press, which kept the public informed of all the composer's dealings. When *Der Rosenkavalier* had its Metropolitan Opera premiere, the New York *Sun* of December 8, 1913, broke the news that "the Metropolitan is said to be paying $1,500 a night or thereabouts for 'Rose Cavalier' in order to soothe the wounded feelings of Strauss after the affair of 'Salome' here. This is ten times what used to be paid for the most popular works of Puccini." Everybody in the world wanted to know the most intimate details, financial or otherwise, about The World's Greatest Composer or, as one newspaper put it, The Musical Man of the Hour.

And if nothing could be found for an article on Strauss, there always was good copy in his wife, Pauline. She was a grasping, strong, determined woman, once a singer, who went through life without thinking much about other people's feelings, least of all her husband's. She was a legend. For some reason, Strauss contentedly put up with her tantrums. He told the Viennese critic Max Graf that as a young man he had a tendency to dissipate and make nothing of himself. Pauline cured him of that. "Richard, go compose!" she would scream, and Strauss would shrug his shoulders, leave his game of skat (his favorite pastime), and go to the workroom. She had him well trained. Deems Taylor, the American composer-critic, once interviewed him at Garmisch. Before Strauss walked into the house, "he paused and wiped his feet carefully on a small square of dampened doormat that lay before the door. Advancing a step, he wiped his feet once more, this time upon a dry doormat. Stepping across the doorsill he wiped his feet for a third and final time upon a small rubber doormat that lay just inside the door."

Up through *Der Rosenkavalier* Strauss was a composer who generated a constant atmosphere of excitement and electricity. After *Der Rosenkavalier* something happened. Some critics consider all of Strauss's post-*Rosenkavalier* works a regression: pallid, repetitive music in which years of skill were operating from sheer habit. "A composer of talent who once was a genius," snorted Ernest Newman. Others insist that once having rid himself of the superficial sensationalism of the symphonic poems, Strauss started to compose the long series of operas that culminated in the "masterly" and "autumnal" and "profound" works of his old age. Strauss himself later indicated that in *Salome* (1905) and *Elektra* (1908) he had come too close to the Pit for comfort and hastily withdrew: "Both operas are unique in my life's works. In them I penetrated to the uttermost limits of harmony, psychological polyphony (Klytemnestra's dream), and of the receptivity of modern ears." The public reaction to Strauss's work after *Der Rosenkavalier*—and also the reaction of most of Strauss's colleagues—were in line with Newman's estimate of genius succeeded by talent. Strauss had existed as a sensationalist, successively topping one work with something even more *outré*. When he could not surpass any of his previous works in daring and sensationalism, there was an unprecedented falling-off in public response. No longer was the premiere of a Strauss opera an international event. The operas were politely received and no more; never again was there the excitement and brouhaha there used to be. Through the years after 1911 Strauss doggedly continued to compose much the same kind of opera, and his colleagues could not have cared less. To them, *Salome* and *Elektra* were the end of the line as far as Strauss was concerned. There were new heroes in international music—Prokofiev, Bartók, and especially Stravinsky. There was also much talk about Arnold Schoenberg, whose music made Strauss's once-revolutionary scores sound old-fashioned.

Richard Strauss was born in Munich on June 11, 1864. His father, a peppery, opinionated, outspoken man, was the most celebrated horn player in Germany, and also a composer who thought that Wagner was subversive and that no true music had been written since Mendelssohn and Schumann. Franz Strauss was the horn player in the orchestra of the Munich opera, and had participated in the world premieres of *Tristan und Isolde* and *Die Meistersinger*. He was always getting into fights with Hans von Bülow and with Wagner himself. Franz simply loathed the horn parts of the Wagner operas, but he played them so beautifully that Wagner ignored his biting asides about the music. There must have been red hot moments when the martinet Bülow, the most dyspeptic conductor of his day, tangled with the fiercely independent Franz Strauss. One argument ended with Bülow telling Strauss to go and apply for his pension. Strauss promptly packed his instrument and did exactly that, "because Herr von Bülow has so ordered." The incident was patched up. Some years later, when Bülow and the young Richard Strauss were working together, Bülow and Franz actually became friends.

Richard inherited his father's musical instincts. He was playing the piano at four and a half, the violin shortly afterward, and was composing at six. Franz Strauss kept his son on a very conservative musical diet, and the result was apparent in Richard's juvenile compositions. They were skillful, but they represented the early part of the nineteenth century. Richard could have been a touring prodigy *à la* Mozart, but his father kept him in Munich and put him into the *Gymnasium*, where the boy received a good general education. There was no rush. It was taken for granted in the Strauss family that Richard would be a musician, but all in good time. From the Gymnasium, Strauss in 1882 went to the University of Munich (he took some courses but never worked for a degree) and then spent some time in Berlin, making the rounds, playing the piano at musical parties. In 1884 Strauss met Bülow in Berlin, and the young composer's Serenade for Winds in E flat (Op. 7) was programmed by Bülow's Meiningen Orchestra. Bülow himself did not conduct; the assistant conductor took over and Bülow sat in the audience, vigorously applauding. So pleased was Bülow with the score that he asked Strauss to compose another like it. The result was the Suite for Winds in B flat (Op. 4). The score was rehearsed by Bülow in Meiningen but, in a pleasant gesture to the talented young composer, Bülow decided that the world premiere should take place in Strauss's own city, Munich. He also suggested that Strauss himself be the conductor. When Bülow "suggested," everybody obeyed. Up to then, Strauss had never held a baton in his hand, but conduct he did—in a state of shock, as he remembered in later years. All he knew was that he had committed no major blunders. After the performance, Franz Strauss thanked Bülow, and the famous conductor exploded in a typically Bülovian outburst: "You have nothing to thank me for. I have not forgotten what you did to me in this damned city of Munich. What I did today I did because your son has talent, and not for you." Suddenly, Strauss wrote in his little memoir about Bülow, "Bülow was in the best of spirits." His nasty remarks had soothed his bad humor and now he was happy.

The approval of so majestic a potentate as Bülow was enough to start Strauss on a promising career. Bülow even saw enough in Strauss to appoint him his assistant at Meiningen in 1885, and, at his debut, Strauss conducted his own F minor Symphony. He was well on his way—but as an academic composer.

The break in this continuity came with acquaintance with Alexander Ritter, a violinist in the Meiningen Orchestra. Ritter had known Wagner and had married Wagner's niece, Franziska. It was Ritter who introduced Strauss to the music of Berlioz, Liszt, and Wagner; who explained what The Music of the Future was all about; who encouraged Strauss to look for new ways of writing. That did not come immediately. The young composer wrote a Brahmsian Piano Quartet in C minor, and concentrated on perfecting his craft as a conductor. When Bülow resigned from Meiningen in November, 1885, Strauss was in sole charge of the orchestra. He finished out the season, went to Italy, returned to Munich, and composed a symphony called *Aus Italien*. The last movement caused great excitement at the premiere in 1887, and there were boos and cheers. Strauss did not worry about the opposition. "I now comfort myself with the knowledge that I am on the road I want to take, fully conscious that there never has been an artist not considered crazy by thousands of his fellow men." But he had not yet found himself, though the wild orchestration of the last movement of *Aus Italien*, in which Strauss quoted Luigi Denza's *Funiculì Funiculà* (under the impression it was a genuine folk song), gives more than a hint of the brilliance that was to come.

Strauss went to the Munich Opera in 1886 as third conductor. Meanwhile, during this period in his life, he continued to compose traditional works. One was the attractive *Burlesque* for Piano and Orchestra (1885). Another was the E flat Violin Sonata (1887)—charming, stylish, even masterly, but still essentially music of the past. In 1886 Strauss met Pauline de Ahna, the soprano he was to marry. She had sung in Munich several times under his direction, and the story goes that they had a violent argument at a rehearsal. Strauss disappeared into her dressing room, and they emerged with an announcement that they were engaged. Pauline was the daughter of a general, and she never let anybody forget that there was noble blood in *her* family. She always looked down at the Strausses and the bourgeois background they represented. Strauss's mother, Josephine Pschorr, came from a wealthy family of brewers (Pschorr beer is still one of the popular brands in Munich). *Brewers!* Strauss's love for Pauline showed itself in the series of songs he composed specifically for her, and which she sang in public with him at the piano. One of those songs, the *Ständchen* of 1866, has remained among the most popular in the repertoire. Strauss continued to write songs all his life, and the world would be considerably poorer without such beautiful pieces of music as *Ruhe, meine seele; Cäcilie; Heimliche Aufforderung; Morgen; Freundliche Vision; Traum durch die Dämmerung* and—to many, the most beautiful of all—the four songs for voice and orchestra he composed in 1948, known as the *Vier letzte Lieder* or *Four Last Songs.*

The first major break in Strauss's music came in 1889, with the tone poem *Don Juan*. Everybody in Europe was writing symphonic poems. The symphonic poem was to the late romantic period what the concerto grosso had been to the baroque. There was prevalent unhappiness with symphonic form among the avant-garde. Beethoven, many felt, had said all there was to say, and had done all there was to do, with the symphony. One way around the problem was an extension of the Lisztian symphonic poem, and in Strauss the right man appeared to do it. On November 11, 1889, *Don Juan* received its premiere in Weimar, and a new force had arrived.

Don Juan was the score that made everybody recognize Strauss as Liszt's natural successor, and, to a point, Wagner's. The score required an orchestra of unprecedented size, handled with unprecedented virtuosity. Its melodic material, with its wide span and unexpected leaps, was something new. And although the work was tied to a specific literary program, the music was yet inventive enough and had enough structural integrity (free sonata form) to stand up as absolute music. *Don Juan* was followed by a series of symphonic poems that set all Europe on its ear: *Tod und Verklärung* in 1890 (the dates are the premieres, not the dates of composition), *Till Eulenspiegels lustige Streiche* in 1895, *Also sprach Zarathustra* in 1896, *Don Quixote* in 1898, *Ein Heldenleben* in 1899, the *Sinfonia Domestica* in 1904. *Eine Alpensinfonie* in 1915 was the last, and a failure. Each of these symphonic poems was progressively bigger and more sensational. It may also be that their musical worth is in inverse ratio to their size and dates of composition. A poll of musicians would probably show that the first four are the most highly regarded.

All of these scores derived basically from Liszt. But whereas the Liszt symphonic poems deal with very generalized programs, Strauss wrote explicit descriptive music: the labored breathing of a dying man, the trial of Till

Eulenspiegel, the hero in *Ein Heldenleben* fighting with his critics, the sun rising in *Zarathustra*, Don Quixote charging the windmill, and so on. His symphonic poems began to get more and more detailed, and the headline in a New York paper of 1904 about the *Sinfonia Domestica* was not far off the mark: "Home Sweet Home as Written by Richard Strauss—Pappa and Momma and Baby Celebrated in Huge Conglomeration of Orchestral Music." Strauss was on the defensive about the *Domestica*, and he wrote about it with characteristic lack of humor:

The symphony is meant to give a musical picture of married life. I know that some people believe the work is a jocular exposé of happiness in the home, but I own that I did not mean to make fun when I composed it. What can be more serious a matter than married life? Marriage is the most serious happening in life, and the holy joy over such a union is intensified through the arrival of a child. Yet life has naturally got its funny side, and this I have also introduced into the work in order to enliven it. But I want the symphony to be taken seriously, and it has been played in this spirit in Germany.

Strauss always blew hot and cold about the importance of the program in his symphonic poems. He supplied detailed scenarios for each one, yet was irritated when analysts and the public made too much of them. In 1905 he tried to explain his theories to Romain Rolland. He wrote a letter to the French writer and critic in which he said that "a poetic program is exclusively a pretext for the purely musical expression and development of my emotions." The program was not, Strauss emphasized, "a simple physical description of precise facts of life. For this would be most contrary to the spirit of music." Music, Strauss continued, has to be contained in "a determining form." But Strauss never felt dependent on classic forms in his series of symphonic poems. "New ideas must search for new forms," he kept on insisting. For the most part he was successful in his formal structures. Whatever the intrinsic value of the musical materials, Strauss put them into well-integrated free forms—modified sonata, variations, rondo. He was a superb technician, and one of the most resourceful orchestrators of all time. Even Debussy, who stood for everything Strauss was not, had to admit the "tremendous versatility of the orchestration, then the frenzied energy which carries the listener with him for as long as he chooses. . . . One must admit that the man who composed such a work [*Ein Heldenleben*] at so continually high a pressure is very nearly a genius." Yet, "modernistic" as his scores appeared to his contemporaries, they were the end of a period, not the beginning. After Strauss, very few composers wrote tone poems, and today practically nobody does. The symphonic poem as a viable medium currently appears as dead as the concerto grosso—deader, indeed, for the concerto grosso at least enjoyed something of a renaissance during the neo-classic period of 1920–1935.

Just as Strauss grew more famous as a composer, so grew his reputation as a conductor. In 1898 he succeeded Felix Weingartner as conductor of the Royal Opera in Berlin, and he remained there until 1918, after which he became co-director of the Vienna Opera. As a conductor, Strauss developed into an exponent of the revolt from romanticism that was beginning to take hold in the early 1900's. Romantic conducting was free, impulsive, often self-indulgent. Strauss, like Weingartner, like Karl Muck and Arturo Toscanini, kept himself out of the music much more than the romantics did. Using a tiny beat, he kept his rhythms regular, adhered closely to the score, and avoided flamboyance. Most of his conducting was done in the opera house, and it was not long before Strauss began to concentrate almost exclusively on composing as well as conducting opera.

During his run of symphonic poems Strauss had composed a Wagnerian opera named *Guntram*. It had its premiere at Weimar in 1894 and achieved only one performance. (Not until 1935 was it again heard, when it had a radio performance in Berlin.) Never was there such a failure. "It is incredible what enemies *Guntram* has made for me," Strauss wrote. "I shall shortly be tried as a dangerous criminal." Strauss was so discouraged that he waited for six years before writing another stage work. That too, an opera named *Feuersnot*, was a failure. At last with *Salome* of 1905 Strauss composed an opera that electrified the public as much as his symphonic poems had done. The subject matter of *Salome* had as much to do with its notoriety as the music. Everybody was eager to see Salome make love to the detached head of Jochanaan, and to watch her take off the seven veils one by one. (Marie Wittich, cast as Salome for the Dresden world premiere, at first refused to learn the role. "I won't do it, I'm a decent woman.") Everybody shivered to Strauss's shrieking, "decadent," near-atonal writing. Here, and in *Elektra*, which followed in 1908, Strauss moved out of the post-romantic castle to do battle with a new kind of harmony, a new and powerful kind of melody, and a progressive style that could have led him into still greater adventures. Both operas were, and to an extent remain, shockers. But, frightened by what he saw, Strauss withdrew, and never again experimented with the kind of jagged harmony and psychological underlining that make *Salome* and *Elektra* two of the most provocative operas of the century.

In its day *Elektra* posed tremendous problems for the singers and orchestra. Strauss wanted a new kind of singing, and the cry went up, just as it had gone up in Wagner's and Meyerbeer's day, that the result would be the permanent ruination of the human voice. Singers brought up in the earlier tradition were appalled. Ernestine Schumann-Heink, the great contralto, sang the role of Klytemnestra in the premiere, and she never got over it. "We were a set of madwomen, truly we were," she reminisced some years later. "He had written us so, and so we became in very truth. . . . The music itself is maddening. He writes a beautiful, beautiful melody, five measures; and then he is sorry for writing something lovely and breaks off with a dissonance that racks you. He does not need singers because his orchestral scores so paint, so draw the picture." She ended with the statement that "If Mr. Hammerstein were to put on that opera tomorrow and offer me $3000 a night to sing Klytemnestra, I would say no. And $3000 is a great deal of money and I have many children."

Elektra brought Strauss and Hugo von Hofmannsthal together. In 1903, Max Reinhardt staged Hofmannsthal's translation of Sophocles' *Elektra*, and Strauss wanted to set it to music. Hofmannsthal made the adaptation, and in that librettist Strauss found his Boito and Lorenzo da Ponte. For almost twenty-five years Strauss and Hofmannsthal worked together, turning out *Der Rosenkavalier* (1911), the first version of *Ariadne auf Naxos* (1912), the *Josefslegende* ballet (1914), the revised *Ariadne* (1916), *Die Frau ohne Schatten* (1919), *Die ägyptische Helena* (1928), and *Arabella* (1933). It is a moot point whether or not Hofmannsthal's influence on Strauss was entirely healthy. Hofmannsthal led the composer away from the *Elektra* style into a kind of literary opera suffused with symbolism. Strauss's natural musical leaning was extroverted, violent, convulsive, sensational, but with Hofmannsthal leading the way, Strauss was diverted into a gray land of allegory and symbolism that did not fit his flamboyant approach. *Der Rosenkavalier* and *Elektra* are the only two of their collaborations that are still extremely popular. *Ariadne auf Naxos* (1916) also has a strong band of admirers, although this opera turns up less frequently. One of the problems with *Ariadne* is to find a competent cast. Strauss wrote here for voices of Wagnerian strength plus, in the role of Zerbinetta, a coloratura soprano who has to conquer incredible difficulties. The second-act aria of Zerbinetta, *Grossmächtigen Prinzessin,* is a set piece in which Strauss used bel canto procedures in twentieth-century terms, and very few singers have been able to sing the long aria with any degree of ease. The other Strauss-Hofmannsthal operas —*Die Frau ohne Schatten, Die ägyptische Helena,* and *Arabella*—even in Germany and Austria live mostly through a small band of fanatical admirers.

The two men had a curious relationship. Hofmannsthal, an Austrian, was one of Germany's most distinguished men of letters. He was quiet, shy, and sensitive, an idealist who at the same time was well aware of his worth. Strauss was his antithesis: hardheaded, practical, more interested in the concrete than the abstract. The two men clearly admired and respected each other. Yet they were never very close, and the relationship was strangely formal. Their lengthy correspondence through the years is fascinating in many ways. Above all, it gives an idea of the eternal tussle between the demands of the music and the demands of the word. Strauss himself pondered the problem for decades, and his last opera, *Capriccio* (1942), to a libretto by Clemens Krauss and himself, is nothing but a long speculation on the subject of words and music. Which is of greater importance? Strauss could not make up his mind, and the opera ends with a question mark.

The correspondence reveals that to Hofmannsthal, Strauss was a tremendous creative figure, one to be feared as much as admired. To Strauss, Hofmannsthal was something like a libretto factory. Strauss had no hesitation about stepping on his colleague's feelings, and during one sticky point in the preparation of *Ariadne* actually suggested that Hofmannsthal get a collaborator. "Such things are usually done best by two people." Hofmannsthal, who stood in awe of Strauss, would never have suggested that the composer get a collaborator. He continued writing for Strauss because he was convinced that the composition of a libretto was as much an art as the construction of a play. "I know the worth of my work," he wrote to Strauss. "I know that for many generations past, no distinguished poet of the rank with which I may credit myself among the living, has dedicated himself willingly and devotedly to the task of working with a musician." He did bow to the music. "I consider Dr. Strauss entirely as the principal partner, and the music as the dominant one of the elements joined together." And so he put up with a frequent lack of comprehension on Strauss's part. Some of his letters trying to justify his approach are sad to read. Strauss, as a practical man of the theater (and he was generally correct in specific criticisms of Hofmannsthal's librettos), would often raise violent objections. Hofmannsthal would defend himself, as in his long account, in July of 1911, about the philosophical import of *Ariadne*. Then, thirsting for some kind of praise, he continues in the vein of a jilted girl writing to the man she still loves: "All this, I must say, seemed to me to deserve some expression of appreciation from the one person for whom my work was visualized, conceived and executed. I doubt, moreover, if one could easily find in any other libretto for a one-act opera three poems of comparable delicacy, and at the same time equally characteristic in tone, as Harlekin's song, the rondo for Zerbinetta, and the Circe song of Bacchus. Not unnaturally, I would rather have heard all this from you than be obliged to write it for myself." One can imagine the exasperated, impatient shrug of Strauss's shoulders while reading this.

The tug of war between the man of words and the man of music was never settled, as it never is. Each considered his own contribution important, and each fought for it. Generally it was Hofmannsthal who gave way, with Old Testament groans and lamentations. Through the years of give and take it was Hofmannsthal who did most of the giving, Strauss most of the taking. By far their most successful collaboration was *Der Rosenkavalier*. After *Elektra*, Strauss decided to compose a comedy, and Hofmannsthal came up with an idea for a work with two main roles, "one for a baritone and one for a young and graceful girl dressed as a man, of the type of a Farrar or Mary Garden. The period: Vienna at the time of Maria Theresa." The German operatic repertory badly needed a new comic work. There had been no internationally successful German comic opera since *Die Meistersinger* in 1868. *Der Rosenkavalier* came into being after much struggle on all sides. Strauss insisted on certain dramatic touches which Hofmannsthal, after a great deal of reluctance, inserted. He finally admitted that Strauss was right: "I see that it is all far more purely theatrical and very much better than the earlier version." One of the things Strauss insisted upon was to have the comic elements emphasized. "Don't forget that the audience should also laugh! *Laugh*, not just smile or grin! I still miss in our work a genuinely comic situation: everything is merely amusing, but not *comic!*" For a while the title of the opera was up in the air. As late as April, 1910, Strauss was thinking of calling it *Ochs*. Hofmannsthal suggested *Der Rosenkavalier* and proposed that it be called a "burlesque opera." Strauss objected to the word "burlesque." He said that once the public heard that word, it would think of Offenbach or Gilbert and Sullivan. They finally settled on *"Der Rosenkavalier,* Comedy for Music by Hugo von Hofmannsthal, Music by Richard Strauss."

Both also agreed that the opera should end not with Octavian the central figure, or even Ochs, but the Marschallin. "She is the central figure for the public," Hofmannsthal wrote, "for the women above all, the figure with whom they feel and *move*." It is interesting that in this letter Hofmannsthal wrote that *Der Rosenkavalier* was "a turning-away from Wagner's intolerable erotic screaming—boundless in length as well as in degree: a repulsive, barbaric, almost bestial affair, this shrieking of two creatures in heat as he practices it." Anti-Wagnerism was setting in, and *Der Rosenkavalier,* whatever Wagnerisms remain in it, follows a different aesthetic. *Die Meistersinger* has a libretto that is heavy German *Pfannkuchen,* while *Der Rosenkavalier* has a sophistication, especially in sexual matters, that Wagner never could have brought off. (Wagner, the great sensualist, was in his operas really a prude.) Hofmannsthal gently deals with young and old love in a civilized, urbane manner. Wagner's sex in *Tristan* is primal, like that of two whales gravely coming together. In *Der Rosenkavalier* there are no Jungian archetypes, only the human condition. Instead of long narratives there are Viennese waltzes. Instead of a monumental *Liebestod* there is a sad, elegant lament from a beautiful, aristocratic woman who begins to see old age. Instead of death, we get a bittersweet and hauntingly beautiful trio that in effect tells us that life will go on as it always has gone on. People do not die for love in Hofmannsthal's world. They face the inevitable, surrender with what grace they can summon up, and then look around for life's next episode. As Strauss himself later said, the Marschallin had lovers before Octavian, and she will have lovers after him.

After *Der Rosenkavalier,* Strauss was an anachronism. European music was headed in a different direction while Strauss was still working his old formulae. Every composer does, in a way, for his music is the man; but a Beethoven, Mozart, Verdi, or Chopin continued to broaden and become deeper, more meaningful, more original. There is little of that kind of growth in Strauss's bland succession of operas, though *Die Frau ohne Schatten* has some exceedingly beautiful things in it (Strauss considered it his best opera.) Post-Hofmannsthal operas included *Die Schweigsame Frau* (1935), *Friedenstag* (1936), *Daphne* (1937), *Die Liebe der Danae* (1940), and *Capriccio* (1942). There also is a strange little opera called *Intermezzo* (1924), for which Strauss himself wrote the libretto. It is an autobiographical opera, a family joke about Strauss and Pauline's jealousy.

Time went on, the Nazis came into power, and Strauss was appointed president of the Reichsmusikkammer. The Nazis did not know exactly what to do with him. He *was* their most important composer, he did elect to stay in Germany, and yet he did and said things that would have put anybody else in a concentration camp. Then he would hastily resume friendly relations with the authorities. Strauss was opportunistic, amoral, and apolitical, and all he wanted was to be left alone to write his music and make money. He would gladly use a Jewish librettist, and did so in Stefan Zweig, much to the unhappiness of the Nazis. On the other hand he never put up much of a fight against the horrors of the Nazi regime. He wanted to have the best of all worlds.

During World War II he composed a series of reflective works mostly for small orchestra—the Oboe Concerto (1946), the Horn Concerto No. 2 (1942), the *Metamorphosen* (1945) for twenty-three solo strings. There also were the *Four Last Songs,* for soprano and full orchestra. About this music there are mixed feelings. Some listeners find in it what they also find in Strauss's late operas—the final flicker of postromanticism, the musings of a great composer in his full, venerable mastery. Others dismiss the music with actual irritation as works of tremendous skill that repeat past formulae and have nothing to say. Strauss died at Garmisch on September 8, 1949. The obituaries all paid tribute to his importance in the music of the late nineteenth and early twentieth centuries, but there was decided hedging about the post-*Rosenkavalier* works, and there still is. In any event, it is clear that Strauss exercised little or no influence on the new school of composers, most of whom disliked or even despised his work. Stravinsky's reaction is typical: ". . . bombast and rodomontade . . . treacly . . . the music [of *Capriccio*] chokes me. Strauss does not know how to punctuate. His musculature is without measure." To the new generation, his symphonic poems were vulgar, overorchestrated, ostentatious bores; and most of his operas tiresome, thick, repetitive works full of fake symbolism and fake philosophy. Which does not leave much of poor Strauss; and, in all truth, it is hard to take the huffings and puffings of the once-electrifying *Ein Heldenleben,* or the nature-painting of *Don Quixote,* or, indeed, most of the music that once meant so much to so many people. Nothing dates as fast as pure sensationalism, and the tragedy of Strauss is the tragedy of a superior musical mind flawed by the desire to put effect over substance.

✥ 9 ✥

Religion, Mysticism, and Retrospection

BRUCKNER, MAHLER, REGER

The year, 1911, of the premiere of *Der Rosenkavalier* was also the year during which Gustav Mahler died. Anton Bruckner had already been dead for fifteen years. Max Reger was to die five years later, in 1916. Those three composers in their day were completely eclipsed by Richard Strauss. Mahler was famous mostly as a conductor, as the central figure in the so-called "golden years" of the Vienna Opera, from 1897 to 1907. His symphonies were played, but performances were relatively few, and they became fewer after his death. Bruckner was regarded by many as some kind of pure fool (in the Parsifallian sense) who by some freak had managed to attract a small, devoted band of followers. Reger, on the other hand, was widely respected, and his music had a strong vogue in Germany for a decade after his death. Then it was dropped, and has remained dropped. To most musicians today, Reger, who was one of the few Brahms followers (as opposed to Mahler and Bruckner, who were Wagnerites out of Beethoven and Schubert), represents everything that is wrong and vulgar with postromanticism.

But the 1960's saw a remarkable renaissance of the music of Bruckner and Mahler. Mahler especially is regarded as a symbol of the second half of the twentieth century, and the process was accelerated when the scholars of the avant-garde decided that he was the spiritual father of dodecaphonism. Mahler's eternal questings, his seeking and searching, his inability to come to terms with society, his guilt complexes, his doubts and anxieties—all these made him, many believed, a prophet for an age riddled also with doubts and anxieties. Earlier ages at least had the comforts of orthodox religion. Mahler, the Jew turned Catholic, and neither a practicing Jew nor a practicing Christian, could find none of the answers. Most people of his time were able to make some kind of peace between themselves and the universe. Mahler never could, just as fewer and fewer people can today.

The meaning of life obsessed Mahler, and he was constantly asking questions. But the questions suggest that Mahler was more a neurotic than a Deep Thinker. There was something of the child in his plaintive queries. "Whence do we come?" he asked Bruno Walter. "Whither does our road take us? Have I really willed this life, as Schopenhauer thinks, before I was even conceived? Why am I made to feel that I am free while yet I am constrained within my character, as in a prison? What is the object of toil and sorrow? How am I to understand the cruelty and malice in the creations of a kind God? Will the meaning of life be finally revealed by death?" Why, why, why? Walter believed that each of Mahler's symphonies was a new attempt to answer the questions eternally plaguing him.

Bruckner too wrote symphonies that reflected an attempt to answer these questions. In Bruckner's case, however, no doubts are expressed. He was a devout man with a simplistic view of the world and the hereafter. God is good. Everything man does should reflect the glory of God. Music should honor Him. The old Bruckner once said to Mahler: "Yes, my dear, now I have to work very hard so that at least the Tenth Symphony will be finished. Otherwise I will not pass before God, before Whom I shall soon stand. He will say: 'Why else have I given you talent, you son of a bitch, than that you should sing My praise and glory? But you have accomplished much too little.' "

Temperamentally no two men could have been as far apart as Bruckner and Mahler. Yet they had certain things in common. Each composed nine symphonies: nine, that mystic Beethovenian numeral. Each composed long works—symphonies that in size, power, and orchestration far exceeded any of Brahms's and even the Beethoven Ninth. Both often fell back on the heritage of Austrian folk song, building entire movements on ländler-like melodies that can be traced back to Schubert. Both were strongly influenced by Wagner. And both were even more strongly influenced by Beethoven—the Ninth Symphony, specifically: the unapproachable ideal, the standard against which all music had to be measured.

In Bruckner's case the Ninth fixation could be seen in conscious or unconscious imitations of technical and melodic devices used in the Beethoven D minor. How many of Bruckner's symphonies start with a tremolo in the low strings, as does the Ninth, and then proceed to melodic material derived from the common triad, again as in the Ninth! How many slow movements of the Bruckner symphonies echo the soaring violin passages of the Beethoven adagio! Mahler had an even greater fixation. In the words of the psychoanalyst Theodor Reik, Mahler was an "obsessive neurotic" who was afraid of the thought of composing a ninth symphony. "The fact that Beethoven, Schubert and Bruckner had died after having touched the number nine in their symphonies made this number a menace." When Mahler did get to work on a ninth symphony, and actually finished it, he crossed out the number and published it as *Das Lied von der Erde*. Then, when composing his next symphony, he told his wife: "Actually, of course, it is the Tenth, because *Das Lied von der Erde* was really the Ninth." When it was near completion he said: "Now the danger is past." As a matter of fact, it was not past. He died a few months after finishing the work that was published as his Ninth Symphony, leaving only two substantially finished movements and a mass of sketches for the work that was to be his Tenth. This confirmed the dark feelings of those in the Mahler orbit. They *knew* that punishment awaited those who challenged certain forces. "It seems," wrote Arnold Schoenberg in 1913, "that the Ninth is the limit. He who wants to go beyond it has to leave. . . . Those who had written a Ninth Symphony were too close to the Beyond."

Whatever similarities Bruckner and Mahler had, their differences were huge. Their music stands for different things, for the opposing social and philosophical polarities of a period. Bruckner stands for repose, Mahler for unrest; Bruckner for certitude, Mahler for doubt; Bruckner for naïveté, Mahler for sophistication; Bruckner for provincialism, Mahler for internationalism.

Anton Bruckner, born in Ansfelden, Upper Austria, on September 24, 1824, studied at nearby St. Florian, where he became choirmaster and organist of the Foundation, a settlement of Augustine monks. In 1856 he moved to Linz as church organist. Once a week he went to Vienna to study counterpoint with Simon Sechter. This was the Sechter with whom Schubert was going to study in the last year of his life.

Bruckner was a simple man, incredibly rustic and naïve. He had a shaven head and a country dialect; he wore homespun and ill-fitting clothes and moved in constant awe of those great city people who knew so much more about everything than he did. A child of nature, he was not well read, was completely unsophisticated, would blurt out the first thing that came into his mind. He tipped the majestic and wealthy Hans Richter at the end of the final rehearsal of his Fourth Symphony. "Take this"—pressing a thaler into Richter's hand—"and drink a mug of beer to my health." The dumbfounded conductor looked at the coin, put it into his pocket, and later had it put on his watch chain. Antics like this amused some, irritated others. Wagner, for one, was amused. Bruckner went to Munich in 1865 to attend the premiere of *Tristan und Isolde,* and the music so overwhelmed him that he became one of the most enthusiastic Wagnerians in Europe. He met Wagner several times. On one occasion, Wagner gave him his hand, and Bruckner, overcome, bent down on his knee, pressed the Hand to his lips and said: "O Master, I worship you!" His Third Symphony shows some of this worship, though in his music Bruckner never was really a Wagnerian. Some analysts have a tendency to read things into it because it was dedicated to Wagner.

Through Johann Herbeck, the Viennese court conductor, Bruckner was appointed teacher of organ and theory at the Vienna Conservatory in 1868, and was made a professor there three years later. He also became organist of the court chapel and lecturer in theory at the University of Vienna. Several important conductors, among them Richter, Artur Nikisch, Hermann Levi, Felix Mottl, and Gustav Mahler, began to take an interest in his music. But whenever it was performed in Vienna, the Establishment critics, headed by Eduard Hanslick, tore it apart. Bruckner was convinced that Brahms was behind the attacks on him. What with the cool reception his music received, and his financial difficulties, his life in Vienna was not pleasant during his early years there. "Had to borrow money already in September, and again later, if I did not choose to starve," he wrote to a friend in Linz. "No man is helping me. Stremayr [the Austrian Minister of Education] promises—and does nothing. Fortunately there have come some foreigners who are taking lessons from me—otherwise I should have to go begging. Hear me further: I asked all the chief professors for pupils. They all promised, but except for some theory lessons I got nothing. . . . I should not have been brought to Vienna so long as I lived had I forseen this. It would be an easy thing for my enemies to drive me out of the Conservatory. I am surprised that this has not already happened. . . ."

Naïve as he was, Bruckner knew what was going on. In the wildly partisan Vienna of the time, there was the Brahms sect and there was the Wagner sect. Bruckner was classified as a Wagnerian. As the press was dominated by the Brahmsians, Bruckner found himself under constant attack. The story went that Bruckner was once asked by the Emperor if there was anything he could do for him. "Yes, Your Majesty, if you could only tell Mr. Hanslick to stop writing such terrible things about me," or words to that effect. The Emperor did grant him a pension, and in 1891 Bruckner was able to resign from the Conservatory, and from the University in 1894. He died on October 11, 1896.

To many, his clumsiness as a human being made him an object of derision. But those exposed to him for any length of time did not go away laughing. Bruckner inspired the same sort of devotion that César Franck did; and, indeed, Bruckner has been called a German Franck by more than one scholar. Max Graf attended several of his University lectures, and wrote that he went to Bruckner's class expecting to be amused. There was Bruckner, wearing the Upper Austrian loose jacket, his big head and wrinkled face peering at the students. When the Angelus would sound from the nearby church, Bruckner would stop his lecture, get on his kness and pray. Then he would resume the lecture. Occasionally he would pass Hanslick (who lectured on musicology) in the hall, and Bruckner would bow and scrape before that dreaded figure. But it did not take Graf long to become first impressed and then worshipful. In Bruckner's theory lectures, the basis was Sechter. Graf, later to become Vienna's most important music critic, has written about Bruckner's approach:

> Sechter's doctrine, which was delivered to us by Bruckner like a holy heritage, was built on two strong pillars. The one that inspired Bruckner with greatest respect was the theory of the "Fundamental Basses," a world of spirits in the bass, which accompanied the harmonies like shadows in the depths; and the theory of "natural harmonies," which form the laws of all beauty of harmonic progression. Everywhere there was law and order, even holiness. The fundamental steps of the bass which Bruckner invariably noted in his scores under the last line of the staff, had cosmic importance. Thus we understood the greatness and sometimes the rigidity and solemnity of Bruckner's harmonies. Bruckner, the pupil of Sechter, who was a kind of architect of harmonies, pondered over chords and chord associations as a medieval architect contemplated the original forms of a Gothic cathedral. They were his path to the Kingdom of God.

It is this slow, inexorable, solemn procession of harmonies that is the essence of Bruckner's music. Everything was deliberate about the man's symphonies and choral music. The Viennese nicknamed him the "Adagio-Komponist"—the composer of adagios. Even his first movements were so big and stately, took so much time to get under way, that they sounded like adagios to the Viennese. Bruckner's music, with its Gothic arch, its tremendous spans, its organlike sonorities, its bigness in time and space, is essentially cathedral-like music of belief, and one probably has to be a believer to identify fully with it. The scherzo movements of the Bruckner symphonies often use Austrian dances, and these too involve belief. Mozart's third movements evoke the court; Haydn's, the peasants; Beethoven's, the gods at play. But Bruckner's evoke some kind of religious ideal involving nature. The religiosity of Bruckner's nine symphonies (and, of course, of his Masses and other religious choral music) suggests to his admirers a kind of message that is allied to the Infinite. Even unbelievers can find themselves carried away by the simple conviction of the man.

Just as Bruckner's music arouses an all but apocalyptic response in the faithful, so it is irritating and even meaningless to another group of listeners. Those who are not attracted to Bruckner's music are not necessarily bothered by its length. Rather they are bothered by the repetition of material that to them is not very stimulating to begin with. They tend to feel that Bruckner wrote the same symphony nine times. Not liking the message, or the thematic material to begin with, they are all but driven out of their minds as a Bruckner symphony makes its slow, inexorable procession. Bruckner admirers and Bruckner doubters are two armed camps glaring at each other, and the music evokes no middle response. What one camp finds noble and uplifting, the other finds long-winded and boring. Power to one is flabbiness to the other. In any case, Bruckner was an isolated figure. He had no followers, as Mahler did. But there is something in his music that appeals to one aspect of the modern psyche, and as a result his symphonies have in recent years become a basic part of the repertory. A good deal of their appeal lies in their unvarnished faith, their repose and unhurried serenity—qualities that so many people today long for. They can live the experience in Bruckner's music.

Bruckner's symphonies are full of textual problems. He was so anxious to get his music played that he would let conductors do anything with it—cut, alter, reorchestrate, smooth out rough harmonies. Bruckner said more than once that the correct performance of his music could await future generations. In the meantime, many of the first published editions of his symphonies, from 1878 to 1903, were unreliable and often actually corrupt. Well-wishers like the conductors Franz Schalk and Ferdinand Löwe decided to "help" the composer, and some of the first published editions are almost as much their work as his. Not until the formation of the International Bruckner Society in 1929 did correct editions of Bruckner's works begin to be issued in a projected twenty-two volume critical edition. Robert Haas and Alfred Orel were the first editors, and were succeeded by Leopold Nowak, who sometimes arrived at different interpretations of the scores. Today all literate conductors use either the Haas or Nowak editions.

If Bruckner's music arouses fanatical devotion in many listeners, Mahler's creates an actual frenzy. Again there are doubters, those who find Mahler's music too neurotic and often too banal for enjoyment. The dedicated Mahlerian regards these unregenerates the way St. Paul regarded the heathen. It is hard to think of a composer who arouses an equal loyalty. The worship of Mahler amounts to a religion. Any music critic will attest to the fact that a response of anything except rapture to the Mahler symphonies will bring long letters of furious denunciation. Much more than even Bruckner's music, Mahler's stirs something imbedded in the subconscious, and his admirers approach him mystically. Thus Arnold Schoenberg wrote:

Actually everything that will characterize him is already present in the First Symphony. Here already his life-melody begins, and he merely develops it, unfolds it to the utmost extent. Here are his devotions to nature and his thoughts of death. He is still struggling with fate here, but in the Sixth he acknowledges it, and this acknowledgement is resignation. But even resignation becomes productive and rises, in the Eighth, to the glorification of the highest joys, to a glorification only possible to one who already knows these joys are no longer for him; who has already resigned himself; who already feels that they are merely an allegory for even higher joys, a glorification of the most supreme bliss . . .

137

Life-melody . . . fate . . . resignation . . . joys . . . death . . . glorification. But this is not analysis. It is sentimental extrapolation, from the black and white symbols and spaces on music paper to a set of conclusions that Mahler's admirers would dearly like to believe; and it ends up making Mahler not merely a composer but a combination of Moses and Christ. Where Bruckner evokes a purely religious impulse, Mahler evokes a moral, psychic, mystic, Freudian one. Mahler's admirers find themselves talking about soul states, inner crises, ecstasy, apotheoses, transfiguration, fate, Nature with a capital N, spirit, the all-in-one and the one-in-all. Mahler's heroic and futile struggle to make sense out of life passes through his music to the listener. It is very easy to identify with the struggle. The question remains whether or not the struggle is worth the experience. Beethoven's struggles were expressed purely in music, and are those of an indomitable hero who not only triumphed but created his own hereafter. Mahler's struggles are those of a psychic weakling, a complaining adolescent who whimpered or blustered or grew hysterical rather than put up much of a fight. Mahler's music can, indeed, be sickening to a certain type of mind—a mind that prefers manliness to anguish. For Mahler was, down deep, a sentimentalist. He *enjoyed* his misery; he reveled in it; he wallowed in it, wanting the whole world to see how he was suffering. In him, the textbook definition of sentimentalism became a living example, for Mahler never transformed the self in terms of the object. He transformed the object in terms of his self.

Perhaps it was this weakness, this basic insecurity, that accounted for his external character. To compensate, he turned out to be an austere, despotic, querulous, and arrogant man, convinced of his moral and musical rectitude. His wife once remarked that he was always telephoning to God. "Thin, fidgety, short, with a high, steep forehead, long dark hair and deeply penetrating bespectacled eyes" (Bruno Walter's description), he was a manic-depressive with a sadistic streak. Musicians respected him but hated to play under his baton. He was the kind of conductor who would pick on individual players; the kind of conductor who would start a rehearsal of the *Lohengrin* Prelude and yell at the players, before a note was sounded, "Too loud!" He was nervous among people and had no small talk, none of the social graces. His musical honesty would not permit him to acknowledge the second-rate. Bruno Walter tells of the time a composer played his new score to Mahler, who hated it. He said nothing. The composer, a friend, was terribly hurt. A curt *"Auf wiedersehen!"* ended the scene. "An entire lifetime of personal relations of all kinds had not supplied Mahler with that modicum of social polish that would have brought the meeting to an ordinary end," Walter wrote regretfully. Of Mahler's dedication to music there was no doubt. He had an ideal, and his life was spent in search of it. As such, it was a noble life.

Mahler, indeed, put so much into his music—as composer, conductor, administrator—that there was very little time for anything else, and that included personal relationships. He ignored his wife, and she resented it. "I knew that my marriage and my own life were utterly unfulfilled," Alma Mahler wrote, many years later. Worried about himself and his wife, Mahler had a session with Sigmund Freud. In a letter to Theodor Reik, dated January 4, 1935, Freud recalled the event:

I analyzed Mahler for an afternoon in the year 1912 (or 1913?) [it was 1910] in Leyden. If I may believe reports, I achieved much with him at that time. The visit appeared necessary for him, because his wife at that time rebelled against the fact that he withdrew his libido from her. In highly interesting expeditions through his life history, we discovered his personal conditions for love, especially his Holy Mary complex (mother fixation). I had plenty of opportunity to admire the capability for psychological understanding of this man of genius. No light fell at that time on the symptomatic façade of his obsessional neurosis. It was as if you would dig a single shaft through a mysterious building.

Reik concludes that Mahler's basic trouble was that in his passionate desire to achieve his ideal, Mahler neglected to live as other men did. While he was lost in his work, life passed him by. "He sought for the hidden metaphysical truth behind and beyond the phenomena of this world, for the ideal. He never tired in his search after that transcendental and supernatural secret of the Absolute and he did not recognize that the great secret of the transcendental, the miracle of the metaphysical, is that it does not exist."

Born in Kalist, Bohemia, on July 7, 1860, Mahler was the second of twelve children. In 1878 he went to the Vienna Conservatory, where he was a good pianist and where he discovered his talent as a conductor. When he was graduated, he started the slow climb from opera house to opera house that was the traditional path of an aspiring conductor. In 1880 he was musical director in the small city of Hall. The following year he went to Laibach (now Ljubljana), and in 1882 he worked in Olmütz. The year of 1883 saw him in Vienna (with an Italian opera company) and Kassel. In 1885 he was in Prague, and in 1886 the second conductor in Leipzig. Mahler remained in Leipzig for two years, but could not get along with Nikisch and left in 1888. His first big chance came in Budapest, where he was musical director of the Royal Opera from 1886 to 1888. Brahms heard him and was greatly impressed with his conducting of *Don Giovanni*. Richard Strauss also was impressed and passed the word to Bülow: "I have made a new, very attractive acquaintance in Herr Mahler, who appears to me a highly intelligent musician and conductor." The next step was Hamburg, from 1891 to 1897. Bülow heard him there and agreed with Strauss: "Hamburg has now secured a really excellent opera conductor in Gustav Mahler (a serious, energetic Jew from Budapest) who in my opinion equals the very best: Richter, Mottl, etc." Then in 1897, with the enthusiastic backing of Brahms, the thirty-seven-year-old conductor from Hamburg was named head of the Vienna Opera.

There, for ten years, Mahler imposed his despotic will. *He* was the opera. He chose the repertory and singers, conducted many of the performances, staged many productions himself, and had his finger in everything that had to do with the house. He even imposed his will on the audience. One stern glance from his thin, nervous, forbidding face, and quiet would mantle the hall. As a conductor, he appears to have been a precisionist on the order of Bülow and, again like Bülow, strongly intellectual in his approach. He insisted on strenuous preparation, driving himself and his singers and musicians to exhaustion. To him there was no such thing as a minor detail, for minor details were important—as every great conductor knows. Mahler would not tolerate inattentive or careless playing. Never in his life did he encounter an orchestra that satisfied him in his search for perfection. Some idea of his ear and musicianship can be gained from what he once wrote about orchestras:

There are frightful habits, or rather inadequacies, which I have encountered in every orchestra. They cannot read the score markings, and thus sin against the holy law of dynamics and of the inner hidden rhythms of a work. When they see a crescendo they immediately play forte and speed up; at a diminuendo they become piano and retard the tempo. One looks in vain for gradations, for the mezzo-forte, forte, fortissimo, or the piano, pianissimo, pianississimo. And the sforzandos, forte pianos, shortening or extension of notes, are even less in evidence. And should one ask them to play something that is not written down—as is so necessary a hundred times when one accompanies singers in opera—then one is lost with every orchestra.

In the ten years of Mahler's administration the Vienna opera was revitalized and cleared of debt. Prominent stage directors, such as Alfred Roller, were brought in, often causing great controversy. Roller's production of *Tristan und Isolde,* with its free forms, advanced lighting effects, and general feeling of avant-garde expressionism, caused a furore. In Vienna, Mahler was a legend, and hansom drivers would single him out as one of the monuments, like St. Stephen's. "Der Mahler!" they would tell their fares, pointing to him in the street. He never stopped working. "I cannot do anything but work. I have unlearned all other things within the course of the years." Bruno Walter never could keep up with him. "At no time during the two years I spent with Mahler in the Hamburg theater or the six at the

Vienna Opera, did I note a lessening of that high-tension speed."

In 1907 he went to the Metropolitan Opera for two full seasons, then returned to New York in 1909 with a two-year contract as conductor of the Philharmonic Society. His American experiences were unhappy. His second season at the Metropolitan coincided with the first season of Giulio Gatti-Casazza and his star conductor, Arturo Toscanini. Friction developed between Mahler and the new management, especially when Gatti-Gasazza assigned *Tristan und Isolde* to Toscanini—after Mahler had already rehearsed the orchestra and prepared the production. It was also apparent that Mahler in New York was not the Mahler of the Vienna Opera. He allowed cuts, which he had not permitted in his own house; and as an excuse for some indifferent performances lamely said that the musicians would not play for him and that there was not enough rehearsal time. The New York critics did not like him, or he them. Worse was to happen when he took over the Philharmonic. His programming displeased the ladies of the board almost as much as his antisocial personality did. He was tactless enough to refer to the Philharmonic as "the true American orchestra—without talent and phlegmatic." That did not increase his popularity. Mahler had to defend himself at a board meeting, and his wife was appalled. "You cannot imagine what Mr. Mahler has suffered," she told the press. "In Vienna my husband was all-powerful. Even the Emperor did not dictate to him, but in New York he had ten ladies ordering him around like a puppet." Mahler already was fatally ill, and had only a few more months to live. He left New York without finishing his Philharmonic season, and died in Vienna on May 11, 1911.

As a busy and successful conductor all of his adult life, Mahler had a minimum of time for his own creative work. He referred to himself as a part-time composer, and indeed the list of his compositions is not large. It consists of the nine symphonies and the unfinished tenth, and *Das Lied von der Erde*, the *Kindertotenlieder*, and other songs with orchestral and piano accompaniment. Many of the songs, and some of the movements in the symphonies, were inspired by the poems of *Des Knaben Wunderhorn*, a collection of folk poetry published in 1805 by Ludwig von Arnim and Klemens Brentano. Like many city people, Mahler liked to get out into the country, persuaded that he was renewing himself; and the use of *Wunderhorn* poems gave him a feeling of identification with Austrian folk elements. There is no real nationalism in his music, however. Pantheism might be a better word to describe it.

As in so much of the music of Mahler's day, there is an implied program running through everything he wrote. These program elements are not specific, as in the Strauss tone poems. They are general, giving the psychic key to the score. Mahler was a child of his time, and the same impulse that made Clara Schumann describe the Brahms Third Symphony as the story of Hero and Leander, the same impulse that made Liszt supply a silly program to Chopin's F minor Fantasy, made Mahler look for an implied program in all music, not only his own. "Believe me," he wrote in 1896, "the symphonies of Beethoven too have their inner program, and when one gets to know such works better, one's understanding of the proper succession of the emotions and ideas increases. In the end that will be true of my works also." Elsewhere he wrote: "Beginning with Beethoven, there exists no modern music that hasn't its inner program." And, "It is therefore good that at the beginning, when my style is still foreign to him, the listener be provided with a few signposts and milestones along the journey, or shall we say a map of the stars to comprehend the night sky with its shining worlds." It naturally followed that he could write "My music is, everywhere and always, only a sound of Nature." By "Nature" Mahler meant the word in its widest sense—life and death, earth and universe. Of his Eighth Symphony: "Imagine the universe beginning to sing and resound. It is no longer human voices; it is planets and suns revolving." He went into great detail about his ideas of program music in a letter to Max Marschalk, dated March 26, 1896:

> . . . My need to express myself musically—symphonically—begins only where the *obscure* perceptions hold sway, at the gate that leads into the "other world;" the world in which things are no longer separable through the agency of time and place.
>
> Just as I think it is a platitude to invent music to a program, so I consider it to be unsatisfying and sterile to want to attach a program to a musical work. This is no way altered by the fact that the *occasion* for a musical creation is doubtless to be found in an experience of the author's, and an actual one, which for that matter might be specific enough to be clothed in words . . .
>
> Having expressed myself in the above terms, you can understand that I find it a little awkward to say something to you now about the C minor Symphony.—I have named the first movement "Funeral Rite," and if you want to know, it is the hero of my First Symphony that I am burying here and whose life I am gathering in a clear mirror, from a higher point of vantage. At the same time it is the great question: *Why have you lived?* Why have you suffered? Is all this merely a great, horrible jest?—We *must* resolve these questions somehow or other if we are to continue living—nay, if we are only to continue dying. Once this call has resounded in anybody's life, he must give an answer; and that answer I give in the last movement.

The letter goes on to describe in even fuller detail what the movements of the Second Symphony mean. All of Mahler's music has this kind of pro-

142

gram, and every one of his symphonies can be described in terms of unrest, struggle, aspiration. Naturally there is a difference between Mahler's first and last works, between the buoyant and athletic writing of the First Symphony to the hushed, motionless pessimism that concludes the Ninth and *Das Lied von der Erde*. Aspiration finally gives way to resignation.

In Mahler's music are many unconventional harmonies, culminating with the mad, macabre *Burleske* of the Ninth Symphony, that weird march with its powerful dissonances and parodistic quality. But the harmonic daring of Mahler has been somewhat overplayed by those scholars too anxious to make him the link between Wagner and Schoenberg. Schoenberg's Five Orchestral Pieces of 1908 are already far more advanced than Mahler's last works of 1910 and 1911. As far as that goes, Alexander Scriabin around 1905 was dispensing with key signatures, using quartal instead of triadic harmonies, and using a type of dissonance that was more prophetic than anything in Mahler.

When history puts Mahler in perspective, it probably will be clear that he was, aesthetically and technically, much more a nineteenth- than a twentieth-century figure. He thought in terms of romanticism and composed in terms of romanticism. His concept of music as program, stemming from Wagner's idiotic exegeses on the Beethoven symphonies, was romantic. His big orchestra, like Strauss's, merely carried Wagner one step further. His harmonies were no more advanced than most of Strauss's, and not as advanced as those in *Salome* or *Elektra*. Schoenberg, Strauss, Scriabin, and Debussy were much more modern than Mahler even in his own day. Even though Mahler's symphonies illustrate the breakup of classical models, they remain symphonies "after Beethoven" in more ways than one, and some of Mahler's slow movements, like Bruckner's, are unconscious attempts to rewrite the adagio of the Ninth. The Mahler symphonies, of course, do not have the tight organization of the Beethoven symphonies. That they also lack the emotional discipline of the Beethoven symphonies goes without saying. The swollen dance movements of the Mahler symphonies are sentimental evocations of an earlier Austria, with its peasants and *Ländler:* those simple tunes, played so thickly by Mahler's immense orchestra, dripping with earnestness. (It may have been this kind of music to which Debussy was referring when he wrote that "The fashion for popular airs has spread quickly throughout the musical world: from east to west the tiniest villages have been ransacked, and simple tunes, plucked from the mouths of hoary peasants, find themselves, to their consternation, trimmed with harmonic frills.") The cosmic movements of Mahler are hysterical. A frightened, tortured Mahler shrinks from the Infinite. With all this, there are sections in most of his symphonies where the undoubted brilliance of Mahler the musician conquers Mahler the Deep Thinker. And in his most moving work, *Das Lied von der Erde*, Mahler for once created an edifice in which form and emotion match each other. The genuine sadness and otherworldly quality of the music do not sound artificial or forced, and the last song is as much a farewell to the end of romanticism in music as it is to the approaching end of Mahler's own life. But to make Mahler, as many have done, a modern symbol is to misunderstand modernism and to misunderstand Mahler. His questions about life were trite, no deeper than those of Dickens's Sairey Gamp: "Sech is life. Vich likewise is the hend of all things."

The turn-of-the-century composer in Germany who defiantly looked back rather than forward was Max Reger, the central figure of the "Back to Bach" movement. He worked almost alone, and outside of Germany his music is all but unknown; nor is it played much any more even in Germany. To most critics of the latter half of the twentieth century, who apparently know Reger only by such pieces as the *Mozart* or *Hiller* variations, he is a monster—a composer of swollen scores with pointless fugues. The mention of Reger's name arouses a conditioned reflex: "Fugue!" Mahler and Bruckner have enjoyed an enormous revival, but Reger, who worked and composed voluminously during the same period, is today ignored, except to appear on critics' lists of the ten most disliked composers.

In his day, Reger was well known. He was a bumptious, outspoken man who for some reason hard to discern today was considered an ultramodernist. A child prodigy, born in Brand (Bavaria) on March 19, 1873, he was a professional organist at the age of sixteen, a teacher in Munich for many years, a professor at the Leipzig Conservatory, and a pianist and conductor. At the age of forty-three he had a heart attack and died, on March 11, 1916.

It was Reger's mission in life to write music in the spirit of Bach and Beethoven. "I can say with good conscience," he wrote in 1914, "that of all living composers I am probably the one who is in closest touch with the great masters of our rich past." He inveighed against the "perverted rubbish of Wagnerites and Straussomania." Where most other German composers of the day followed the line from Berlioz through Liszt and Wagner, his ancestry started with Bach and worked through Beethoven to Mendelssohn and Brahms. As a romantic who flourished in the day of the great post-Wagnerian orchestra, Reger did not hesitate to put it to use. Where Brahms would write a series of orchestral variations on a theme by Haydn, keeping everything direct and lyrical, Reger did not hesitate to take the opening theme of Mozart's A major Piano Sonata and subject it to a series of gargantuan variations culminating in a colossal fugue. The idea was similar to that of Brahms; the execution suffered from gigantism. Some German-oriented musicians continue to admire this type of writing, but it is precisely scores like the *Mozart* Variations that have given Reger a bad name, and most musicians today consider them the epitome of shocking taste. Mozart's pretty, slender theme put through such elaborate, heavy-footed paces! Decked with such inappropriately scented, lush harmonies!

But the *Mozart* Variations are by no means typical of Reger's work. That score represents only one side of his output. A good deal of his music is devoid of counterpoint. His chamber music, of which the Clarinet Quintet is a representative example, is nothing more than an extremely chromatic Brahms, just as his F minor Piano Concerto is a massive work that goes the Brahms B flat Concerto one better in size and sonority. This is not to say that Reger was a mere imitator of Brahms. His intense chromaticism is handled in a very individual manner (some of his chromaticism sounds like, of all composers, Delius, who was very popular in Germany before World War I). Reger's melodies also manage to maintain purity despite their heavy lacquer of postromanticism. As a technician he was masterful. Still another side of Reger is encountered in the unaccompanied sonatas for violin. The composer who is associated in so many musicians' minds only with fugue and overloaded orchestral scores here composed a set of tiny sonatas, none much over five minutes long, of delicacy and charm. His songs and piano pieces, while they reflect the period, are elegant and often beautiful. Reger did not have the originality to be one of the great masters, but his secure workmanship and honest fund of melody should have prevented his music from falling so low in professional esteem. As with many of the minor romantics and post-romantics, a shift in aesthetic values from objectivism to subjectivism will have to take place before Reger's music begins to be reexamined.

Reger was a plucky man and a scrappy fighter who had no hesitation about speaking his mind. He has achieved a kind of fame through an episode that concerned his dismissal of a music critic: scatological but perfect. He read a review of one of his pieces that outraged him, and presently that critic received from Reger the following note: "Dear Sir: I am sitting in the smallest room of my house. Your review is before me. Shortly it shall be behind me." In his day, Reger did not lack champions. Arnold Schoenberg held his music in very high esteem; and in the conductor Fritz Busch, Reger found a musician who was frequently presenting his music. Busch believed that Reger was the greatest composer after Brahms. He described the composer as "an extraordinarily tall man with tiny feet and an ugly, child-like face." Busch once invited Reger to participate in a concert at Bad Pyrmont. He told Reger that there would be no fee, but that the Prince would give him a decoration. Reger had to know exactly what kind of decoration. "He wanted to know whether it would be the *gold* medal for art and science? Whether it would be the *large* gold medal? Whether it would be the large gold medal with the red ribbon?" During Reger's stay at Bad Pyrmont, the Princess asked him why he played an Ibach rather than a Steinway piano. Reger, as always, spoke his mind. "You know, Your Highness," he boomed, "they pay much more."

❧ 10 ❧

Symbolism and Impressionism

CLAUDE-ACHILLE DEBUSSY

"*A tout Seigneur, tout l'honneur,*" runs the French proverb. Honor to whom honor is due. It is not that Claude Debussy lacked honors in his own day. After a slow start, this *musicien français* (so he described himself) was recognized as the greatest French composer of his time. But today he is more than that. He is considered not only the greatest French composer who ever lived; he is considered the revolutionary who, with the *Prélude à l'après-midi d'un faune* of 1894, set twentieth-century music on its way. The younger critics are ecstatic now when they discuss the contributions of Claude Debussy. He is, they say, the one who destroyed nineteenth-century rhetoric; the one whose harmonic and melodic innovations led to the breakup of the scale as used in the nineteenth century; the one whose new concepts of orchestration led straight into Webern; the one whose piano music gave pianists more to think about than any other composer since Chopin; the one who reinstated the power of sound for sound's sake: the Rimbaud, the Verlaine, the Cézanne of music. Pierre Boulez, that outspoken exponent of the serial school, has written that certain of Debussy's last works "will be almost more astonishing than the final works of Webern." To Boulez, these late Debussy works are pieces in which all elements of the past have been discarded, pieces illustrative of "the total overthrow of notions that had remained static up to that time." Even as early as in *L'après-midi*, Boulez says, "all of Wagner's heavy heritage was discarded. . . . The Debussy reality excludes all academism."

Debussy is the greatest of the musical impressionists, though symbolist might be a better word. The impressionist painters—Manet, Monet, Cézanne, Renoir, Pissarro, and the other members of the *Société Anonyme des Artistes, Peintres, Sculpteurs et Graveurs*—had three famous shows from 1874 to 1877, and after 1877 the term "impressionism" stuck. It was derived from a painting by Monet named *Sunrise—an Impression*. Debussy disliked the term in relation to his own music. As a matter of fact, his tastes in painting were more in the direction of Whistler and Turner than of the impressionists. The symbolist poets—Mallarmé, Verlaine, Rimbaud, Maeterlinck—meant more to Debussy than painting. Another writer who fascinated him, as he fascinated all the French symbolists, was Edgar Allan Poe. Debussy worked for a while on an orchestral work based on *The Fall of the House of Usher,* and in 1908 he actually signed a contract with the Metropolitan Opera for operas on *Usher* and *The Devil in the Belfry* (and also for one on a non-Poe subject named *The Legend of Tristan*). But impressionism and Debussy are forever intertwined, and with good reason. Just as the impressionist painters developed new theories of light and color, so Debussy developed new theories of light and color in music. Like the impressionist painters, and like the symbolist poets, he tried to capture a fleeting impression or mood, tried to pin down the exact essence of a thought as economically as possible. He was far less interested in classical form than in *sensibilité.* He was from the beginning a boy, then a man, of *sensibilité.* Even as a child he had the tastes of an aristocrat. At Bourbonneux's famous pastry shop, his friends would gorge themselves on the cheapest candy, the most they could get for a few centimes. Debussy would choose a tiny sandwich, or a little *timbale aux macaronis,* or a delicate bite of pastry. Later in life his tastes were equally exquisite. He had to surround himself with fine prints and books. He was a gourmet with a notable appetite for caviar. He dressed to the point of dandyism, complete with carefully selected cravat, cape, and broad-brimmed hat *à la* Western. He knew exactly what he wanted from life and he took it, ignoring the rest.

Born on August 22, 1862, in St.-Germain-en-Laye, just outside of Paris, he grew up to be a strange-looking boy with bony protuberances on his forehead—*un double front.* He became a brilliant pianist and was admitted to the Conservatoire at the age of ten. Two years later he was skillful enough to be playing Chopin's F minor Concerto. He also started to compose at that time. He had no close friends, and a fellow student described him as "uncommunicative, not to say surly; he was not attractive to his friends." He studied theory with Alfred Lavignac, piano with Antoine Marmontel, harmony with Émile Durand, composition with Ernest Guiraud. Even at that time he was a natural rebel, one with the kind of questioning mind that did not hesitate to ask embarrassing questions of his elders. At the Conservatoire he sat in on some of César Franck's classes and recoiled in horror. "*Modulez, modulez,*" Franck would say, looking over Debussy's exercises. Debussy shocked the class by facing directly up to the famous and venerable *maître.* "Why should I modulate when I am perfectly happy in the tonality I am in?" He poked fun at Franck, calling him a modulating machine. In Guiraud's composition class he would sit at the piano making up outlandish chords and refusing to resolve them. He was asked by an exasperated teacher what rules he followed. *"Mon plaisir,"* Debussy curtly answered. Nevertheless, his talent was recognized, and after winning many prizes he finally was awarded the greatest of all, the Prix de Rome, in 1884.

Debussy grew into a complicated and reserved man, one whose shell was hard to penetrate. He had few friends and fewer intimates. Erik Satie and Pierre Louÿs were among the few intimates. His private life was very private and rather deplorable—at least, according to customary canons of behavior. After returning from Rome in 1887 he lived with Gabrielle Dupont—Gaby of the green eyes—for ten years. Where she came from nobody knew. He settled in with her in a miserable room just off Montmartre and for those ten years she took care of him, supported him (What did she do? Was she a washerwoman? A *midinette*? Did she scrub floors? Nobody knows.), and shooed away creditors. He rewarded her in 1899 by marrying Rosalie Texier. Even before that, he had been unfaithful, and Gabrielle shot herself after an argument with him. She lived, briefly returned to him, and then disappeared as mysteriously as she had entered his life. Many years later, the pianist Alfred Cortot ran across her in a theater in Rouen. She was in the dress of a working woman.

Debussy's marriage to Rosalie did not last very long. After a while, Debussy once said, the sound of her voice made his blood run cold. He threw her over in 1904 for the married Emma Bardac, whereupon Rosalie, like Gaby, shot herself. When Debussy married Emma in 1905, most of intellectual Paris sided with Rosalie and felt that Debussy had married for money. Emma was older than Debussy and had several grown children. She bore Debussy a daughter—Chouchou, whom he adored—before her divorce from the banker Raoul Bardac. It is very possible that Debussy was interested in her money, but he also liked her as much as he could like anybody. Emma was a singer and a witty, sophisticated, artistic woman, where Rosalie had been a sweet, unintellectual provincial.

In every respect Debussy's tastes were not as other men's. While musical Europe was worshiping Wagner, Debussy had his brief fling with the operas of the German master and then fought Wagnerism for the rest of his life. Satie claimed credit for giving Debussy the final push from Wagner into a "purer" style. Erik Satie (1866–1925) was an eccentric pianist and composer who entertained the customers at *Le Chat Noir* and also managed to secure for himself a prominent position in French aesthetic life. He composed stripped-down, short pieces in "white-key" harmony, was an ardent anti-Wagnerian, and proclaimed a kind of music that in a way was antimusic, deliberately so. His *"musique d'ameublement"* was to be played without being listened to, like looking at wallpaper without seeing it. Satie was one of the early Dadaists and surrealists, and he composed music with such surrealistic titles as *Pièces en forme de poire* (*Pieces in the form of a pear*) or *Embryons desséchés* (*Desiccated embryos*). His music, which is a link between Chabrier and Poulenc, is of striking individuality. Throughout his life, Satie influenced the advanced French school, first Debussy, then the composers of *Les Six*. He represented a complete break from tradition.

Debussy and Satie first came together at *Le Chat Noir* around 1890.

When I first met Debussy [Satie later wrote] he was full of Mussorgsky and very deliberately seeking a way that wasn't very easy for him to find. In this problem I was well in advance of him. I was not weighted down by the Prix de Rome or any other prize, for I am a man like Adam (of Paradise) who never won any prizes—a lazy fellow, no doubt. At that time I was writing *Le Fils des étoiles* to a libretto by Joseph Péladan, and I explained to Debussy that I was in no way anti-Wagnerian but that we should have a music of our own—if possible, without any sauer-kraut. Why could we not use the means that Claude Monet, Cézanne, Toulouse-Lautrec, and others had made known? Why could we not transpose those means to music? Nothing simpler.

Debussy himself was coming to the same conclusion independently. As early as 1894 he found his love affair with Wagner coming to an end. "Having been an impassioned visitor to Bayreuth for several years, I began to doubt the Wagnerian formula—or, rather, it seemed to me it fitted only the particular genius of that composer, who was a great collector of clichés that he summed up in a formula which seemed unusual only because people did not know music well enough." Debussy concluded that it was necessary to go beyond Wagner rather than follow in his path. More and more, Debussy began to find inspiration in Mussorgsky rather than in Wagner. He had heard Mussorgsky's music in Russia, where he had spent some time in 1881 as piano teacher to the children of Nadjeda von Meck, Tchaikovsky's patroness. (When he fell in love with Sonia, her eldest daughter, she sent him packing.) Another strong musical influence, one that immensely touched the nerves of his *sensibilité*, was the exotic ethnic music represented by the Javanese gamelan orchestra he had heard at the Grande Exposition Universelle, in 1889. At that time he noted that Javanese music employed a counterpoint "in comparison to which that of Palestrina is a child's game." Primitive and medieval music always interested him.

With these superrefined tastes ran a corresponding dislike of the academic composers. Brahms meant nothing to him, Tchaikovsky he disliked, Beethoven bored him. He seldom worked in sonata form, the prevailing form since Mozart. He believed that the symphony as a form was dead. "It seems to me that the proof of the futility of the symphony has been established since Beethoven. Schumann and Mendelssohn did no more than respectfully repeat the same forms with less power." His was a music of personal, all but tactile, sensation ("Formless!" cried the academicians), a music that lacked "proper" resolution of chords, a music in which tonality began to be broken up, in which certain twentieth-century ideas of form and technique were first put on display. He was the first of the post-Wagner composers to work in an entirely new style, and *L'Après-midi d'un faune* has a place in musical history comparable to the *Eroica* Symphony and Monteverdi's *Orfeo*. Each of those epochal works shook a fist at the past and made it clear that the old rules no longer applied.

Debussy *thought* in a new manner. "I am more and more convinced that music, by its very nature, is something that cannot be cast into a traditional and fixed form. It is made up of colors and rhythms. The rest is a lot of humbug invented by frigid imbeciles riding on the backs of the Masters— who, for the most part, wrote almost nothing but period music. Bach alone had an idea of the truth." There was very little music that Debussy liked, and he was as contemptuous of his French contemporaries and immediate predecessors as he was of some of the revered figures of the past. Massenet was "a master in the art of pandering to stupid ideas and amateur standards." *Faust* was "massacred" by Gounod, and Shakespeare's *Hamlet* was "most unfortunately dealt with by M. Ambroise Thomas." Charpentier was "downright vulgar." In general: "Our poor music! How it has been dragged in the mud!"

It was not for nothing that Debussy called himself *musicien français*. Mostly the label was a defiant affirmation of his anti-Wagnerianism, and later included his anti-German feeling during the First World War. In any case, his music is the essence of everything French. He once made a lengthy statement on what the Gallic ideals were, comparing French clarity and elegance with German length and heaviness. "To a Frenchman, finesse and nuance are the daughters of intelligence." A French musician should not pile sonority upon sonority: that would be un-French. Artists should use self-control. At that time, Debussy was looking for a libretto. "I am dreaming of poetry that would not condemn me to contrive long and heavy acts, poetry that would offer me scenes which move in their locality and character, and where the characters do not argue but submit to life and their fate."

These lines were written in 1889. In 1893 he found his dream poetry. It was Maurice Maeterlinck's play *Pelléas et Mélisande*, produced in 1892. Debussy saw it and was enraptured. It exactly fit his ideas of a libretto. Even as a conservatory student he had been looking for a libretto that had "no place, no time, no big scene." He told his teacher that the musical element in opera was far too prominent, that there was too much singing. "The blossoming of the voice into true singing should occur only when required. A painting executed in grey would be the ideal." There should be, Debussy said, "no developments merely for the sake of development." *Pelléas et Mélisande* could have been written to order for Debussy, and he immediately asked the author's consent to set it to music—a brash request from a little-known composer to a world-famous playwright. The result, ten years later, was a masterpiece. It was also a sore period for Debussy and Maeterlinck, a comedy of errors and ruffled pride, of bitterness, heroics, and sheer silliness.

They got along very well at the beginning. Debussy paid Maeterlinck a visit to discuss the libretto. He wrote to a friend that at first Maeterlinck "assumed the air of a young girl being introduced to her future husband." Debussy found him charming, knowledgeable in general, but musically illiterate. "When he speaks of a Beethoven symphony he is like a blind man in a museum." Debussy finished the score in 1895, was dissatisfied, and rewrote it completely. It was not until 1901 that he wrote the last notes. In the meantime he had published his String Quartet, the three Nocturnes for orchestra, some amazing songs, and was by then a famous composer.

When he played the score to Maeterlinck, the dramatist almost fell asleep from boredom. His wife, Georgette Leblanc, kept prodding him awake. Leblanc was an actress who had achieved stardom in Maeterlinck's plays. She also was a singer, and she hoped to create the operatic role of Mélisande. That was where the trouble started. According to her story—and most people believed her—Debussy was "enchanted" with the suggestion that she sing the premiere, and they had a few rehearsals together. But Albert Carré, director of the Opéra-Comique, had different ideas. He wanted Mary Garden, and Garden got the assignment. Neither Maeterlinck nor Leblanc knew anything about it until they picked up the paper one day. Then there was an explosion. Maeterlinck immediately tried to stop the production. Debussy denied that he had promised Leblanc the role. Maeterlinck went to court, and the court decided for Debussy. On receiving this news, Maeterlinck's fine Belgian temper boiled over. He brandished his stick and threatened to thrash Debussy. In a roaring rage, Maeterlinck jumped out of the window of his home (not as grand a gesture as it sounds, for he lived on the ground floor) and hastened to Debussy, breaking into his apartment. Debussy cut something less than a heroic figure. Confronted by the furious and formidable Maeterlinck, he refused to fight and sank prostrate into an armchair while his wife rushed to him with smelling salts. The baffled Maeterlinck took his leave saying, "All crazy, all sick, these musicians." There was talk of a duel between Debussy and Maeterlinck, or Carré and Maeterlinck. But there was no duel. Instead, Maeterlinck went to a fortuneteller. He did not believe in clairvoyance, he said, but then again he did not disbelieve in it. The clairvoyant supplied him with an answer that nobody could dispute. "The forces of nature are well balanced," said the clairvoyant. "According to human logic it is impossible to predict the outcome."

The affair ended with Maeterlinck writing an open letter to *Le Figaro*, telling the world that the performance was going to be given against his wishes. He accused Debussy of butchering the libretto "with arbitrary and absurd cuts." In the circumstances, said Maeterlinck, "I am reduced to wishing its immediate and decided failure."

Maeterlinck's wish was almost granted. *Pelléas et Mélisande* was not a success at its premiere on April 30, 1902, though it caused a great deal of comment. It soon took hold, however, even if it puzzled some fine musicians, especially German musicians. It ran so counter to what the Germans of the day considered opera that there was nothing for them to hold on to. Richard Strauss attended a performance of *Pelléas et Mélisande* in 1907 with Romain Rolland, who has written a very funny account of the evening:

Strauss arrived at the end of the first scene and seated himself between Ravel and myself. Jean Marnold and Lionel de la Laurencie [two music critics] sat behind. . . . In his usual uninhibited manner with no regard for conventional courtesy, Strauss hardly speaks to anybody but myself, confiding his impressions of *Pelléas* to me in a whisper. (Since all the gossip in the papers he has become distrustful.) He listens with the greatest attention and, with his opera glasses up to his eyes, follows everything on the stage and in the orchestra. But he understands nothing. After the first act (the first three scenes), he says, "Is it like this all the time?" "Yes." "Nothing more? There's nothing in it. No music. It has nothing consecutive. No musical phrases. No development." Marnold tries to bring himself into the conversation and says, in his usual heavy manner, "There are musical phrases, but they are not brought out or underlined in a way that the ordinary listener would appreciate." Strauss, rather put out but very dignified, replies, "But I am a musician and I hear nothing." . . .

To this day, listeners conditioned by orthodox singing opera respond as Strauss did. *Pelléas et Mélisande* has never been popular in the sense that the operas of Verdi, Puccini, and Wagner are popular. It is too refined, too lacking in red blood. These attributes are, of course, the very things that attract the minority who consider *Pelléas et Mélisande* the most subtle and atmospheric opera ever written. It is an opera in which all traditional arias are banished. Instead, the characters declaim in a kind of speech-song. Before the premiere, Debussy called the cast together and begged everybody to forget they were singers. Mussorgsky, not Wagner, is the progenitor of the vocal line in this opera, though it also is the kind of integrated opera, complete with leitmotifs (which Strauss gleefully pointed out), that in theory closely approximates the Wagnerian ideal of a fusion of music, drama, and décor. In sound and concept, however, *Pelléas et Mélisande* altogether differs from Wagner. It is set in a dream world, a world of pianissimo sounds, diaphanous colors, subtlety, and restraint. It is an opera of *sensibilité*. Debussy was content. "I have tried to beat out a path where others can follow by adding their own discoveries and by ridding dramatic music of the heavy constraint from which it has suffered for so long a time."

Some years after the premiere he wrote for the Opéra-Comique an introduction to *Pelléas et Mélisande* that is of unusual interest. He said that he had always wanted to compose an opera. "But the form I wished to employ was so unusual that after various efforts I had almost abandoned the idea. Previous research in pure music had led me to hate classical development, whose beauty is merely technical and of interest only to the highbrows of our class. I desired for music that freedom of which it is capable perhaps to a greater degree than any other art, as it is not confined to an exact reproduction of nature, but only to the mysterious affinity between Nature and the Imagination." Wagner's theories were not the answer. "The thing, then, was to find what came *after Wagner's time* but not *after Wagner's manner*." Maeterlinck's play suited Debussy because "in spite of its fantastic atmosphere" it contained "much more humanity than the so-called *documents of life*." In his opera, Debussy said, he tried

to obey a law of beauty which appears to be singularly ignored in dealing with dramatic music. The characters of this drama endeavor to sing like real persons, and not in an arbitrary language built on antiquated traditions. Hence the reproach levelled at my alleged partiality for monotone declamation, in which there is no trace of melody. . . . To begin with, this is untrue. Besides, the feelings of a character cannot be continually expressed in melody. Then, too, dramatic melody should be totally different from melody in general. . . . The people who go to listen to music at the theater are, when all is said and done, very like those one sees gathered around a street singer! There, for a penny, one may indulge in melodic emotions. . . . By a singular irony, this public, which cries out for something new, is the very one that shows alarm and scoffs whenever one tries to wean it from old habits and the customary humdrum noises. . . . This may seem incomprehensible; but one must not forget that a work of art or an effort to create beauty are always regarded by some people as a personal affront.

Pelléas et Mélisande had no followers. It was unique and has remained unique. Debussy himself never made much of an attempt to push his one opera or, indeed, any of his music. His attitude toward life was something of a sullen I don't-care viewpoint. Anyway, he did not like people very much, and that alone would have prevented him from the personal contacts that most composers have found indispensable for promoting their music. When he won the Prix de Rome in 1894 and had to live in the Villa Medici, he was miserable. He hated the villa, hated his fellow students, hated Rome, and fled to Paris without finishing his three-year term of what he called "forced labor." He always was abnormally touchy—quick to take offense, sensitive to the point of mania, uncomfortable with people he did not know. Naturally he hated to appear in public, hated to conduct, hated to play the piano at concerts. He preferred cats to people, and was never without one or more Siamese cats. Perhaps he saw reflected in cats the reserve, independence, and lack of morality of his own nature. Debussy did have the habits and morals of a tomcat, and there was something feline about the character of the man, though there was nothing feline about his physique. He was short, plump, flabby, pale, and indolent; he had heavily lidded eyes under his huge, bulging forehead; he wore a beard that reminded many of Christ in Italian renaissance paintings. He trained his hair to hide the bulges, but it did not work, and he was called "*Le Christ hydrocéphalique.*" He was indeed an unusual-looking man, and Colette referred to his "Pan-like head. . . . In his unrelenting gaze the pupils of his eyes seemed momentarily to dart from one spot to another like those of animals of prey hypnotized by their own searching intensity." Like a cat, he pampered himself and thought only of himself. "I don't know whether his egoism will ever be subdued," his schoolmate Paul Vidal had written. "He is incapable of any sacrifice whatever. Nothing has any hold over him. His parents are not rich. Instead of using the money from his lessons to support them, he buys for himself many books, curios, etchings and all that sort of thing. His mother has shown us drawers full of them." When his friends gave him "loans," they knew they would never be repaid.

The chain-smoking Debussy was a sybarite, a sensualist, an ironist, and not the most pleasant of men. It followed that he would be very choosy about his friends. Marcel Proust admired him, wanted to know him better, and once even cornered him and drove him home in his carriage. The meeting between the two great exemplars of *sensibilité* was not happy. Proust complained that Debussy did not listen to him. Debussy thought Proust was "long-winded and a bit of the concierge." Nevertheless Proust, always the snob, persisted, and asked Debussy to a party he wanted to give in his honor. Debussy refused to attend. "I know I am a bear, I much prefer to see each other again in a café. Don't hold it against me. I was born that way." · And he was also born a genius with two of the most sensitive ears any musician ever had. No composer ever had a more infallible instinct for the one chord that would supply exactly the right touch of color. These touches of color make his music, and especially his piano music, unique. Debussy composed a great deal of piano music, from the rather conventional *Pour le piano* to the austere Études. His piano music was as original as his own way of playing the piano. Alfredo Casella, the Italian composer, was spellbound when he heard Debussy play: "No words can describe his playing of some of the Préludes. He did not have the virtuosity of the specialist, but his touch was extremely sensitive. One had the impression that he was actually playing on the strings of the instrument, without the mechanical aid of keys and hammers. He used the pedals as nobody else ever did. The result was pure poetry."

Debussy would have been pleased with these words. His entire approach was aimed at liberating the piano from its percussive sound. That meant an approach derived from Chopin rather than from Beethoven. "I became finally and completely convinced," he wrote in 1909, "that Beethoven definitely wrote badly for the piano." And to the pianist Marguerite Long, "I heartily detest the piano concertos of Mozart, but less than those of Beethoven." Chopin had showed how, through pedal effects and delicate varieties of touch, the piano could be made to "sing." Debussy carried this one step further. Indeed he insisted that the piano should sound as though it were an "instrument without hammers." The fingers should "penetrate into the notes." Effects were to be obtained through use of the pedal—Debussy called it a "breathing pedal." In 1903 he started his mature series of piano works. In *Estampes, L'Isle Joyeuse,* the *Images, Children's Corner,* the two books of Préludes and the two of Études, a new style of piano writing was invented, the most significant since Chopin. Often the music is technically difficult, but technique is the least of it. Pianists of the day had to struggle with a new type of fingering, new spacings, new sonorities, and the revolutionary use of the pedal. Tones and chords now floated in air; melodies darted through blocks of suspended harmonies. (Later musicians like Pierre Boulez who loftily say that in their interpretations they want to "burn the mist off Debussy" ignore the fact that Debussy very consciously set out to create that very mist.) The piano pieces of Debussy are as much "impressions" as the canvases of the impressionist painters. They had no "development." Instead, these pieces seized upon a single idea, saw it through, and stopped. Harmonically the music followed no rule. Debussy's exquisite ear was the only rule, and it was an infallible ear. Tonality was not abandoned, but it did verge on dissolution. Chords did not necessarily resolve. They were often an end in themselves. A work like *Voiles* seems to operate in three keys at once—A minor, C major, and B flat major.

Debussy's songs also have this kind of tonal ambiguity. In the songs, the exquisite feeling for declamation heard in *Pelléas et Mélisande* is even more refined. The vocal line is largely a form of recitative, in which the words take on a heightened value, perfumed by Debussy's unerring ear for prosody and the exotic-sounding, sensual accompaniments. Debussy was always the sensualist. Even when he used ancient devices—modal scales, Gregorian chant, orientalisms of a pentatonic nature—the music sounded sensual. Or it sounded sensual when he used the whole-tone scale, a new device in which the scale was built on major seconds. There is in Debussy's music a languorous kind of veiled sound and, in the orchestral music, an absolutely new kind of approach. Debussy's orchestration is subtle, resilient, and original. As in his piano music, he *heard* differently from other composers. He gives us a series of sense impressions; and even in *La Mer*, the closest he came to writing a symphony, there is a feeling of improvisation rather than development. Color, timbre, and rhythm take on an importance equal to harmony and melody. To many of today's younger generation, a score like *Jeux* of 1912 is more revolutionary than anything by Schoenberg or Stravinsky.

Of course, Debussy pondered his aesthetic a good many years before starting to produce his great sequence of works. He did not write anything really significant until he was past thirty. Ravel, thirteen years his junior, started producing around 1900 at twenty-five, and the careers of the two were parallel. By 1907 the Debussy and Ravel cliques were having at each other, and musical Paris rocked with the battle. Debussy, who usually stood aloof from public controversy, was disgusted. He met a friend in the street one day, and the man said something about being annoyed by the·Debussyists. "They annoy you?" said Debussy. "They are killing me."

When Debussy did start composing steadily, it was clear that his was not an abstract musical mind. He needed a trigger to set off a chain reaction, and it is significant that almost all of his works have names—*Printemps, Iberia, Children's Corner, Estampes, La Mer, Suite bergamasque, En blanc et noir*, and so on. Each of the twenty-four Préludes has a name, though the titles are placed *after* the music, not before. By doing this, Debussy clearly showed that he did not intend to write program music. He never tells a story. Rather he gives an impression—an impression of the sea, of moonlight, of goldfish, of Spain. He is the musical painter and epigrammatist *par excellence*. Even his most ambitious orchestral work, *La Mer*, is almost completely unprogrammatic, much less programmatic than Beethoven's *Pastoral Symphony* (which was also an "impression" of nature), for Beethoven has specific indications of bird calls, a thunderstorm, and a peasant's frolic. *La Mer*, on the other hand, is a series of tonal impressions in which one does not see waves but feels them, a series of impressions in which the images are implied rather than specific. "I have the greatest contempt for music that has to follow a bit of literature which they've been careful to hand out when you come in," Debussy once wrote.

It is interesting to note that in this great score the free impressionism of

156

Debussy is tempered with something like classic form. There are three movements that bear a passing resemblance to the classical symphony. When he died on March 25, 1918, in Paris, while it was being bombarded by the Germans, Debussy was turning to a new idea of classical form and was germinating six instrumental sonatas, of which three had been completed. The Sonata for Cello and the Sonata for Flute, Viola and Harp are infrequently played, but the Violin Sonata is often heard and it is a lovely work that looks back to the early String Quartet. It might have been that Debussy would have revolutionized classic form as much as he had revolutionized other aspects of music.

He was irritated with the term "impressionism," much as Schumann three generations before him had been irritated by the term "romanticism." When he composed *Images* he tried to explain his theories. "What I am trying to do is something different—an effect of reality, but what some fools call impressionism, a term that is usually misapplied, especially by the critics who don't hesitate to apply it to Turner, the greatest creator of mysterious effects in the whole world of art." But what it comes down to is a matter of semantics. Whatever it be called—impressionism, superreality, or what you will—Debussy worked as did the great poets or painters, heightening reality by giving a new aural picture of the world. From his exquisitely sharpened sensibilities came a new vocabulary. His was not the grand-thewed music of a Bach or Beethoven, and some of it is even precious. But in its taste, color, and fragrance there never has been anything like it. His work has a texture—transparent, glowing, vaguely modal, exotic, unerringly precise—that is one of the most original in music. So is his harmony original, with its hitherto unheard-of parallel chordal movement, unresolved dissonances, arbitrary scales, and a new grammar.

It is the beginning of the twentieth-century breakup of music. No longer was there a great structure assembled like a cathedral. No longer were there to be set rules by which this modulation or progression was allowed, that one not. Debussy did to tonal relationships what Monet and Cézanne did to traditional color relationships. *Pouf!* and out they went. Art and music became insinuation rather than rhetoric or illustration, the haiku rather than the sonnet. One magical, spiced chord was enough to set the mood. Why bother about unnecessary development? Debussy never forgot the remark of Verlaine that one must wring the neck of eloquence.

❧ I I ❧

Gallic Elegance and the New Breed

MAURICE RAVEL AND LES SIX

Claude Debussy and Maurice Ravel were to each other in France what Anton Bruckner and Gustav Mahler were to each other in Austria. Their careers overlapped, and they had certain things in common, representing much the same backgrounds and traditions. Debussy and Ravel are classified as impressionists—indeed, the only two impressionists of importance. But, as with Bruckner and Mahler, their differences were vaster than the things they had in common.

Where Debussy was a sensuous composer, in the line from Chopin to Gounod to Massenet, Ravel was much the more objective, a precisionist whose line runs from Liszt to Saint-Saëns to Fauré. Debussy's music floats on a cushion of air. Ravel's ticks away like a well-assembled chronometer— Stravinsky once called Ravel "a Swiss watchmaker." His music contains a great deal of artifice, and he was accused in his day of being artificial. "Has it ever occurred to them," he said of his detractors, "that one may be artificial by nature?" Ravel never minded being called artificial, but he very much minded being called imitative. Many critics in the first decade of the twentieth century wrote that Ravel copied Debussy. Ravel deeply resented the charge.

The relationship between the two greatest French musical figures at the beginning of the new century is a little clouded, and not much is known about it. Debussy and Ravel did not even correspond; no letter is known to have passed between them. Debussy, in letters to other people, had some snide remarks to make about his younger colleague. Ravel, much more temperate, had nothing but praise for Debussy throughout his life, though sometimes the praise had a curious cutting edge.

Ravel and Debussy probably met in 1901. At that time, Ravel, who had been born in Ciboure in the Basses-Pyrénées on March 7, 1875 (and thus thirteen years younger than Debussy), was still in the Paris Conservatoire, which he had entered in 1889. Although he had started to play the piano at the age of seven, Ravel was not a child prodigy, and he remained in the Conservatoire for sixteen years, an unusually long time. In 1898 he began to be performed, and in 1901 he composed his *Jeux d'eau*, which was published the following year. Debussy at that time had composed no piano music of any importance. In later life Ravel, politely but firmly, kept insisting he had priority; that if it was a matter of copying, Debussy had copied from *him*. Thus, in a letter to Pierre Lalo in 1906: "You propound at length on a rather special kind of piano writing, the invention of which you ascribe to Debussy. But *Jeux d'eau* appeared at the beginning of 1902, when the only known piano works of Debussy were the three pieces forming the suite *Pour le piano* which, I hardly need say, I deeply admire but which from a purely pianistic point of view conveyed nothing really new." And, as late as 1928, ten years after Debussy's death, Ravel was still desperately anxious to keep the record straight:

> For Debussy the musician and the man, I have had profound admiration, but by nature I am different from Debussy, and while I consider that Debussy may not have been altogether alien to my personal inheritance, I should identify also with the earliest phases of my evolution Gabriel Fauré, Emmanuel Chabrier and Erik Satie. . . . I believe that I myself have always followed a direction opposite to that of Debussy's symbolism. . . . It has been claimed with some insistence that the earlier appearance of my *Jeux d'eau* possibly influenced Debussy in the composition of his *Jardins sous la pluie,* while a coincidence even more striking has been suggested in the case of my *Habanera;* but comments of this sort I must leave to others. It could very well be, however, that conceptions apparently similar in character should mature in the consciousness of two different composers at almost the same time without implying direct influence of either one upon the other.

At the beginning, Debussy seems to have encouraged Ravel. He is said to have sent a letter to Ravel about the String Quartet of 1904: "In the name of the gods of music, and in my name, do not touch a single note." This sentence is quoted in many biographies of the two composers, but nobody has come up with the actual letter. Ravel's reputation grew very fast, and Louis Laloy, the French musicologist and critic, said in his memoirs that the friends of Debussy and Ravel took sides so furiously, that there were so many "silly meddlers," that after a while the two men simply stopped seeing each other. It was Romain Rolland's opinion that the coolness stemmed mostly from Debussy, "who has, I know, a violent antipathy for the music (or the success) of Ravel. Ravel speaks of him with great dignity and modesty." Debussy, who was terribly catty about almost all music but his own, had some nasty things to say about Ravel when Laloy reviewed Ravel's *Histoires naturelles* in 1907. Laloy wrote that the songs were in the spirit of Mussorgsky, only better. Debussy was furious and sent Laloy a note. He wrote that he was "amazed to see that a man of your taste deliberately sacrifices such a pure, instinctive masterpiece as *The Nursery* to the artificial Americanisms of the *Histoires naturelles* of M. Ravel. Despite Ravel's unquestioned skill, these songs consist of music that we must call unwarranted." Ravel, on the other hand, never ceased to admire Debussy's music, and in 1909–10 transcribed for two pianos the Nocturnes and *L'Après-midi d'un Faune.*

Ravel in 1910 was a famous man and had been so ever since 1905, when a scandal erupted over his failure to win the Prix de Rome. He had first competed in 1901. Amused by the stuffiness of the text to which he had to write a cantata, he submitted a manuscript largely in waltz time. The jury huffed and puffed. "M. Ravel should not think he can ridicule us. M. Ravel may well consider us flatfooted pedants, but he will not go unpunished for taking us for imbeciles." Ravel was awarded the second prize, and comforted himself with all the publicity he had received. He remained at the Conservatoire and competed again in 1902 and 1903, receiving no prize at all. When he applied for the Prix de Rome in 1905 he was not permitted to compete, on the grounds that he was over thirty. There was an immediate uproar from the press, and the case became a *cause célèbre.*

For Ravel was not merely a young, talented composer. He was far more than that. He had proved himself, and already was the most-discussed young composer in France. As early as 1895 he was in print with his *Menuet antique,* a short piano piece that already had the sophisticated precision of his mature style. His *Les Sites auriculaires* had been played at a concert of the Société Nationale in 1898. Ricardo Viñes, the Spanish pianist who had been a classmate of Ravel's at the Conservatoire and who eventually was to play the premieres of nearly all of Ravel's and Debussy's piano music, had introduced *Jeux d'eau* in 1902. In 1903 Ravel composed the fine song cycle *Shéhérazade,* and in 1904 the String Quartet in F. This was the composer who was not considered competent enough for the Prix de Rome in 1903, and who was not allowed to compete in 1905. There was indignation not only in musical circles, and the newspapers seized the story, siding with Ravel. For a few months Paris buzzed with the dispute. Ravel was interviewed by *Le Temps* and issued a dignified statement:

I am not going to Rome. This was decided by the institute, which is the only one with the power to open to young composers the road to the Villa Medici. This misfortune upsets me. The award of the second prize; my diligent work, encouraged and appreciated by my professor, M. Gabriel Fauré; my works, published and favorably received by the public, allowed me to hope, without any ridiculous presumption of writing a perfect cantata, or one superior to my comrades, that I would be permitted to join the competition. . . .

One result of *l'affaire Ravel* was the resignation of Théodore Dubois as director of the Conservatoire, and the appointment of Fauré in his stead. But none of this directly affected Ravel, who left the Conservatoire. From that point to the end of his life, he lived quietly as a composer. He was a tiny man, just about five feet tall, elegant, a natty dresser to the point of dandyism. "I would at any time rather have been Beau Brummel than Maurice Ravel," he once said. There was a good deal of gossip about him in his day. He claimed Basque ancestry through his mother, but nobody has been able to trace the family line far enough back to see if the claim had any validity. There were those who called Ravel a Jew. Again there is no proof, though it appears unlikely. It was whispered that he was a homosexual. Again there is no evidence one way or the other. He never married, and his name was never linked to a woman or a man.

For a long time he was a member of a group known as the "Apaches," along with the composer Florent Schmitt, the poet Tristan Klingsor, the pianist Viñes, the writer Léon-Paul Fargue, the critic Dimitri Calvocoressi, and others famous in French intellectual life. This was a French *Davidsbund*, and Schumann would have been delighted. Much of Ravel's music was first heard by the Apaches, and he listened very carefully to their criticisms. His Sonatine and the five *Miroirs* were composed in 1905; the Introduction and Allegro for harp, flute, clarinet, and string quartet was finished in 1906, the same year as the song cycle, *Histoires naturelles. Miroirs* puzzled the Apaches; and, indeed, only one of the set has achieved much popularity—*Alborado del Gracioso,* with its Spanish snappiness and brilliant piano layout. The other pieces—*Oiseaux tristes, Noctuelles, La Vallée des cloches,* and *Une Barque sur l'océan*—seemed to wander in a no-man's land between music and painting. Where *Miroirs* bored most listeners of the day, the *Histoires naturelles,* set to poems by Jules Renard, caused a scandal. Jane Bathori sang them early in 1907 at a Société Nationale concert, and it was a wild evening. The Debussyists screamed at the Ravelites, and vice versa. Newspapers referred to the concert and the commotion it created as the second *Affaire Ravel*. Lalo added to the fire with articles accusing Ravel of imitating Debussy without knowing what he was doing.

Ravel, after entering the dispute himself and writing a few letters to the newspapers, started work on a one-act comic opera, *L'Heure Espagnole*. He finished it in 1907 and then had to wait four years to see it on stage. Other major works up to the beginning of World War I included the three-movement *Gaspard de la Nuit* in 1908 and the *Valses nobles et sentimentales* in 1911 (both for solo piano), *Ma Mère l'Oye* in 1908 (piano duet), the *Rapsodie Espagnole* in 1907 (for orchestra), and the ballet *Daphnis et Chloë*. The ballet was composed for Diaghilev's Ballets Russes, receiving its premiere in 1912. Unlike Stravinsky's two blockbusters for Diaghilev—*Firebird* in 1910 and *Petrushka* in 1911—*Daphnis et Chloë* has never been a popular ballet. Its story is too static, its choreography by Vaslav Nijinsky is too awkward, and its Grecian poses do not go very well with Ravel's score. But the two orchestral suites arranged from the ballet immediately started to make the rounds, and the *Daphnis et Chloë* Suite No. 2 became one of the most popular orchestral works of the century. The ballet itself was soon withdrawn from the Ballets Russes repertoire. But Ravel's association with Diaghilev did result in one of the most spectacular orchestral scores of the twentieth century, and it also served to bring Ravel and Stravinsky together. The two composers admired each other and in 1913, even worked together on an orchestration of Mussorgsky's *Khovantchina* to be used for a ballet. Ravel and the Apaches all turned out for the premiere of Stravinsky's *Sacre du Printemps* on May 29, 1913, at the Champs-Elysées Théâtre, cheering their new champion.

The last work Ravel completed before the war was the fine Trio in A minor, one of his most polished and elegant scores (the opening theme of the first movement may well be his greatest lyric inspiration). Ravel tried to get into the army but was rejected. He was too short, and he was underweight. Finally, early in 1916, he was accepted as a truck driver and even got to the front lines. In 1917 he was transferred to Paris and discharged because of ill health. Among other symptoms, it was feared that he had developed tuberculosis. He went to Normandy to convalesce, and worked on *Le Tombeau de Couperin,* finishing both the piano solo version and its arrangement for orchestra in 1917. Then, back in Paris, he composed *La Valse* (1920), which he originally named *Wien. La Valse,* a "choreographic poem," was composed for Diaghilev, who paid for it but never used the music. Ravel was hurt. (The two men met in 1925, and Ravel refused to shake hands. Diaghilev was insulted and challenged Ravel to a duel. As customary, the challenger was talked out of it. They never met again.) He purchased a little villa, Le Belvédère, at Montfort l'Amaury and stocked it with a collection of mechanical toys, which he loved to wind up and operate for his friends. In 1920 he was awarded the Legion of Honor—and refused to accept it. He had not forgotten the way he had been finessed out of the Prix de Rome. Later, showing what he thought of the French government, he accepted a decoration from King Leopold of Belgium and an honorary doctorate from Oxford.

In the meantime, *Les Six* were coming into international attention. They were grouped around Erik Satie and represented an aesthetic that differed considerably from Ravel's. He showed them a thing or two in 1925 with his opera-pantomime, *L'Enfant et les sortilèges*, as sophisticated a work as any turned out by *Les Six*. There followed the *Chansons madécasses* (1926), a violin sonata (1927), a trip to the United States in 1928, the famous *Bolero* (1929), and two piano concertos (1931). One of those concertos, in D for the left hand alone, was commissioned by the Austrian pianist Paul Wittgenstein, who had lost his right arm during the war. The other was the more orthodox Concerto in G.

In 1932, perhaps as a result of an automobile accident, perhaps from a disease more deeply functional, Ravel had a nervous breakdown. His injuries from the crash appeared to be superficial, and Ravel made light of them: "a few cracks, an arched nose to persuade the Americans of my Hebrew origin, but particularly some bruises on my chest that force me to cough in a crooked way." The following year, 1933, he began to lose control of his arms and legs. This was followed by memory loss and an inability to coordinate. Though his mind remained normal, he could not compose or play the piano. In 1937 he underwent brain surgery, from which he never recovered. His malady has been kept secret. On December 28, 1937, Ravel died in a Paris hospital.

He left a small quantity of music, little of it large-scale. And a good deal of his orchestral music was originally composed for the piano. This includes *Ma Mère l'Oye*, the *Pavane pour une infante défunte*, *Alborado del Gracioso*, the third movement (*Habanera*) of the *Rapsodie espagnole*, *Le Tombeau de Couperin*, and the *Valses nobles et sentimentales*. One of his most popular pieces involves another piano work, his orchestration of Mussorgsky's *Pictures at an Exhibition*. The flashy *Tzigane* was originally composed in 1924 as a piece for violin and piano, and later that year transformed into one for violin and orchestra. All of this music is of a piece; there is very little variation in quality. From the very beginning, Ravel worked out an individual style, and it varied surprisingly little through the years. His early influences were Liszt, Chabrier, Mussorgsky, and Fauré and, of course, Debussy played a part in his development. No young composer growing up in Paris after *L'après-midi* could entirely escape those new sounds.

But in essence, Ravel's aesthetic worked on different premises from Debussy's. Ravel was more precise, and a more orthodox formalist, using sonata form and forms derived from classical and baroque models. His music, personal as it is, has a strong feeling of objectivity. Ravel's music never had the languorous sensuousness of Debussy's; it was an etching against the watercolors of his great contemporary. Debussy's forms were often evolved from colors and textures, and followed no known rules. Ravel worked from themes rather than colors and textures. Much more than Debussy he looked to his

predecessors, often writing pieces "in the manner of." His very first important work, *Jeux d'eau*, was a water piece inspired by Liszt's *Jeux d'eaux
à la Villa d'Este*. "It should be played the way you play Liszt," Ravel told
Viñes. Ravel never conceived of the piano, as Debussy did, as an instrument
without hammers. In *Gaspard de la Nuit* he specifically set out to write a
post-Lisztian virtuoso piece "to be more difficult than Balakirev's *Islamey*."
Scarbo, the last of the three pieces of *Gaspard de la Nuit*, is one of the
most prodigious finger-twisters of the repertory. It came into special favor
after World War II. The new generation of pianists loved it and made *Gaspard*
one of the most-performed of twentieth-century piano works.

Having been triggered by Liszt and Balakirev, Ravel next turned to
Schubert in his *Valses nobles et sentimentales*. "The title. . . . shows
clearly enough my intention to compose a chain of waltzes in the style of
Schubert [who had composed a series named *Valses Nobles*]. In the place
of the virtuosity that characterized *Gaspard de la Nuit*, there was a style
clearer, brighter, that emphasized the harmonies and brought them into re-
lief." The *Valses nobles et sentimentales* ended up as French as Schubert is
Viennese. The idea may come from Schubert, but the execution is perfumed
French, especially the last of the waltzes, which in a dreamlike manner rem-
inisces about the previous waltzes. Schubert was not the only Austrian
composer who prompted a Ravel work. There also were Johann Strauss and
Mozart. *La Valse* stems from the former, the Piano Concerto in G from the
latter. Ravel described *La Valse* as "a sort of homage to the memory of the
Great Strauss, not Richard, the other—Johann. You know my intense sympathy for this admirable rhythm, and that I hold *la joie de vivre* as expressed by the dance in far higher esteem than as expressed by the Franckist
puritanism. I am so little a Catholic." As for the G major Concerto, Ravel
claimed that it was "a concerto in the truest sense of the word, very much in
the same spirit as those of Mozart and Saint-Saëns. The music of a concerto
should, in my opinion, be light-hearted, brilliant and not aim at profundity
or at dramatic effects." Ravel makes it clear that he does not like the piano
concertos of Brahms; he said that they are against the piano, not for it.

The restless, inquisitive Ravel looked elsewhere for other works. He went
back to the clavecinists for *Le Tombeau de Couperin*. In the United States
he met George Gershwin, listened to a great deal of jazz, and incorporated
it, with other American devices, into his music. He said that he had tried to
compose *L'Enfant et les sortilèges* "in the style of an American operetta."
The slow movement of his Violin Sonata is named *Blues*, and there is some
jazz in his G major Concerto. For the *Rapsodie espagnole* and *L'Heure espagnole* he turned to Spain, as so many French composers before him had
done.

His prime period ended in 1914. Later, in ill health, he found it harder and harder to write. It bothered him. "I have failed in my life," he told the composer Claude Delvincourt. "I am not one of the great composers. All the great have produced enormously. There is everything in their work—the best and the worst, but there is always quantity. But I have written relatively very little . . . and at that, I did it with a great deal of difficulty. I did my work slowly, drop by drop. I have torn all of it out of me by pieces . . . . and now I cannot do any more, and it does not give me any pleasure." Nevertheless he went on during the following twelve years to compose some fine music that shows no diminution in his powers. Some critics maintain that the Piano Concerto for the Left Hand, one of his last works, is one of the most exciting and significant he ever composed.

All of this music, no matter what its inspiration (Liszt, Schubert, or Spain), ends up filtered through Ravel's imagination and technique into a consistent amalgam. It all has the Ravel sound. He was a musician pure and simple, working directly with the materials of music, and, unlike so many of the composers of the period, he had no theories about music, nor did he involve himself with the various aesthetic movements. There seldom is the feeling of instinct in his music; everything is too carefully arranged and balanced. It is even, in a way, a reticent music, in that Ravel seldom bared his emotions. Some critics have complained that Ravel was too detached, and he most definitely *was* detached. But with this objectivity, the music also has charm, extraordinary finish, wit (as in the *Histoires naturelles*), and color. As an orchestrator he was even more inventive than Debussy, from whom he learned a great deal. Compare Ravel's *Rapsodie espagnole* with Debussy's *Iberia*, two great scores inspired by Spain, and composed within a year of each other—1907 and 1908 respectively. The Ravel orchestration has a springier, lither quality.

Ravel was not a creator on the mighty level of a Debussy. His mind worked along somewhat more conventional paths, and he was just a shade too conscious of his own style. But in his range he worked with surety and perfection, and his music has dated very little.

It has dated far less than the music of most of the members of *Les Six*, the darlings of Paris in the 1920's, the youngsters who were really "modern," who were going to lead French music into new paths. The genesis of *Les Six* goes back to 1917, when Diaghilev staged *Parade*, with music by Erik Satie, book by Jean Cocteau, décor by Pablo Picasso. *Parade* created one of those scandals so dear to the hearts of the French public. A group of young composers, vociferous in their admiration of the score, gathered around Satie. These youngsters, whom Satie called his *nouveaux jeunes*, were the Swiss-born Arthur Honegger, Georges Auric, Louis Durey, and Germaine Tailleferre. A year later, Francis Poulenc and Darius Milhaud joined the *nouveaux jeunes*. "We were tired of Debussyism, of Florent Schmitt, of

Ravel," Poulenc wrote. "I wanted music to be clear, healthy and robust—music as frankly French in spirit as Stravinsky's *Petrushka* is Russian. To me, Satie's *Parade* is to Paris what *Petrushka* is to St. Petersburg." Under this aesthetic, the young composers joined forces. Milhaud has described how *Les Six* became consolidated:

> After a concert at the Salle Huyghens [in 1919], at which Bertin sang Louis Durey's *Images à Crusoë* on words by Saint-Léger and the Capelle Quartet played my Fourth Quartet, the critic Henri Collet published in *Comoedia* a chronicle entitled "Five Russians and the Frenchmen." Quite arbitrarily he had chosen six names: Auric, Durey, Honegger, Poulenc, Tailleferre and my own, merely because we knew each other, were good friends and had figured on the same programs: quite apart from our different temperaments and wholly dissimilar characters. Auric and Poulenc were followers of Cocteau, Honegger derived from the German romantics, and I from Mediterranean lyricism. . . . But it was useless to protest. Collet's article excited such worldwide interest that the "Group of Six" was launched, and willy-nilly I formed part of it.
>
> This being so, we decided to give some *Concerts des Six*. The first was devoted to my works, the second to foreign music. . . . Satie was our mascot. He was very popular among us. He was so fond of young people that he said to me one day: "I wish I knew what sort of music will be written by the children who are four years old now." The purity of his art, his horror of all concessions, his contempt for money and his ruthless attitude toward the critics were a marvellous example for us all.

Cocteau became the intellectual leader of Les Six, much as Satie was its spiritual leader. Stravinsky was the third guru, but only as an influence. *Les Six* admired his music more than the music of any other living composer. To them, Debussy was "dead," and Ravel's music was "arty," "excessively refined," "outworn." Music in general, they said, was sterile, living on formulae of the old masters. Intermarriage and fresh blood were needed: the intermarriage of "serious" music with jazz, popular music, vaudeville, music hall, the circus, commercial music. To be lowbrow was to be highbrow. One had to thumb one's nose at tradition. One did not write symphonies. Instead one wrote foxtrots, satires, burlesques, caricatures, short pieces, dance music. It was the Jazz Age: a merry period that produced some merry works, most of which are now forgotten.

Durey and Tailleferre soon dropped from sight, and Auric never produced anything of much value. The one who first came to international attention was Darius Milhaud (born on September 4, 1892). Honegger was slow developing, and the facile Poulenc was regarded as a clown. Milhaud attracted a great deal of attention in the early 1920's, especially for his polytonal experiments. Stravinsky had started things off with the famous F sharp major against C major episode in *Petrushka*. Milhaud took it from there, developing the concept. "I set to work to examine every possible combination of two keys superimposed and to study the chords thus produced. . . . Then I did the same thing in three keys. What I could not understand was why, though the harmony books dealt with chords and their inversions and the laws governing their sequence, the same thing could not be done for polytonality. I grew familiar with some of these chords. They satisfied my ear more than the normal ones, for a polytonal chord is more subtly sweet and more violently potent."

Milhaud, incredibly fluent and industrious, applied his polytonal theories to every type of music, and his scores—*La Création du monde* (1923), *Le Boeuf sur le toit* (1919), *Les Choëphores* (1919), the so-called "minute operas"—were the last word in chic avant-gardism of the 1920's. They were spicy, they were clever, they were sophisticated, they were dissonant, they shocked the bourgeoisie. Endlessly inventive, Milhaud came up with effect after effect. But eventually the shock value and novelty wore off. Today the Milhaud scores of the 1920's and 1930's tend to sound like Stravinsky pressed through a filter made in Paris. Very little of Milhaud's music remains in the permanent repertory.

Arthur Honegger (March 10, 1892–November 28, 1955) became allied to *Les Six* despite pronounced differences in style and outlook. He was close to the Central European tradition, and he wrote in a busy, angry-man, tightly compressed kind of way. There is very little humor in his music, and that alone almost immediately separated him from *Les Six*. Another point of difference was his penchant for working in sonata form: five symphonies, three string quartets, and the like. In the early 1920's he became famous for an age-of-steel tone poem, *Pacific 2-3-1* (1923). That has long since disappeared from concert programs. His large-scale choral works—*Le Roi David* (1921) and *Jeanne d'Arc au bûcher* (1938)—attracted a good deal of interest in their day and are still occasionally heard. But on the whole Honegger has slid from his once-high position, and his music is vanishing fast from the halls.

It seems clear that Francis Poulenc (January 7, 1889–January 30, 1963) has emerged as the strongest and most individual member of Les Six. Nobody would have guessed it in the 1930's. The betting would have been on Milhaud or Honegger. Poulenc was considered the comic (he even had a marked facial and physical resemblance to the great French comic Fernandel), the court jester, the sophisticate. So charming and amusing! So lightweight! So chic! As a corollary, so unimportant, *au fond!* To the world Poulenc was the musical soft-shoe man, dancing away at his music-hall routines with not a care in the world, a grin permanently plastered on his face.

As it turned out, neither Milhaud nor Honegger had much staying power. Poulenc was the one who kept growing. From the *enfant terrible* of *Les Six* he developed into a skilled composer whose outlook and technique developed with the years. And even from the beginning it was apparent that Poulenc was a fine composer of songs. He developed into a great one. Some insist he was the greatest since Fauré, and that includes Debussy. He had style; he had taste; his ear for the accent of the word, for the patterns of prosody and its relationship with the note, was unparalleled. Above all, he had a fresh and original fount of melody. As a melodist, Poulenc was more than a mere entertainer. He had a distinguished gift. Never a composer comfortable with large structures until near the end of his life, Poulenc found the lyric forms—songs, piano pieces—best suited to his intense but narrow talent. Poulenc's songs soon became firmly established in the repertoire, and they promise to be a permanent fixture.

A great deal of his other music also seems to have become fixed in the repertoire. Perhaps this is because of the basic conservatism of his idiom. True, it is smart and undeniably modern, what with its constant references to Stravinsky's neoclassicism, its titillating dissonances, and unexpected harmonic darts. One of Poulenc's favorite devices, to the point of mannerism, was his use of unprepared modulations a half step down. It is his fingerprint, found in virtually every piece he composed. But Poulenc was conservative in that he never lost contact with the past—with Schumann, and Fauré, and Chabrier, and the mainstream of nineteenth-century harmony. Despite his flirtations with polytonality and other then-advanced devices, Poulenc thought tonally and composed tonally. As often as not he composed in triadic, tonic-dominant harmony. That is one reason the 1920's and 1930's refused to take him very seriously. Those were the great days of "modernism," and modernism was equated with dissonance (or what was considered dissonant in those days; ears have since been stretched). It had to follow that anybody bucking the trend and, in effect, composing "white-key music," could not conceivably be accepted as an important creator.

But Poulenc went his own way and had the last laugh in the long run, for he outlived certain revered twentieth-century figures just as Berlioz outlived Meyerbeer, Offenbach outlived Halévy, Sullivan outlived Stanford, and Fauré outlived d'Indy. Poulenc's talent might have been restricted, and nobody ever claimed that he was a universal composer in the sense that Beethoven and Mozart were; but at the same time there was something genuine, something very valuable, about his talent. He had something to say, and he said it with style and personality.

At the beginning of his career, from the end of World War I to the early 1930's, he wrote flip, fashionable, brittle, but jewel-like music. The *Aubade* for small orchestra, the ballet *Les Biches,* the *Mouvements perpetuels* for piano, *Le Bal masqué,* a series of songs including the cycle *Le Bestiaire*—all these were the work of a brash, talented young man with a propensity for teasing his elders and poking fun at the verities. So clever is this music that even today it continues to charm. A little later came more substantial works like the Mass in G (1937) and the Organ Concerto (1938), less flip, trying for more serious things. A superb series of song collections date from this period, including *Banalités, Chansons villageoises, Tel jour, telle nuit, Caligrammes.* During World War II Poulenc composed an opera named *Les Mamelles de Tirésias.* This was a throwback to his tomfoolery days. As such, it was exceptional, but it also turned out to be a neo-Offenbachian romp, naughty and delicious. During the last twenty years of his life he seldom worked this vein. There was a broadening-out, a new dimension, an emphasis on religious music. These religious works culminated in the simple and beautiful Gloria (1961), and in the opera *Les Dialogues des Carmélites* (1957).

The opera is, like most of his music, intimate. Poulenc was never one for the big gesture. Indeed, in a curious way, *Carmélites* recalls such earlier and light-hearted works as *Les Biches* and *Aubade,* in that Poulenc's melodic habits changed very little through the years. He had his little tricks and was constantly repeating them. But toward the end, his short-breathed, delicate melodies were put to new uses, intensified, made to express something more than easy badinage. In the first dialogue between Blanche and Constance in the *Carmélites,* the exquisite, tiny theme (almost a motto) that comes up whenever death is mentioned is startling in its emotional impact, its focus of concentration. But it happens to be first cousin to a theme that can be found in the salonlike Sextet of 1940, and later in the Gloria of 1961. In each case the theme has an entirely different emotional meaning.

Many musicians still refuse to take Poulenc seriously. Part of the trouble stems from our musical phylogeny, so closely imbred to Germanic ideas about form, structure, and "sublimity." Poulenc did not compose orthodox, completely developed sonatas and symphonies; he had little truck with fugue and canon; he specialized in pretty songs and sophisticated piano pieces. *Ergo,* he must have written *Kitsch.* But this kind of *Kitsch,* as represented in Poulenc's vocal music, will live as long as there are singers around to sing songs.

❦ 12 ❧

The Chameleon

IGOR STRAVINSKY

Igor Stravinsky, born on June 17, 1882 in St. Petersburg, lived to be universally recognized as the world's greatest living composer. He all but started out at the top. There was no doubt of his stature after the three Russian ballets he wrote for Serge Diaghilev between 1910 and 1913 in Paris. *Firebird,* which had its premiere on June 25, 1910, was the first, and it made the twenty-eight-year-old composer famous overnight, as Diaghilev had predicted the day before the performance. The score was a brilliant exercise in Russian nationalism, derived from Rimsky-Korsakov in general and Rimsky's *Coq d'Or* in particular. But it was far more daring and original than any work by Rimsky, and everybody knew that an unusual composer had arrived. Debussy's keen ears picked out the essential quality of *Firebird:* "It is not a perfect piece, but from certain aspects it is nevertheless very fine, for here the music is not the docile servant of the dance. And at times you hear altogether unusual combinations of rhythms." On June 13, 1911, came *Petrushka,* and it solidified Stravinsky's position as the coming man of European music. Like *Firebird, Petrushka* was a ballet on a Russian subject, but it moved with more confidence and mastery, and it had some ideas that were to affect the course of European music, especially its polytonality. There was one section in which two unrelated harmonies, C major and F sharp major, joined forces, and the effect came as a revelation to young European composers. For the next two decades there were numerous polytonal experiments stemming from *Petrushka.* To listeners of 1911, the Stravinsky ballet had a barbarous quality eclipsing anything that had come out of Russia before, and the tiny composer took on the dimensions of a giant. Even Diaghilev had not expected the fuss raised by *Petrushka.* Its great success was a surprise.

But all the excitement was nothing against the impact of *Le Sacre du Printemps,* which had its premiere on May 29, 1913. Stravinsky had conceived the idea for it while working on *Firebird*. "I dreamed of a scene of pagan ritual in which a chosen sacrificial virgin danced herself to death." Work on *Le Sacre* was dropped for *Petrushka*, but Stravinsky soon resumed work on the new ballet. (He has said that *The Coronation of Spring* would be closer to his original meaning than the usual translation, *The Rite of Spring*.) Vaslav Nijinsky was the choreographer, and the premiere resulted in the most famous *scandale* in the history of music. Hardly anybody in the audience was prepared for a score of such dissonance and ferocity, such complexity and such rhythmic oddity. Nobody connected with the production had the faintest idea that the music would provoke a visceral reaction. As soon as the bassoon ended its phrase in the high register, at the very opening of the ballet, laughter broke out. Soon there were whistles and catcalls. Nobody could hear the music. Diaghilev had the electricians switch the house lights off and on, in an effort to restore order. Nijinsky, in the wings, yelled the rhythms to the dancers. The Comtesse de Pourtalès stood in her box, brandishing her fan, and shouted: "This is the first time in sixty years that anybody has dared make fun of me." People hurled insults at each other. The Apaches, headed by Ravel, shrieked their praise. Stravinsky himself, in his *Expositions and Developments*, has described the famous evening at the Théâtre des Champs-Elysées:

That the first performance of *Le Sacre du Printemps* was attended by a scandal must be known to everybody. Strange as it may seem, however, I was unprepared for the explosion myself. The reactions of the musicians who came to the orchestra rehearsals were without intimation of it, and the stage spectacle did not appear likely to precipitate a riot. The dancers had been rehearsing for months and they knew what they were doing, even though what they were doing often had nothing to do with the music. . . . Mild protests against the music could be heard from the very beginning of the performance. Then, when the curtain opened on the group of knock-kneed and long-braided Lolitas jumping up and down (*Danse des adolescents*), the storm broke. Cries of "*Ta gueule*" came from behind me. I heard Florent Schmitt shout "*Taisez-vouz garces du seizième;*" the "*garces*" of the sixteenth arondissement were, of course, the most elegant ladies in Paris. The uproar continued, however, and a few minutes later I left the hall in a rage; I was sitting on the right near the orchestra, and I remember slamming the door. I have never again been that angry. The music was familiar to me; I loved it, and I could not understand why people who had not yet heard it wanted to protest in advance. I arrived in a fury backstage, where I saw Diaghilev flicking the house lights in a last effort to quiet the hall. For the rest of the performance I stood in the wings behind Nijinsky holding the tails of his *frac* while he stood on a chair shouting numbers to the dancers like a coxswain.

Le Sacre du Printemps hit Europe with unprecedented force. It was to the first half of the twentieth century what the Beethoven Ninth and *Tristan* were to the nineteenth. For decades there were repercussions as composers all over the world imitated the new Stravinsky rhythms and sonorities. In Prokofiev's *Scythian* Suite, in Bartók's *Miraculous Mandarin*, in the Milhaud "minute operas," in music everywhere one could hear *Sacre* rhythms. They entered the musical subconscious of every young composer. *Le Sacre du Printemps*, with its metrical shiftings and shattering force, its near-total dissonance and breakaway from established canons of harmony and melody, was a genuine explosion. After the score had its premiere in Boston, a poem appeared in the *Herald* that was widely reprinted. It presented a prevailing audience attitude toward the Stravinsky work:

> Who wrote this fiendish *Rite of Spring*,
> What right had he to write the thing,
> Against our helpless ears to fling
> Its crash, clash, cling, clang, bing, bang, bing?
>
> And then to call it *Rite of Spring*
> The season when on joyous wing
> The birds harmonious carols sing
> And harmony's in everything!
>
> He who could write the *Rite of Spring*
> If I be right, by right should swing!

Stravinsky became the new apostle of modernism, replacing the fading Richard Strauss. Stravinsky was being discussed much more even than Debussy. The French composer was jealous, and wrote of Stravinsky in a nasty way not to be surpassed until Stravinsky himself in the latter part of his life started writing about musicians in his series of books with Robert Craft as collaborator. Debussy and Stravinsky met and socialized, and it was to Debussy that Stravinsky bore the completed *Sacre* in a four-hand version. He and Debussy played it through (Debussy was a fabulous sight reader), and Debussy went to all of the *Sacre* rehearsals. Obviously he respected Stravinsky. He also may have noted in the *Sacre* some of his own music, as Stravinsky pointed out in his *Expositions and Developments* of 1962: ". . . *Le Sacre* owes more to Debussy than to anyone except myself, the best music (the Prelude) as well as the weakest (the music of the second part between the first entrance of the two solo trumpets and the *Glorification de l'Élue*)." The opening of the *Sacre*—the famous bassoon solo—is not far distant from the theme that opens *L'après-midi d'un faune*. Yet there was tension between Debussy and Stravinsky, as indicated in the curious letter, one that mixes pettiness with grudging praise, that Debussy wrote to Robert Godet in 1916:

> I have recently seen Stravinsky. He says, my *Oiseau de Feu*, my *Sacre*, just as a child says "My toy, my hoop." And that is exactly what he is—a spoiled child who sometimes cocks a snook at music. He is also a young barbarian who wears flashy ties and treads on women's toes as he kisses their hands. When he is old he will be unbearable, that is to say, he will admit no other music, but for the moment he is unbelievable. He professes a friendship for me because I have helped him to mount a rung of the ladder from which he launches his squibs, not all of which explode. But once again, he is unbelievable. You have really understood him and, even better than I, have been able to understand the unrelenting workings of his mind.

In St. Petersburg, it is safe to say, nobody would have guessed that Stravinsky would have developed into the *enfant terrible* of music. As a child, he showed some talent, but certainly not of a spectacular order; nor did his early compositions hint at the musical revolution to come. But from the beginning he was exposed to music. His father, who died in 1902, was a bass singer at the St. Petersburg Opera, and musicians from Russia and abroad were constantly visiting the house. Thus Igor heard a great deal of music, and had piano lessons, but until the age of twenty-three was a law student at the University. About 1900, while still a student, he was introduced to Rimsky-Korsakov, showed him some of his attempts at composition, and was taken on as a private pupil in 1903. The lessons continued until Rimsky's death in 1908. One of the results, finished in 1907, was a grand Symphony in E flat, a richly scored, traditional work that any diligent student could have produced. It contains nothing of the Stravinsky sound or the Stravinsky style. On the whole it is an essay in the sterile academism of Alexander Glazunov.

In 1908, Stravinsky composed an orchestral work named *Fireworks*, which brought him to the attention of Serge Diaghilev, who had a genius for spotting talent. The history of music in the first quarter of the twentieth century would be considerably poorer without his presence. An intellectual, a man who thought big, an impresario willing to gamble, a man vitally interested in all of the arts, Diaghilev became active in Paris, where in 1906 he sponsored a show of Russian art. The following year he presented five concerts of Russian music at the Opéra, and followed that in 1908 with a staged performance of *Boris Godunov* with Feodor Chaliapin in the title role. In 1909, Diaghilev introduced Paris to Russian ballet, and the success was such that he organized the Ballets Russes as a permanent organization. From this company stemmed some of the great works of the century. Diaghilev made the Ballets Russes a center of the avant-garde. Debussy, Falla, Stravinsky, Prokofiev, Ravel—the greatest and most progressive composers of the day wrote for it. Picasso, Bakst, and other great artists were called in for scenery and costumes. The dancers of the company, headed by Nijinsky and Karsavina, were a legend. This was a company with style, glamour, *goût*, and imagination; and it all revolved around the figure of the saturnine, powerful, and aristocratic Serge Diaghilev.

For his 1910 season, Diaghilev wanted a Russian ballet to a scenario on the Firebird legend to be choreographed by Michel Fokine. Anatol Liadov was approached and accepted the assignment to compose the music. He delayed and delayed. In desperation Diaghilev, remembering the impression that Stravinsky's *Fireworks* had made on him, turned to the young composer. Stravinsky whipped out the score in short order and went to Paris to be present at the rehearsals. *Firebird*, to Stravinsky's eternal disgust, turned out to be the most popular work he ever composed. He went on to create greater works, but it is *Firebird* in its orchestral suite (the full-length ballet is seldom performed) that still leads all Stravinsky works in number of annual performances.

The first three Stravinsky ballets are examples of Russian nationalism. After them, Stravinsky proceeded to an entirely different kind of music, turning from superscores with superorchestras to scores for small groups and a pointed, precise way of writing. From these came the neoclassic works. Transitional compositions between Stravinsky's nationalism and neoclassicism were *L'Histoire du Soldat* (1918), the ballet *Renard* (1922), the one-act opera *Mavra* (1922), the *Symphonies of Wind Instruments* (1921), and the cantata *Les Noces* (1923). All of these still have nationalistic elements, but the forces employed were small, and the workmanship heading in a new direction. For *L'Histoire du Soldat*, Stravinsky used a tiny orchestra that had analogies to a jazz group; for *Les Noces*, the dance cantata on the subject of a Russian wedding, a percussion orchestra and four pianos. *Les Noces* has some of the primitive, earthy, Russian feeling of *Sacre*, and something of its rhythmic impact; but *L'Histoire*, a dance pantomime based on a Russian fairy tale about a soldier and the devil, points to something altogether new—a stylized treatment of various musical forms with a completely different rhythmic and textural organization. Everything is in miniature—a miniature waltz and tango, a miniature chorale, a miniature march. Jazz played a part. "My knowledge of jazz," Stravinsky wrote in 1962, "was derived exclusively from copies of sheet music, and as I had never actually heard any of the music performed, I borrowed its rhythmic style not as played but as written. I *could* imagine jazz sound, however, or so I like to think. Jazz meant, in any case, a wholly new sound in my music, and

174

L'Histoire marks my final break with the Russian orchestral school in which I had been fostered."

Those who complained of the complexity of *Le Sacre du Printemps* could not have found much to object to in *L'Histoire*, with its clean sound and modesty of means. This work, and the *Symphonies of Wind Instruments*, led to the Octet of 1923, in which Stravinsky for the first time since his E flat Symphony worked in sonata form. Stravinsky was launched on neoclassicism: historical manner expressed in contemporary language. The clear forms of the baroque and classic appealed to Stravinsky's logical mind, and the following years saw a series of works—the Piano Concerto (1924), *Oedipus Rex* (1927), the Capriccio for Piano and Orchestra (1929), the *Symphony of Psalms* (1930), the Violin Concerto (1931), the *Duo Concertante* (1932), the Symphony in C (1940), the Symphony in Three Movements (1945)—in which old forms were revitalized and transformed in the alchemy of Stravinsky's workshop. The forms were old; the treatment and modification of the forms were ultramodern. There also were works in which Stravinsky arranged music of other composers—Pergolesi, in the ballet *Pulcinella* (1919); and Tchaikovsky, in another ballet, *Le Baiser de la Fée* (1928). Whatever the source of the music, it had the typical lean sound, idiosyncratic orchestral spacings, spiky dissonances, and asymmetrical rhythms that represented Igor Stravinsky.

As early as 1921 Stravinsky, in the *Symphonies of Wind Instruments* (the term "symphonies" is used in the sense of instruments sounding together and has nothing to do with sonata form), predicted that he was embarked on a type of music that would not be as popular as the early ballets. He said of the *Symphonies* in his autobiography (1935) that "It lacks all those elements that infallibly appeal to the ordinary listener, or to which he is accustomed. It is futile to look in it for passionate impulse or dynamic brilliance. . . . The music is not meant to 'please' an audience, nor to arouse its passions. Nevertheless, I had hoped that it would appeal to some of those persons in whom a purely musical receptivity outweighed the desire to satisfy their sentimental cravings."

These words could stand as a summary of what all of Stravinsky's post-*Sacre* music represents. He was correct in his feeling that audiences would have trouble identifying with such antiromantic, antisentimental writing. Many of his admirers were disconcerted. Stravinsky's neoclassicism was taken up by some composers, and elements of his language entered the thinking of all composers, but his music after 1920 never caused the upheaval that his Russian ballets had caused. The new works were considered cosmopolitan and generally abstract, just as Stravinsky himself was a cosmopolitan, a Russian expatriate living mostly in Switzerland from 1914 to 1920, in France from 1920 to 1939 (he became a French citizen in 1934), and in the United States from 1939 (he became an American citizen in 1945). Certainly the public did not especially care for the majority of Stravinsky's neoclassic scores, a fact of which he was well aware. As he noted in the autobiography:

> At the beginning of my career as a composer I was a good deal spoiled by the public. . . . But I have a very distinct feeling that in the course of the last fifteen years my written work has estranged me from the great mass of my listeners. . . . Liking the music of *Firebird*, *Petrushka*, *The Rite of Spring* and *The Wedding*, and being accustomed to the language of those works, they are astonished to hear me speaking in another idiom. They cannot and will not follow me in the progress of my musical thought. What moves and delights me leaves them indifferent, and what still continues to interest them holds no further attraction for me.

What Stravinsky represented, among many other things, was a complete rupture with romanticism. Everything about the man and his music was antiromantic. In the 1930's there was a great stir when Stravinsky said that it was not music's job to "express" anything. For years those remarks were hurled back at him by the traditionalists. What he had meant was that music by its very nature cannot express anything but music. "Composers combine notes. That is all." It was a neo-Hanslickian notion. Hanslick, in his treatise *The Beautiful in Music*, had based his entire argument on the theory that music was a completely abstract art, incapable of painting pictures or conveying anything except broad emotions. His, and Stravinsky's, remarks are probably accurate, though aestheticians have devoted much study to the meaning of meaning in music, and have never been able to arrive at a satisfactory answer. Stravinsky was never reticent about his belief that music is primarily form and logic. His antiromanticism extended to fierce attacks on performers and conductors who overinterpreted his music. This sort of thing irritated Stravinsky as much as did most romantic music. His main interest continued to be in structure, in texture, in balance, in rhythm. His music is the work of one of the supreme logicians.

Everything about Stravinsky pointed to an intellectual tidiness, and that included his work habits. Those were tidy to the point of compulsion. In 1916, the Swiss writer C. F. Ramuz, who was working with Stravinsky on *L'Histoire du Soldat*, looked at Stravinsky's work table and marveled:

> Stravinsky's scores are magnificent. He is above all (in all matters and in every sense of the word) a calligrapher. . . . His writing desk resembled a surgeon's instrument case. Bottles of different colored inks in their ordered hierarchy each had a separate part to play in the ordering of his art. Near at hand were india-rubbers of various kinds and shapes, and all

sorts of glittering steel implements: rulers, erasers, pen-knives, and a roulette instrument for drawing staves, invented by Stravinsky himself. One was reminded of the definition of St. Thomas: beauty is the splendor of order. All the large pages of the score were filled with writing in different colored inks—blue, green, red, two kinds of black (ordinary and Chinese), each having its purpose, its meaning, its special use: one for the notes, another the text, a third the translation; one for titles, another for the musical directions. Meanwhile the bar lines were ruled, and the mistakes carefully erased.

(Thirty years later, nothing had changed. Nicolas Nabokov visited Stravinsky in Los Angeles. "I believe," he noted, "Stravinsky has in his study all the instruments needed for writing, copying, drawing, pasting, cutting, clipping, filing, sharpening, and gluing, that the combined effects of a stationery and hardware store can furnish." Life in the Stravinsky workshop continued to revolve around the piano. "The piano itself is the center of my musical discoveries," Stravinsky has written. "Each note that I write is tried on it, and every relationship of notes is taken apart and heard on it again and again.")

After his early successes in Paris, Stravinsky was constantly on the move. Up to the beginning of World War I he was resident in Russia, France, and Switzerland. The war years he spent in Switzerland, remaining there until 1920. Because of the 1917 Revolution in Russia, he did not return there (and he stayed away permanently until a visit in 1962). From 1920 to 1939 he lived in France, making concert tours through Europe and the United States. World War II sent him to the United States for good, and he settled in Hollywood.

In the United States, Stravinsky entered on a fruitful relationship with the Russian-born choreographer George Balanchine, with whom he had previously worked in Europe. There were the ballets *Jeu de cartes* (1936; originally choreographed by Stravinsky himself in collaboration with M. Malaïev), *Danses Concertantes* (1942), *Orpheus* (1948), *Agon* (1957), *Movements* (1958), and others. Several scores, including the *Danses Concertantes* and *Movements,* were not originally composed as ballets, but in Balanchine's choreographic realizations they achieved a popularity denied them in the concert hall. There also was one bizarre Stravinsky-Balanchine collaboration, composed in 1942 for the Barnum and Bailey Circus. The dancers in Stravinsky's *Circus Polka* were elephants, and the event was advertised as "a choreographic tour de force," a description against which few would argue. Collaboration with W. H. Auden and Chester Kallman resulted in a large-scale opera, *The Rake's Progress.* Friendship with the young American conductor, Robert Craft, resulted in a switch to serial composition and also a series of tart books in which Stravinsky had his

177

say about everything from the genesis of everything he composed to his opinions of other composers and his observations on life. Stravinsky-Craft pulled no punches, and musicians approached the books, when published, as though a live hand grenade were under the covers. Some eminent music critics had special cause to shudder. These books provide an unusual look into a major composer's mind.

Until the end of World War II, Stravinsky was the symbol of progressiveness in music. Prokofiev, Bartók, Schoenberg, and Webern were still active, but to the public Stravinsky represented modernism in music. By and large, musicians were content to accept Stravinsky as the leader of the avant-garde. But with the rise of the serial movement and the emergence of an articulate group wedded to the ideas of Schoenberg and the serial school, Stravinsky for the first time came under attack by young composers and critics. His entire post-*Noces* body of work was questioned, especially by the polemicists of the school of Paris. André Hodeir and Pierre Boulez led the charge. They took the attitude that Stravinsky's aesthetic was invalid, that his scores, a case of "accelerated exhaustion," represented "a sclerosis of all realms: harmonic and melodic, in which one arrives at a faked academism; and even rhythmic, in which one sees a painful atrophy produced." Those words came from Boulez, who insisted that Stravinsky's neoclassicism was retrogressive rather than forward-looking. "Incapable by himself of reaching the coherence of a language other than the tonal one, Stravinsky dropped the unwisely-attempted struggle and began to employ his expedients—which became arbitrary and gratuitous gestures intended to delight the already perverted ear." Boulez charged Stravinsky—*Stravinsky!*—with "intellectual laziness, pleasure taken as an end in itself."

It was not long after these attacks that Stravinsky dipped partially into the waters of serialism and eventually took the plunge. Nothing in his career caused more gossip in musical circles than his entry into serial writing, into the world of Schoenberg and Webern. Stravinsky and Schoenberg had never been close, and Schoenberg had no great liking for Stravinsky's music. At least, Schoenberg wrote a satire about Stravinsky and his neoclassicism in 1926, and even set it to music:

> Ja, wer trommelt denn da?
> Das ist ja der kleine Modernsky!
> Hat sich ein Bubikopf schneiden lassen;
> sieht ganz gut aus!
> Wie echt falsches Haar!
> Wie eine Perücke!
> Ganz (wie sich ihn der kleine Modernsky vorstellt),
> ganz der Papa Bach!

Which Eric Walter White, in his biography of Stravinsky, translates as:

> But who's this beating the drum?
> It's little Modernsky!
> He's had his hair cut in an old-fashioned queue,
> And it looks quite nice,
> Like real false hair—
> Like a wig—
> Just like (at least little Modernsky thinks so)
> Just like Father Bach!

In Europe, Stravinsky and Schoenberg met a few times, but never after 1912. Stravinsky heard *Pierrot Lunaire* and admitted that "it was beyond me" as it was "beyond all of us at the time." For many years Stravinsky did not hear a note of Schoenberg's music. In Los Angeles, where they both lived, they never saw each other. Previously, Stravinsky never had anything favorable to say about serial music. But after being introduced by Craft to dodecaphonic music, and especially the music of Webern, he revised his opinion. In an interview in 1952 he said that while he himself was not interested in writing serial music, "the serial composers are the only ones with a discipline that I respect." Stravinsky made an intensive study of Webern's music. Then he experimented with serial elements in several works, notably the *Canticum Sacrum* (1955) and *Agon* (1957). Finally came *Threni* (1958), the *Movements* for Piano and Orchestra (1959), *A Sermon, A Narrative, and A Prayer* (1961), the Variations in Memory of Aldous Huxley (1964), and the *Requiem Canticles* (1966), all serial works.

Naturally there was a great outcry that Stravinsky had gone over to the "enemy." Stravinsky was accused of jumping on the serial bandwagon, of abdicating his position, of an unseemly ambition to keep his place as leader of the avant-garde. What was overlooked in the hubbub was that, serial or not, *Threni* and the other works still had the old Stravinsky sound; that his serial scores were no more Webernish than *Le Baiser* was Tchaikovskian, or the Violin Concerto was Bachian. Stravinsky merely did with serialism what he had done with any other form of style that passed his way: put it through the Stravinsky filter. No composer with the overpowering personality of a Stravinsky could suddenly begin to write music reflective of any other mind but his own. In any case, the serial compositions are only a very small part of his work.

Through the years Stravinsky's position has been, in a way, perplexing. From 1911 to the end of World War II he was the acknowledged leader of the musical avant-garde and by common consent the world's greatest living composer. To the public he remained the apostle of modernism. To his colleagues, he was the most precise and finished technician of the day. Certainly up to 1945 he was the strongest influence on the contemporary musical scene. That alone would be enough to make secure his place in history. Minor composers may achieve great popularity in their day, but they never influence the course of music. Stravinsky did. He always was at the end of the rope, pulling everybody along with him. (In this, his career greatly resembled that of his good friend Pablo Picasso. There are many parallels between the two: their almost simultaneous entry into various stylistic periods, their use of distortion for expressive purposes, their brilliant craftsmanship, the influence they had on the avant-garde.)

But the curious thing is that Stravinsky, after his post-*Sacre* works, was greatly admired more by fellow musicians and a handful of vociferous followers than by the public. It is not that Stravinsky lacked public performance. His stature and reputation were too great. Everything he composed was immediately performed, and recordings automatically followed. He is one of the few contemporary composers represented on records by, substantially, his complete works, most of them recorded under his personal supervision. Yet his music has always commanded more respect than love. The majority of his works after *Sacre* seem to hang around the rim of the repertoire rather than being down in the nucleus. Remove the three Russian ballets and his two other most popular works, *Oedipus Rex* and the *Symphony of Psalms,* and his music suddenly drops near the bottom of the annual list in the survey of American symphony orchestra programs published by the American Symphony Orchestra League and Broadcast Music, Inc. Stravinsky has ended up a musician's musician rather than one who was major musical box office. His music may be too sharp, pointed, reserved, balanced, intellectual (if you wish). It is not music to everybody's taste. "I've come to the conclusion," wrote Aaron Copland in 1943, "that Stravinsky is the Henry James of composers. Same 'exile' psychology, same exquisite perfection, same hold on certain artistic temperaments, same lack of immediacy of contact with the world around him."

Nor does Stravinsky's music have the kind of melody that would attract a wide following, though it is an error to say, as some have done, that there is no melody in his music. An aria like the Jocasta plaint in *Oedipus Rex,* or the melody that starts the slow movement of the Symphony in Three Movements, or the scene in *Orpheus* where the protagonist serenades the Underworld, or the *Sur le lit elle repose* from *Perséphone* (is this not an unconscious echo of Tchaikovsky's *June Barcarolle?*)—these are melodies as pronounced as *Casta Diva.* Stravinsky could be as melodic as any composer if he wanted to. But he has not always wanted to. He never was a heart-on-sleeve composer, and often he cold-bloodedly discarded an obvious type of melody in favor of other elements of music. Thus his scores have been called "intellectual," in the pejorative sense. Nothing more aroused Stravinsky's anger than to be chastized for being intellectual. What's wrong with the intellect? he demanded to know. To condemn Stravinsky's music for being "intellectual" is to condemn it for the very thing for which it should be praised. Of course it is intellectual, in the best sense of the word. It is a music in which the formal elements are cunningly in balance, in which patterns are juggled with virtuosity, in which a strong mind, going out of its way to avoid nineteenth-century concepts, sets out to exploit certain musical ideas with brevity, objectivity, and unromantic notions. Has there been a composer in the history of music, Bach and Webern included, who has displayed the sheer logic of Stravinsky? One doubts it. Much of the pleasure in listening to his music comes from sharing the mental processes of a superbly organized mind—a mind with a good deal of perkiness, to be sure; a fascinating mind; a witty and aphoristic mind; but above all, an organized mind. In his music there is no padding, no inflated or uneasy "developments." Stravinsky's music can communicate strongly, but only to a certain type of mind, a kind of mind equivalent to Stravinsky's own—which means a mind that responds to form, technique, rhythm, stylization. Where a Beethoven, Schubert, or even Bach appears to appeal to all listeners on all levels, Stravinsky does not have that universal quality. He can all but hypnotize a music lover who has a high degree of sophistication; but the sophisticates are, after all, a minority of the musical public. It may be that Stravinsky, "the world's greatest living composer," will end up living more for what he did to music rather than for what his music did to the majority of his listeners.

181

✣ 13 ✣

The English Renaissance

ELGAR, DELIUS, VAUGHAN WILLIAMS

By rights, England in the nineteenth century should have developed as strong and individualistic a school of composers as Germany, France, or Russia did. The roots were there, the tradition was there, and in Henry Purcell (1659–1695) England had produced a major figure. Long before Purcell, however, English composers of importance had made their contribution to the development of music. Such skilled contrapuntists as John Dunstable, who died in 1453 (the date of his birth is unknown), John Taverner (1495–1545), and Thomas Tallis (c. 1505–1585) produced a strong body of church music. The latter part of the reign of Queen Elizabeth I saw a brilliant group simultaneously active in London. There were William Byrd, Orlando Gibbons, Thomas Morley, John Dowland, John Wilbye, and Thomas Weelkes, among others, composing madrigals, ayres, lute and other instrumental music, and church music. Shakespeare, Marlowe, Jonson, Donne, Herrick, and the rest of the galaxy of great Elizabethan writers often worked closely with these composers. What a wonderful period it was, and how exciting it must have been!

English music culminated in the figure of Purcell. In the thirty-six years of his life, he turned out an enormous quantity of music in all forms— church music, odes, incidental music to plays, the first English opera (*Dido and Aeneas,* 1689), chamber music, part songs (some of them deliciously naughty), works for the harpsichord. His music has an unusual degree of personality, and some of it is startlingly modern. Aside from Purcell's striking melodic ideas and a harmony that at times anticipated the chromaticism of the romantics, he was unusual for his day in that his music speaks directly to the modern listener. The Elizabethan madrigals, for instance, lovely as they can be, call for an acquired taste because of their archaic modalities. It takes a listener with a certain amount of sophistication to respond to them. But Purcell's music, to a large extent, speaks the language of

Everyman. His successors should have developed and refined his techniques, bringing English music to even greater heights. But, unfortunately, he had no successors. Instead, George Frideric Handel came to England.

Handel's impact on music in England was cataclysmic. One might even say catastrophic. The massive figure of the burly Saxon pressed heavily on his successors, to a point where creative effort seemed to be stifled. The English could not get enough choral writing in the Handel manner; and since Handel, not unexpectedly, composed in that manner better than anybody else, it was Handel who was constantly played. It is true that romanticism did finally come to England. Indeed, Wordsworth started the entire romantic school with his *Lyrical Ballads* of 1798. Had British musical romanticism been as imaginative and creative as literary romanticism, England would have taken the lead throughout the world. Instead, the musical romanticism that most of the British pursued was in the Mendelssohn rather than the Chopin-Liszt-Wagner line.

Mendelssohn exerted as strong a force upon British musical thinking in the nineteenth century as Handel previously had done. There was something about the bourgeois, competent, academic Mendelssohn with which musical England completely identified. He was more of a god there than he was even in Leipzig. England was a conservative country, rich, with a powerful upper class; and it feared change. Mendelssohn was undeniably a genius, but such a *proper* genius! He was a gentleman, he was wealthy, he was a conservative, and he did not rock the boat. It was inevitable that Mendelssohn and Queen Victoria should become friends. They had a great deal in common—caution, conventionality of mind, breeding, a very conservative outward surface, and they took to each other very strongly. There is something sweet, innocent, and charming about the relationship, about Queen Victoria and Prince Albert, both music lovers, joining forces with Mendelssohn for a musicale like a good middle-class family. Everything was polite and cozy at Buckingham Palace when the nice Mr. Mendelssohn dropped in to pay his respects:

Prince Albert had asked me [Mendelssohn wrote in 1842] to go to him on Saturday at two o'clock, so that I might try his organ before I left England. I found him all alone; and as we were talking away, the Queen came in, also quite alone, in a house dress. She said she was obliged to leave for Claremont in an hour. "But, goodness! how it looks here," she added, when she saw that the wind had littered the whole room, and even the pedals of the organ (which, by the way, made a very pretty feature in the room), with leaves of music from a large portfolio that lay open. As she spoke, she knelt down and began picking up the music. Prince Albert helped and I too was not idle. Then Prince Albert proceeded to explain the stops to me, and while he was doing it, she said that she would put things straight alone.

But I begged that the Prince would first play me something, so that, as I said, I might boast about it in Germany; and thereupon he played me a chorale by heart, with pedals, so charmingly and clearly and correctly that many an organist could have learned something; and the Queen, having finished her work, sat beside him and listened, very pleased. Then I had to play, and I began my chorus from *St. Paul*—"How Lovely Are the Messengers." Before I got to the end of the first verse, they both began to sing the chorus very well, and all the time Prince Albert managed the stops for me so expertly—first a flute, then full at the forte, the whole register at the D major part, then he made such an excellent diminuendo with the stops, and so on to the end of the piece, and all by heart—that I was heartily pleased. . . .

Queen Victoria wanted all music to sound like Mendelssohn's. Her subjects obliged, writing very proper and not very original music. Between the death of Handel in 1759 and the emergence of Edward Elgar in the 1890's, England did not produce one major musical figure. There were good composers in the country during the nineteenth century—William Sterndale Bennett, Arthur Sullivan, Alexander Mackenzie, Charles Hubert Parry, Charles Villiers Stanford. All were academicians, and the music of these worthy composers seldom was heard outside of England. This was true even of Schumann's protégé, Sterndale Bennett, while Sullivan lives only through his operetta music. The counterpart to this group of composers would be the Boston Classicists in the United States. Some accomplished and even lovely music came out of the London group, just as it came out of Boston, and the music in both cases is better than its reputation, but it is a music too powerfully dominated first by Mendelssohn, later by Schumann and Brahms.

Elgar, born in Broadheath on June 2, 1857, broke the mold. He became recognized as England's greatest composer, and his reputation in his day was enormous. Then it rapidly declined, to rise up again in the 1960's. During the modernism of the 1920–40 period, the great days of Stravinsky, Bartók, Prokofiev, and Milhaud, most musicians would have ridiculed the very idea of Elgar being an important composer. He was considered an inflated provincial, popular in his day only because England was so desperately anxious to claim an important composer for her own. He was Edwardian, stuffy, a relic of Colonel Blimp and Empire. What else could be expected of a man who indulged in fox-hunting, golf, fishing, and kite-flying? Even Elgar's very appearance was held against him. He was tall, straight, heavily moustachioed, with a hooked nose and flaring nostrils; he carried his umbrella at the furl; his entire bearing was military; his clothes were proper;

he was the very model of an Edwardian clubman. It followed that he was a musical wallah who composed vulgar and jingoistic music (*Pomp and Circumstance:* really!). His music could no more be listened to than the poetry of Kipling could be read. And so mounted the catalogue of sins.

It was not only the aesthetic of a neoclassic age, with its revulsion against romanticism, that helped put Elgar among the discards for several decades. There also was the interest in nationalism, as represented in England by Ralph Vaughan Williams and the revival of the Elizabethan school. Nationalism was sweeping the entire musical world, what with Bartók in Hungary, Janáček in Czechoslovakia, Nielsen in Denmark, Sibelius in Finland, and Ives in the United States (though hardly anybody knew Ives's music). The nationalists immersed themselves in the native font, piping their native wood-notes wild. But Elgar would have none of this. He believed that it was a composer's business to invent tunes, not to quote them or base them on the quaint sounds of the past. Like Strauss and Mahler, he was a composer who delighted in massive effects. "If a composer writes for forty harps, get him forty harps." But this kind of thinking was long out of fashion at the time of Elgar's death, in Worcester on February 23, 1934. All his contemporaries could see were the Wagner, Strauss, and Brahms derivations of his music. His major works—the two symphonies, the Violin Concerto and Cello Concerto, the enormous symphonic poem *Falstaff*—all went into prompt decline. Only his *Enigma Variations* and *The Dream of Gerontius* had much currency among his serious works, and *Gerontius* was seldom played outside of England. Young musicians went around calling *The Dream of Gerontius* a "nightmare."

Yet to the musicians of the 1890's, Elgar was an individualist, and one of the greatest living masters of the orchestra. He was almost a self-taught composer. His father, an organist, violinist, and piano tuner, encouraged his early experiments in composition, which started as a child. Young Elgar studied violin and piano, went to work in a lawyer's office, and then decided to concentrate on music. He became a violinist in the Worcester Philharmonic, taught as a provincial musician, and turned out a large quantity of music, much of it salon, all of it unimportant. There was nothing to distinguish him from any other hard-working but hack composer. If he had any reputation at all, it was through sentimental little pieces like the *Salut d'Amour* for piano, a work that occupied the position in the drawing rooms of Victorian England that the Gottschalk piano pieces of the *Last Hope* variety occupied in American drawing rooms of the period.

Then, in 1889, came the *Froissart Overture*, Elgar's first significant work, and it revealed a composer with a brilliant feeling for the sonorities of the big postromantic orchestra. The *Black Knight* (1893), *King Olaf* (1896), and *Caractacus* (1898), all for chorus and orchestra, attracted further interest. By

1900, Elgar was the most famous composer in England, especially after the tremendous success of the *Enigma Variations* in 1899. This orchestral work was a musical picture of his friends. Elgar also said that the main theme itself had for a counterpoint "a theme that is not heard." Nobody has identified that mysterious unheard theme, the enigma of the *Enigma*. Hans Richter conducted the premiere in London, and the work was taken up on the continent. Fritz Steinbach, the Brahms specialist, called Elgar "an unexpected genius and pathbreaker in the field of orchestration. . . . Entirely original effects with almost unique virtuosity." Which was indeed a compliment from a conductor in the land of Richard Strauss.

Elgar clearly was influenced by Strauss. Some of his melodies have the characteristic Strauss contour, with their skips, large range, and unexpected landing spots. Elgar's orchestration also owes something to the composer of *Ein Heldenleben*. But Strauss's orchestration, effective as it is, often makes its point through sheer size and volume. Elgar achieved a more luminous sound. As Vaughan Williams remarked: "I have found that with Wagner the extra instruments could almost be dispensed with altogether, with a little loss of color, it is true, but with no damage to the texture. But when it came to Elgar, the case was quite different. Even in the accompaniments to choral movements there was hardly anything that could be left out without leaving a hole in the texture."

Elgar followed the *Enigma Variations* with what many consider to be his greatest work, the oratorio *Dream of Gerontius* to Cardinal Newman's text. The premiere at the Birmingham Festival was little short of a disaster. Richter was unprepared, the chorus did not understand the music, and the soloists were not up to its demands. (From that point on Elgar himself conducted most of his premieres.) Subsequent performances of *Gerontius* went better, and England, with its tradition of choral singing, took to the score. (The English, George Bernard Shaw somewhere observed, always "took a creepy sort of pleasure in Requiems.") *Gerontius* does have moments of great nobility and beauty. It also has a pious stuffiness about it; and while it is Elgar's most ambitious score, it is not, despite the claims of his admirers, his best. It occupies the position in his music that *A Mass of Life* occupies in the music of Delius: a big attempt that does not always come off.

Cockaigne: In London Town came in 1901. Elgar never pretended to be a nationalistic composer. But in *Cockaigne,* as in his later *Falstaff* of 1913, he wrote a kind of music that strongly evokes a national spirit. It may be more Merrie England than the real thing, but nobody but an Englishman could have conceived it. The same can be said of the four *Pomp and Circumstance* Marches. No. 1 in D was to Elgar what the *Valse Triste* was to Sibelius and the Prelude in C sharp minor was to Rachmaninoff. To people everywhere, Elgar was the composer of *Pomp and Circumstance*. The first two marches had their premiere at a Proms concert in 1901. "I shall never forget the scene at the close of the first of them, the one in D major," Elgar wrote in his autobiography. "The people simply rose and yelled. I had to play it again—with the same result; in fact, they refused to let me go on with the program. . . . Merely to restore order, I played the piece a third time." Not much later, Edward VII suggested that *the* tune be provided with words, and it was, as *Land of Hope and Glory*. If Elgar had been well-known before that, now he was wildly famous. Honors came his way, including degrees from American universities and, in 1904, a knighthood. That was the year that saw a three-day festival of his music at Covent Garden.

Pomp and Circumstance may have brought Elgar fame and money, but musically it did him much more harm than good. The march tarred him with a Kiplingesque kind of jingoism, and there were those who refused to take seriously any music by the composer of *Pomp and Circumstance*. Musicians would not accept it for what it was—a rattling good march. In the meantime, Elgar was producing a fine series of works—the superb Introduction and Allegro for string orchestra (1905), the First Symphony (1908), the Violin Concerto (1910), the Second Symphony (1910), and the Cello Concerto (1919). Elgar also worked on a major choral trilogy. *The Apostles* came out in 1903, and *The Kingdom* in 1906. Neither work is in the international repertory. Part III of the trilogy never was finished.

The two symphonies are broad postromantic works, vigorous, very much in the Brahms tradition with some touches of Strauss. Both are fine, sturdy pieces, redeemed from their obvious derivations by the gusto of the writing and the typically Elgarian kind of melody. These symphonies are coming back into favor again, and so is the Violin Concerto, even with its unconscious references to the Brahms Violin Concerto. Possibly the best of Elgar's late works is the Cello Concerto, an elegiac, strongly personal work with hauntingly beautiful themes. The sustained lyricism of the opening theme is unusual even for Elgar, who liked long-phrased melodies. It goes on, generating from itself, for an incredible length of time. The Elgar Cello Concerto ranks with Dvořák's in B minor as the greatest of its species.

With the Cello Concerto and the Piano Quintet of 1919, Elgar's creative period stopped. He did compose a few things in the fifteen years remaining to him, but none of those works is heard. Like Rossini and Sibelius, Elgar decided to call it a day at the height of his career. He never recovered from the loss of his wife, in 1920. And he did not like the direction music was taking. Very likely he considered himself an anachronism. Certainly he was made to feel so. The hectic age after World War I dismissed his music, and the public ignored it. At his seventieth birthday concert in Queen's Hall, the house was only half full. Elgar said that he had composed a third symphony but would not waste time scoring it, as nobody wanted his music any more. He was a lonely old man. He withdrew from all musical contact, never went to a concert, said that he disliked music, and preferred to talk about cricket or horse-racing.

What the 1930's could not see through Elgar's glowing postromanticism was that his music had something very special. Unlike his Victorian predecessors, Elgar spoke with an unusual degree of individuality. He may have based his orchestra on Strauss and Wagner, and his symphonic and concerto forms on Brahms, but his melodies and his handling of the forms were very much his own. An Elgar melody, with its curious tension, its wide intervals and exuberant leaps, its confident, strong, British feeling (hard to describe in words, but it is there), immediately stands out, recognizable as the work of but one composer and no other in the history of music. That alone would suffice to put his music above that of a better technician or a more advanced experimenter. For music without personality, no matter how skillful, does not live. Elgar's music may be Edwardian and bourgeois, it may celebrate British imperialism (explicitly or, more often, implicitly), it may even have its share of conventional rhetoric (*Gerontius* certainly does). But it abounds in vitality and personality. It is no coincidence that Elgar's rehabilitation started with the revival of Kipling and other figures of the period. The spate of Edwardian studies in the 1950's showed that those bearded gentlemen and bustled ladies could be quite interesting, if not to say racy.

The element of Edwardian rhetoric in Elgar's music can make it hard to conduct. He used an immense orchestra, and the conductor is tempted to overstress. Then the music really sounds vulgar. Elgar himself recognized the problem and was greatly concerned about it. He told the critic Ernest Newman that the expression was written into his music, and all a conductor had to do was follow directions. "If only," he wistfully said, "people would be content to play the music as it is written down in the score." Otherwise Elgarian sentiment, Newman observed, has a habit of slobbering over, for which Elgar wrongly was blamed. "Few composers," Newman wrote, "suffer as much in this way from their uncomprehending interpreters as Elgar does; his exquisite sensitiveness is turned into sentimentality, his high spirits into vulgarity, his *nobilmente* into theatrical bombast—all because the conductor does not know where to stop." To which it can be added that Elgar himself conducted the orchestra in recordings of his Violin Concerto (with the young Yehudi Menuhin) and both symphonies, among other works, and his tempos and phrasings are there for all to study.

Elgar was one of a trinity of British composers, all active at the same time, who lifted British music from its post-Handel and post-Mendelssohn doldrums. The other two were Frederick Delius and Ralph Vaughan Williams, and no three composers could have been more different. Elgar, hearty and exuberant, was content to accept the England around him and to glorify it in music. Vaughan Williams, the outspoken nationalist, went back to the Tudor England of the sixteenth century for his inspiration. Delius fled the country, and the only inspiration he found was in himself. He did not like England very much, he was more an intellectual aristocrat than a bourgeois or commoner, and he wrote an entirely personal music that was as close to pantheism as music can get.

In some respects Delius was a composer like Fauré—highly personal, sometimes delicate, elegant, traditional without being academic. He did not compose a large body of music, and he had to wait a long time for recognition. By the time he had reached the age of forty he had written some significant music, but nothing was in print except a few songs. Not until 1905 did his music begin to take hold, and in Germany. Even then he did not enjoy international fame. He kept writing, polishing, and repolishing his music in his home at Grez-sur-Loing, about forty miles outside of Paris. In 1924, paralysis and blindness set in. A dedicated British musician, Eric Fenby, offered his services to the stricken Delius, and they worked out a system so that the composer could dictate his music. Several works did result from this effort, but fortunately Delius by that time had already finished all the music on which his fame rests.

It is difficult to describe this music. Some have called it English impressionism, but that does not fit too well. Many influences went to make up the complex man known as Frederick Delius. He was born in Bradford, near Manchester, on January 29, 1862. His family, wool merchants of German descent, were wealthy. Delius showed an aptitude for music and wanted to devote himself to it. His father, instead, decreed that Frederick enter the family business. Delius did, and turned out to be the worst businessman since the invention of money. After a time, his father was glad to get rid of him. Delius and a friend went off to Florida in 1884 to make their fortune growing oranges. They settled in at Solano Grove, near Jacksonville. Very few oranges were shipped to market. Instead, Delius concentrated on music. He became acquainted with a musician from New York named Thomas Ward, and they became friends. Delius said that the only teaching of real value he ever received was from Ward, who appears to have been a sound theorist and harmonist.

For a while, Delius taught music in Jacksonville, and later in Virginia. He also spent some time in New York. Then, in 1887, he went to the Leipzig Conservatory, where he was financed by his father. Delius never had to worry about money. The attractive *Florida Suite* was composed in Leipzig. Next, in 1888, came a visit to Paris. He lived there for a while with an uncle, and decided to make France his home. In France he married the painter Jelka Rosen, and he composed two wonderful orchestral works—

Over the Hills and Far Away (1895) and *Paris* (1899). These two works mark his mature style. He was slow in developing, but once he found his *métier* it remained unaltered all his life. "It came to me very slowly what I wanted to do, and when it came, it came out all at once." There followed an opera, *Irmelin* (1892), which was not staged until 1953, long after his death, and a series of other operas, orchestral pieces, and a piano concerto. At the age of forty-one, Delius had composed five operas, six large works for orchestra, about fifty songs and miscellaneous works, but virtually nothing, was in print. Suddenly he began to be played in Germany. His opera *Koanga* was produced in Elberfeld in 1904, and another opera, *A Village Romeo and Juliet,* was produced in Berlin in 1907. The choral works *Appalachia* (1902) and *Sea Drift* (1903) were taken up by German conductors. In England, Thomas Beecham became interested in Delius's music and did everything in his considerable power to further its cause. Little by little, Delius made headway in England. In Germany he was considered one of the most important living composers. Beecham states that only Richard Strauss was more popular in the decade preceding the war. The violent anti-English feeling in Germany after 1914 removed Delius from the German repertory.

A work that attracted great attention, and one that has been called Delius's masterpiece, was *A Mass of Life* (1905). In all truth it is not Delius's masterpiece, no more than *The Dream of Gerontius* is Elgar's, except to those who equate masterpieces with length and breadth. But it does aim high and has some tremendous moments. The text of *A Mass of Life* comes from Nietzsche, a writer Delius adored. He would take a chapter from Nietzsche's works and study it, perhaps for weeks on end, then turn to another. "I hail him as a sublime poet and a beautiful nature," Delius said.

The genesis of *A Mass of Life* was Nietzsche's *Night Song of Zarathustra.* Beecham conducted the premiere in 1905. It is not a religious work, nor was Delius a religious man. He told Eric Fenby that he had no use for religion or creeds. "There is only one real happiness in life, and that is the happiness of creating." (A surprising number of the great composers have been freethinkers or downright atheists. Verdi, Saint-Saëns, Debussy, Brahms, Wagner, probably Schubert, Berlioz, and Chopin, come to mind.) If anything, Delius was a solipsist. He and his music existed for themselves, feeding on each other, closed in a little circle.

Delius was a striking figure. When Beecham met him for the first time, he thought he was a cardinal or at least a bishop in mufti, for, as he wrote,

> . . . his features had that mingled cast of asceticism and shrewdness one mentally associates with high-ranking ecclesiastics. I was also struck by a general air of fastidiousness and sober elegance rarely to be observed in

artists of any kind. Unexpectedly contrasting, but not unpleasing, was his style of speech, of which the underlying basis was recognizably provincial. Not for him was the blameless diction so laboriously inculcated and standardized in our leading public schools and ancient universities. He loyally preserved his preference for the Doric dialect of that great northern country of broad acres, which looks down with compassion upon the niminy-piminy refinements of the softer south. Upon this had been grafted a polyglot mish-mash, acquired during his twenty-four years of self-imposed exile from England. Both French and German words interlarded his sentences, and he always spoke of the "orchester." . . . In public he was invariably dignified, reticent and well mannered; and of Bohemianism there was no visible sign.

The rest of his life, after the outbreak of World War I, Delius alternated between England and France, spending most of his time at Grez-sur-Loing, where he lived quietly with his wife. He never paid much attention to the music written during his day. Indeed, he actively disliked most music except his own. His career was fulfilled in some fifteen years, roughly from 1900 to 1915. On June 10, 1934, he died, at Grez.

Delius's music owed nothing to anybody. Like Debussy, he completely broke away from established form, and there is a free, improvisatory quality about his music that sounds as if it had resulted from experimenting with voluptuous, exotically chromatic chords at the piano. It is a rhapsodic kind of music, in free forms, and is altogether free of classicism. The harmonies can be overwhelmingly rich and even dissonant at times, but they were unlike the harmonies of any other composer. "I don't believe in learning harmony or counterpoint," Delius said. "Learning kills instinct. Never believe the saying that one has to hear music many times to understand it. It is utter nonsense, the last refuge of the incompetent. . . . For me, music is very simple. It is the expression of a poetical and emotional nature." To Delius, "a sense of flow" was the only thing that mattered. Music had flow or it didn't. If it had, it was good music. If it didn't, it was bad. In 1920 he reacted violently to the advanced music of his day, in a long article he wrote for *The Sackbut:*

There is room in the world for all kinds of music to suit all tastes, and there is no reason why the devotees of Dada should not enjoy the musically imbecile productions of their own little circle as much as the patrons of musical comedy enjoy *their* particular fare. But when I see the prophets of the latest clique doing their utmost to pervert the taste of the public and to implant a false set of values in the rising generation of music lovers by sneering at the great masters of the past, in the hope of attracting greater attention to the *petits maîtres* of the present—then I say it is time to speak openly and protest. . . .

This is an age of anarchy in art; there is no authority, no standard, no sense of proportion. Anybody can do anything and call it "art" in the certain expectation of making a crowd of idiots stand and stare at him in gaping astonishment and admiration. . . .

Music does not exist for the purpose of emphasizing or exaggerating something which happens outside its own sphere. Musical expression only begins to be significant where words and actions reach their uttermost limit of expression. Music should be concerned with the emotions, not with external events. To make music imitate some other thing is as futile as to try and make it say *Good morning* or *It's a fine day*. It is only that which cannot be expressed otherwise that is worth expressing in music.

Delius observed his own precepts. Basically he was a tone painter who expressed himself in rapturous improvisations. The tiny tone poems—*Brigg Fair* (1907), *Summer Night on the River* (1911), *On Hearing the First Cuckoo in Spring* (1912)—sound like improvisations; and more extended works sound merely like more extended improvisations. It is music "concerned with the emotions," and it expresses things "which cannot be expressed otherwise." Delius was a wonderful melodist, almost a Tchaikovskian melodist. But he never was as plangent as the great Russian, and his melodies do not have that kind of immediate impact. Delius, despite his defiant words about the immediate impact of good music, takes a little more time to assimilate. Once assimilated, his music never seems to wear off. And if the listener likes one Delius work, the chances are that he will like them all, for Delius wrote almost consistently in the same style. He was, of course, far from being a universal composer. His equivalents in the other arts might be a Gerard Manley Hopkins, a Mary Cassatt, or a James Branch Cabell. (The last-named, to some, might be the kiss of death; but how many more elegant prose stylists are there? Delius's magical landscapes are of the same romantic country as Cabell's Poictesme.)

What Delius did, he did perfectly, and he wrote beautifully of beautiful things. Above all, his music has an exquisite refinement, frequently with an undercurrent of tragedy. Often it is sensuous, sometimes strong, but always elegiac and elegant. It is never program music but it is at all times evocative music—music of lakes, sunsets, landscapes, of the Paris sky and the Atlantic Ocean off the coast of America. Even his operas are intimate. *A Village Romeo and Juliet* is not for big houses. Delius lived much of his life in privacy, and something of this reserve, this reluctance to wear his heart on his sleeve, comes out in everything he wrote. Delius was not a composer who went to the people. They had to come to him. Those who did, like Beecham, discovered that the music of Delius is a unique experience. "Opinions are bound to differ, and widely," Beecham wrote in his biography of the composer. "For myself, I cannot do other than regard him as the last great apostle in our time of romance, beauty and emotion in music."

Ralph Vaughan Williams, who followed Elgar by fifteen years and Delius by ten, was a big, burly, indestructible man who had one of the longest creative spans in history. He was born in Gloucestershire on October 12, 1872, and died in London on August 26, 1958, finishing his Ninth Symphony only a short time before his death at the age of eighty-six. As he was already in print when he was nineteen years old, his was a sixty-five-year record of productivity. There was money in the family, and Vaughan Williams was able to take his time before settling on the idiom he was so faithfully to pursue. As a boy, he learned several instruments, none of them professionally. "I had been taught the pianoforte, which I never could play, and the violin, which was my musical salvation." At the Royal College of Music he studied with Stanford and Parry, and was especially indebted to the latter. "We pupils of Parry have, if we have been wise, inherited from Parry the great English choral tradition which Tallis passed on to Byrd, Byrd to Gibbons, Gibbons to Purcell, Purcell to Battishill and Greene, and they in turn through the Wesleys to Parry. He has passed the torch to us, and it is our duty to keep it alight." Unlike Elgar, Vaughan Williams rejected the German nineteenth-century tradition in favor of the English folk song and choral tradition. Temperamentally he was never able to identify with the German school. "To this day the Beethoven idiom repels me," he wrote as an old man, adding, "but I hope I have at last learnt to see the greatness that lies behind the idiom that I dislike, and at the same time to see an occasional weakness behind the Bach idiom which I love."

For some strange reason, considering his opinion of nineteenth-century German music, he went to Berlin to have a few lessons with Max Bruch. Nothing much came of these. He took a degree of Doctor of Music in Cambridge in 1901. Shortly thereafter he joined the English Folk Music Society. That was to be the turning point of his life. Like Bartók and Kodály, Vaughan Williams and his friend Gustav Holst went into the field to collect native music in as pure a state as it could be found. Holst was a well-known composer in his day, though little of his music is heard any more. He was considered an aggressive modernist, and was one of an important group of post-Elgar composers—a group that included Samuel Coleridge-Taylor, Arnold Bax, John Ireland, and, a little later, Arthur Bliss.

Vaughan Williams saturated himself in folk song. Through these studies he was able to free himself of foreign influences, as he explained in a lecture:

In the days when Elgar formed his style, English folk song was not "in the air" but was consciously revived and made popular only about thirty

193

years ago. Now what does this revival mean to the composer? It means that several of us found here in its simplest form the musical idiom which we unconsciously were cultivating ourselves. It gave a point to our imagination. . . . The knowledge of our folk songs did not so much discover for us something new, but uncovered something which had been hidden by foreign matter.

His attitude toward musical nationalism represented as much a conscious flight from foreign domination as from any philosophy of composition involving the music of a people. Vaughan Williams had seen too many British composers end up as captives dragged on a rope behind the chariot of German academism, and he fiercely resisted capture. "As long as composers persist in serving up at second hand the externals of the music of other nations, they must not be surprised if audiences prefer the real Brahms, the real Wagner, the real Debussy or the real Stravinsky to their pale reflections." Better a limited but honest music than imitation. "Every composer cannot expect to have a world-wide message, but he may reasonably expect to have a special message for his own people." Anybody can write in the style of Wagner or Strauss, but that should not tempt the British composer. "Is it not reasonable to suppose that those who share our life, our customs, our climate, even our food, should have some secret to impart to us which the foreign composer, though he be perhaps more imaginative, more powerful, more technically equipped, is not able to give us?" That, Vaughan Williams concluded, was the secret of the national composer. He got to the point, as do so many men riding a hobbyhorse, where only music with a national tinge interested him. Thus it followed that most of Stravinsky's music bothered him, except for such scores as *Les Noces* and the *Symphony of Psalms,* in which Stravinsky's Russian heritage was so strongly emphasized. Otherwise, Vaughan Williams argued, Stravinsky was merely a clever and fashionable composer who relied on a bag of sophisticated tricks. As for the atonality of Schoenberg and his school, Vaughan Williams stood away. "Schoenberg meant nothing to me— but as he apparently meant a lot to other people, I dare say that it is all my own fault."

Buoyed by his overriding interest in British folk music, Vaughan Williams started writing scores that he hoped would spearhead a national movement. Two of them—the three *Norfolk Rhapsodies* and *In the Fen Country*—attracted a great deal of attention in 1906 and 1907 respectively. But Vaughan Williams felt that he needed more study and decided to take some lessons with, of all people, Maurice Ravel. "In 1908 I came to the conclusion that I was bumpy and stodgy, had come to a dead end, and that a little French polish would be of use to me." Off he went to Paris—a big, stout, bearlike man, dressed with cheerful sloppiness (Vaughan Williams always dressed "as though

194

stalking the folk song to its lair," somebody once remarked)—to confront the tiny, dandified Ravel, who did not know exactly what to make of the invader. He looked at some of Vaughan Williams's music and told him to write a little minuet in the style of Mozart. Vaughan Williams met this head-on. "Look here, I have given up my time, my work, my friends and my career to come here and learn from you, and I am *not* going to write a *petit menuet dans le style de Mozart*." Ravel guided Vaughan Williams away from "the heavy contrapuntal Teutonic manner." After Ravel, Vaughan Williams considered his musical education complete.

He returned to England and started to compose in all forms. His series of symphonies was inaugurated with *A Sea Symphony* (1910), *A London Symphony* (1914), and the *Pastoral* Symphony (1922). There also was an opera, *Hugh the Drover* (1914), in addition to choral pieces, incidental music to plays, the *Fantasia on a Theme by Tallis* (1910) for double string orchestra (one of his most popular works), and the beautiful song cycle *On Wenlock Edge* (1909), for tenor, string quartet, and piano. A sharp break in his style came with the Fourth Symphony in 1935. This departed from the folk-derived idiom of the previous symphonies in favor of a knotty, dissonant, and all but abstract style. The music is supposed to reflect Vaughan Williams's agitation over the Italian invasion of Abyssinia. "I don't know whether I like it," Vaughan Williams said of this symphony, "but this is what I meant."

From that point there was an ever-increasing harmonic tension in his symphonies. Some, like the Sixth, were abstract. Others, like the Fifth and Ninth, reverted to the folk idiom. But even in the abstract symphonies there was an underlying Englishness, with harmonic and melodic transformations that could be traced back to the Tudors. It was not nice-Nelly music. Vaughan Williams was not interested in writing "pretty" evocations of the past or present, and no British composer has so managed to steer clear of Ye Tea Shoppe school of music. The Vaughan Williams symphonies are rugged affairs with a strong dose of dissonance and often a type of construction that turns "sonata form" upside down. It is uncompromising music that follows no fashion of the day and is, in the best sense of the word, original.

The Fifth Symphony of 1943, with its return to the folk tradition, pastoral-sounding, idyllic, might well be Vaughan Williams's orchestral masterpiece. The abstract Sixth Symphony has an amazing last movement marked "always pianissimo, without a crescendo." It is a crepuscular, spooky movement, and its only equivalent in sonata-form history would be the last movement of Chopin's B flat minor Sonata. For his Seventh Symphony, the *Sinfonia Antartica* (not Antarctica), Vaughan Williams in 1953 adapted music from his film score *Scott of the Antarctic*. The Eighth Symphony (1956) is an unconventional work that Vaughan Williams described as "seven variations in search of a theme." Four months before his death came the Ninth Symphony (1958), a retrospective work rich in reminiscence and full of the sublimated nationalism of his best music.

The Ninth Symphony is a big work in every way, but it is seldom played. There has been a reaction against Vaughan Williams's music equivalent to the reaction that set in against Elgar's. Elgar, however, has been rediscovered, and Vaughan Williams also will be. He may yet turn out to be hailed as the most important symphonist of the century. Neither an academic nor an avant-gardist, he wrote emotionally uncluttered music that was set forth in old forms considerably modified for expressive ends. It is easy to overplay his nationalism. If patriotism, as Dr. Johnson said, is the last refuge of a scoundrel, it is also true that nationalism in music can be the refuge of a chauvinist, as was proved so convincingly during the period of Socialist Realism in Russian music. It is the easiest thing in the world to write "national music" of a certain kind. All that is necessary is to take a folk tune and dress it in an orchestral coat of many colors. But Vaughan Williams did not operate that way. His nationalism, like Bartók's or Dvořák's, was as much the expression of the inner state of a man as of the outward state of his country's culture. Whatever the initial impulse that triggered Vaughan Williams's music, it ended up as music first, nationalism second—the music of a big man, a big spirit, and a very original thinker. Vaughan Williams was fond of a quotation of Gustav Stresemann, and it can serve as a summation of what he was trying to do: "The man who serves humanity best is he who, rooted in his own nation, develops his spiritual and moral endowments to their highest capacity, so that growing beyond the limits of his own nation he is able to give something of the whole to humanity."

❧ 14 ❧

Mysticism and Melancholy

SCRIABIN AND RACHMANINOFF

After Tchaikovsky and The Five came two Russian composers whose lives for a while were linked: Alexander Scriabin, born in Moscow on January 6, 1872, and Serge Rachmaninoff, born in Oneg, near Novgorod, on April 1, 1873. Both were students together, both were formidable pianists, and both were the most important men of Russian music in the two decades up to World War I. Scriabin died in Moscow on April 27, 1915, and Rachmaninoff, twenty-eight years later and almost half a globe away, in Beverly Hills, California, on March 28, 1943. Scriabin was a flaming, mercurial, probably insane (toward the end) man, who started as a composer of charming little piano pieces and ended up a mystic who wrote near-incomprehensible music that was going to pull together all the arts and religions. Rachmaninoff wrote his C minor Piano Concerto in 1901 and never deviated from the pattern, writing essentially the same kind of music throughout his life. The public liked his music, but to many professionals around the world he was a creative nobody, crying his Russian tears at the feet of Tchaikovsky. It was to Serge Prokofiev that the world looked in the 1920's when the subject of Russian music came up—Prokofiev, the meteor from the East, the age-of-steel composer, the cubist in music. And after Prokofiev there was his natural successor, Dmitri Shostakovich. Rachmaninoff? *Really!*

Rachmaninoff and Scriabin first encountered each other in the piano class of Nikolai Zverev. Rachmaninoff was twelve years old, Scriabin thirteen. Both were formidable talents, with perfect pitch, supple hands, all-encompassing memories, and creative aspirations. It was no easy life in Zverev's school. He was a hard taskmaster. His students were up at 6 A. M. to start the day, and they worked for the next sixteen hours. They wore uniforms, had to take language lessons, and were brought up as gentlemen. Zverev, who was rich, took no money for his lessons, and his pupils had to come from good families. He was a homosexual, and it was whispered in Moscow that he taught certain of his pupils other things than music. Scriabin and Rachmaninoff, at any rate, apparently came through physically untouched. They entered the Moscow Conservatory, Rachmaninoff in 1887, Scriabin in 1888. Both were composing at the time. Scriabin was the more precocious. He was in a period of great love for Chopin, often slept with a volume of Chopin's music under his pillow, and at the age of fourteen composed his Étude in C sharp minor (Op. 2), Chopinesque, but a little masterpiece.

At the Conservatory, Rachmaninoff studied piano with Alexander Siloti. Scriabin went to Vassily Safonov. Both also had lessons in counterpoint with Taneiev, and with Arensky studied theory and composition. Among the Safonov pupils was the fabulous Josef Lhevinne, and Scriabin nearly ruined his right hand trying to emulate Lhevinne's thunderings in the Liszt *Don Juan Fantasy*. He had trouble with the hand for years. Rachmaninoff and Scriabin swept easily through the Conservatory, grabbing prizes as they went. Rachmaninoff won the Great Gold Medal in 1892 and Scriabin won the Little Gold Medal. Then after graduation, their paths diverged for some years. The slight, elegant, convivial, party-going, and alcoholic-prone Scriabin started to tour Europe as a pianist. Rachmaninoff stayed in Moscow for the most part, where he was better known as a composer and conductor than as a pianist. He was a completely different kind of man from Scriabin. Rachmaninoff was dour, serious, taciturn, and open to only a very few close friends. He was stubborn and would not be pushed around, even as a student. He was one of the few who dared stand up to Zverev; and in the Conservatory he insisted on his rights. When he was seventeen he composed his First Piano Concerto (later it was revised), and it had a tryout at the Conservatory the following year. His fellow student, Mikhail Bukinik, has left an account of that premiere:

At the rehearsals the 18-year-old Rachmaninoff showed the same stubbornly calm character that we knew from our comradely gatherings. Safonov, who ordinarily conducted the compositions of his students, would brutally and unceremoniously change anything he wished in these scores, cleaning them up and cutting parts to make them more playable. The student composers, happy to have their creative efforts performed . . . did not dare contradict Safonov, and readily agreed to his comments and alterations. But Safonov had a hard time with Rachmaninoff. This student not only refused categorically to accept alterations, but also had the audacity to stop Safonov (as conductor), pointing out his errors in tempo and nuance. This was obviously displeasing to Safonov, but being intelligent, he understood the rights of an author, though a beginner, to make his own interpretation, and he tried to take the edge off any awkwardness. Besides, Rachmaninoff's talent as a composer was so obvious, and his quiet self-assurance made such an impression on all, that even the omnipotent Safonov had to yield.

Rachmaninoff's graduation work was a one-act opera, *Aleko,* which Tchaikovsky admired. Rachmaninoff had been introduced to Tchaikovsky by Zverev. "He listened to me, a young beginner, as if I were his equal," Rachmaninoff once said. Later Tchaikovsky arranged for the production of *Aleko* at the Imperial Theater, and did even more: "Timidly and modestly, as if he were afraid I might refuse, he asked me if I would consider having my work produced with one of his operas. To be on a poster with Tchaikovsky was the greatest honor that could be paid to a composer." There was much in common between the two composers, and Tchaikovsky may have seen his successor in Rachmaninoff. Both represented Russian melancholy expressed in German forms. Throughout his career Rachmaninoff was content to work within a completely traditional framework.

His career moved slowly. He did some teaching and playing, composed the famous Prelude in C sharp minor in 1892, completed a Symphony in D minor in 1895, and attended its premiere in St. Petersburg in 1897. The symphony was a fiasco. It was not that hardly anybody liked it. It was that *nobody* liked it. Rachmaninoff lost confidence and went through a terrible period. For almost three years he wrote nothing. "I felt like a man who had suffered a stroke and had lost the use of his head and hands." Instead of composing, he turned to the piano. When he appeared in London in 1899, he found that he was famous. His C sharp minor Prelude had preceded him. Still he could not compose. Finally he went to a Moscow specialist named Dr. Nikolai Dahl, who worked with him on a form of psychiatric treatment coupled with hypnosis and autosuggestion. Rachmaninoff would lie on a couch under hypnosis, and Dr. Dahl would repeat: "You will write your Concerto. . . . You will write your Concerto. . . . You will write your Concerto. . . . You will work with great facility. . . . The Concerto will be of excellent quality." The treatment worked. Rachmaninoff started his C minor Concerto and finished it in 1901. It remains the most popular work he ever composed. European and American tours followed. At these, Rachmaninoff played or conducted only his own music. He was at the piano for the world premiere of his D minor Concerto, in New York in 1909. Up to World War I he had composed three concertos, two symphonies (No. 2 in E minor has retained its popularity), the symphonic poem *Isle of the Dead,* and a large quantity of songs and piano music. The piano music was tailored to his own spectacular hands. It is extremely difficult, demands wide stretches, and has tremendous virtuosity without indulging in Lisztian pyrotechnics. On the whole it is an original body of piano music, owing little to the nineteenth-century romantic school, yet part of the family. It also is strongly Russian in flavor. If it has a predecessor, it would be the piano music of Balakirev and of Adolph Henselt, the Bavarian pianist-composer who settled in Russia in 1838.

In the meantime, Scriabin was making a different kind of sensation in

Russia and abroad. Subsidized by the publisher Mitrofan Belaiev, he was playing all over Europe and demonstrating a sensuous, colorful kind of pianism, one altogether different from Rachmaninoff's clear, precise, strong, and logical work at the keyboard. At the age of twenty-six he became a professor of piano at the Moscow Conservatory, his base of operations when he was not concertizing. (He resigned in 1903.) He also was turning out a series of neo-Chopin piano works—Chopin with a Russian undercurrent. These works were graceful, lyric, full of personality, aristocratic, and by no means mere Chopin imitations. They exuded their own kind of charm. He also composed the Piano Concerto in F sharp minor in 1897, a work that gave many ideas to Rachmaninoff.

In 1898 came a shift in his style. The Third Piano Sonata showed a tendency to break textures into pointillistic bits of color. Outlines became vague, the content began to sound cryptic. Scriabin called the work *États d'Ame*. It was a decided break not only in his music but in all music. Nobody had conceived of this kind of piano writing. Spurred by his work along these lines, he started to turn to big forms, composing two symphonies by 1901. He also started to read Nietzsche and from there drifted into mysticism, inspired by the theosophical writings of Helena Blavatsky. He began to think in terms of sound and ecstasy, of music as a mystic ritual. It was as if Parsifal had gone to the East. The jargon of theosophy entered his speech. "In these mysteries of antiquity there was real transfiguration, real secrets and sanctities."

His Third Symphony and Fourth Sonata of 1903 began to break free of all conventions. Scriabin experimented with harmonies built on fourths instead of thirds, and the writing, especially for piano, became incredibly difficult and complex. He developed his "mystic chord"—C, F sharp, B flat, E, A, D—and worked out entire compositions based on it. Key signatures were dropped, and dissonance was piled on dissonance. His music began to explore a rapprochement with the other arts. In the Third Symphony, named *The Divine Poem,* an immense orchestra was used, and the music had to do with "Man-God," sensual pleasures, divine play, the Soul, the Spirit, the Creative Will. Scriabin considered *The Divine Poem* the turning point in his career. "This was the first time I found light in music, the first time I knew intoxication, flight, the *breathlessness* of happiness." His scores became peppered with such markings as "Luminously and more and more flashing." It might be that Scriabin also suffered from a rare genetic peculiarity known as synesthesia, in which sound is translated directly into color. People with synesthesia cannot hear music without seeing colors.

Scriabin's private life underwent stresses as his mysticism developed. Some peculiar traits developed. He became a compulsive hand-washer, and would put on gloves before touching money. He spent as much time at his toilette as an actress, looking for wrinkles, worried about baldness. He developed extreme hypochondria. His amorality approached Wagner's; and, like Wagner, he found it easy to rationalize and justify his actions. "Since it is far more difficult to do all one wants to do than *not* do what one wants, it is nobler to do what one likes." He seduced a former pupil, and there was a major scandal in Moscow. He left his wife, Vera (she was also a pianist), and their four children for another woman, telling Vera that he was going to live with Tatiana Schloezer as "a sacrifice to art." His friends received strange letters from him: "I can't understand how to write only 'music' now. How uninteresting it would be. Music, surely, takes on idea and significance when it is linked to one, single plan within the whole of a world-viewpoint. . . . Music is the path of revelation." He kept notebooks in which he jotted down his musings in a kind of disturbed prose-poetry that shows a mind anything but normal:

> Something began to glimmer and pulsate and this *something was one*. It trembled and glimmered, but it was one. I do not differentiate multiplicity. This *one* was all with nothing in opposition to it. It was everything. I am everything. It had the possibility of anything, and it was not yet Chaos (the threshold of consciousness). All history and all future are eternally in it. All elements are mixed, but all that can be is there. It exudes colors, feelings and dreams. I wish. I create. I differentiate. I distinguish unclearly. Nothing is delineated. I know nothing, but all seems foreboding and I remember. Instants of the past and future come together. Confused presentiments and recollections, frights and joys.

Scriabin began to think that he was absorbed into the rhythm of the universe, and became megalomaniacal on the subject. He identified with God:

> I am freedom, I am life, I am a dream, I am weariness, I am unceasing
>   burning desire, I am bliss, I am insane passion, I am nothing, I am
>   atremble.
> I am play, I am freedom, I am life, I am a dream, I am weariness, I am
>   feeling,
> I am the world. I am insane passion, I am wild flight, I am desire, I am
>   light,
> I am creative ascent that tenderly caresses, that captivates, that sears,
>   Destroying,
> Revivifying. I am raging torrents of unknown feelings, I am the boundary,
> ·I am the summit. I am nothing.

> You, depths of the past born from the rays of my memories, and you,
>   heights of the future and creations of my dreams! You are not you.

I am God!
I am nothing, I am play, I am freedom, I am life.
I am the boundary, I am the peak.

I am God!
I am the blossoming, I am the bliss,
I am all-consuming passion,
     all engulfing,
I am fire enveloping the universe,
Reducing it to chaos.
I am the blind play of powers released.
I am creation dormant, Intellect quenched.

From 1904 he lived openly with Tatiana. His wife would not divorce him, so he and Tatiana left Russia from 1904 to 1909. In 1906 he was invited to the United States by Modest Altschuler, a classmate of Scriabin's who had gone to New York and formed the Russian Symphony Orchestra. Altschuler was one of the less talented conductors of his time, or any other time, but he introduced a great deal of Russian music to America. Scriabin arrived in New York in December and promptly gave a recital. Immediately the newspapers referred to him as "The Cossack Chopin." Scriabin liked America but could not understand American morality as explained to him by Altschuler. It seemed that Maxim Gorky had a great deal of trouble when he came to the United States with his mistress, and was evicted by several hotels. Scriabin revealed his findings to Tatiana: "Altschuler says that if Gorky had had a different whore in his room every day, and they had known ALL about it, they wouldn't have thought a thing of it or persecuted him to such an extent. That would have been natural. However, it is considered a crime now to live faithfully with a beloved woman out of wedlock." Nevertheless, early in 1907, Tatiana joined Scriabin in New York. Newspapers found out about it. Altschuler, crying that he would be ruined, put Scriabin and Tatiana on the next boat to Europe. Scriabin had been in the United States only for about four months. He never returned, though his impressions of the country were not unfavorable. "America has a great future," he told friends. "There is a very strong mystic movement there."

Scriabin and Tatiana lived briefly in Paris and then, late in 1907, settled in Lausanne. There they heard that Altschuler had conducted the world premiere of *The Poem of Ecstasy* in New York on December 10, 1908. Altschuler notified Scriabin that the work had not been reviewed, which was not true. It had been poorly received, but Altschuler wanted to spare Scriabin the details of its reception. At that time, Scriabin was desperately short of money, but there was a turn in his fortune with his liaison with the wealthy (by marriage) conductor, Serge Koussevitzky. They met in the summer of 1908. Koussevitzky, in Berlin, had started the Russian Music Edition and was looking for important scores. He visited Scriabin in Lausanne, and also invited him to appear with his orchestra as piano soloist. Scriabin accepted and, as Faubion Bowers relates in his biography of the composer, "overflowed with plans. He spoke of tactile symphonies. He called incense an art which joins earth and heaven. He described the *Mysterium* [a work about which Scriabin had been thinking for many years]. He explained this great, final, cataclysmic opus as synthesizing all the arts, loading all senses into a hypnoidal, many-media extravaganza of sound, sight, smell, feel, dance, décor, orchestra, piano, singers, light, sculptures, colors, visions. Koussevitzky brought rights to it then and there." The two men worked out an agreement through which Scriabin would be paid 5,000 rubles a year for five years, the time necessary for the completion of the *Mysterium*. Koussevitzky also agreed to publish all of Scriabin's other compositions during that five-year period, at good royalty terms. One of those works was the Fifth Symphony, which Scriabin named *Prometheus: The Poem of Fire*. This had an elaborate program, ending with the world's beginning and a cosmic dance of the atoms. In addition to the full symphony orchestra, *Prometheus* used a piano, a chorus, and a color organ. It was Scriabin's first actual attempt to synthesize music and colors, and he worked out a chart:

Note	Vibrations per second	Color
C	256	Red
C sharp	277	Violet
D	298	Yellow
D sharp	319	Glint of steel
E	341	Pearly white and shimmer of moonlight
F	362	Deep red
F sharp	383	Bright blue
G	405	Rosy orange
G sharp	426	Purple
A	447	Green
A sharp	469	Glint of steel [for some reason, the same as D sharp]
B	490	Pearly blue

Koussevitzky conducted the world premiere of *Prometheus* in Moscow, on March 2, 1911. But there was no color organ; the instrument turned out to be impractical and was dropped. Scriabin was back in Russia for the premiere. He had broken up his Lausanne establishment in 1910 and returned to his own country for good. Naturally his path again crossed Rachmaninoff's. Russia was split into two musical camps. Scriabin and Rachmaninoff: which was the greater composer? the greater pianist? Scriabin was much the more discussed, if only because of the strangeness of his music. By now he was using the intervals of seconds and ninths in addition to fourths, and was living in a strange world of his own. "My Tenth Sonata is a sonata of insects. Insects are born from the sun . . . they are the sun's kisses . . . How unified world-understanding is when you look at things this way." He spent a great deal of time working on the *Mysterium*—not composing any music, but thinking about its locale and the extramusical accompaniments to the spectacle. The *Mysterium* involved the end of the world and the creation of a new race of man. At the climax of the *Mysterium* the walls of the universe would cave in. "I shall not die," Scriabin said. "I shall suffocate in ecstasy after the *Mysterium*." He thought of himself as the true Messiah and wanted his *Mysterium* to be performed in a temple in India, a temple hemispherical in shape. To prepare himself for India, he went out and purchased a sun helmet and a Sanskrit grammar. As Bowers describes the *Mysterium:*

Bells suspended from the clouds in the sky would summon the spectators from all over the world. The performance was to take place in a half temple to be built in India. A reflecting pool of water would complete the divinity of the half-circle stage. Spectators would sit in tiers across the water. Those in the balconies would be the least spiritually advanced. The seating was strictly graded, ranking radially from the center of the stage, where Scriabin would sit at the piano, surrounded by hosts of instruments, singers, dancers. The entire group was to be permeated continually with movement, and costumed speakers reciting the text in processions and parades would form parts of the action. The choreography would include glances, looks, eye motions, touches of the hands, odors of both pleasant perfumes and acrid smokes, frankincense and myrrh. Pillars of incense would form part of the scenery. Lights, fires, and constantly changing lighting effects would pervade the cast and audience, each to number in the thousands. This prefaces the final Mysterium and prepares people for their ultimate dissolution in ecstasy.

Goodness knows how far Scriabin would have gone with the project. Had not Wagner created Bayreuth against all inconceivable odds? But Scriabin died while all of the *Mysterium* was in his head. He died in a ridiculous manner. People like him should go up in a blaze of fire. Scriabin died from blood poisoning, the result of a carbuncle on his lip. Rachmaninoff sorrowed. He, who up till then had played only his music in public, gave a series of Scriabin recitals in his memory. The Scriabin fans honored the idea but did not like the execution. Rachmaninoff's playing was not to their taste. Young Serge Prokofiev was in the audience for one of the recitals. Rachmaninoff played, among other things, the Fifth Sonata. When Scriabin played it, the music was all allure and suggestion, in subtle tints. It flew, Prokofiev said. "But with Rachmaninoff, all its notes stood firmly and clearly on the ground." Scriabin's friends were outraged. Ivan Alchevsky, the tenor, had to be restrained from running to the stage and telling Rachmaninoff what he thought of him. Prokofiev tried to smooth things out, saying that there were more ways than one to play a piece of music. He went to the green room and, with his typical lack of tact told Rachmaninoff that he had played very well. That was all the young man had to say. "And you probably thought I'd play badly?" Rachmaninoff icily inquired. That ended Rachmaninoff's relations with Prokofiev for many years.

Shortly after the 1917 Revolution, Rachmaninoff left Russia for good and settled in Switzerland, starting a new life as a piano virtuoso. He was about forty-five years old and had virtually no repertory aside from his own music. His reputation as a conductor was good—he had been a first-line conductor at the Imperial Theater and the Moscow Philharmonic—and several major American orchestras offered him positions, but he decided to concentrate on the piano. It probably was the better choice, for he was one of the colossal pianists in history. In 1935 he settled permanently in the United States. Of course through the years he continued to compose as well as concertize. Significant works were the Piano Concerto No. 4 (1926), the Variations on a Theme by Corelli, for solo piano (1931), the Rhapsody on a Theme of Paganini, for piano and orchestra (1934), the Third Symphony (1936), and the Symphonic Dances (1940).

There was never a time when the music of Rachmaninoff was out of the repertory. This is in sharp contrast with the music of Scriabin, for there never was a time when the music of Scriabin was really in the repertory, though his early piano pieces achieved some popularity, and *The Divine Poem* and *The Poem of Ecstasy* were played once in a while. Not until the late 1960's was there the beginning of a Scriabin rediscovery. Scriabin has suddenly begun to be studied very seriously. But Rachmaninoff, so often played, has had hardly any critical appraisal at all. He was a composer who unabashedly used nineteenth-century models for his music, and as a result has been all but dismissed by scholars, historians, professionals, and tastemakers.

Typical of the attitude is the sneering reference in the fifth edition of Grove's *Dictionary of Music and Musicians*. It is one of the most outrageously snobbish and even stupid statements ever to be found in a work that is supposed to be an objective reference. Rachmaninoff rates only five paragraphs in this august nine-volume encyclopedia. It is worth reproducing the last two paragraphs complete:

> As a pianist Rachmaninoff was one of the finest artists of his time; as a composer he can hardly be said to have belonged to his time at all, and he represented his country only in the sense that accomplished but conventional composers like Glazunov or Arensky did. He had neither the national characteristics of the Balakirev school nor the individuality of Taneiev or Medtner. Technically he was highly gifted, but also severely limited. His music is well constructed and effective, but monotonous in texture, which consists in essence mainly of artificial and gushing tunes accompanied by a variety of figures derived from arpeggios.
>
> The enormous popular success some few of Rachmaninoff's works had in his lifetime is not likely to last, and musicians never regarded it with much favor. The third pianoforte Concerto was on the whole liked by the public only because of its close resemblance to the second, while the fourth, which attempted something like a new departure, was a failure from the start. The only later work that has attracted large concert audiences was the Rhapsody (variations) on a Theme by Paganini for pianoforte and orchestra.

Much of this is nonsense, but it represents a prevalent view of Rachmaninoff and his music. It blames him for not being Mussorgsky. It comes up with the astounding statement that he did not have the individuality of Taneiev or Medtner. Sergei Taneiev (1856–1915) was a Russian academician and specialist in fugue, whose music, if his Second Symphony is a fair example, was devoid of life and character and is as individual as a toothpick nestled in a box of toothpicks. Nicolai Medtner (1880–1951) was another Russian eclectic who, like Rachmaninoff, was a pianist-composer and who did Rachmaninoff the great honor of imitating him. Medtner's music has all but disappeared from the repertory. He was a composer on the order of an Ernö von Dohnányi—a good craftsman who seldom came up with an original idea. To call these two men more individual than Rachmaninoff displays ignorance and a blind reluctance to accept an unpalatable verdict of history.

For the facts are that Rachmaninoff is as popular as he ever was; that his music stubbornly refuses to go away; that, far from regarding his music with disfavor, every young pianist has in his repertory the C minor and D minor Concertos; that the C minor has had (at the point of writing) almost seventy years of exposure and the D minor almost sixty, with neither one showing any perceptible signs of waning; that in addition to the concertos the E minor Symphony also continues to make a great effect; that a good deal of Rachmaninoff's solo keyboard music continues to be well represented on programs throughout the world; and that many of his songs are still beloved. What more does a composer have to do to prove himself?

The point about Rachmaninoff's music is this: within its limitations it moves with perfect security and, yes, with much individuality. As with any major composer, it takes but a few measures of his work to establish its identity (Medtner and Taneiev would fail this test). Rachmaninoff may have contributed nothing to twentieth-century form or harmony, but he did suffuse the old forms with something highly personal, as Tchaikovsky did; and, in addition, he was one of the better melodists of his time. Nor was his melody as sentimental as writers like that in Grove's would have us believe. A good case can be made that Rachmaninoff was less sentimental than Tchaikovsky or Mahler. It is his followers who have made him sentimental: those minor composers who drifted off to write hack or movie music and helped make Rachmaninoff's name anathema.

Nor is it even true that his music is international as opposed to national. A strong Russian quality is the essence of Rachmaninoff's music, and that is part of its appeal. But whether or not it is nationalistic, whether or not it "belongs to its time"—all that is beside the point. A lot of music that "belongs to its time" is trash, and in any period of history there has been significant music that looked back rather than forward. The important thing about any composer is how individual he is, how well he expresses himself, how strong his ideas are. Rachmaninoff comes out better than most. His ideas did not have the universality of the great composers. Emotionally (and technically, too) he was apt to repeat himself. But the ideas themselves have validity and strength—as well over a half-century of delighted listeners continue to testify—the melodies have authentic sweep, and they always evoke a response. Ferruccio Busoni, it is said, had ten times Rachmaninoff's intellect, and he may have been an even more interesting pianist. But it is Rachmaninoff's music that continues to live, while Busoni's is hardly alive at all. The reason is that Rachmaninoff expressed himself, while Busoni had a tendency to express everybody from Bach to Liszt. (Busoni's music has a fascination of its own, but for different reasons.) Rachmaninoff's music has been around for a long time. If it did not have something to say, it would have disappeared long ago.

Rachmaninoff's music, of course, poses no problems. Scriabin's does. Almost as much as Schoenberg's it illustrates a break from the musical thinking of the past. Indeed, there is a strong parallel between the music of Schoenberg and the late Scriabin. Neither was influenced by the other, but both at almost the same time started to break away from triadic harmony and explore a harmony based on fourths instead of thirds. In the process the music of both composers became more dissonant. Schoenberg made the plunge into atonality and Scriabin did not, but he came very close, and orthodox key relationships were abolished. Scriabin's late music is a black mass of accidentals, fearsome-looking chords, and murderously difficult piano figurations. A work like the Tenth Sonata, with its strange trillings, its quartal harmonies, its disjunct melodic line, its dissonance and complete disregard for the amenities, is amazingly close to Schoenberg. One section near the end of the Tenth Sonata sounds as though Webern were the composer.

Another aspect of Scriabin that interested the late 1960's was his use of supplementary media. The concept of mixed media fascinated composers after 1965, and they began to experiment with lights, tape, speech and other sounds, in their scores. Scriabin, of course, had done much the equivalent prior to 1910. One of the key words of the late 1960's was "psychedelic," and it was found that Scriabin was the most psychedelic of all previous composers, dealing with visions, hallucinations, colors, smells, and tastes. There even was an element of Dada in Scriabin's musical thinking. He spoke about writing a sonata based on the pain of a toothache, or of dissolving a melody into an aroma.

Yet with all Scriabin's wildness in his late music, there are aspects that link up with his early music. To the very end his harmonies—no matter how complicated, no matter how divorced from key relationships—have a sensuous quality. Scriabin's music can be called erotic. It may be that music by itself cannot be erotic; it becomes so only through association; but some composers have more of a feeling for rich harmonic combinations than have others, and this is often termed erotic. Scriabin had this quality as much as any composer in history. There also is a certain kind of melody characteristic of Scriabin, and those big, sweeping gestures of *The Poem of Ecstasy* or *Prometheus* are but expansions of such works as the early *Poème* in F sharp.

In his early works there sometimes is a nationalistic quality. Later that was to disappear. Scriabin is not one of the Russian nationalists, though he did influence some of them. Stravinsky has called Scriabin a case of "musical emphysema," and his music "bombastic," but when Stravinsky came to write his *Firebird,* he had not only Rimsky-Korsakov in his blood. He also knew *The Poem of Ecstasy.*

It would be idle to deny that Scriabin's music, especially his orchestral music, suffers from self-indulgence. It is also true that in his mysticism he can be all but incomprehensible. Richard Anthony Leonard, in his book on Russian music, suggests a parallel between Scriabin and William Blake. Both were mystics, both were actuated by a personal vision, both talked with God, both produced works of art that can be explained only in terms of religious ecstasy, and both invented their own symbolism. Thus neither can be approached superficially. Their work has to be studied, and an understanding of what they were trying to do involves an understanding of what they thought about matters outside their art. Blake has won his battle in the eyes of posterity. Scriabin has yet to win his. But he was one of the most original, fascinating, enigmatic, revolutionary, and rewarding composers of the turn of the century.

❧ 15 ❧

Under the Soviets

PROKOFIEV AND SHOSTAKOVICH

In the days before World War I, when Rachmaninoff and Scriabin were riding high in Russia, there was a student at the St. Petersburg Conservatory named Serge Prokofiev. He was a stubborn, ill-tempered, obstinate, and surly young man of undeniable talent. Some said genius. He was born in Sontsovka, in the Ukraine, on April 23, 1891. At the age of six he was a facile pianist, and at nine he was trying to compose an opera. When he entered the Conservatory, at the age of thirteen, everything about him attracted attention, including his looks. His head was set on a pipe-stem neck; he had pink skin that would turn red when he was in a rage (which was often), piercing blue eyes, and thick, protruding lips. He brought along with him to the Conservatory four operas, a symphony, two sonatas, and other piano pieces. Rimsky-Korsakov, Nicolai Tcherepnin, and Anatol Liadov were among his teachers. "I don't show my compositions to Liadov," Prokofiev said, "because if I did he probably would expel me from the class." He studied piano with Annette Essipov. She had been one of the many wives of the famous teacher Theodore Leschetizky, from whose atelier had come such famous pianists as Paderewski, Schnabel, Gabrilowitsch, and Friedman; and she herself was recognized as one of the best pianists of the day.

Prokofiev disturbed little Essipov. He disturbed everybody. Prokofiev was like King Gama in *Princess Ida*, always ready with a crushing repartee, with an irritating chuckle and a celebrated leer. He was a man who never could temporize, and he did not suffer fools gladly. He had to say exactly what he thought, and even as a student he was alienating his superiors by his sharp judgments on their music or their teaching methods. (He was to be like that all his life, and had to be approached cautiously. If he took a dislike to anybody, he could be savage. Typical was his reply to an admirer, who gushed over him and shook hands saying "What an infinite pleasure to meet you!"

Prokofiev turned away, growling "On my part there is no pleasure.")

As one of the new breed of antiromantics in a romantically oriented conservatory, Prokofiev composed music that appalled his venerable betters. His *Suggestion diabolique* (1909) and Piano Concerto No. 1 (1911), both composed while he was at the St. Petersburg Conservatory, set the institution on its ears, and he was denounced as "an extreme leftist." At the piano, Prokofiev was an ice-cold demon—throwing out bleak dissonances (or what were in those days considered bleak dissonances) and propulsive rhythms with complete control and emotional detachment. He would have none of the tradition that stemmed from Chopin and Liszt. The piano, he insisted, was a percussion instrument and had to be played percussively. Anyway, Prokofiev did not like the music of Liszt and Chopin, and was constantly poking fun at them. "They say you can't give a recital without Chopin? I'll prove that we can do very well without Chopin." No wonder Essipov in her report called him "very talented but rather unpolished." Nevertheless he won the Rubinstein Prize for piano playing in 1914, and on his own terms. Instead of playing the prescribed classical concerto, he insisted on playing his own, No. 1 in D flat. There was grumbling, but somehow Prokofiev bulled his way through. One of the best descriptions of Prokofiev in action as a young man comes from the composer Vernon Duke, who in those days was named Vladimir Dukelsky and was making up his mind to be a composer. His mother took him to a concert to hear the St. Petersburg Gold Medalist play his own concerto. Reinhold Glière conducted:

Glière bowed and shortly reappeared with a tall young man of extraordinary appearance. He had white-blond hair, a small head with a large mouth and very thick lips. . . . (Prokofiev was then nicknamed the "White Negro") and very long, awkwardly dangling arms, terminating in a bruiser's powerful hands. Prokofiev wore dazzlingly elegant tails, a beautifully cut waistcoat, and flashing black pumps. The strangely gauche manner in which he traversed the stage was no indication of what was to follow; after sitting down and adjusting the piano stool with an abrupt jerk, Prokofiev let go with an unrelenting muscular exhibition of a completely novel kind of piano playing. The prevailing fashion in those days was the languorous hothouse manner of a Scriabin or the shimmering post-Debussy impressionist tinklings of harp and celesta. This young man's music and his performance of it reminded me of the onrushing forwards in my one unfortunate soccer experience—nothing but unrelenting energy and athletic joy of living. No wonder the first four notes of the concerto, oft-repeated, were later nicknamed *"po cherepoo"* ("hit on the head"), which was Prokofiev's exact intention. . . . There was frenetic applause, and no less than six flower horseshoes were handed to Prokofiev, who was now greeted with astonished laughter. He bowed clumsily, dropping his head almost to his knees, and recovering with a yank.

The Russian Revolution came, and Prokofiev headed for the United States by way of Japan. With him were some major compositions. The Revolution may have sent him out of the country, but 1917 was also a great creative year for him. It saw many of the *Visions fugitives* for solo piano, the D major Violin Concerto, and the *Classical Symphony,* all of which have remained among his most popular works. The *Classical Symphony* was a *jeu d'esprit.* "It seemed to me that if Haydn had lived in this century, he would have retained his own style of writing while absorbing certain things from newer music. I wanted to write the kind of symphony that would have such a style." The *Classical* also was Prokofiev's first work written away from the piano. "I wanted to establish the fact that thematic material worked out away from the piano is better."

In the United States, Prokofiev was greatly discussed, somewhat admired, and not generally liked. His sharp, brittle, percussive, wildly propulsive playing was something new, and so was his music. "The Bolshevik pianist," he was called. Or, "Steel fingers, steel biceps, steel triceps—he is a tonal steel trust." To those used to the romantic meanderings of the Liszt and Leschetizky pupils, Prokofiev's playing was poison. Here were no romantic landscapes but pistons, clankings, the machinery of a new age. America did not like him, and he did not like America, especially after the failure of his opera, *The Love for Three Oranges,* when it was staged by the Chicago Opera in 1921. Prokofiev had some hard words to say about the United States:

I wandered through the enormous park in the middle of New York and, looking up at the skyscrapers bordering it, I thought with fury of the wonderful American orchestras that cared nothing for my music; of the critics who were repeating for the hundredth time, "Beethoven is a great composer," while balking violently at new works; of the managers who arranged long tours for artists playing the same hackneyed programs fifty times over.

In disgust, he went to Paris and made his headquarters there. Diaghilev became interested in the young Russian and commissioned two ballets from him, *Le Pas d'acier* (1925) and *L'Enfant prodigue* (1929). He worked on his opera *The Flaming Angel,* finished his Third Piano Concerto, did a good deal of concertizing, and became one of the most-discussed composers of his period. In some respects, he was *the* composer. His music was not played as often as he would have liked, but it nevertheless created an enormous stir in the 1920's, and it made a great many people uncomfortable.

Those who felt uncomfortable had good cause to be; their instincts were correct. For Prokofiev *was* the Age-of-Steel composer, and his music did reflect the new antiromanticism. In a day when Schoenberg's advanced theory was not understood and little encountered, in a day when Stravinsky had "retreated" into neoclassicism after the colossal explosions of *Petrushka* and *Le Sacre du Printemps,* Prokofiev was to many the exemplar of the new era following World War I and the Russian Revolution. People could despise his music, could hate it, could deride it, but it could not be dismissed.

Today we can see that Prokofiev composed within a traditional framework. He used, for the most part, nineteenth-century forms; and his music, despite the many pile-ups of dissonance, was tonal. It is music of a powerful personality, and has many qualities that set it apart. Among those qualities are celerity, dash, confidence, and an enormous athleticism. Prokofiev was not a profound composer, but at its best his lean, clear, pointed music has a remarkably bracing quality. He could invent fine melodies when he wanted to. Melody, however, is not what Prokofiev's music is about. What Prokofiev represented was a sharp, eager, slashing attack on the romantic musical conventions. If in the long run it did not prove to be as revolutionary as many people thought it was, it has remained powerful and muscular, outliving most music of its time.

While Prokofiev was in Paris, a new hero arose in Russia. Dimitri Shostakovich, born in Petersburg on September 25, 1906, was the first important musical child of the Revolution. Like Prokofiev, he had been admitted to the Conservatory at the age of thirteen. There he studied with Maximilian Steinberg and was encouraged by Glazunov. Thin, serious, bespectacled, nervous, shy, chain-smoking, he impressed everybody with his talent. As a senior at the Conservatory in 1925 he composed his First Symphony, which had its premiere the following year, and it bore out all the good predictions that had been made about him. The First Symphony is a remarkable work for a nineteen-year-old—a symphony on a grand scale, with wit and an irrepressible *joie de vivre,* with irony and elements of parody, with juicy melodic content and rich-sounding orchestration. Immediately Shostakovich was established as an important composer. He followed the First Symphony with a series of works that cemented the initial impression. There was the satirical opera *The Nose* (1928), after the Gogol story; and in one interlude of the opera, a section scored for percussion orchestra, Shostakovich showed that he could be as modern as any of his colleagues in the West. There was a smart-aleck Piano Concerto which suggested that Shostakovich could have followed in the footsteps of *Les Six* had he so wanted. There was a ballet named *The Golden Age* (1930), from which the Polka achieved a great deal of fame at one time. Shostakovich also composed a pair of symphonies based on recent Russian history. One was subtitled *October* (1927) and the other

May Day (1931). In 1932 he finished an opera named *Lady Macbeth of Mzensk*, a sort of Russian verismo based on adultery and murder, and expressed in music of powerful dissonance.

It was this opera that got Shostakovich into trouble, for the new leadership in Russia did not look kindly on either the morality or the musical idiom of *Lady Macbeth of Mzensk*. In the early 1920's, experimental work in all the arts had been encouraged in Russia. The theater, headed by such creative forces as Vsevolod Meyerhold, Vladimir Mayakovsky, and Nicolai Okhlopokov, was smashing every tradition in sight. Sergei Eisenstein was bringing new horizons to the cinema. In painting and sculpture, modernism all but became the official style, and the constructivists, headed by Naum Gabo, were emerging as a major force. The creators who came out of the Revolution honestly believed that their art and Russian politics were headed in the same direction. As the artist Kasimir Malevich said, "Cubism and futurism were the revolutionary forms of art in foreshadowing the Revolution in political and economic life of 1917." But by 1930 the entire scale of values had shifted. Through one of the ironies of history, revolutionary Russia began to turn out art of a banality and uniformity of expression that represented the antithesis of revolution.

Some of this shift represented the bourgeois character of Stalin. But more than that, it represented official Soviet doctrine stemming from the words of Lenin, and the words of Lenin meant sanctification. Russian aestheticians and bureaucrats took as their starting point Lenin's statement that "Art belongs to the people." Art was turned into a vehicle for Soviet propaganda, and Socialist Realism came into being. In dictatorships, art always is disposed of much the same way. Only the terminology is different. Where Hitler was to ban avant-garde art and music on the premise that it represented decadent cultural Bolshevism, Stalin banned it on the grounds that it represented decadent imperialistic capitalistic formalism. Any kind of adventurous music was banned in Russia. Composers could not write it, audiences could not hear it. All twelve-tone music, all Bartók and Hindemith, all Stravinsky after *Petrushka* (which did not leave very much), anything that had any hint of abstractionism was banned. The country was closed. No foreign publications were admitted, and all foreign radio broadcasts were jammed. Soviet composers had little way of knowing what was going on in the world. A dreadful pall of uniformity fell over Russian art, literature, and music; and critics—all official spokesmen of government doctrine—developed a weird jargon in which music was evaluated not on its own merits but on its doctrinal purity. Yuri Keldish, in his *History of Russian Music*, denounced Stravinsky's music as the "reactionary essence of modernism as an anti-folk end in art, reflecting the decadent ideology of the imperialist bourgeoisie." All Russian critics wrote like this. The most dreaded charge against a com-

214

poser was "formalism." Nobody knew exactly what it meant, except that if a composer was accused of formalism he had better start mending his ways. In general, formalism in music was anything modern or dissonant, anything that was "pessimistic," anything that did not reflect the heroic ideals of the Soviet worker. "Formalism," said Prokofiev, "is the name given to music not understood on first hearing."

Prokofiev was back in Russia at that time. He had made a visit in 1927, was enthusiastically welcomed, and in 1932 returned for good. Stravinsky for one, in his *Memories and Commentaries,* flatly states that Prokofiev's return to Russia was "a sacrifice to the bitch goddess, and nothing else. He had no success in the United States or Europe for several seasons, while his visit to Russia had been a triumph. When I saw him for the last time in New York in 1937, he was despondent about his material and artistic fate in France. He was politically naive, however, and he had learned nothing from the example of his good friend Miaskovsky. He returned to Russia, and when finally he understood his position there, it was too late." Nicolai Miaskovsky (1881–1950) was a prolific composer of symphonies (he wrote twenty-seven) and an eminent teacher who learned to dance to the Russian tune.

At first, Prokofiev was happy. He was celebrated and honored, he was kept busy, and until 1937 he was allowed to leave the country for concert tours. He told his friend Vernon Duke that he was content:

. . I asked Serge a difficult question then uppermost in my mind. I wanted to know how he could live and work in the atmosphere of Soviet totalitarianism. Serge was quiet for a moment and then said quietly and seriously: "Here is how I feel about it: I care nothing for politics—I'm a composer first and last. Any government that lets me write my music in peace, publishes everything I compose before the ink is dry, and performs every note that comes from my pen is all right with me. In Europe we all have to fish for performances, cajole conductors and theater directors; in Russia they come to *me*—I can hardly keep up with the demand. What's more, I have a comfortable flat in Moscow, a delightful *dacha* in the country and a brand-new car. My boys go to a fine English school in Moscow. . . .

But Prokofiev could not have been happy about the restrictions that were beginning to handcuff Russian musicians. Shostakovich was the first to feel the blow, and his antagonist was Stalin himself. The occasion that drew forth Stalin's wrath was a performance of *Lady Macbeth of Mzensk* in Moscow in 1936. Stalin is said to have stormed out of the theater in a fury after the first act, livid with rage about the "degenerate" music. He immediately postulated three criteria for Soviet opera: subjects must have a Socialist theme; the musical language must be "realistic," *i.e.*, without dissonance and based on Russian folksong; and the plot must be "positive," *i.e.*, with a happy ending in which the State is eulogized. With these postulates came an attack on Shostakovich in *Pravda*. This was serious. A Soviet musician coming under official disapproval could lose his job and could find all outlets for publication and performance closed. He also could lose his home and such perquisites as a car and his *dacha*. In Stalin's day, he even could be jailed. Shostakovich rehabilitated himself in 1937 with his Fifth Symphony. But to all intents and purposes, he was ruined as a composer. Never again would he write with the dash, sparkle, and modernity he had shown in the First Symphony, *The Nose, Lady Macbeth*, and the Piano Concerto. Instead he was to write nothing but safe music, repeating old formulas, imitating some of Prokofiev's mannerisms.

In the 1930's and 1940's, with Shostakovich in full retreat, Prokofiev was the dominant force in Soviet music. His harmonic ideas and melodic idiosyncracies could be found echoed in the music of every important Soviet composer of the day—in Shostakovich, in Dmitri Kabalevsky, in Aram Khachaturian, in Tikhon Khrennikov. They all composed watered-down Prokofiev. Prokofiev himself composed watered-down Prokofiev. They all also acted as spokesmen for the State and its propaganda—all but Prokofiev, who was big enough and stubborn enough to do nothing but compose. And compose he did. He wrote film scores, of which *Lieutenant Kije* (1934) and *Alexander Nevsky* (1939) are the most popular. He finished his Violin Concerto No. 2 (1935), *Peter and the Wolf* (1936), and his ballet music for *Romeo and Juliet* (1935). All of these turned out to be international favorites. An opera, *Semyon Kotko* (1939), did not work out. Another opera, *Betrothal in a Monastery* (1931), adapted from Sheridan's *The Duenna,* received only a few performances. The war years saw a series of important works—the huge opera *War and Peace,* the Piano Sonata No. 7, the String Quartet No. 2, the Flute (Violin) Sonata in D, the ballet music to *Cinderella*, and the Fifth Symphony. These were clearly the scores of a master, and also somewhat different from the music of Prokofiev's French and American period. It carried all of Prokofiev's rhythmic, melodic, and harmonic mannerisms, but sounded less modern, less age-of-steel. Emotionally it was a gentler kind of music, staying close to the principles of Socialist Realism.

Yet even so famous and internationally respected a composer as Prokofiev was not immune to criticism, and in 1948 the roof fell in. Prokofiev and every important Soviet composer of the day were attacked by the regime. The event that touched off the explosion was the premiere, on November 7, 1947, of Vano Muradeli's opera *Great Friendship*. It was reviewed as historically and ideologically incorrect, with "inexpressive, poor, unharmonious, muddled music . . . confused and discordant, built on continuous dissonances and ear-splitting combinations of sounds." Three months later the

Central Committee of the Communist Party held a meeting at which charges were preferred against Muradeli, Prokofiev, Shostakovich, Khachaturian, Miaskovsky, Vissarion Shebalin, and others. The Central Committee published a Resolution accusing all these composers of formalism, "anti-democratic tendencies that are alien to the Soviet people and its artistic tastes," and of writing music "strongly reminiscent of the spirit of contemporary modernistic bourgeois music of Europe and America." For page after page the Central Committee's diatribe went on. Critics also came under attack. "Musical criticism has ceased to express the opinion of Soviet society." The document contained a threat to the effect that such music "cannot be tolerated any longer," and ended with a four-point program:

(1) To condemn the formalistic movement in Soviet music as anti-national and leading to the liquidation of music.

(2) To urge the Department of Propaganda and Agitation of the Central Committee and the Committee of the Fine Arts to correct the situation in Soviet music, to liquidate the defects pointed out in the present Resolution of the Central Committee, and to secure the development of Soviet music in the realistic direction.

(3) To call upon Soviet composers to realize fully the lofty requirements of the Soviet people upon musical art, to sweep from their path all that weakens our music and hinders its development, and assure an upsurge of creative work that will advance Soviet musical culture so as to lead to the creation, in all fields of music, of high-quality works worthy of the Soviet people.

(4) To approve organizational measures of the corresponding Party and Soviet organs, designed to improve the state of musical affairs.

That was on February 10, 1948. From February 17 to 26 there was a meeting of Soviet musicians in Moscow, at which Andrei A. Zhdanov, the Politburo spokesman for cultural ideology, amplified some of the Central Committee's points. Khrennikov added to Zhdanov's remarks, attacking his colleagues and accusing them of formalism. Khrennikov specifically cited Shostakovich's Eighth and Ninth Symphonies and Second Piano Sonata, and Prokofiev's *War and Peace,* Sixth Piano Sonata, and a number of other piano works, as formalistic. He said that Soviet composers "must reject as useless and harmful garbage all the relics of bourgeois formalism in musical art." (Khrennikov soon became a powerful figure in the Soviet musical bureaucracy.) One by one the composers under attack got up and apologized. Muradeli: "How could it have happened that I failed to introduce a single folk song into the score of my opera? . . . I have before me a definite task, to realize fully and unequivocally the seriousness of my creative errors, and to correct these errors with ideological honesty in my future work." Shostakovich: "I am deeply grateful for . . . all the criticism contained in the Resolution. . . . I shall with still more determination work on the musical depiction of the images of the heroic Soviet people." Khachaturian: "How could it happen that I have come to formalism in my art? . . . I want to warn those comrades who, like myself, hoped that their music, which is not understood by the people today, will be understood by future generations tomorrow. It is a fatal theory. In our country, millions of people, the entire Soviet nation, are now arbiters of music. What can be higher and nobler than writing music understandable to our people and to give joy by creative art to millions?" Prokofiev: "The Resolution . . . has separated decayed tissue in the composers' creative production from the healthy part. . . . The Resolution is particularly important because it demonstrates that the formalist movement is alien to the Soviet people. . . ." All the composers wrote a joint letter to Stalin, thanking him for the public spanking: "We are tremendously grateful to the Central Committee of the All-Union Communist Party (Bolsheviks) and personally to you, dear Comrade Stalin, for the severe but profoundly just criticism of the present state of Soviet music. . . . We shall bend every effort to apply our knowledge and our artistic mastery to produce vivid realistic music reflecting the life and struggles of the Soviet people. . . ."

Small wonder that any lingering ideas of individuality were squashed after the 1948 Central Committee Resolution. If the skillful puerilities of Prokofiev's *War and Peace* were to be condemned as formalistic, what was left for the Soviet composer to do but orchestrate folk songs and let it go at that? A period of complete uniformity followed. Russian music, like Russian painting, had nothing to offer to the world. Even the best composers of the Soviet Union—Prokofiev and Shostakovich—were reduced to turning out pallid and uncontroversial scores of artistic inconsequence—the musical equivalent of the agriculture paintings that the artists were turning out. Shostakovich embarked on chamber music, more symphonies, and film scores. Prokofiev wrote such rehashed music as the *Stone Flower* ballet in 1948, the Cello Concerto No. 2 in 1950 (later revised as the Sinfonia Concertante for cello and orchestra), and the Symphony No. 7 in the last year of his life. He died in Moscow on March 5, 1953, the same day that Stalin died.

Prokofiev left a group of works that show no signs of diminished popularity. He is one of the most-played of twentieth-century composers. Two of his five piano concertos, both violin concertos, the Fifth Symphony, a good deal of piano music (especially the third and seventh sonatas), and at least three ballet scores of importance—*L'Enfant prodigue, Romeo and Juliet,* and *Cinderella*—are constantly heard. It may be that a large percentage of Prokofiev's music eventually will die. He often did feature effect above substance in his early works; while in his later ones he was forced to compose a bland, written-down kind of music that is actually cynical. Works like the Piano Sonata No. 7, the D major Violin Sonata, or the G minor Violin Concerto do not wear well. Prokofiev's emotional range was limited and often, as in *The Flaming Angel*, he deliberately set out to shock. Once the shock value wears off, there is not much left. But in his best music he did hit an exposed nerve of the century.

A more liberal artistic policy struggled to come into being after Stalin's death. The second All-Union Congress of Composers actually spoke up for more freedom in 1957. But Nikita Khrushchev, who came into power in 1958, continued to espouse the cause of Socialist Realism. At least there was, during the Khrushchev regime, a party decree of 1958 that exonerated Muradeli and the others who had been attacked in 1948. Shostakovich's *Lady Macbeth of Mzensk* was brought back with a few revisions and a new title, *Katerina Ismáilova*, and a film was even made of it. Shostakovich grew a little more confident in the post-Stalin era, and composed a symphony—his thirteenth—based on five poems by Yevgeny Yevtushenko. One of those poems, "Babi Yar," dealt with the massacre of the Jews in Kiev during World War II. Word got out that Khrushchev disapproved of the subject matter, and the premiere in 1962 was an occasion of gloom. Government officials did not attend, even though the work was the product of two of the cultural stars of the Soviet Union. Official disapproval was unofficially expressed, and the symphony was retired after a second performance. It was again performed the following year, in revised form. But even in its first version it was music of Socialist Realism, an example of poster-propaganda music. It has received very few performances in or outside of Russia.

Not until Khrushchev was deposed by Alexei Kosygin and Leonid Brezhnev in 1964 was there a relaxation in artistic doctrine. Radio jamming was stopped, and students and young composers were able not only to listen to foreign broadcasts of the latest avant-garde music, but also to copy it on tape. A dozen or so composers even started to write a form of serial music, working without textbooks and getting as much information as they could from visiting musicians. The music of Stravinsky and Bartók could be heard once more, and the new generation of composers started to imitate *Le Sacre du Printemps* and *Music for Strings, Percussion, and Celesta* instead of Prokofiev and Shostakovich. But after the Czechoslovakian uprising of 1968 there followed a freeze in the Soviet Union, and a crackdown on artistic freedom. Once again a form of curtain descended, and radio jamming was resumed. The future of music in the Soviet Union again looks bleak. Not until there is a major upheaval and reorientation in the aesthetic and political thinking of the Soviet Union will the country produce music that has any chance of survival.

219

❧ 16 ❧

German Neoclassicism

BUSONI, WEILL, HINDEMITH

The early years of the twentieth century saw a few composers deliberately look back rather than forward. There was Stravinsky with his neoclassicism. There was Reger with his "Back to Bach" movement. There was Paul Hindemith and his evocation of the baroque. And there was Ferruccio Busoni, who was the apostle of Young Classicism (sometimes called New Classicism).

Busoni, one of the greatest and most original of pianists, an intellectual, a composer of music that was little heard in its day and is little heard in ours, was one of those transitional figures with a restless mind whose theories outstripped his actual music in interest. Such advanced composers as Debussy, Stravinsky, and Schoenberg were content to work within the traditional octave. But Busoni as early as 1906 was postulating that the octave could be divided into thirty-six intervals, and he was thinking of the creation of new instruments to play such finely graded microtones. (The idea of microtonal music goes back to the early Greeks, and some medieval composers discussed it, but their theories had long been forgotten.) Busoni, in his search for an extension of the musical vocabulary, also worked out 113 scales by raising and lowering normal intervals. Some examples: C, D flat, D, F flat, G, A, B, C; or C, D, E flat, F flat, G, A sharp, B, C; or C, D flat, E flat, F sharp, G sharp, A, B flat, C. In his *Sketch of a New Esthetic for Music* (1911) he called for "a wealth of harmonic and melodic expression" by splitting the tone into three parts. When Thaddeus Cahill in the United States invented an instrument called the Dynamophone, which transformed electric current into a fixed and mathematically exact number of vibrations, Busoni seized upon this as a possibility for microtonal music. More: the Dynamophone operated independently of any musical instrument, and therefore Busoni was the first to envisage the possibility of electronic music. Busoni's ideas led directly into the work of the Czech composer Alois Hába, who started experimenting with quartertones and sixth tones around 1920; and

Busoni also anticipated some of the work of Edgard Varèse.

But Busoni's own music is neither microtonal nor electronic. He was content to theorize, and he never composed the daring kind of music that his ideas would indicate. He was born in Empoli on April 1, 1866, and died in Berlin on July 27, 1924. His father was Italian, his mother half German, half Italian. Busoni was one of those fantastically gifted children who need no lessons because they already seem to know everything about music. He was playing in public at eight and was a veteran of the concert stage at ten. He had no piano teacher besides his mother, and his only instruction in composition came in 1886, during a short stay at the Leipzig Conservatory, when he was already twenty years old. He was a handsome, virile-looking young man who should have had the world at his feet as a hero of the keyboard, but there was something a shade reserved, a shade too intellectual for tastes of the day, that kept him from wide public success. For a long time he taught—in Helsingfors, in Moscow, in Boston—alternating his teaching with long concert tours. But Berlin was his real home, and he was active there from 1894 to 1914, composing and holding master classes. As a pianist he was the exponent of the grand manner. He had a colossal technique and specialized in the big works of the repertoire, playing them with a combination of neo-Lisztian virtuosity and twentieth-century intellectuality. He thought nothing of putting on one program the Beethoven *Hammerklavier* Sonata followed by the four Ballades of Chopin. The war brought an end to his activities in Berlin, and he settled in Zurich. After 1920 he returned to Berlin, where he taught composition rather than the piano.

It was Busoni's aim as a composer to combine Italian warmth with German forms. Despite his far-out theories, he was basically a traditionalist and even a conservative. When he coined the term Young Classicism in 1919 he wrote that it meant "the mastery, the sifting, the turning to account of all the gains of previous experiments and their inclusion in strong and beautiful forms." Part of Young Classicism was "the definite departure from what is thematic and the return to melody. . . . the casting-off of what is 'sensuous' and the renunciation of subjectivity and the reconquest of serenity." Among other things about Young Classicism, "It does not know the future at all but represents the present at its time of origin. . . . It is ripe through experience gained and supported by tradition." This was a mild call to arms compared to the manifestos that the Futurists, the Second Viennese School, and the Primitivists were putting out, and it is small wonder that not many paid much attention to Young Classicism.

Because of the avant-garde theories scattered through Busoni's prose writings and letters, some musicians have read into Busoni's music things that are not there. The fact is that his music, though often extremely interesting, represents an eclectic approach to the new problems of form that agitated the first half of the twentieth century. Creators like Stravinsky and Schoenberg came up with a specific solution. Busoni, like Reger, offered an escape, the one with his Young Classicism, the other with his Back to Bach movement, but in essence they had little to offer that was of interest to the radicals of the day. Busoni's early music, much of which he later disavowed, is frankly postromantic, with a noticeable debt to Brahms. A transitional work was the tremendous Piano Concerto of 1904, which ends with a choral finale. The three composers who meant the most to Busoni were Bach, Beethoven, and Liszt. One of his aphorisms was: "Bach is the foundation of piano playing, Liszt the summit. The two made Beethoven possible." Busoni's idols, Bach, Beethoven, and Liszt, are all present in the Piano Concerto. There even is a hint of Tchaikovsky. If Tchaikovsky could write a popular piano concerto with smashing opening chords, Busoni could go him one better with a series of gigantic chords that go on ten times as long as Tchaikovsky's famous opening splurge. The piano writing is Liszt-derived, and one movement of the Busoni concerto is based entirely on a Liszt theme, the Tarantella from *Venezia e Napoli*. Busoni must have had a mind like a blotter, and he never seems to have forgotten a note he ever heard, nor could he entirely shake himself free from the themes and ideas of other composers. His Piano Concerto, despite what some critics have said, is nothing more than a large-scale, ambitious postromantic work in which Busoni was determined to outdo Liszt, Rubinstein, Tchaikovsky, and all the other composers of virtuoso concertos. The finale for male chorus is merely tacked on. Interesting as it is in itself, it has no place in this concerto, and it gives the work an air of fake sublimity.

Later Busoni was able to shake off the obvious postromanticisms of much of his music. He began to write a series of works that are reserved, enigmatic, and full of novel twists. It is a very personal kind of music that ran counter to every trend of the day. Where Stravinsky was startling the world with the rhythms and barbarisms of *Le Sacre du Printemps,* where Schoenberg was breaking off into atonalism and expressionism, where Debussy was creating a new world of sensuous, antiacademic color, Busoni was working in a medium that was more intellectual than sensuous: a medium that took old forms and translated them into more modern terms. But Busoni's was a timid kind of neoclassicism, unlike Stravinsky's revolutionary filtration of classic and baroque elements into a dissonant and polyrhythmic language. Busoni's harmonies and rhythms were of the past, never far removed from the nineteenth century.

Nevertheless his music has its own personality and probity. His idolatry of Bach is reflected in the remarkable *Fantasia Contrappuntistica* for solo piano (later arranged for two pianos). In its twenty-five minutes it takes Bach from the 1740's to the beginning of the twentieth century. Reger at that time was also writing Bach-derived pieces, but Reger's were all but Franckian, with their juicy chromatic harmonies and cheerful self-indulgence. Busoni's ideas about Bach were stringent, powerful, and intellectual. The *Contrappuntistica* is in twelve sections—a series of variations on Bach's *Ehre sei Gott in der Höhe*, followed by four fugues interspersed with an intermezzo and variations, and ending with a chorale and stretta. The first fugue is an attempt to finish the uncompleted fugue in Bach's *Die Kunst der Fuge*. This part of the *Fantasia Contrappuntistica* is severely Bachian. But then come some startling shifts. As the work progresses one can hear a Beethovenian development of the fugal subject: *Die Kunst der Fuge* heard through Beethoven's *Grosse Fuge*, full of enigmatic, dissonant trills and a few stabbing harmonies. Busoni eventually gets around to Busoni, and the end of the *Fantasia Contrappuntistica* is extremely personal. The harmonies become dry and somewhat dissonant, and the entire feeling passes from Bach baroque to Bach with something completely alien superimposed on it. Liszt shows up in some of the writing—the Liszt of the *Weinen, Klagen* Variations —especially in the version for two pianos. But what is heard is a modern Liszt—the Lisztian textures without the Lisztian glitter and exhibitionism. Difficult and virtuosic as the *Fantasia Contrappuntistica* is, it is not a show-piece. Still another composer figures in the piano writing of this work— Charles Alkan (1813–1888), the almost-forgotten French pianist-composer so admired by Liszt and Busoni. Alkan was called the Berlioz of the piano and composed eccentric, monstrously long and complicated works that Busoni played in public once in a while. The amalgam of Liszt and Alkan in Busoni's piano style leads to a massive, fluent, orchestral manner of writing. Some of Busoni's elegies can be traced back to the shorter Alkan pieces.

In addition to his considerable number of piano works, Busoni composed several operas—*Die Brautwahl* (1912), *Arlecchino* and *Turandot* (1917), and *Doktor Faust* (1925), which he left unfinished at his death. As such his last opera joins the company of Puccini's *Turandot*, Boito's *Nerone*, and Berg's *Lulu*. Busoni's pupil Philipp Jarnach, working from his master's sketches, finished the last scene. Busoni had written his own libretto in 1914, but he was a busy touring pianist with a heavy teaching schedule, and he could work on his ambitious opera only at intervals. Long gone were the days when a Rossini or Donizetti could whip out a full opera in three weeks.

Doktor Faust is a remarkable opera with some very modern ideas. Busoni himself had a good deal of Faust in his makeup, and also a touch of Hamlet: "a weak man, yet a stout wrestler, whom doubts drive hither and thither; master of thought, slave of instinct, exhausting all things, finding no answer." Thus Busoni himself wrote about his nature. *Faust* is in line with this summing up: a tortured, complicated work that looks to the past

223

and yet has sections that are prophetic. Busoni has left some comments about his opera. He was afraid to touch Goethe, he said, but he had fallen under the fascination of the Faust idea. His solution was to incorporate features of the medieval puppet show, which he filled with symbolism. At the end of the opera Faust passes his own spirit into the body of his dead child by the Duchess of Parma. Busoni's explanation is that "after Faust in his last approach to God has also thrown away belief, he proceeds to mystical deeds, which renew his exhausted life."

Busoni would have nothing to do with opera composers who wrote merely descriptive music, as Gounod had done in his setting of *Faust*. Busoni, in his opera, sought for a large outline, creating "musically independent forms which at the same time suited the words and the scenic events, and which also had a separate and sensible existence detached from the words and the situations." Thus the scene of the demons is in variation form, the scenic intermezzo is a rondo, and so on. This is exactly what Berg was to do in *Wozzeck* and it is one of the most original things about *Doktor Faust*. The music itself is varied. There are certain obvious derivations. Berlioz, Liszt, Wagner, and Strauss play a part. The derivations are easy to point out. But even they are used in an unusual, original manner. The whole *feeling* of the opera is original, derivations and all, nineteenth-century harmonies and all. It is post-Wagnerism without Wagner, post-Straussian without Strauss. It has a melodic line that resembles early Schoenberg here and there. And in one startling instance, in the second Prelude (starting with section 2 of the Breitkopf vocal score), there is an anticipation of the Dr. Schoen love motive in Berg's *Lulu*.

Like Mahler, Busoni believed that his music was for a later day, and he indicated as much in the epilogue of *Doktor Faust:*

> Still unexhausted, all the symbols wait
> Still in this work are hidden and concealed.
> Their germs a later school shall procreate
> Whose fruits to those unborn shall be revealed.
> Let each take what he finds appropriate:
> The seed is sown; others may reap the field.

But Busoni, unlike Mahler, has never had his day, although the late 1960's saw a slight interest in his music. His *Doktor Faust* has received very few performances in Europe and no staged performance at all (thus far) in the United States. The opera composer in Germany who achieved the smash hit of the 1920's was not Busoni but his pupil Kurt Weill, whose *Die Dreigroschenoper* (*The Three-Penny Opera*) was a wild international success that has yet to run its course.

Weill was born in Dessau on March 2, 1900, and died in New York on April 3, 1950. At first he composed respectable "modern music" that always turned up at the various festivals of the International Society for Contemporary Music. These works were well received and were never heard of again. (After Weill's death an attempt was made to revive them, but they were much too weak to gain a foothold.) It was not until Weill collaborated with Bertolt Brecht that he found his métier. In 1928 Brecht adapted—very closely indeed; it was actually a rewrite—John Gay's ballad opera of 1728, with new music by Weill, who scored the work for a small jazz combination. *Die Dreigroschenoper* had a predecessor in Ernst Krenek's jazz opera *Jonny spielt auf* (1927), but that work, so popular for a decade or so, has vanished for good and is much too dated to be revived, whereas *Die Dreigroschenoper* continues to retain its fierce and venomous punch. In a way *Die Dreigroschenoper* was a German equivalent of what *Les Six* were doing at the same time in Paris. But where the music of *Les Six* was Stravinsky-derived, often neoclassic, light and entertaining, Weill's little opera was bitter, anti-Stravinsky, anti-Wagner, anti-everything that was considered opera. It also was as much a social as a musical document, reflecting the terrible postwar period in Germany. It was to German music what the line drawings of George Grosz were to German art.

Weill never duplicated the success of *Die Dreigroschenoper*, though he composed several works in the same vein, including the longer and more ambitious *Mahagonny*. All are in essence rewrites of his great success. In 1933 Weill left Germany, went to France, then settled in New York, where he became a very popular composer for the Broadway stage. He also tried his hand at "American opera," and both *Street Scene* and *Down in the Valley* are attempts along that line. They do not work, and the composer of the biting *Dreigroschenoper* descended into cheap platitudes. At least in that opera Weill added a remarkable work to the lyric stage, and the word masterpiece is not too strong.

The most important man of German music in the 1920's was neither Busoni nor Weill but the short, bald, cherubic-looking, incredibly gifted Paul Hindemith. Germany was full of composers at the time, but the music of very few has lived. Eugen d'Albert, Hans Pfitzner, Franz Schmidt, Paul Graener, Walther Braunfels, Max von Schillings, Manfred Gurlitt, Artur Schnabel, Heinrich Kaminski—where is their music today? Hindemith and Weill are virtually the only ones of the period whose music has survived.

If ever there was a musician's musician it was Paul Hindemith. The man had perfect pitch, was a professional violinist and violist, a good pianist, could play virtually every instrument in the orchestra (if he was unfamiliar with one he would take off a week or so and master it), was a good musicologist, could compose with incredible facility, and had stored in that bald head of his an overwhelming knowledge of music. In the 1920's he was to German music what Prokofiev was to Russian music—a young revolutionary, impatient with the postromantic tradition, who was composing music that was regarded as the last word in acid dissonance and atonality (he never composed atonal music, but that is how it sounded to his contemporaries). His sharp, even savage, scores made him the *enfant terrible* of the decade. Well known is Richard Strauss's complaint to Hindemith: "Why do you have to write this way? You have talent." Less known is the cocky Hindemith's answer: "Herr Professor, you make your music and I'll make mine."

If Busoni represented a diluted form of neoclassicism, Hindemith represented the neobaroque. He worked in old classic forms—fugue, sonata, suite —and produced an enormous quantity of music, just as the baroque composers did. Throughout his entire creative span—he was born in Hanau on November 16, 1895, and died in Berlin on December 28, 1963—he represented the baroque. Like the baroque composers he adopted a utilitarian, practical view toward music. His philosophy was antiromantic and so was his music, which had its roots in the great German tradition of Bach through Beethoven. In his youth he was an avant-gardist, and his severe, dissonant music was never really close to the public's heart, even though his great talent was recognized almost immediately. He went on to compose a handful of scores that have become repertory items—the *Mathis der Maler* Symphony (1934), the *Kleine Kammermusik* for Wind Quintet (1922), the song cycle *Das Marienleben* (1924), the Violin Concerto (1939), *The Four Temperaments* (1944), the *Symphonic Metamorphoses* on Weber themes (1943), the Third String Quartet (1922), the *Ludus Tonalis* for piano (1943), the ballet *Nobilissima Visione* (1938)—but on the whole he was more admired by professionals than by the public. For professionals respond to craft; and Hindemith was one of the century's greatest craftsmen and most learned musicians.

His music was a model of workmanship in the mainstream of baroque and classic German music. Bach was probably the composer to whom Hindemith was closest. From the very beginning Hindemith shunned program music, just as he derided the theories of Schoenberg and Stravinsky. He was an academician and proud of it. And, working academically, he did put his mark on the music of the twentieth century. He showed that the German tradition was not exhausted and that it had vitality when properly approached. The old forms were generally his means of expression. But those old forms sounded anything but old as treated by Hindemith. Unlike the eclectic Busoni, who also was interested in old forms, Hindemith evolved a most unusual harmonic and melodic language, and any phrase he wrote can instantly be recognized as his. He evolved a tonal system based on the natural laws of sound, on the fundamental note and its overtone series; and it was as distinctive in its way as Scriabin's fourths and mystic chords, or as Stravinsky's rhythmic legerdemain. Above all, there was in his writing that sheer expertise. Of all the great figures of his day, he may have been the most complete musician *qua* musician.

As a theoretician, Hindemith was the author of some valuable and provocative books. Nor was he merely an ivory-tower theoretician. For several years after 1933—he did very little work in Germany after the Nazis branded his music as degenerate art—he busied himself reorganizing musical education in Turkey. In 1939 he settled in the United States, becoming head of the music department at Yale University in 1942 and an American citizen in 1946. In 1953 he returned to Europe.

Throughout his career, Hindemith was desperately anxious to write music that would be played not only by the professional but also by the amateur. It was Hindemith who was responsible for the term *Gebrauchsmusik,* or utilitarian music. As early as the 1920's Hindemith had become concerned about the ever-increasing schism between composer and public. Consequently he started composing, in addition to concert works, a long series of scores intended for amateur players. For them he wrote pieces for virtually every instrument, singly or in combination. It is not, in this case, important whether or not this kind of utility music is great. The significant thing is that a major composer turned his attention to it; and even the slightest work of a major composer is of greater musical value than the slickest work of a hack.

As it happens, much of Hindemith's *Gebrauchsmusik* is better than it sounds, as is so much of his other music. A good deal of Hindemith's music on first hearing is forbidding: pungent in its dissonance, austere in its form, acerbic in its melodic content. It is anything but loveable music. Indeed, it can impress one as downright unloveable. But, somehow, exposure to Hindemith's music always brings its own rewards. What at first seems forbidding soon turns out to be strong, subtle, curiously fascinating, and highly stimulating in its logic, organization, and integrity. It was only toward the end that Hindemith began to turn out scores almost by rote, much like Milhaud—competent but dry scores in which the flywheel seemed disconnected from the motor.

It is difficult to guess Hindemith's ultimate place in music. Perhaps he will end as the Max Reger of the 1920–40 period. Or it may be that a future age will put greater stress than the 1960's has done upon his solidity, impeccable workmanship, evocation of the baroque, and reserved but nevertheless pronounced melodies. After 1945 his music had little to offer to the new generation. Anything derived from the baroque or classic (and that included even the music of Stravinsky) was frowned upon. But fashions and fads change, while craft—real craft—will always be appreciated. Purely as a craftsman, Hindemith was on a transcendental level. True, it must be conceded that craft alone, unsupported by cogent ideas, is not enough; and Hindemith in the last years of his life was often guilty of mechanically stringing together notes. But at his best he was a strong creative figure with something positive to offer. The urgency and propulsion of some of his *Kammermusik* writing, the big conception of the symphony extracted from the opera *Mathis der Maler*, the lean, medieval-impregnated quality of such a score as *Der Schwanendreher*, the fascination of the deft contrapuntal writing in *Ludus Tonalis*—all these are reflective of an art and a mind that will live when most of the ephemera around it is long dead.

❦ 17 ❧

Rise of an American Tradition

FROM GOTTSCHALK TO COPLAND

While Europe was busily producing great composers, the United States during most of the nineteenth century was occupied in opening its frontiers. Muscles were bunched for a mighty effort, and amazing things were accomplished, but the national spirit was turned to matters other than the development of a serious musical culture. It was not that the United States lacked music. There was a strong body of folk music derived from the English, from the African slaves, and from the Caribbean area. At least two composers did take advantage of that material—Louis Moreau Gottschalk and Stephen Foster. Foster (1826–1864), who has come down in history as "America's minstrel," was one of the few composers to suggest something specifically personal and American in his music. He also was extremely popular. The whole country was singing "Old Folks at Home," "Old Black Joe," "Camptown Races," "Come Where My Love Lies Dreaming," and the other Foster favorites. Foster was a true lyricist, and his songs have never lost their authentic, gentle beauty.

But during the nineteenth century in the United States, "serious" music was by and large a foreign art, practiced by imported professors. The major symphony orchestras were staffed mostly by foreign-born musicians. Soloists and teachers were immigrants, many of them German, who represented a tradition stemming from Beethoven and his successors. American composers based their work on foreign models. When William Mason (1829–1908) wrote piano music, it was a synthesis of Schumann and Chopin. When William Henry Fry in 1845 composed the first American grand opera, *Leonora,* he went to Bellini for inspiration. Not until the appearance of Charles Ives late in the century did an American composer begin to speak with an individual, powerful voice. But Ives had been preceded by the fascinating Louis Moreau Gottschalk, a composer who trembled on the verge of a breakthrough but who never fully lived up to his potential.

229

Gottschalk might have been an American Glinka, but a combination of circumstances prevented it. Among those circumstances was his death at the early age of forty. In Rio de Janeiro, where he died in 1869, he was beginning to compose large-scale works, and had he had more time he conceivably could have added significantly to the repertory. As it is, he was a very interesting figure whose music started to be rediscovered in the United States after the Second World War.

He was born in New Orleans on May 8, 1829, the son of a British father and a Creole mother. Soon he learned everything his local teachers could give him, and at the age of thirteen was sent to Paris, where he was refused admittance to the Conservatoire on the grounds of his nationality. Pierre Zimmerman, head of the piano faculty, refused to listen to the boy. "America is only a country of steam engines." Gottschalk had to take private lessons, first a few with Charles Hallé, then with Camille Stamaty. Among the pupils in Stamaty's class was the seven-year-old Camille Saint-Saëns, and one wonders what young Gottschalk's reaction must have been the first time he heard the genius of an infant. But Gottschalk's talent at the keyboard also was of a supreme order. He soon became not only a good pianist, but a great and celebrated one. Among his admirers were Berlioz and Chopin, and for a while he had a tremendous vogue in Europe. He was slim, handsome, aristocratic, extraordinarily talented, and he blazed a trail through early romantic pianism. Many competent critics called him the equal of Liszt and Thalberg. The flashy young American, the first internationally famous pianist to come out of the United States, was the man of the hour.

In the late 1840's Gottschalk started to compose. In his background were the plantation melodies with which he had grown up, and also the snappy Cuban and Caribbean rhythms he had heard in New Orleans. Inspired by the nationalistic quality of the Chopin mazurkas, Gottschalk began to write music that was reflective of *his* ethnic background and environment. Native tunes and rhythms were put into a sophisticated piano layout stemming from Chopin and Liszt, to which Gottschalk added a device of his own later to be described as the "style pianola." It was so called because it resembled the tinkling of the player piano. Gottschalk had a great fondness for the upper two octaves of the piano keyboard, and was constantly producing from it cascades of silvery sound. His initial series of piano pieces, which he started to compose in Paris when he was sixteen years old, was based mostly on Negro and plantation melodies, with titles like *Bamboula, Le Bananier,* and *La Savane.* Later Gottschalk was to spend much time in the West Indies and South America, where a different type of nationalism entered his music. Even today some of his nationalistic music sounds sophisticated; it has dated very little, and the rhythmic flair of the writing, with its sharp syncopations, is surprisingly modern. A work such as *Souvenir de Porto*

Rico, written in the middle 1850's, is not very different from many pieces in Milhaud's *Saudades do Brasil,* written about seventy years later.

When Gottschalk's music began appearing in Europe, audiences could not get enough of it, and celebrated pianists jostled one another in their rush to play these exotic, colorful pieces from the New World. For several decades there was a run on them. Gottschalk was the first composer with the imagination to take advantage of the American and Caribbean folk material, and he had the skill to touch it up without losing its basic quality.

Gottschalk returned to the United States in 1853. He lived a busy life, concertizing steadily, writing large quantities of music, traveling through the country and in the West Indies, getting mixed up in love affairs (one of those, with the actress Ada Clare, shook the foundations of New York society). He loved the West Indies, Havana in particular, and he absorbed the native music he constantly was hearing. He kept a diary, posthumously published as *Notes of a Pianist,* in which a very literate, appealing personality comes through. Gottschalk was a good reporter, and his book is source material on the America of the Civil War period. As a composer, he was very popular with his countrymen. He wrote a good deal of salon music, and two of his salon pieces—*The Last Hope* and *The Dying Poet*—graced the pianos of every genteel household in the country. He was constantly on the move, as though fleeing from something. Before and during the war he toured the eastern and central states (always with supporting musicians; there was no such thing as a solo recital in those days). In 1865 he went to the Far West, playing in San Francisco and the mining towns. In San Francisco he got into trouble. The citizens were stirred up when there were reports that Gottschalk had made free with one of the respectable young ladies of the city. He hadn't, but rather than face a posse of vigilantes, he fled to a ship and sailed to South America. Beating his way through the continent, he ended up in Rio de Janeiro. There he arranged big concerts —"monster festivals," they were called—that would have made his friend Berlioz proud. Romantic to the end, he collapsed at the piano while playing one of his pieces, a work named *Morte.* Shortly after, he died. Some said it was of yellow fever. Some said that he had been assassinated by a jealous husband. The true cause appears to have been peritonitis.

A large part of Gottschalk's music was ephemeral. His dated salon pieces have little to offer except a nostalgic glimpse at a type of music that so delighted our forebears. More interesting are his big virtuoso pieces, which are in the mainstream of romantic pianism. Some of them are worth revival. Most important of all are his nationalistic works for piano, for orchestra, even for voice. These are prophetic. Gottschalk wrote them to entertain and probably had no delusions about their worth, but they have come down the generations not only as an authentic whiff of a vanished America but as significant creations in their own right. Probably no composer in the world at the time, not even Berlioz or Liszt, had Gottschalk's rhythmic freedom. His rhythms were profoundly original because he was working in an Afro-Cuban rhythmic world that had not been explored by any serious composer up to that time. Unfortunately, he lacked the independence of mind to follow this to its logical end; and he was too restless, too careless, a person to make full use of his natural abilities. At that, he could sometimes write with a breathless disregard for the amenities, as in the crazy discords at the end of the four-hand version of *La Gallina,* which all but anticipate Ives. He could also attempt works on a big scale, and his two-movement symphony (a symphony only because he called it so), *A Night in the Tropics,* has a broad, well-planned and rich-sounding first movement in which Berlioz figures, as well as the Félicien David of *Le Désert.* This movement is followed by a Cuban dance that crackles its jaunty, irresistible way.

Naturally this music was scorned within a few decades after Gottschalk's death, and all of it slipped into obscurity. It was considered trash, and serious composers were ashamed of it. Could such lightweight, commercial stuff represent American music? The trend was toward weighty writing in the German manner. In the last quarter of the century rose the group known as the Boston Classicists. Nearly all of them went abroad to complete their musical education in Germany, and they returned to the United States eager to pass on to their pupils the thrilling precepts of the Leipzig, Berlin, or Munich professors. John Knowles Paine (1839–1906) studied with Karl August Haupt in Berlin and in 1862 became director of music at Harvard. George Chadwick (1854–1931) worked under Solomon Jadassohn in Leipzig and Josef Rheinberger in Munich. Arthur Whiting (1861–1936) was a Rheinberger product, and so was Horatio Parker (1863–1919). Others in the group were Arthur Foote (1853–1937), who did *not* study in Europe, and Charles Martin Loeffler (1861–1935), the Alsatian-born violinist who came to Boston at the age of twenty. All of these composers were active in the New England area, all were conservatives, all but Loeffler were influenced by Brahms, and all composed good academic music that at the very least ranked with the good academic music of Europe.

All were put in the shade by Edward Alexander MacDowell, who was born in New York on December 18, 1861, and died there on January 23, 1908. Few composers have been so idolized during their lifetime. MacDowell occupied a position in the United States like Elgar's in England. He was not only hailed as America's greatest composer; he was firmly believed to be the equal of any composer anywhere. That was while he was alive. Few composers of equivalent fame in their day have been so soon forgotten. Of MacDowell's rather large output, what remains in the active repertoire? The D minor Piano Concerto (1890), a few of the *Woodland Sketches* (1896), the

Indian Suite (1897). That is about all. Every once in a great while there is a revival of one of the big symphonic poems. *Lamia* (1908) might turn up, or *Hamlet and Ophelia* (1895). They sound like faded, forgotten curiosities. Even the four piano sonatas, which used to appear occasionally, seem to have vanished.

The irony about MacDowell is that he was accepted as America's greatest composer without in reality having anything specifically American about his music. He realized that as well as anybody, and one can understand why he protested violently, in speech and in print, against being called a nationalist. Time and again he insisted that his music had to be accepted on its own terms, and he raised a fierce row when his music was included on an American program. MacDowell energetically rejected the idea of nationalism in music. "So-called Russian, Bohemian or any other national music has no place in art, for its characteristics may be duplicated by anyone who takes a fancy to do so. On the other hand, the vital element in music—personality —stands alone." MacDowell did not want to be judged as an American composer; he wanted to be judged as a composer, without any special or chauvinistic favors. Another reason he so strongly railed against nationalism was his eagerness to justify his use of German models. There is very little local color in MacDowell's music. Works like the *New England Idylls* (1902) or *From Uncle Remus* (1898) could have been written by any German composer of the period.

This is not surprising, for aside from a year spent at the Paris Conservatory (1876), MacDowell was German-trained—at Stuttgart, Wiesbaden, Frankfurt, and, briefly, with Liszt at Weimar. His big inspiration was Joachim Raff, a very popular composer of the day. MacDowell studied with him in Frankfurt, and Raff showed great interest in the handsome, tall, red-headed American. In 1881 MacDowell became head piano teacher at the Darmstadt Conservatory and produced a great deal of music that interested Liszt. Liszt also enjoyed MacDowell's clever piano playing. It was not until 1888 that MacDowell returned to America for good. He had been in Europe for twelve years. Now he settled down in Boston, taught privately, and composed. In 1896 he went to New York to become chairman of the newly formed Department of Music at Columbia University. Seven years later he clashed with Nicholas Murray Butler, the president of Columbia, and resigned in 1904, charging Butler and Columbia with "materialism." MacDowell, a brokenhearted and emotionally shattered man after this experience, died in 1908 feeling that he had failed in life.

A through-and-through romantic, MacDowell was perfectly content to write scores that were safely derived from Schumann, Liszt, Grieg, Raff, and Rubinstein. Especially Rubinstein. MacDowell's two piano concertos have often been compared with the Grieg A minor, but in fact they are closer to the conventional display concertos that Rubinstein had written. And they —the MacDowell as well as the Rubinstein—are very good concertos of their genre, though in MacDowell's case, his D minor is a much better realized and more spontaneous-sounding work than the companion A minor. The last movement of the D minor has a snappy buck-and-wing hint of the American scene rare in MacDowell's music.

Conventionality: that is the word that is, unfortunately, descriptive of MacDowell's music. He had gifts, but daring did not go with them. His harmonies are always derivative, and what saves his music from total extinction is an unusually sweet and genuine melodic power. It is in salon music like the *Woodland Sketches* that this kind of melodic gift best comes through. Of course, at the turn of the century, the tastemakers were apt to sneer at the *Woodland Sketches,* which contained works like *To a Wild Rose* and *To a Water Lily.* These were considered unimportant chips, sentimental effusions, and MacDowell was going to live by his great *Sonata Tragica* (1893) or *Sonata Eroica* (1895). It is easy to see how those two works commanded the respect they once did. MacDowell had ambitious dreams here, and attempted an equally big canvas. Critics spoke of his four piano sonatas—the other two are the *Norse* (1900) and the *Keltic* (1901)—in terms reserved for the Liszt B minor. They raved about the workmanship, the brilliant pianistic layout, the depth and passion of the music. What they did not see, because they were too close, was that the workmanship creaks, the passion is sham, and the difficulties are unsupported by cogent musical ideas.

But there is nothing sham about the lovely *Woodland Sketches* and some of the other piano pieces. Some of his songs, too, are of real beauty and would repay the attention of recitalists. For MacDowell, who so desperately wanted to be a "big" composer, was essentially a miniaturist. And, curiously, it was here that whatever national traits there were in him came out. The *Woodland Sketches* are much more than period pieces (just as Mendelssohn's *Songs Without Words* and Grieg's *Lyric Pieces* transcend their period). They are more than period pieces because they are perfect and individual of their kind, and have a melodic flavor that is altogether honest. *To a Wild Rose* is worth all the four sonatas rolled together, on the premise that an honest dime is worth more than a counterfeit $100 bill.

Thus, where MacDowell's orchestral music is mostly embarrassing, and where his large-scale compositions (the D minor Piano Concerto excepted) are mostly rhetoric unsupported by content, his shorter piano pieces and songs do deserve a niche in the repertory. It remained for Charles Ives, born thirteen years after MacDowell, to be the first great American national composer; but what MacDowell did was to show the world that the United States was not devoid of creative musical talent; and to show the United States that the career of a composer was one that could command a respect-

234

ed social status. Through his activities as a composer of world-wide reputation, and as pianist and as teacher, he crystallized an emergent national pride. He came on the scene just as America was conquering its last frontiers and for the first time beginning to think of things that were beyond pure materialism. It was the time when the industrial barons were beginning to separate Europe from its art treasures; when some wealthy people banded together to make for themselves a great opera house in New York; when there was great talk of a national academy of music; when Theodore Thomas was bringing the best in symphonic music to the people. The pot was ready to boil, and Edward MacDowell was one of the chief cooks.

Charles Ives, whose early career coincided with MacDowell's last period, cannot be judged in any rational manner. His music was so far ahead of its time that it was mutated rather than composed. He was everything Mac-Dowell was not, and was a bewildering combination of seer and practical man, mystic and democrat, sentimentalist and businessman. His music is a constant reflection of his New England youth: remembrances of life in a simpler age. He yearned for the virtues of an older, town-hall-meeting, village-band, transcendentalist, Emersonian America, and expressed those yearnings in the most advanced, unorthodox, ear-splitting, grating music composed by anybody anywhere up to that time.

This was the composer who, with his partner Julian Myrick, ran one of the most successful insurance agencies in the country at the time (forty-eight million dollars worth of new business in 1929, the year he retired). This was the composer who was captain of the baseball and football teams at Danbury High School, who pitched a winning ten-inning game against the Yale freshmen, and later made the Yale football team. This was the composer who avoided most professional musicians, seldom went to a concert, published his own music, refused royalties and copyrights, delved into atonality before Schoenberg, into dissonances that made most contemporary music sound Victorian, into tone clusters long before Henry Cowell, into polytonality long before Stravinsky and Milhaud, into polyrhythms that remained for the postserialists to investigate. Quarter tones, asymmetrical rhythms, disjunct melodies, jazz and ragtime elements, anticipations of aleatory— name it, and Ives was doing it, usually long before anybody else.

So advanced was his idiom, so convulsively dissonant and complicated, so full of unusual textures and devices, that hardly anybody could grasp its significance. Stravinsky's reaction was typical. He first heard music by Ives in 1942. "I wish I could say that I was attracted by what I heard, for I respected Ives as an inventive and original man, and I wanted to like his music. It seemed to me badly uneven in quality, however, as well as ill proportioned." On further exposure to Ives, Stravinsky decided that though his original objections had not changed:

I think I now perceive the identifying qualities which make those objections unimportant. The danger now is to think of Ives as a mere historical phenomenon, "The Great Anticipator." He is certainly more than that, but nevertheless, his anticipations continue to astonish me. Consider, for example, the "Soliloquy, or a Study in 7ths and Other Things." The vocal line of this little song *looks* like Webern's *Drei Volkstexte*, albeit the Ives was composed a decade and more before the Webern. The retrogrades are of the sort Berg was concerned with in the *Kammerkonzert* and *Der Wein*, though the "Soliloquy" was composed a decade and more before the Berg pieces. The rhythmic devices such as "4 in the time of 5" are generally thought to be the discoveries of the so-called post-Webern generation, but Ives anticipates this generation by four decades. The interval idea itself, the idea of the aphoristic statement, and the piano style all point in the direction of later and more accepted composers. But Ives had already transgressed the "limits of tonality" more than a decade before Schoenberg, had written music exploiting polytonality almost two decades before *Petrushka*, and experimented with polyorchestral groups a half century before Stockhausen.

Small wonder that Ives has been canonized as the saint of American music. Very few composers write in his style, but he has become one of the spiritual fathers of all composers active in America. To them, he is the symbol of daring and independence, of uncompromising genius decades ahead of his time, of a complete break from academism; and also, incidentally, as the composer of a body of music that finally has come into its own—a body of music unique in the literature, sometimes flawed but always vital. Ives's music in a way reflects the American unconscious, drawing together as it does the hymnodists from Billings on, the Negro and his music, Stephen Foster, the American folk music, even the academic tradition. Ives's music is also the history of American music.

He was born in Danbury, Connecticut, on October 20, 1874, and died in New York on May 19, 1954. At a time when all good American composers were going to Leipzig and Munich, dutifully studying the mysteries of fugue and sonata under Rheinberger and other academicians, Ives was putting two bands against each other, each band playing different American tunes in a different key. At the age of twenty, he composed a *Song for Harvest Season* for voice, cornet, trombone, and organ pedals, each in a different key: complete polytonality in 1894. MacDowell and Paine, the then leading American composers, with their *allegros* and *quasi sostenutos* and *andante con motos*, spoke a different language from Ives, who was writing such musical directions as "roughly and in a half-spoken way," or "The piano should be played as *indistinctly* as possible," or "In a gradually excited way." One of his songs is named *A Son of a Gambolier,* and toward the end Ives inserts a "Kazoo chorus with flutes, fiddles and flageolets." A few measures on, he directs: "And piccolos, ocarinas and fifes."

He did not expect the singer to run out and collect kazoo players. He wrote the direction because it was an indication of the type of tone color he wanted (though he would have been delighted had the singer actually come on stage with kazoo and ocarina virtuosos). Leopold Stokowski, who in the 1950's wanted to program an Ives piece, had a hard time locating a jew's harp player for a certain effect that Ives requested. Local 802 of the American Federation of Musicians had thousands of members, but not a single jew's harp player. Stokowski had to advertise before one was found.

The bulk of Ives's music falls between 1896 and 1916. His work was so unconventional and eccentric, and so impossibly hard to perform, that he did not get a public hearing of an orchestral work until 1927. It took John Kirkpatrick about ten years to learn the Piano Sonata No. 2 (the *Concord*). In 1947 Ives was given a Pulitzer Prize for his Third Symphony—forty-three years after he composed it. He was seventy-three years old then, and his style had been substantially formed by the middle 1890's. "I found I *could not* go on using the familiar chords early," he once explained. "I *heard* something else." In Yale, he had taken a composition course with Horatio Parker in 1898. Parker would look sorrowfully at the exercises submitted by the young maverick. "Ives, *must* you hog all the keys?" he would ask, with a sigh.

Very little of Ives's music has been published. His manuscripts, a wild collection of scarcely decipherable notes, prose (he had a worse handwriting than Beethoven's), marginalia, erasures, and scratches, are all but impossible to decipher. There are completed compositions, rough drafts, compositions started and abandoned, ideas of genius, and ideas of banality. On one manuscript he scribbled: "May not be good music, but true sounds make beauty to me." He writes, at the end of one of the *Tone Roads,* "There are many Roads, you know, besides the Wabash." One of his most haunting pieces is *The Unanswered Question.* The strings, Ives wrote, "are to represent the Silences of the Druids—Who Know, See and Hear Nothing." The trumpet intones "The Perennial Question of Existence," while "The Flying Answerers (flutes and other people)" run around in vain trying to discover the invisible reply to the trumpet. Nonsense? Profundity? Mysticism? Tongue in cheek? All things to all men, perhaps; but all men would agree that this was strange language indeed to emanate from the Ives and Myrick agency of Mutual Life.

He starts a composition in wedge formation after seeing a Yale-Princeton football game. "Trumpet running halfback," he suggests. Another unfinished composition is named *Giants vs. Cubs, August, 1907, Polo Grounds.* Partly decipherable among the frenzied scribblings are: "A—1st Mike jaunts [?] out to CF. Johnny at bat. Hits over Mike's head. Pitcher on mound. Ball. Strike. Ball. Ball. Strike." The classic 3-and-2 situation. "Johnny comes sliding home safe. Tune: *Johnny Comes Marching Home*." A little pleasant research in newspapers of the day reveals that Ives probably went to the Polo Grounds on Saturday, August 17, 1907. The Cubs played the Giants only one series at the Polo Grounds that August. There were no Sunday games in the National League on August 18, and the chances are that Ives, a working man, could attend only the Saturday game of the series. The score was 3-2 in favor of the Cubs; they won when the great Christy Mathewson weakened in the twelfth inning. Ives, incidentally, appears to have been a little off the mark in his description of the action. The only player in that game who slid home (the only player, indeed, in the four-game series between August 17 and August 21) was William "Spike" Shannon, the left fielder of the Giants.

Ives did not especially care if his music was considered unplayable. "The impossibilities of today are the possibilities of tomorrow," he insisted. Himself an individualist, he did not even care if musicians bobbled the notes as long as they understood what the composer was trying to say and the general effect he was trying to achieve. At one of his infrequent performances, in 1931, the orchestra, struggling with his adventurous way of writing, ended up in chaos. "Just like a town meeting—every man for himself. Wonderful how it came out!" he admiringly said. Like Beethoven, whom he so greatly admired, Ives pursued an Idea, in the Platonic sense. But he was not an ivory-tower composer. He accepted art as a natural function of humanity, and looked forward to the day when "every man, while digging his potatoes, will breathe his own Epics, his own Symphonies (Operas if he likes); and as he sits of an evening in his own back yard in shirt sleeves, sucking his pipe and watching his children in *their* fun of building *their* themes for *their* sonatas of *their* life, he will look over the mountains and see his visions, in their reality." Above all, he despised the "pretty music" admired by the public. The typical music-lover, he who sits and inhales the "pretty sounds," he called Rollo, a name taken from the series of books for children written by the Reverend Jacob Hallowell Abbott between 1834 and 1858. Rollo was a nice, dull, mama's boy. Rollos *en masse* Ives called ladybirds. "Keep up our fight—*art!*—hard at it—don't quit because the ladybirds don't like it." He accuses "Richie Wagner" of false nobility. Debussy to him was "a city man with his week-end flights into country esthetics." Chopin was "soft . . . with a skirt on." Ravel was "weak, morbid, and monotonous." Stravinsky's *Firebird* kept "going over and over and it got tiresome." Mozart was effeminate and a bad influence on music.

Ives stands for a fierce musical integrity and a unique type of nationalism. He had been brought up on Emerson, idolized the man and his philosophy, and tried to express an Emersonian kind of transcendentalism in his music. Almost every Ives work contains references to his own New England background—to the tunes, hymns, patriotic songs, dances, and marches he heard in his youth. His entire approach can be summed up in his own notes to his Fourth Violin Sonata: "The subject matter, such as it is, is a kind of reflection, remembrance, expression, etc., of the children's services at the outdoor summer camp meetings held around Danbury and many of the farm towns in Connecticut in the Seventies, Eighties and Nineties . . ." *Reflection, Remembrance, Expression:* that is the key to Ives, whether to his Second Symphony, Second String Quartet, *Three Places in New England,* or the *Concord* Sonata. The Second Symphony tries to express "the musical feelings of the Connecticut country around here in the 1890's. . . . It is full of the tunes they sang and played then. . . . The part suggesting a Steve Foster tune, while over it the old farmers fiddled a barn dance with all its jigs, gallops and reels, was played in Danbury on the old Wooster House bandstand in 1889." The movement of the *Holidays* Symphony named *Washington's Birthday* describes a "barn dance at the Centre. The village band of fiddles, fife and horn keep up an unending 'break-down' medley. . . ." *Central Park in the Dark* is "a picture in sounds of the sounds of nature and of happenings that men would hear thirty or so years ago (before the combustion engine and radio monopolized the earth and air)." Some of those sounds are street cries, night owls from Healey's, the elevated train, newsboys yelling "uxtry!" pianolas, fire engines, a runaway horse, an echo over the pond—"and we walk home."

Everything Ives heard as a child seems to have made a permanent impression on him. Once, at a baseball rally in Danbury, he heard two marching bands, playing different music, approach and recede. As they came together there was a frightful dissonance. Ives thought the sound delightful, and he reproduced it again and again in his music. He would attend revival meetings where singers yowled lustily out of tune. This to Ives was life; people sounded like this, so why shouldn't his music? In the preface to the Fourth Violin Sonata he explains ". . . The second movement is quieter and more serious except when Deacon Stonemason Bell and Farmer John would get up and get the boys excited. But most of the movement moves quietly around that old favorite hymn of the children—'Yes, Jesus Loves Me, the Bible Tells Me So,' while mostly in the accompaniment is heard something trying to reflect the outdoor sounds of nature on those summer days. . . ." All this is in the music. Yet it is not at all program music. It has flavors and colors rather than story content.

Reflection, Remembrance, Expression. It all sounds simple enough as described. Hearing it and understanding it is not so simple. Ives was not out to make what he called "sissy sounds" for Rollo. It is true that he is constantly using familiar tunes—tunes like "America"; "Columbia the Gem of the Ocean"; "Tenting Tonight on the Old Camp Ground"; "Rule, Britannia"; "Good Night Ladies"; favorite hymns and ragtime melodies. But what he does with them is another matter. The ending of the Second Symphony has fragments of "Columbia the Gem of the Ocean," some barn fiddling, and "De Camptown Races" all going on in different keys at once. But familiarity with the Ives idiom permits the listener to pull the polyphony apart. This unselfconscious, unabashed handling of the sentimental old melodies (never quoted in full but always allusively) put through a sieve of dissonance is what separates the Ives national idiom from that of the other American composers. Compared to him, Roy Harris is a tub-thumping chauvinist, Virgil Thomson a Parisian aesthete who dreams of the Middle West while sipping tea, and Copland is a cowboy from Brooklyn. Ives had an authentic Yankee voice, speaking the accent pure and communicating the belief and dignity of an entire people.

He had a right to his Yankee accent. His ancestors had come to New England in 1653. Ives's father, George, was a remarkable man who had been a bandmaster during the Civil War and later a bandmaster and teacher in Danbury. "Pa taught me what I know," Ives was to say. Part of his father's instruction was completely orthodox. He insisted that Charlie learn the rules before breaking them. But the better part of George Ives's instruction was unheard-of in his day. He was interested in new tonal relationships and had a completely open mind about them. "Nothing but fools and taxes are absolute," he said. He tried to work out a system of microtones, with twenty-four notes to the octave. Like his son, he was impatient with people who thought and heard conventionally. When Charles was ten years old, his father would make him sing "Swanee River" in the key of E flat and accompany him in C major. This was, Ives said many years later, "to stretch our ears . . . to be less dependent on customs and habits."

With this kind of background it is no wonder that Ives developed as he did. (Henry Cowell, his biographer, suggests that Ives was really writing his father's music for him.) But Ives soon gave up the idea of becoming a full-time composer. "Father felt that a man could keep his music interest stronger, cleaner, bigger, and freer if he didn't try to make a living out of it." Ives never regretted going into the insurance business, and came to believe that there was more open-mindedness in the business world than in the music world. "My work in music helped my business, and my work in business helped my music." He married in 1908, adopted a daughter, went to the office, composed industriously on weekends and holidays (he had a farm in West Redding, near Danbury), and shrugged off the laughter his few public performances evoked. His wife, Harmony Twitchell, was the daughter of a Hartford clergyman. "She never told me to be good and write something nice that people would like," he said gratefully. In 1951, when Leonard Bernstein conducted the New York Philharmonic in Ives's Second

Symphony, Mrs. Ives, who had had sad experiences with audiences and her husband's music, timidly sneaked into a box. The symphony created a furor, and Mrs. Ives could not at first accept the idea that a work of Charles's was being applauded. Ives did not attend the concert. He heard the Sunday broadcast in his home on East Seventy-fourth Street, listening in the kitchen to the maid's table radio. (That was the only radio in the Ives home.) When the symphony was over, Ives, according to Henry Cowell, "did an awkward little jig of pleasure and vindication."

The Second Symphony was the first of Ives's four to come into favor. His First was a graduation piece, tuneful enough, full of reminiscences of Beethoven, Brahms, and Dvořák. The Second, composed in 1902 and not performed until Bernstein "discovered" it in 1951, moves with much more assurance. It is one of Ives's blander works, but it is authentic Americana, sweet and flowing. The Third, composed in 1911 and not performed until 1945, is something like a hymn-tune symphony, and it too is a sweet, flowing score written with spiky harmonic independence. It would have sent listeners of 1911 screaming out of the hall. The Fourth Symphony is wild. It is Ives's biggest, most sonorous, and most complex. He finished it in 1916, and its first complete performance came with Leopold Stokowski and the American Symphony Orchestra in 1965. Copyists had to work for a long time to get it into shape; the notation frequently was all but undecipherable, and there were no parts. The symphony is a compendium of what Ives was trying to do, alternating massed dissonance and polyrhythms with moments of Sunday-to-church calm (Stokowski had to use two assistant conductors at the premiere). It is an amazing work, and by far the greatest symphony ever composed by an American.

During his creative period Ives heard only a tiny handful of the scores he had written. When he did begin to receive performances, he was an old man with a bad heart and sight diminished by cataracts, and he was unable to leave his house to attend concerts. To the public he was an unknown figure. There are very few photographs of him, and he shunned publicity. Only once in his long life, in 1949, did he ever give a newspaper interview. As nobody wanted to hear his music, Ives published some of it himself: "privately printed and not to be put on the market. Complimentary copies will be sent to anyone as long as the supply lasts." Among his few supporters were the poet-novelist Henry Bellamann, the pianist E. Robert Schmitz, the composer Henry Cowell, and the composer-conductor Nicolas Slonimsky. Slonimsky programmed the *Three Places in New England* for a Town Hall concert on January 10, 1931. The music was resoundingly booed, and Carl Ruggles's *Men and Mountains,* on the same program, got an even more uproarious reception. Ives bore his own failure stoically, but during the screaming over the Ruggles he got to his feet and yelled "Stop being such a

God-damned sissy! Why can't you stand up before fine, strong music like this and use your ears like a man!" (Ives really spoke like this.) Slonimsky later conducted some Ives music in Europe, and while it was ridiculed, it also caught the ears of some responsible musicians and critics. The one major American critic to take up the Ives cause was Lawrence Gilman of the New York *Herald Tribune*. When fame and recognition finally did come, during the last decade of his life, Ives may have had some resentment about its tardy appearance. He did accept the Pulitzer Prize in 1947 for his Third Symphony, but told the committee that "Prizes are for boys. I'm grown up." He told a reporter that "Prizes are the badges of mediocrity," and he gave away the $500 he received for the award. He also said that many composers, perhaps of genius, had been started on the downward path by trying to win a $10,000 prize for an opera. The reference here was to Horatio Parker, whose opera *Mona* won a $10,000 prize offered by the Metropolitan Opera in 1911.

This attitude is basic Ives. It can, of course, be pooh-poohed away by pointing out that he was independently wealthy and could afford to scorn commercialism. (Mozart or Beethoven would have been the last men in the world to turn down $10,000 commissions.) But Ives's remark cannot be thrown aside so easily. What he meant was that pretty-pretty music for the Rollos of the world flourishes under conditions of patronage, that he who pays the piper calls the tune, and that a gifted composer would be tempted to prostitute himself. As far as Ives was concerned, there was no such thing as a part-time prostitute: you were pure, or you were not. Pretty-pretty music meant compromise. Ives considered it his duty as a Yankee and a Puritan to scorn comfort in listening; and he also believed that the public, which was spoiled enough as it was, had a similar duty to listen hard to new tonal relationships. What he did musically—those amazing innovations—he did despite himself. He did not have a very good technique; in some respects he had a terrible technique. What he had was genius and a new way of hearing. It is fascinating to speculate on how Ives would have composed had he received performances, worked with orchestras and musicians. Would he have gone into a smoother kind of writing? Would his notation have been clearer? It is hard to say, but probably not. Ives was too stubborn a man, and he came from a background where, as he noted on the manuscript of his *Tone Roads No. 1*, people "got up and said what they thought regardless of the consequences."

With Ives an almost unknown factor until his discovery in the 1950's, the composer who best represented the United States in the public and professional eye was Aaron Copland, born in Brooklyn on November 14, 1900. Copland made the break that took American music away from the tarnished provincialism of MacDowell into a powerful, modern, very personal kind of speech. He also helped break the stranglehold of the German domination on American music. As a young pianist and aspiring composer, he did at first study with Rubin Goldmark (nephew of Karl Goldmark, the composer of *The Queen of Sheba*), but abruptly shifted and went to Paris in 1921. There he studied with Nadia Boulanger at the new School of Music for Americans at Fontainebleau. Those studies with Boulanger were later described by Copland as the most important musical experiences of his life. Boulanger became the teacher of virtually every important American composer of the period from 1920 to 1940; she was to those two decades what Rheinberger and Jadassohn previously had been to theirs. So numerous were her students that it was said every American town had two things—a five-and-dime, and a Boulanger pupil.

Boulanger led her pupils away from nineteenth-century models. She was just as much interested in Mussorgsky and Stravinsky as she was in Brahms and Beethoven, and she was fully in sympathy with the new experiments springing up all over the world. Copland was in Paris at a good time, and was intellectually stimulated. Stravinsky, Ravel, Prokofiev, *Lex Six*, the Ballets Russes—all had their headquarters there. Picasso, Hemingway, Gertrude Stein and her circle, Joyce, and the other heroes of the Left Bank made Paris in the 1920's the most exciting city in the world. Copland, brash, breezy and confident, full of ideas about music, interested in American jazz, started turning out a kind of music that was his own. It was a music that reflected the new age. Copland was not the only American to work in an avant-garde style. Henry Cowell had experimented with tone clusters and sound for sound's sake. Leo Ornstein, the brilliant young pianist, was smashing keyboards and getting a good deal of publicity about his rhythmic, dissonant music. But Ornstein soon disappeared, and Cowell seemed at best to be a minor talent. Copland was the one who had the brains, determination, and skill to arrive at his goal.

At first he was influenced by Stravinsky and *Les Six*, and composed poly-rhythmic music that played with jazz elements. The ballet *Grohg*, later worked into the *Dance Symphony* (1925), belongs to this period, and so do *Music for the Theater* (1925) and the Piano Concerto (1927). It was clear that a major talent had arrived. After 1927, Copland dropped jazz. "With the Concerto I felt I had done all I could with the idiom, considering its limited emotional scope. True, it was an easy way to be American in musical terms, but all American music could not possibly be confined to two dominant jazz models: the 'blues' and the snappy number." Many other composers of the period had come to the same conclusion. During the 1920's some of the international stars, including Stravinsky, had a brief fling with jazz, but nothing much came of it.

After the Piano Concerto, Copland turned to a completely different form

243

of expression, one that stimulated every young American composer. With the Piano Variations (1930), the *Short Symphony* (1933, later reduced to a Sextet), and *Statements* for orchestra (1935), Copland became the leader of the new American school.

These new products from Copland's pen were stripped-down scores, dissonant, percussive, powerful, abstract. Pattern and rhythm were the main preoccupations, much more than melody. The Russians would have called them "formalistic." A strong mind was at work, manipulating the musical elements in forms that amounted to pure logic. Even Stravinsky had not gone so far. "They are difficult to perform, and difficult for an audience to comprehend," Copland said of this music. The public did not respond; it seldom does to abstract music—that is, music in which the rigorous development of an idea occupies more importance than melody (in the traditional sense of the word). To many audiences, this kind of music is considered too "intellectual," abstruse, and ungrateful. But elements of the new Copland style crept into the writing of many American composers. These were the days when everybody was desperately anxious to be "modern," and Copland was the most modern of all the Americans.

Suddenly Copland changed his style once again. He shifted from abstractionism to a more popular idiom. Copland felt that the new music could be dangerous in that it might end up completely alienating the public. In *The New Music* he pointed out that during the early 1930's

> I began to feel an increasing dissatisfaction with the relations of the music-loving public and the living composer. The old "special" public of the modern music concerts had fallen away, and the conventional concert public continued apathetic or indifferent to anything but the established classics. It seemed to me that we composers were in danger of working in a vacuum. Moreover, an entirely new public for music had grown up around the radio and the phonograph. It made no sense to ignore them and to continue writing as if they did not exist. I felt that it was worth the effort to see if I couldn't say what I had to say in the simplest possible terms.

Thus came into being the music by which Copland is best known and best loved. With *The Second Hurricane* (1935), *El Salón México* (1936), and above all with his three "American" ballets—*Billy the Kid* (1938) for Eugene Loring, *Rodeo* (1940) for Agnes de Mille, and *Appalachian Spring* (1944) for Martha Graham—he moved out of a small circle into a position as not only the most respected American composer, but also the most popular, by far. Other works that can be added to this list would include *A Lincoln Portrait* (1942), the opera *The Tender Land* (though it was not a success when it was produced in 1954), *Quiet City* (1940), and the *Twelve*

Poems of Emily Dickinson (1950). All of these are sophisticated, tuneful, and atmospheric scores, popular but not written-down. All bear the Copland imprint, with his characteristic harmonies and rhythmic breaks. In other words, Copland did not follow the material; he bent it to his will. Once again young American composers rushed to imitate the Master.

The 1930's saw a group of prominent American composers attracting attention with Copland. Few have had his staying power. It was hoped in those days that Copland, Roy Harris, Walter Piston, William Schuman, Samuel Barber, and Virgil Thomson would spearhead the new American school. Things did not work out that way, and history will put the group (Copland excepted) in an analagous position to the Boston Classicists— worthy and skillful musicians who lacked the individuality to create a lasting body of music. Harris turned out work after work, but only his Third Symphony achieved much currency, and today that work is only on the fringe 'of the repertory. Piston turned out polite, well-tailored classistic music of no particular urgency or individuality. Schuman's music, lean and athletic, well-organized and smartly orchestrated, was discussed but never much liked. Perhaps its melodic inhibition was the reason. Thomson at least composed two operas to Gertrude Stein librettos—*Four Saints in Three Acts* (1934) and *The Mother of Us All* (1947)—that had something sweet and genuine. They are rather precious works and not to everybody's taste but, with all their Satie-like "white-key" harmonies, they are immensely sophisticated and appealing. Barber, the most traditional of all, enjoyed great popularity and still remains very much in the repertory, though he composed less and less after 1960.

Music had changed. Instead of being the spearhead of the American movement, Copland and the other big American composers of the 1920–40 period found themselves in the backwash. The younger men turned to serial music and its derivatives, and instead of an American style there suddenly was an international style. Copland, never a very prolific composer, made a few attempts at a form of serial composition, as in the Piano Fantasy and the *Connotations* for orchestra, composed in 1962 for the opening concert at Philharmonic Hall, in New York's Lincoln Center. Neither work has had many performances, and Copland too has composed less and less. He busied himself other ways. As the most articulate of spokesmen for American music and musicians, he has been writer, critic, analyst, educator, and administrator. In his books and articles he has for years been explaining new music; as an educator he has guided the young students at the Berkshire Music Center in Tanglewood, which he headed from its inception in 1940 to 1969. Counselor and elder statesman, Aaron Copland is the urbane, respected symbol of a half century of American music.

❧ 18 ❧

The Uncompromising Hungarian

BÉLA BARTÓK

It is generally agreed that the three greatest post-Debussyian composers of the first half of the twentieth century were Igor Stravinsky, Arnold Schoenberg, and Béla Bartók: each a powerful individualist, each a significant innovator. If Stravinsky represents logic and precision in music, and if Schoenberg represents the break from tonality into an entirely new philosophy of musical composition, Bartók represents the fusion of nationalism and nineteenth-century musical forms into a convulsively powerful means of expression.

Bartók was a tiny, frail man with explosive psychic force, prepared to go his own uncompromising way even if his music was never played. A stubborn integrity and an all-encompassing humanism animated the man, and he would not swerve from his ideal of truth, even when it involved resisting the Nazis and making a new home elsewhere. He was prepared at all times to stand up to the Establishment in defense of his music and in defense of his liberty. In this determination to maintain his personal and artistic integrity he was much like Schoenberg, and some of his letters even read like Schoenberg's. In 1915, when Bartók was getting hardly any performances, his First Suite was played, but in a mutilated form. Bartók immediately got off a letter of protest to the directors of the Budapest Philharmonic Society, pointing out that "the thematic interdependence of each movement is so close that there are measures in certain movements that simply cannot be understood unless they have been preceded by the earlier movements." Bartók added a final paragraph; and the directors of the Budapest Philharmonic Society, who probably honestly thought they were doing Bartók a favor by programming several movements of his Suite, must have been startled to read the composer's *fiat:*

> I must, under the circumstances, declare that I should be exceptionally grateful to you if you would never again perform any of my works. I can

make this request all the more, since the regrettable state of musical affairs in Budapest has in any case forced me to withdraw completely from public participation as a composer for the past four years, and to refrain from producing any of the compositions I have written during that period.

Bartók was a nationalist composer, probably, with Mussorgsky, the greatest who ever lived, and there is scarcely a note of his music that is not impregnated with the feeling of the Hungarian *melos*. It was not that he invented or quoted folk melodies, though once in a while that could happen. It was something far deeper than that. As one of the world's most knowledgeable ethnomusicologists—Bartók had an international reputation for his scholarly researches in folk music—the sound, rhythms, and scales of the music of his native Hungary were so much a part of him that he automatically thought in those terms. And what he expressed was the real, undiluted thing. Most nationalists of the previous century used a westernized, smoothed-out version of folk elements. Bartók went down to basics, to the raw material, the *Ur*-folk. He often put these materials into forms derived from the mainstream of Western music. "Kodály and I," he said, "wanted to make a synthesis of East and West." Zoltan Kodály too used folk elements in his music. But his works sound tame next to Bartók's. Kodály had a more polite and more conventional mind, and while he was a fine composer, he could not break entirely away from the academic or nineteenth-century formulae. Bartók did, changing the sonata and other forms as suited him, and using folk elements in a new and daring manner.

From the beginning he was exposed to folk music. He was born in Nagyszentmiklós, in the Torontál district of Hungary (now Rumania), on March 25, 1881. He was a serious child who developed into a serious man, and though his figure was slight, and his features delicate, he nevertheless gave the impression of unyielding strength. His father died when he was seven years-old, and his mother, a piano teacher, moved around the country. Bartók thus during his childhood had the opportunity of hearing several varieties of folk music. His mother started him on piano when he was five, soon discovering that he had absolute pitch and amazing aptitude. At the age of eleven he was playing in public. In 1899 he entered the Budapest Academy of Music. Those were the days when the major Hungarian talent was Ernö von Dohnányi (1877–1960). Dohnányi was a remarkable pianist, and a composer who worked skillfully in the Brahms tradition. Later he became the czar of Hungarian music. He and Bartók were rivals, and their paths were to cross many times throughout the years. When Bartók was graduated in 1901 and gave his public concert, the critics could find no higher words of praise than to say that Bartók was the only piano student at the Academy who might follow in Dohnányi's footsteps. (Dohnányi had been graduated from the Academy in 1897, winning a great number of prizes.)

Bartók had started to compose as a child. He stopped for a while, to concentrate on the piano. In 1902 he heard Strauss's *Also sprach Zarathustra,* and became wildly excited. "Straightaway I threw myself into a study of Strauss's scores and began again to compose." The pieces he wrote in those days, such as the *Kossuth* Symphony (really a symphonic poem in ten parts), reflected the German tradition in general and Strauss in particular. More work at the piano followed, including some lessons with Dohnányi. There also were periods of bad health; throughout much of his life, Bartók was ailing in one way or another. In 1904 he composed his Op. 1, a Rhapsody for piano and orchestra. This again was a German-derived work, though with a strong nineteenth-century type of Hungarian nationalism. Liszt might have written it had he lived another twenty years; it is somewhat in the style of Liszt's *Hungarian Fantasia.* Bartók composed it as a vehicle for himself. Like any pianist-composer from Mozart on, he needed material to demonstrate his own wares, and it was this work, among others, that Bartók carried with him in 1905 to Paris, to compete for the Rubinstein Prize. He took second place in composition, to an Italian named Attilio Brignoli; and in the piano competition he lost out to Wilhelm Backhaus, which was no disgrace.

The big break in Bartók's line of development came in 1905, when he and Zoltán Kodály went into the field to collect folk music. They had with them an Edison machine on which they recorded hundreds of cylinders, and they took voluminous notes. The study and classification of folksong was to occupy a good part of Bartók's energy for the rest of his life. His first publication, with Kodály, was the collection named *Twenty Hungarian Folksongs,* which came out in 1906. Bartók and Kodály discovered that there were several categories of Hungarian folksong—the old style, largely pentatonic in melody; a new style, with mixed modes and heptatonic scales; and a class in which both elements were combined. To his friend Stefi Geyer, the violinist, Bartók wrote an amusing letter in dialogue form, discussing the difficulties in pulling old music out of the peasants. Bartók is "T" (The Traveler):

T.: The neighbor's wife here said you'd know the sort of old, old songs you learned in your youth from the old folks.

P.: Me?! Old songs?! The gentleman mustn't pull my leg. Hee-hee-hee-hee-hee!

T.: But look here, this isn't a lark! I'm speaking quite seriously. I've come from far away, very far away, from Budapest, just to look for these old, old songs that are known only hereabouts!

P.: Well, and what do they do with those songs then—are they going to be put in the newspaper?

T.: Not at all! The point of this work is to preserve these songs, to put them down in writing. Because if we don't write them down, people won't know, later, what used to be sung here in our day. Because, you see, young folk know quite different songs; they don't even have any use for the old ones, they don't even learn them, though they're much lovelier than the ones made nowadays. Well, isn't that right? So fifty years from now, no one will know that they even existed, if we don't write them down now.

P.: Is that so? [Pause.] Bruhahahaha—heeheeheehee! No, I still don't believe it!

T. (desperately): But just look at this booklet, Auntie—see, I've written down all this. [He whistles a tune.] This one was sung by Mrs. András Gegö [he whistles another] and this by Mrs. Bálint Kosza. Well, you know them also, don't you?

P.: Eh, my day is over. It's not for an old woman to spend her time singing such songs; all I know now is church songs.

Bartók can get nothing from the lady but church songs, which he does not want, and adulterated folk songs, which he wants even less. He goes away "crushed," but he has squeezed out of Auntie an introduction to Mrs. Gyurka Sándor, who lives up the street at the corner and knows so many old songs she could sing them from sunup to sunset without repeating any.

In what he called "peasant music," Bartók found a rejuvenating force. He argued (in a long article in the German magazine *Melos,* published in 1920) that at the beginning of the twentieth century there was a turning point in music: "The excesses of the romantics began to be unbearable to many." But where to turn? "Invaluable help was given this change (or rather let us call it rejuvenation) by a kind of peasant music unknown up till then." In the best of this music, said Bartók, the forms were varied but perfect. In addition, the expressive power was "amazing," and at the same time the music was "devoid of sentimentality and superfluous ornaments." Here, claimed Bartók, was "the ideal starting point for a musical renaissance, and a composer in search of new ways cannot be led by a better master." What the composer has to do is "assimilate the idiom of peasant music so completely that he is able to forget all about it and use it as his mother tongue." Ralph Vaughan Williams in England at much the same time was arguing along the same lines. The concept of assimilation was integral to Bartók's way of thinking, as it was to Vaughan Williams and the other nationalists of the day, including Janáček, with his Czech speech patterns in music. All agreed that peasant music had to be studied in the field, as it actually existed, and that life had to be shared with the peasants. "It is not enough," wrote Bartók, "to study it as it is stored up in museums." Using peasant music in a superficial manner will only supply music with a few new ornaments and gewgaws: nothing more. An entirely new approach to folk music had to be developed, Bartók insisted. For instance, take the strange notion of the nineteenth century that only simple harmonizations were suited for folk melodies. That is all very wrong. "It may sound odd, but I do not hesitate to say that the simpler the melody, the more complex and strange may be the harmonizations and accompaniments that go well with it."

But if a composer wanted to work in this idiom, it was necessary for him to work in a tonal medium. That was where Bartók and the Viennese atonalists parted company. Bartók was adamant about the "truism" that folk music, which was tonal, could not be reconciled with Schoenberg's atonality. Bartók, anyway, was a little irritated by the claims of Schoenberg and his followers, who were insisting that there was One method and One method only. "Far be it from me to maintain that the only way to salvation for a composer in our day is for him to base his music on folk music," Bartók wrote in 1931. "But I wish that our opponents had an equally liberal opinion of the significance of folk music." Bartók tried to clarify a few points. Nationalist composers were charged by the atonalists with using borrowed materials. But the use of borrowed materials has nothing to do with the artistic results of a piece of music. When you come down to it, Bartók pointed out, Shakespeare borrowed, and so did Molière, Bach, and Handel. Everybody has his roots in the art of some former time. It so happens that in Bartók's case, "It is peasant music that contains our roots." It is no sign of barrenness or incompetence if a composer bases his work on folk music rather than taking Brahms or Schumann as his model. On the other hand, it is just as bad if a composer takes folk music and puts it into stereotyped musical forms. In both cases the basic conception is a mistake, for "It stresses the all-importance of themes and forgets about the art of form that alone can make something of those themes." Ultimately, of course, the merit of any piece of music is in direct ratio to a composer's talent. "In the hands of incompetent composers, neither folk music nor any other musical material will ever attain significance. . . . The result will in every case be nothing."

Bartók's theories worked for him. The Viennese atonalists could not have been less interested. They of course went their own way and, as it turned out, history was on their side. After World War II and Bartók's death, his music, while popular, exerted very little influence upon the thinking of young composers. Exponents of the serial school found Bartók's music interesting only in those areas where a relationship could be traced with the work of Schoenberg and his school. Thus Pierre Boulez has dismissed Bartók as "a kind of synthesis of late Beethoven and the mature Debussy," and has praise only for that Bartók music which "arrived at a phase of very specially chromatic experiments not far from Berg and Schoenberg." Otherwise Bartók's music, to Boulez, "lacks interior coherence;" and as for the Bartók works that have found most favor with audiences—the Piano Concerto No. 3 and the Concerto for Orchestra—they exhibit "doubtful taste." Bartók's nationalism is described by Boulez, rather sneeringly, as "only a residue of the nationalistic thrusts of the nineteenth century."

So doctrinaire an approach toward the Bartók aesthetic ignores the fact that starting in 1906 Bartók began to compose a body of music in which folk elements were transmuted into something universal. His style did not evolve all at once, and there was a period of consolidation. As he became less interested in the music of Strauss, he became more interested in the music of Liszt and Debussy, and in the Russian music of Stravinsky up to *Les Noces*. He became a piano teacher at the Budapest Academy (never did he teach composition) and started composing—the *Portraits* (1908), the *Bagatelles* (1907), the First String Quartet (1908), and a great deal of piano music in which the instrument was treated with a sharp, percussive attack. A one-act opera, *Bluebeard's Castle* (1911); the ballet-pantomime, *The Wooden Prince* (1917); and a ballet, *The Miraculous Mandarin* (1919) were among his bigger works. None of these achieved much popularity, and the ballet, with its neo-*Sacre* rhythms, ferocious dissonance, and sex-ridden plot, was universally condemned. Other works of the period from 1907 to the early 1920's include two Violin Sonatas (1921–1922) and the Second String Quartet (1917).

If Bartók received few performances, at least his music made a strong impact upon European professionals. It was much more discussed outside of Hungary than in his own country, where he was very much a prophet without honor. His music was considered atonal, which it was not despite its powerful dissonance. Not until 1920 did Bartók write a work that had any degree of popularity. That was his *Dance Suite*. The latter half of the 1920's saw Bartók's style come to full maturity. A series of major works ensued: the *Cantata Profana* (1934), the first two Piano Concertos (1927 and 1931), the last four String Quartets (1927, 1928, 1934, and 1939), the Sonata for Two Pianos and Percussion (1938), the *Music for Strings, Percussion, and Celesta* (1937, considered by many his masterpiece), the Violin Concerto No. 2 (1939), and the Divertimento for String Orchestra (1940). The music of this period had enormous thrust, personality, and virility, all enclosed in a savage kind of dissonantal nationalism. It was more dissonant than anything Stravinsky, Prokofiev, or the French school were writing, and its slashing sound was immediately recognizable as Bartókian. Only the Viennese atonalists and Charles Ives were capable of such uncompromising dissonance.

Naturally Bartók was attacked because of his lack of melody. He liked to build works from motto themes, sometimes only a few notes long, and from Liszt he developed a kind of cyclic form that would unify all elements. As Halsey Stevens, in his biography of Bartók, has written: "His motives, frequently of two or three notes only, are in a constant state of regeneration. They grow organically; they proliferate; the evolutionary process is kinetic. No doubt many motivic manipulations which seem carefully calculated were brought about intuitively: the line between reason and intuition is never sharply defined, but the compact thematic logic cannot be denied."

A politically sensitive man, Bartók was appalled by the spread of Nazism. After the *Anschluss* on March 11–13, 1938, Bartók knew that he would be forced to leave his country, for after Austria would come Hungary. As he wrote to a friend in Switzerland, "There is the imminent danger that Hungary will also surrender to this system of robbery and murder. How I could then continue to live or—which amounts to the same thing—work in such a country is quite inconceivable." Yet Bartók was fifty-eight years old and was supporting his mother in addition to his wife and family. He made some wry remarks about the Nazis and their ideas of racial purity. His publisher was Universal, of Vienna, and when the Nazis took Austria, all composers on the Universal list received a questionnaire—"an infamous questionnaire," Bartók exploded—asking "Are you of German blood, racially related, or non-Aryan?" Bartók and Kodály refused to fill it out on the grounds that such questions were illegal and unconstitutional. It was, in a way, a pity they so decided, Bartók wrote, because one could make such lovely jokes:

For example, say that we are non-Aryan—for, after all, "Aryan," as my dictionary tells me, means "Indo-European." We Hungarians, however, are Finno-Ugric, indeed perhaps even North Turkic, racially, and so in no way Indo-European, consequently not Aryan. Another question goes: "Where and when were you wounded?" Answer: "On 11, 12, and 13 March in Vienna."

Bartók left Universal to go to the British publishing firm of Boosey and Hawkes. In 1939, when his mother died, he decided to leave Hungary, and the following year he was in the United States, where he was to spend the last years of his life. Before he left, he wrote a will, and in it is one paragraph that fully illustrates Bartók's libertarianism and hatred of dictatorship:

If after my death they want to name a street after me, or to erect a memorial tablet to me in a public place, then my desire is this: as long as what were formerly Oktogon-tér and Körönd in Budapest are named after those men for whom they are at present named [Hitler and Mussolini], and, further, as long as there is in Hungary any square or street, or is to be, named for those two men, then neither square nor street nor public building in Hungary is to be named for me, and no memorial tablet is to be erected in a public place.

In the United States, he was given a position at Columbia University, where he worked on a collection of folk songs. He had very little money, but stories of his sheer penury are a romantic invention. He was never in actual want. For a while he lived in Forest Hills, in an apartment house, and on Christmas Eve, 1940, wrote a charming letter to his sons in Budapest describing his new home and his American experiences:

> On Dec. 7 we moved into a furnished apartment at the above address. It is 16 km. from the center of New York, but the subway (express) station is in front of our door, so that for 5 cents we can be in the city in 20 minutes, at any time. Trains run constantly, and day and night without interruption. . . . There are shops and all conveniences nearby. The heating is so excessive that we have to turn off ¾ of the radiators; we can keep one of our bedroom windows wide open (if there's no wind). We are beginning to be Americanized, e.g., in the matter of food. In the morning, grapefruit, puffed *wheat* (!) with cream, brown bread and butter, eggs or bacon or fish. . . . My head is filling up with all sorts of new words: subway stations, street names, subway-system plans, a mass of possibilities for changing trains: absolute necessities in order to live here. . . . We've had enough trouble learning how to cope with various gadgets of the electric, gas, corkscrew, can-opener type, etc., and with means of transportation, but we are managing now. Only once in a while is there any inconvenience; so, for inst., we recently wanted to take the subway to New York's southernmost part: I didn't know exactly where to change to what (the directions aren't much in evidence; in fact, they are sparse and muddled), so that we jaunted around for 3 hours under the ground; finally, our time having run out, we sneaked shamefacedly home, underground of course, without having achieved our purpose.

In addition to his job at Columbia, Bartók composed and did some concert work. But bad health set in, and his last public appearance took place in New York, on January 21, 1943. He and his wife Ditta played his Two-Piano Concerto (originally the Sonata for Two Pianos and Percussion) with the New York Philharmonic under Fritz Reiner. Doctors could not diagnose the cause of the illness, or so they told Bartók. He had leukemia, and no cure was possible. Bartók's weight dropped alarmingly, down to 87 pounds, and he also suffered from a constant fever. The American Society of Composers, Authors and Publishers (ASCAP) supplied money to see him through his bad period. Serge Koussevitzky came to Bartók with a commission of one thousand dollars for an orchestral work. (This was done at the promptings of Reiner and the violinist Josef Szigeti.) The Concerto for Orchestra resulted; it turned out to be Bartók's most popular orchestral work. For Yehudi Menuhin he composed a Sonata for Unaccompanied Violin; and for his wife he worked on the Third Piano Concerto. At the end of 1944, things were looking up. Money from royalties and performing fees was coming in; a new agreement with Boosey and Hawkes promised a great deal more; he worked on a Viola Concerto for William Primrose; and he started thinking about a concerto for two pianos for Bartlett and Robertson. But as his prospects began to improve, he grew progressively weaker. Desperately he tried to finish two large-scale works at the same time—the Viola Concerto, which was left incomplete, and the Third Piano Concerto, of which all but a few measures of scoring were finished. On September 26, 1945, he died in New York. On his deathbed he lamented, like Schubert, "The trouble is that I have to go with so much still to say."

Within a few years after his death Bartók was among the most-played of all modern composers. The Concerto for Orchestra not only entered the repertory, it almost elbowed aside *Petrushka* and the *Classical* Symphony. Beginning pianists began to cut their eyeteeth on the six volumes of *Mikrokosmos,* those 153 pieces ranging from simple to difficult, all intended to introduce youngsters to modern keyboard sounds. They became standard teaching material. Young virtuosos began to play the last two piano concertos, especially the Third. There was a run on that work, and it vied with Prokofiev's C major Concerto and the ones by Rachmaninoff as the most popular of twentieth-century works for piano and orchestra. Especially admired were the six string quartets. Cycles of the six were played with increasing frequency after Bartók's death, and they were considered by many the greatest body of chamber music after the last quartets by Beethoven.

The first two Bartók quartets, of 1908 and 1917, are relatively conventional, though the harmonies are of a dissonant type of chromaticism. The third of 1927, and the three after that, are in a new, wild, cataclysmic world, full of chamber-orchestra sonorities and a series of effects that frightened listeners and players of the day. Bartók asks for glissandos for all instruments, *ponticello* bowings (close to the bridge), harmonics, *col legno* (using the wooden part of the bow), complicated multiple stoppings, quarter tones, and a variety of percussive sounds that include the famous "Bartók snap"—the rebound of the string against the finger board. Coming to this music unprepared, with the quartets of Brahms or even late Beethoven in mind, can be a disconcerting experience for listeners. These quartets can no more be understood on one hearing than the Beethoven quartets can be. The same can be said of Bartók's *Music for Strings, Percussion, and Celesta* and of the Sonata for Two Pianos and Percussion. The opening movement of the former, with its muted polyphonic flow and rarefied, austere world, has been compared with the opening of the Beethoven Quartet in C sharp minor. The idiom of these works has to be absorbed, and it takes many hearings to do so. Once it is, the music clears up. Rich and complicated as it is, it is nowhere near so difficult as it sounds at first. The ever-present Magyar rhythms and fragments of folklike melody come strongly to the fore, and the dissonances begin to sound pungent instead of fearsome. Those grating seconds and sevenths, those big interlocking chords, those harmonies stemming from the modalities of peasant music, those savage and eccentric rhythms in fives and sevens—all clear up into a direct emotional utterance.

As Bartók himself was so careful to point out, he was not primarily a "nationalist." He was a composer who merely happened to believe that folk music in its pure state was a fructifying force. Thus he wanted to be assessed as a composer, not as a folklorist. He composed rugged music that asked no quarter of anybody, and his best works are the reflection of one of the strongest musical minds of the twentieth century.

✎ 19 ✎

The Second Viennese School

SCHOENBERG, BERG, WEBERN

The first decade of the twentieth century saw a series of convulsive changes in human thought. So radical were those changes that the implications of their full impact were not recognized at the time, and they took years to make their effect. In 1900, Sigmund Freud published *The Interpretation of Dreams,* after which mankind found a new way to probe into the human mind. In the same year, Max Planck published his quantum theory, which destroyed Euclidean geometry and Newtonian physics. Working with Planck's equations, Albert Einstein in 1905 evolved his special relativity theory, after which mankind's understanding of the rules governing the universe were changed. In 1903 the Wright brothers got an airplane into the air, ending man's ages-old search for powered flight. In 1910, Vassily Kandinsky painted his first fully nonrepresentational work, after which painting could never be the same. For the first time, a painting could be regarded purely as a formal assemblage of shapes and colors without reference to anything in nature. And in 1908 Arnold Schoenberg composed his *Buch der hängenden Gärten,* destroying the ages-old concept of tonality as effectively as Einstein had destroyed Newton's macrocosmos. All this in one decade, perhaps the most revolutionary decade in recorded history.

Arnold Schoenberg, who was born in Vienna on September 13, 1874, was a revolutionary who all his life kept insisting he was a traditionalist. Even though he had to admit that he had discarded the musical aesthetic of the past, he nevertheless maintained that all of his works had "arisen entirely from the traditions of German music. . . . My teachers were primarily Bach and Mozart; secondarily Beethoven, Brahms and Wagner." Or, "I am a conservative who was forced to become a radical!" He was a short, bald-headed man with the face of a fanatic: a strong, heavily lined, messianic, uncompromising face; a face with a mouth twisted into a tight-lipped grimace of permanent distrust; a face with huge, glaring, magnetic eyes. "His eyes were protuberant and explosive, and the whole force of the man was in them" (Stravinsky).

Schoenberg felt himself to be a man with a mission. "Once, in the army, I was asked if I was the composer Arnold Schoenberg. 'Somebody had to be,' I said, 'and nobody else wanted to be, so I took it on myself.' " He conceived of music as an art that conveyed "a prophetic message revealing a higher form of life toward which mankind evolves." Schoenberg, of course, was the prophet bearing the message. A higher force was directing him. When he finished his Chamber Symphony he told his friends that he had now established his style. "But my next work showed a great deviation from this style; it was my first steps toward my present style. . . . The Supreme Commander had ordered me on a higher road." His letters are full of an insistence on the unalterable rightness of his music. Schoenberg's egomania approached Wagner's. ". . . I believe what I do and do only what I believe; and woe to anybody who lays hands on my faith. Such a man I regard as an enemy, and no quarter given! You cannot be with me if you are also with my opponents." Or, "Views divergent from my own are something I should never resent, as little as I resent anyone's having any other disability! one short leg, a clumsy hand, etc. I could only be sorry for such a person, but I couldn't be angry with him." In 1942 he was asked by a candidate for a master's thesis to supply certain information about himself and his music. His reply was devastating: "The composer of *Pierrot Lunaire* and other works which have changed the history of music thanks you for the honorable invitation of participating in the production of a Master Thesis. But he thinks it is more important that he writes those works which candidates for a master degree will never know; and, if they know them, will never feel the distance which would forbid them to bother him with such questions." It followed that very little—if any—of the music composed in his time satisfied him. He poked fun at Stravinsky's neoclassicism and satirized him personally. For those composers who piled discords on discords, "like gluttons (wishing to pass as 'moderns') but do not have the courage to draw the consequences from them," he had nothing but contempt. He jeered at the "pseudo-tonalists," and at such neobaroque composers as Busoni and Hindemith, "who claim to make 'a return to So and So' " (though, inconsistently, he regarded Reger, the leader of the Back-to-Bach movement, as a genius). His dislikes included the folklore school headed by Bartók, "who try to apply to the ideas of popular music, which are by nature primitive, a technique that is only appropriate to a more evolved type of thought." Finally, as if to make sure he had not overlooked anybody, Schoenberg in one sweeping condemnation attacked "all the 'ists,' whom I can see only as mannerists."

In the beginning Schoenberg wrote more or less conventional music of a lush chromatic texture that stemmed from Wagner and Mahler. Yet from his first scores Schoenberg was regarded as a subversive. In 1900 a group of his songs created a public outburst at a recital. "Since then," Schoenberg said many years later, "the scandal has never ceased." Even *Verklärte Nacht* caused a near-riot at its premiere in 1903. Today a score like *Verklärte Nacht* is regarded as the essence of late romanticism, but audiences at the turn of the century did not see it that way, and the lack of firm tonality was unsettling to them.

Schoenberg came to music as a self-taught composer. Although he was playing the violin at the age of eight, he had very little training. When he tried to compose, as a teen-ager, it was in imitation of music that he had heard. For a while he worked in a bank, though he became part of the intellectual life of Vienna, mixing with artists, writers, and musicians. He met the composer and conductor Alexander von Zemlinsky and took some counterpoint lessons with him. As far as anybody knows, Schoenberg never had any other instruction. He is one of the few important composers in history who was a complete autodidact. Schoenberg married Zemlinsky's sister in 1901. (She died in 1923, after which Schoenberg married the sister of the violinist Rudolf Kolisch.)

Schoenberg's early works included a string quartet and a group of songs. In 1899 he composed the voluptuous string sextet *Verklärte Nacht,* which is a long, languorous post-*Tristan* sigh. (In 1941 Schoenberg rescored it for string orchestra.) One oddity about *Verklärte Nacht* is that it is a piece of chamber music set to a program (the only other example that comes readily to mind is Smetana's E minor Quartet, *Aus meinem Leben*). The story came from a poem by Richard Dehmel. Schoenberg later went on to compose music that ruptured all the "rules," and eventually he created an organizational system—the so-called "twelve-tone method"—that was to be the most important single influence on the musical thinking of the generation after World War II. But, ironically, the rather conventional *Verklärte Nacht* is the Schoenberg work that has remained the most popular, just as of all the Stravinsky scores *Firebird* is first in public favor.

For a brief time after his marriage Schoenberg worked in Berlin, conducting music-hall and operetta performances. He worked on his symphonic poem *Pelleas und Melisande* and on the enormous *Gurrelieder* in 1900, which was not scored until many years afterwards. In 1903 he returned to Vienna and began to teach. Among his first pupils were Anton von Webern and Alban Berg. Webern was born on December 3, 1883. He was a quiet, scholarly man who in 1906 took a doctorate in musicology. For many years he made his living as conductor of the Vienna Workers' Symphony Concerts. Berg, born on February 9, 1885, was a tall, handsome, aristocratic young man whose family had money. As a musician, he was a complete dilettante when he came to Schoenberg. "The state he was in," Schoenberg wrote in 1910, ". . . was such that his imagination apparently could not work on anything but songs. Even the piano accompaniments for them were song-like in style. He was absolutely incapable of writing an instrumental movement or inventing an instrumental theme. You can hardly imagine the lengths I went to in order to remove this defect in his talent." Schoenberg had other talented pupils, but none on the order of a Berg or Webern. They worshiped him, which was just as well, for Schoenberg exacted worship. Schoenberg's teaching was rigorous and demanding, but not doctrinaire. He insisted on the pupil's using his own imagination, even as a beginner. Exercises were not to be written by rote. They were, even in their simplest form, to be exercises in expression. "Hence," Webern later wrote, "he [the pupil] must actually create, even in the most primitive beginnings of musical construction. What Schoenberg explains to the student is altogether bound up, then, with the work in hand. He brings no external dogmas. Thus Schoenberg educates actually through creating. He follows the traces of the students' personality with the utmost energy, tries to deepen them, to help them break through . . ." Schoenberg all his life remained the spiritual father of Berg and Webern. He preached, they obediently listened.

Schoenberg's music soon began to drift away from the colossal orchestral concepts of *Pelleas und Melisande* and *Gurrelieder*. It became more compact, aphoristic, and dissonant. The Chamber Symphony of 1906 experimented with fourths, much as Scriabin was doing at the same time in Russia. In 1908 Schoenberg had arrived at the point where tonality was abolished. He realized that the songs in the *Buch der hängenden Gärten* (Op. 15) had led to something new:

> With the songs Op. 15 I have succeeded for the first time in approaching an ideal of form and expression that has hovered before me for years. . . I am conscious of having removed all the traces of a past esthetic; and if I am in the process of going towards a goal which seems certain to me, I already feel the opposition I shall have to overcome. . . . I think that even some people who have believed in me up to now will not realize the necessity of this evolution.

These songs were followed by the short one-act opera *Erwartung*, the Five Orchestral Pieces (both in 1909), the Six Little Piano Pieces of 1911 and, above all, *Pierrot Lunaire* in 1912. Schoenberg was now writing expressionistic rather than postromantic music. This was no accident. He was closely allied with the German painters of *Die Brücke*, the group that put expressionism on the rails; and he himself even painted some intense, though ama-

259

teurish, canvases, including a self-portrait. Kandinsky's definition of expressionist painting contained the statement: ". . . the presentation of an internal expression in external, visible form;" and Schoenberg very consciously tried to do in music what the expressionists were doing in painting. "Everything I have written has a certain inward similarity to myself." Expressionism is intensified romanticism, the exploration of inner states. All expressionistic art and music are very serious. Expressionism avoids the superficially pretty and attempts to transcend nature. It often deals with social commentary, psychological commentary, the soul, the psyche, the subconscious. Kokoschka once painted a portrait. "Those who knew you will not recognize you," he told the sitter, "but those who do not know you will recognize you very well." Where the impressionists tried to evoke an ideal state through transparent and sensual textures, and an avoidance of black pigments ("Black does not exist in nature"), expressionism is stark, often brutal, purposely distorted in line and texture, full of nervous tension. Impressionistic music is smooth and never entirely breaks away from tonality (=nature); expressionistic music is dissonant, atonal, with jagged melodic leaps, and deals with an intensified realism rather than idealism.

Schoenberg was steadily moving toward completely atonal textures—"the emancipation of the dissonance," as he put it—and he realized them in the Op. 11 piano pieces and *Pierrot Lunaire*. His opera *Erwartung* was a significant step in the aesthetic that finally resulted in Berg's *Wozzeck*. Schoenberg composed *Erwartung* in seventeen hectic days, between August 17 and September 12, 1909. (Then he had to wait fifteen years for a staged performance of the 30-minute-long work.) The text is by Marie Pappenheim. A woman seeks her lover in the forest. She finds him dead, near the house of the woman who has stolen him from her. That is all the story. The music reflects the woman's states of mind, in a vocal line that is largely declamatory, and in a harmony that is largely fourths and altered fourths, sevenths, and complexes of notes. The entire work is athematic. That is, there is no repetition of any theme, and melody in the accepted sense has disappeared. Yet the work, after one has become immersed in its idiom, looks back as much as it looks forward. Indeed, it is heavily Wagnerian. Wagner is apparent in the big orchestra, in the rich textures, and in many aspects of the libretto. *Tristan und Isolde* is full of night-and-day symbolism, and so is *Erwartung*. *Tristan und Isolde* ends with a love-death, and so does *Erwartung*: when the woman in the Schoenberg opera finds her dead lover, she sings a long passage that is nothing less than a *Liebestod*. Through Schoenberg's new and unconventional language, something very traditional can be experienced.

Just as *Erwartung* looks back to Wagner, so it also looks forward to *Pierrot Lunaire*, which many consider to be Schoenberg's most significant score.

Pierrot Lunaire is composed for speaker (it was commissioned by an actress rather than a singer), flute (doubling on piccolo), clarinet (doubling on bass clarinet), violin (doubling on viola), cello, and piano. For the twenty-one songs of *Pierrot Lunaire* Schoenberg used a poem by Albert Giraud in a German translation by Otto Erich Hartleben. The poem is a parallel to T. S. Eliot's later *Waste Land* and is a series about the decadence of modern man. Schoenberg's settings were unprecedented for their daring and novelty, and for the first time the words *Sprechstimme* (literally, "speak voice") and *Sprechgesang* (literally, "speak song") entered the language. The vocal line calls for a heightened kind of song-speech—*Sprechgesang*—in which speech patterns rise and fall. It is not singing, nor is it speaking, but it is something in between, with the voice at times swooping up and sliding down in sounds of approximate pitch (and, here and there, also ascending to an unearthly high falsetto sound). Some of the music in *Pierrot Lunaire* is based on traditional forms—passacaglia, canons, and the like. But where the forms may be classically precise, the harmonic and melodic idiom break all the known rules. Musicians immediately realized that here was a new world of sound. But it is more than that. *Pierrot Lunaire* is a magical and evocative score that inhabits a ghostly, miniature, imagery-ridden world full of blood symbolism. Today it is recognized as being as seminal a work as *Le Sacre du Printemps*, Joyce's *Ulysses*, Picasso's *Les Demoiselles d'Avignon*, and the reasoning that led to $E = mc^2$. In particular, the vocal style of *Pierrot Lunaire* exerted an overwhelming influence on many composers of the post-World War II period.

In his book, *Style and Idea*, Schoenberg traced his development from the composer of *Verklärte Nacht* through *Pierrot Lunaire* and dodecaphony. One important passage deals with the concepts in Schoenberg's mind that led to *Pierrot*:

In the last hundred years the concept of harmony has changed tremendously through the development of chromaticism. The idea that one basic tone, the root, dominated the construction of chords and regulated their succession—the concept of *tonality*—had to develop first into the concept of *extended tonality*. Very soon it became doubtful whether such a root still remained the center to which every harmony and harmonic succession must be referred. Furthermore it became doubtful whether a tonic appearing at the beginning, or at the end, or at any other point really had a constructive meaning. Richard Wagner's harmony had promoted a change in the logic and constructive power of harmony. One of its consequences was the so-called *impressionistic* use of harmonies, especially practiced by Debussy. His harmonies, without constructive meaning, often served the coloristic purpose of expressing moods and pictures. Moods and pictures, though extra-musical, thus became constructive elements, incorporated in the musical functions; they produced a sort of emotional comprehensibility in practice, if not in theory. This alone would perhaps not have caused a radical change in compositional technique. However, such a change became necessary when there occurred simultaneously a development that ended in what I call the *emancipation of the dissonance*.

The term, "emancipation of the dissonance," Schoenberg explains, refers to the comprehensibility of dissonance, "which is considered equivalent to the consonance's comprehensibility. A style based on this premise treats dissonances like consonances and renounces a tonal center. By avoiding the establishment of a key, modulation is excluded, since modulation means leaving an established tonality and establishing *another* tonality." It was in 1908, says Schoenberg, that the first compositions in this style were written by him and, soon afterward, by Webern and Berg.

Needless to say, this kind of music encountered tremendous hostility, and it still does. Even in the 1960's, during the height of the Schoenberg and Webern craze among composers, their music seldom was performed. In the first decades of the century, nearly every Schoenberg premiere was accompanied by a *scandale*. Not that there were many premieres. The music was strange, very difficult, not liked by audiences, and therefore most musicians and conductors avoided it. Schoenberg was confident that his music would become the normal language. "In ten years," he wrote in 1910, "every talented composer will be writing this way, regardless of whether he has learned it directly from me or only from my works." Later he was not so confident. "Today," he wrote in 1924, "I realize that I cannot be understood, and I am content to make do with respect." Several years before his death he was resigned to his fate. In a letter written in 1947 he said that "I am quite conscious of the fact that a full understanding of my works cannot be expected before some decades. The minds of the musicians, and of the audiences, have to mature ere they can comprehend my music. I know this, I have personally renounced an early success, and I know that—success or not—it is my historic duty to write what my destiny orders me to write."

Like any composer, Schoenberg eagerly sought performances. Unlike most composers, he insisted that performances be true to the music—that is, thoroughly prepared—or else no performances would be allowed. "I will not be bullied by anyone," he wrote to his publisher in 1913, after the composer-conductor Franz Schreker threatened to cancel a performance. "I am not *so* eager for success. In particular: what I am interested in is not *a* performance, only a good performance. . . . Please do not hesitate to cancel the performance." He would not permit his operas, *Erwartung* or *Die glückliche Hand*, to be given once and then dropped. "I would let a theater have them only for inclusion in the repertory." Irritated and insulted because the Vienna Philharmonic had never played his music, he notified Wilhelm Furt-wängler that "I would not let a new work have its first performance in Vienna. The fact is I am the only composer of any reputation at all whom the Philharmonic has not yet performed. And it may as well rest at that!" In the United States he learned that Otto Klemperer had expressed a dislike for his music, that Klemperer had said it was "alien" to him. When Klemperer got in touch with Schoenberg about conducting a work, he received a letter bitterly accusing him of the alleged statement. "I then consider that you should cease to conduct my works. For what can a performance be like if the music has become alien to you?" In 1922 Edgard Varèse decided to perform *Pierrot Lunaire* and received a stiff letter from Schoenberg. Among other things, there was this paragraph:

What offends me equally, however, is that without asking me whether you *can and may* do so, you simply set a definitive date for my *Pierrot Lunaire*. Have you already got a suitable speaker; a violinist, a pianist, a conductor, etc.? How many rehearsals do you mean to hold, etc., etc. In Vienna, with everyone starving and shivering, something like 100 rehears-als were held and an impeccable ensemble achieved with my collabora-tion. But you people simply fix a date and think that's all there is to it! Have you any inkling of the difficulties, of the style, of the declamation, of the tempi, of the dynamics, and all that? And you expect me to asso-ciate myself with it? No, I'm not *smart* enough for that. If you want to have anything to do with me, you must set about it quite differently. What I want to know is: 1. How many rehearsals? 2. Who is in charge of the rehearsals? 3. Who does the *Sprechstimme*? 4. Who are the players? If all this is to my satisfaction, I shall give my blessing. But for the rest I am, of course, powerless and you can do as you like. But then kindly re-frain from asking me about it. I regret not being able to say anything more obliging. But I must reject this exclusively business approach. I sin-cerely hope that another time I may have occasion to be more cordial.

During World War I, Schoenberg was in service for two spells, between 1915 and 1917. He composed very little, not publishing again until 1923. Of his two famous pupils, Berg was in the army for three years, and Webern for a short time. The big, handsome Berg, healthy looking but never a well man, was discharged because of his asthma. Webern was released because of bad eyesight. Berg, Webern, and Schoenberg remained in constant touch during the war years and afterward, when Schoenberg moved to Berlin, al-ways corresponding, describing, and analyzing one anothers' latest composi-tions. Berg was the most romantic of the three, the one most suggestive of

Wagner, Mahler, and postromanticism. Like Schoenberg, Berg had his roots in the German tradition and was constantly working in old forms. He did not compose much. In 1912 came the *Altenberg* songs, in 1914 the Three Orchestral Pieces, and in 1914 he started work on *Wozzeck,* adapting the Georg Büchner play to his purposes. He finished the libretto in 1917, the score in 1922. It was characteristic that Berg erect his opera on classical and preclassical forms. This atonal, expressionistic opera was described by its composer as a sonata, the first act being an exposition, the second a development, and the third a form of recapitulation. Act I, in five scenes, contains a suite, rhapsody, military march, lullaby, passacaglia, and rondo. The five scenes of Act II are in effect five movements of a symphony: sonata movement, fantasy and fugue, largo, scherzo, and rondo (with an introduction). Act III, also in five scenes, is a series of inventions: on a theme, on a tone, on a rhythm, on a chord, on a tonality.

Few are conscious of this construction when listening to *Wozzeck*. It had its premiere in 1925 at the Berlin State Opera, Erich Kleiber conducting, after an unprecedented series of rehearsals. It cannot be said that the opera was liked, but it created such a furor that other European opera houses hastened to produce it. Critics attacked it as degenerate art and chaos in music; but *Wozzeck* also had its admirers and defenders. So powerful and original an opera naturally had some perceptive listeners on its side. The more sensitive listeners decided that there was method in Berg's madness. Max Marschalk, in the *Vossiche Zeitung*, pointed out that in *Wozzeck* dissonance had been elevated to a very principle; that "forms resolve into continuity, colors coalesce, and there results something which, by its very oscillation and nebulous atmosphere, is probably exactly the music which justifies the transformation of *Wozzeck* into an opera." Adolf Weissman in *Die Musik* wrote about the spiritual values of the opera and its "instinctive perception."

Other critics felt uneasy. "The listener attains an hypnotic state in which he believes the walls of the theater are about to crash down on him," wrote Erich Steinhardt in *Der Auftakt*. And, of course, there were the old-line critics who frothed at the mouth. Paul Zschorlich of the *Deutsche Zeitung* was one: "As I was leaving the State Opera, I had the sensation of having been not in a public theater but in an insane asylum. On the stage, in the orchestra, in the stalls—plain madmen. . . . We deal here, from a musical viewpoint, with a capital offence." Naturally the Soviet critics saw in *Wozzeck* the decline of the West, and expressed their opinions in the approved ideological language: "Berg's opera . . . reveals the helplessness of the Western-European petty-bourgeois intellegentsia before oncoming fascistization, and demonstrates the crisis not only in the individual consciousness of the Western-European bourgeois composer, but in Western-European musical culture in general" (Boris Asafiev, in *Sovietskaya Musica*).

Berg in 1928 explained what he was trying to do, in language that goes back to Gluck and Wagner:

> I never entertained the idea of reforming the artistic structure of the opera with *Wozzeck*. . . . I wanted to compose good music, to develop musically the contents of Büchner's immortal drama, to translate his poetic language into music; but other than that, when I decided to write an opera, my only intentions, including the technique of composition, were to give the theater what belongs to the theater. In other words, the music was to be formed as consciously to fulfill its duty of serving the action at every moment. Even more, the music should be prepared to furnish whatever action needed to be transformed into reality on the stage. . . .
>
> That these purposes should be accomplished by use of musical forms more or less ancient (considered by critics as one of the most important of my ostensible reforms of the opera) was a natural consequence. For the libretto, it was necessary to make a selection from twenty-six loosely constructed, sometimes fragmentary, scenes by Büchner. Repetitions that did not lend themselves to musical variations had to be avoided. Finally the scenes had to be brought together, arranged and grouped in acts. The problem therefore became, utterly apart from my will, more musical than literary, one to be solved by the laws of musical structure rather than by the rules of dramaturgy. . . .
>
> No matter how cognizant any particular individual may be of the musical forms contained in the framework of this opera, of the precision and logic with which everything is worked out, and the skill manifested in every detail, from the moment the curtain parts until it closes for the last time, there must be nobody in the audience who pays any attention to the various fugues, inventions, suites, sonata movements, variations and passacaglias—nobody who heeds anything but the idea of this opera, which by far transcends the personal destiny of *Wozzeck*. This I believe to be my achievement.

Webern, meanwhile, was exploring a different kind of world—the world of the microcosm instead of the macrocosm; a world of delicate, ephemeral, pointillistic sounds, silences, new pitch relationships, constant aphoristic distillation, daintily shimmering orchestration. In his Passacaglia for Orchestra, in the *Stefan George* songs, in the Five Movements for String Quartet and Six Pieces for Orchestra, all composed between 1908 and 1909, he worked with tiny fragments, mottos, and cells rather than themes. He worked out a new method of scoring, in which almost every note of a phrase was given to a different instrument, with consequently changing colors. Webern got the idea from Schoenberg, who had talked about "a melody of tone colors," or *Klangfarbenmelodie*. Webern's music continued to become more and more compact and brief. With his song cycles of 1914–17 he all but (in the estimation of Pierre Boulez) anticipated the serial system with his "assimilation of rigid counterpoint to fundamental serial forms." To Boulez, Webern here created a new dimension: sound-space. "The genius of Webern appears unprecedented, both for the radicalism of his points of view and for the novelty of his sensibility."

In 1923 Schoenberg again started composing, and gave to the world a new way of musical organization. "I called this procedure 'Method of Composing with Twelve Tones Which are Related Only with One Another.'" A composer named Josef Matthias Hauer had been evolving a comparable system, but it was Schoenberg's that took hold. Briefly, Schoenberg's twelve-tone (or dodecaphonic) method involved basing a composition on a "series" made up from the twelve notes of the chromatic scale, arranged in such a way that no note was repeated within the basic set, or tone-row, or series (hence the term "serial composition"). Thus no single note was more important than any other note. This basic set, the tone-row, functioning in the manner of a theme or motive, could be manipulated in three ways. It could be played upside down (inversion), backwards (retrograde), and backwards upside down (retrograde inversion). All these are mirror forms, and are not new. Bach had used them in the *Kunst der Fuge* and elsewhere. What Schoenberg was looking for—as, indeed, what Bach was looking for—was a way to achieve complete unity within a piece of music. Schoenberg felt that his new method "corresponds to the principle of *the absolute and unitary perception of musical space.*" But however the music was composed, whatever its system, Schoenberg insisted that listeners and musicians should forget about the system and judge the music as music, "I can't say it often enough: my works are twelve-tone *compositions,* not *twelve-tone* compositions."

This new music was, basically, horizontal (contrapuntal) as against the vertical (harmonic) writing of the romantics. Its melodic line was disjunct, with wide leaps. The tone-row was arranged so that there was no feeling of triadic (traditional) harmony, (Berg was to break this rule.) Instruments and the voice were used in unusual registers. Instead of recognizable themes, there were cells derived from the tone-row. The last movement of Schoenberg's Piano Pieces (Op. 23) and sections of the Serenade, both published in 1923, contained twelve-tone elements; and the Piano Suite (Op. 25), also published in 1923, was a twelve-tone work throughout. (British writers refer to "twelve-note" rather than "twelve-tone" music. Schoenberg himself, in letters and essays written in English, and in conversation, used the term "twelve-*tone.*" The difficulty comes with the German word *Ton,* which can be translated as "tone" or "note.")

Schoenberg's two disciples enthusiastically adopted the new technique. Berg never entirely divorced himself from postromanticism, and later serial purists have called his work a hybrid, because even within the serial technique it often sounds tonal. Berg set to work on the *Lyric Suite* for string quartet, and on the Chamber Concerto, both of which incorporate serial principles. He then started a serial opera, *Lulu;* and his last work, the Violin Concerto, was also serial. For *Lulu,* Berg brought together two dramas by Frank Wedekind—*Erdgeist* and *Die Büchse der Pandora.* Lulu is an embodiment of Lilith: an amoral temptress who ruins all she touches; and yet she has a curious innocence because she is unconscious of her evil. She is the serpent in the menagerie of life. Berg derived the entire opera from the initial row of twelve tones, but as customary with him, the note to note relationships often have a feeling approaching tonality. He never finished the last act, though many sketches and a short score are in existence. Berg scholars claim that Act III of *Lulu* could easily be completed in a manner entirely faithful to the composer's intentions, but permission to do so has not been granted by the Berg estate.

Webern during the 1920's kept refining his style into what Boulez calls "a new manner of musical *being.*" Webern, he says, "was the first to explore the possibilities of a dialectic of sound and silence," with silences as integral parts of the rhythmic cells. Webern also evolved a new structure of pitches, rethinking "the very idea of polyphonic music on the basis of the principles of serial writing" (Boulez). Where Schoenberg and Berg never could discard romanticism, Webern was the one who worked in pure tonal organization, rejecting completely the romantic rhetoric. It could be said that there was no rhetoric at all. So condensed was the writing that a piece might last only a few minutes, and every once in a while under a minute. Forms so highly concentrated cannot stand lengthy developments. Boulez, Webern's most articulate spokesman, points out that Webern's adoption of serial technique helped unify his vocabulary but did not fundamentally alter his musical thinking: his style had been revolutionary before dodecaphonism and remained revolutionary after it. Boulez claims that in Webern's mature works, between 1927 and 1934—those works would include the String Trio, the Symphony, and the Concerto for Nine Instruments—"each sound becomes a phenomenon in itself, linked to the others . . . . He aerates his positionings in time and space as well as in their instrumental context." Instrumentation itself takes on a structural function. Boulez summarizes Webern's contributions as an art of unprecedented refinement and concentration of musical materials, in which relationships are so rigorously organized that melody, harmony, and even rhythm become indissoluble from each other. From there it was only a short step to the totally organized music of Olivier Messiaen, Milton Babbitt, and Boulez himself, which came into being shortly after World War II. In totally organized music, even dynamics, tone colors, and silences are serially handled.

The transition from serial music to totally organized music might have come earlier had not the Nazis and seven years of war intervened. With Hitler's rise to power, the music of the Second Viennese School—as the Schoenberg-Berg-Webern group came to be known—was banned as cultural Bolshevism. Berg died in 1935, before the full impact of the Nazi horror became apparent. Webern was forced to live in obscurity, doing editorial work for Universal Edition. He was accidentally shot and killed in Mittersill during the night of September 14, 1945, by an American soldier who was working on a black market case in which Webern's son-in-law was involved. Schoenberg, who was a Jew, had to flee from Berlin in 1933. He had been there since 1926, teaching at the Prussian State Academy of the Arts. He went to France and then to the United States, where in 1933 he settled in Boston as a teacher in the Malkin Conservatory. Because of ill health, he went to Los Angeles a year later, where he taught at the University of California in Los Angeles and gave private lessons. He became an American citizen in 1941 and changed his name from Schönberg to Schoenberg. "My name is to be spelled with 'oe.' I changed it when I came to America because few printers have the 'ö' type, and I wanted to avoid the form 'Schonberg.' " In 1944, at the age of seventy, he had to retire from the University, but his pension— $38 a month—was so small, because he had been a faculty member for only eight years, that he was forced to continue private teaching. During the seventeen years he lived in California he was so busy as a teacher that he had relatively little time for composition, though he did finish the Violin Concerto, the String Quartet No. 4, the Theme and Variations for band, the Piano Concerto, and *A Survivor from Warsaw* for speaker, men's chorus, and orchestra. He also worked on his opera *Moses und Aron*, which he had started in 1927. Two acts had been completed by 1932. Schoenberg was anxious to complete *Moses und Aron*, but he never did. He died in Los Angeles on July 13, 1951.

There is a good deal of Schoenberg himself in *Moses und Aron*. At the end of his life he was a bitter man, acutely conscious of his worth and resentful of his neglect: a man of the highest ideals who tried to give the world a message that most found unpalatable or incomprehensible. Small wonder that he should have identified with Moses. Schoenberg had left his religion, but as anti-Semitism mounted in Germany, he returned to it, proudly proclaiming his Jewishness. There are two fascinating and revealing letters he wrote to Kandinsky in 1923. Kandinsky had been one of the founders of the *Blaue Reiter*, a group of avant-garde artists (Franz Marc used to paint blue horses, hence the name, "Blue Riders") with whom Schoenberg had been associated, and he and Kandinsky were close friends. After World War I, Kandinsky entered the Bauhaus group, and there were reports that some of the Bauhaus members were anti-Semitic. But they rationalized their beliefs, and some of their best friends were Jews. On April 20, 1923, Schoenberg wrote an anguished letter to Kandinsky: "I have at last learned the lesson that has been forced on me during the years, and I shall not ever forget it. It is that I am not a German, not a European, indeed perhaps scarcely a human being (at least, the Europeans prefer the worst of their race to me), but I am Jew. . . . I have heard that even a Kandinsky sees only evil in the actions of Jews and in their evil actions only Jewishness, and at this point I give up the hope of reaching any understanding. . . . I should like the Kandinsky I knew in the past and the Kandinsky of today each to take his fair share of my cordial and respectful greetings." Kandinsky answered, explaining that Schoenberg was not representative of most Jews. Schoenberg exploded:

Dear Kandinsky:
  I address you so because you wrote that you were deeply moved by my letter. That was what I hoped of Kandinsky, although I have not yet said a hundredth part of what a Kandinsky's imagination must conjure up before his mind's eye if he is to be my Kandinsky. Because I have not yet said that for instance when I walk along the street and each person looks at me to see whether I'm a Jew or a Christian, I can't very well tell each of them that I'm the one that Kandinsky and some others make an exception of, although of course that man Hitler is not of their opinion.
  . . .

This was in 1923, and *Moses und Aron* was still to come. Schoenberg, after finishing the second act in 1932, never could figure out how to end the opera. He ran into the problem of how to reconcile what he called "some almost incomprehensible contradictions in the Bible." In any event, Schoenberg was not trying to compose a Biblical opera à la *Samson et Dalila*. With that kind of opera, all kinds of liberties can be taken with the text. In an opera that seeks a philosophical truth, as does *Moses und Aron,* there has to be some kind of support for the conclusions. And while Schoenberg became strongly religious after World War I ("In these years religion has been my only support—I confess that here for the first time"), his was a religion based on ethical teaching, not external conformity. What seemed to interest Schoenberg particularly about Moses was a little passage in the Bible where Moses says to the Lord: "I am not eloquent, neither heretofore, nor since Thou has spoken unto thy servant, but I am slow of speech, and of a slow tongue." Schoenberg in his libretto set up a dualism between Moses and his brother Aaron. Moses sees and understands the God of the Jews, but cannot convey his vision. Aaron, a man of less vision and insight, is a politician-demagogue who can act as Moses's tongue and sway his people. But he can act only as long as Moses is at his side to prompt him.

269

Thus there are God and Moses on one side, Aaron and the people (mob?) on the other. A conflict ensues. Moses understands the Oneness of God. But such understanding is given to few men. Perhaps it is an understanding at which the masses will never arrive. Even Aaron, so close to Moses, is ready not only to compromise but to go back to idol worship when the spiritual leader is not beside him. Aaron realizes that the masses have "naught but their feeling." To Moses this is anathema. "My love is for the idea. I live only for it." Aaron points out that the tablets containing the Ten Commandments are also images, "just part of the whole idea." Then, says Moses. "I shall smash to pieces both these tablets, and I shall also ask Him to withdraw the task given me." At the end of the second act, Moses falls to the ground in despair. It is not that he doubts the existence of the One God. It is that he despairs of ever being able to explain the Idea to the people. "Oh word, thou word that I lack." The allegory is clear enough. Will Moses-Schoenberg ever find the Word?

Schoenberg did try to finish the opera, rewriting the last act four times. "Here," he wrote to an expert on the Bible, "I have so far encountered great difficulties because of some almost incomprehensible contradictions in the Bible. For even if there are comparatively few points on which I strictly adhere to the Bible, still, it is precisely here that it is difficult to get over the divergence between 'and thou shalt smite the rock' and 'speak ye unto the rock.' You have worked on this material for so long: can you perhaps tell me where I could look up something on this question? Up to now I have been trying to find a solution for myself. . . . It does go on haunting me."

But Schoenberg never did find the solution, and thus *Moses und Aron* remains a torso. It also remains, however, one of the most personal operas ever written; and, unfortunately, so static, wordy, and unoperatic an opera that it probably never will command much of an audience. Through it is seen the figure of Moses-Schoenberg pleading mutely for the people to follow him, never beset by doubts concerning the Message he was carrying, but wondering if the Message would ever be accepted. Could spiritual principle ever triumph over matter and the Golden Calf? Schoenberg himself never doubted the eventual triumph of principle. And he died just as his vision was beginning to come true for him, just at the moment when his Message was beginning to dominate the thoughts of every avant-garde composer in the world. If the period from 1830 to 1860 was the Early Romantic Period, if the latter half of the century was the Age of Wagner, if the period from 1915 to 1945 was the Age of Stravinsky, then the decades from 1950 were the period of Schoenberg and his school; and the final returns are not yet in.

≫ 20 ≪

Postlude

Many things happened to music after World War II, but they are not within the scope of this book. It will take a generation or more to sort out the new theories, to separate the real from the ephemeral. The period after World War II was a period of unrest; and music, like the other arts, reflected that unrest. Old values no longer applied, and on all sides there was a search for style. Some composers found it in rigid control over all aspects of music. Some found it in precisely the opposite manner, by relaxing all controls. Some looked toward the electronic medium. A new kind of music developed, and also a new terminology. There was much talk of post-Webernism, post serialism, *musique concrète,* open forms, closed forms, Dada, total organization, indeterminacy, randomness, stochastic music, environmental music, total theater, aleatory, improvisation, rock. So radical were some of the changes, so unusual the new sounds, that a new definition was needed for music. Stravinsky suggested "meta-music." Whatever it was, a good deal of it stemmed from the theories of Schoenberg and Webern, and a good deal of it also resulted from technological advances in electronics. Machines were developed by means of which composers could synthesize their own sounds—dispensing altogether, if they so wanted, with the performer.

But there came about a schism between the avant-garde composer and the public. With all the activity that went on in the international avant-garde, with all the publicity that the new music received, with all the many recordings available, it remained a frightening fact that hardly any music in the new idiom was able to establish itself in the permanent repertory of symphony orchestras, opera houses, and concert halls of any country in the world. Explanations were suggested for the breakdown in communication. Perhaps the conductor Ernest Ansermet was correct in the conclusions he drew in his book *Les fondements de la musique dans la conscience humaine*

(1961); perhaps the new music was so alien to the normal processes of thought and aural experience that it was based on a faulty aesthetic. Or perhaps, on the other hand, there was a great composer working under everybody's nose, with a message too subtle for his contemporaries. Perhaps music was developing into a collective effort, in which composer, sound engineer, physicist, film expert, and theater man pooled talents. Perhaps music was passing through a period of agonized experimentation, waiting for the new Berlioz or Wagner to fuse everything into an expression of power and personality that would also mean something to the public. But whatever the complex of reasons, it seemed apparent twenty-five years after the end of World War II that there was a hiatus in the mighty line of powerful, individualistic composers that extended from Johann Sebastian Bach through Igor Stravinsky and Arnold Schoenberg.

A Selected Bibliography
of Books in English

1

Darlington, W. A.   *The World of Gilbert and Sullivan* (New York, 1950)
Fitz-Gerald, S. J. Adair   *The Story of the Savoy Opera* (New York, 1925)
Gilbert and Sullivan   *Complete Plays* (Modern Library, New York, n.d.)
Goldberg, Isaac   *The Story of Gilbert and Sullivan* (London, 1928)
Hughes, Gervaise   *The Music of Gilbert and Sullivan* (New York, 1960)
Kracauer, S.   *Offenbach and the Paris of His Time* (London, 1937)
Pastene, Jerome   *Three-Quarter Time* (New York, 1951)
Sitwell, Sacheverell   *La Vie Parisienne: A Tribute to Offenbach* (London, 1937)

2

Bovet, M. A. de   *Charles Gounod* (London, 1891)
Cooper, Martin   *French Music* (London, 1951)
                 Georges Bizet (London, 1938)
Curtiss, Minna   *Bizet and His World* (New York, 1958)
Finck, Henry T.   *Massenet and His Operas* (New York, 1910)
Glinka, Mikhail   *Memoirs*, trans. R. B. Mudge (Norman, Oklahoma, 1963)
Gounod, Charles   *Autobiography* (London, 1875)
Hewes, Arthur   *Saint-Saëns* (London, 1921)
Harding, James   *Saint-Saëns and His Circle* (London, 1965)
Saint-Saëns, Camille   *Musical Memories* (London, 1921)
                      Outspoken Essays on Music (New York, 1922)

3

Calvocoressi, M. D.   *Modest Mussorgsky: His Life and Works* (London, 1956)
Calvocoressi, M. D., and Abraham, Gerald   *Masters of Russian Music* (New York, 1936)
Diehl, A. M.   *Musical Memories* (London, 1897)

Garden, Edward *Balakirev* (New York, 1967)

Leyda, Jay, and Bertensson, Sergei *The Mussorgsky Reader* (New York, 1947)

Rimsky-Korsakov, Nikolai *My Musical Life* (New York, 1923)

Rubinstein, Anton *Autobiography* (London, 1890)

Seroff, Victor *The Mighty Five* (New York, 1948)

4

Abraham, Gerald (ed.) *The Music of Tchaikovsky* (New York, 1946)

Bowen, Catherine Drinker, and Meck, Barbara von *Beloved Friend: The Story of Tchaikovsky and Nadejda von Meck* (New York, 1946)

Lakond, Wladimir (trans. and ed.) *The Diaries of Tchaikovsky* (New York, 1945)

Newmarch, Rosa *The Life and Letters of Peter Ilich Tchaikovsky* (London, 1906)

5

Abraham, Gerald (ed.): *Grieg: A Symposium* (London, 1948)

The Music of Sibelius (New York, 1947)

Clapham, John *Antonin Dvořák* (New York, 1966)

Finck, Henry T. *Grieg and His Music* (New York, 1929)

Fischl, Viktor (ed.) *Antonin Dvořák: His Achievement* (London, 1942)

Gray, Cecil *Sibelius* (London, 1931)

Johnson, Harold E. *Jean Sibelius* (New York, 1959)

Robertson, Alex *Dvořák* (London, 1945)

Simpson, Robert *Carl Nielsen: Symphonist* (London, 1952)

Stefan, Paul *Anton Dvořák* (New York, 1941)

Trend, J. B. *Manuel de Falla and Spanish Music* (New York, 1929)

Vogel, Jaroslav *Leos Janáček* (London, 1962)

6

Barricelli, Jean-Pierre, and Weinstein, Leo *Ernest Chausson* (Norman, Oklahoma, 1955)

Cooper, Martin *French Music* (London, 1951)

Demuth, Norman *César Franck* (New York, 1949)

Indy, Vincent d' *César Franck* (London, 1910)

Koechlin, Charles *Gabriel Fauré* (London, n.d.)

Meyers, Rollo *Emmanuel Chabrier and His Circle* (London, 1969)

Northcote, Sydney *The Songs of Henri Duparc* (New York, 1950)

Suckling, Norman *Fauré* (New York, 1951)

Vallas, Léon *César Franck* (New York, 1951)

7

Carner, Mosco *Puccini: A Critical Biography* (New York, 1959)

Fiorentino, D. del *Immortal Bohemian: An Intimate Memoir of Giacomo Puccini* (London, 1952)

Hopkinson, Cecil *A Bibliography of the Works of Giacomo Puccini* (New York, 1968)

Marek, George R. *Puccini* (New York, 1951)

Seligman, Vincent *Puccini Among Friends* (New York, 1938)

Specht, Richard   *Giacomo Puccini* (London, 1933)

8

Hammelmann, Hans, and Osers, Ewald (trans.)   *A Working Friendship: The Correspondence Between Richard Strauss and Hugo von Hofmannsthal* (New York, 1961)

Mann, William   *Richard Strauss: A Critical Study of the Operas* (New York, 1966)

Mar, Norman del   *Richard Strauss*. 2 vols. (New York, 1962 and 1969)

Marek, George   *Richard Strauss: The Life of a Non-Hero* (New York, 1967)

Strauss, Richard   *Recollections and Reflections* (London, 1953)

9

Engel, Gabriel   *The Life of Anton Bruckner* (New York, 1931)
 The Symphonies of Anton Bruckner (Iowa City, 1955)

Graf, Max   *Legend of a Musical City* (New York, 1945)

Mahler, Alma   *Gustav Mahler: Memories and Letters* (New York, 1946)

Mitchell, Donald   *Gustav Mahler: The Early Years* (London, 1958)

Newlin, Dika   *Bruckner, Mahler, Schoenberg* (New York, 1947)

Reik, Theodor   *The Haunting Melody* (New York, 1953)

Schoenberg, Arnold   *Style and Idea* (New York, 1950). See pp. 7–36 for essay on Mahler.

Walter, Bruno   *Gustav Mahler* (New York, 1941)

10

Boulez, Pierre   *Notes of an Apprenticeship* (New York, 1968)

Cortot, Alfred   *The Piano Music of Debussy* (London, 1922)

Debussy, Claude   *Monsieur Croche* (New York, 1948)

Lockspeiser, Edward   *Debussy* (New York, 1949)
 Debussy: His Life and Mind. 2 vols. (New York, 1962 and 1965)

Meyers, Rollo H.   *Erik Satie* (London, 1948)

Seroff, Victor   *Debussy: Musician of France* (New York, 1956)

Vallas, Léon   *The Theories of Claude Debussy* (London, 1929)

11

Demuth, Norman   *Ravel* (New York, 1962)

Hell, Henri   *Francis Poulenc* (New York, 1959)

Honegger, Arthur   *I Am a Composer* (New York, 1966)

Lockspeiser, Edward   *Debussy: His Life and Mind*. 2 vols. (New York, 1962 and 1965). See Vol. II, pp. 36ff., for study of Debussy and Ravel.

Myers, Rollo H.   *Ravel: His Life and Works* (London, 1960)

Seroff, Victor   *Maurice Ravel* (New York, 1953)

12

Boulez, Pierre   *Notes of an Apprenticeship* (New York, 1968)

Duke, Vernon   *Listen Here!* (New York, 1963). See pp. 149–189 for essay on Stravinsky.

Lambert, Constant   *Music Ho! A Study of Music in Decline* (London, 1934)
Lang, Paul Henry (ed.)   *Stravinsky: A New Appraisal of His Work* (New York, 1963)
Lederman, Minna (ed.)   *Stravinsky in the Theatre* (New York, 1949)
Lifar, Serge   *Serge Diaghilev: An Intimate Biography* (New York, 1940)
Stravinsky, Igor   *Autobiography* (New York, 1936)
                    Poetics of Music (New York, 1956)
Stravinsky, Igor, and Craft, Robert   *Conversations With Igor Stravinsky* (New York, 1959)
Dialogues and a Diary (New York, 1963)
Expositions and Developments (New York, 1962)
Memories and Commentaries (New York, 1960)
Themes and Episodes (New York, 1966)
Retrospectives and Conclusions (New York, 1969)
White, Eric Walter   *Stravinsky: The Composer and His Works* (Los Angeles, 1966)

13

Beecham, Thomas   *Frederick Delius* (New York, 1960)
Colles, H. C.   *Essays and Lectures* (London, 1945)
Day, James   *Vaughan Williams* (New York, 1961)
Fenby, Eric   *Delius as I Knew Him* (London, 1936)
Foss, Hubert   *Ralph Vaughan Williams* (New York, 1950)
Holst, Imogen   *The Music of Gustav Holst* (London, 1951)
Howes, Frank   *The Music of Ralph Vaughan Williams* (London, 1954)
Kennedy, Michael   *Portrait of Elgar* (New York, 1968)
                    The Works of Ralph Vaughan Williams (New York, 1964)
Schwartz, Elliott   *The Symphonies of Ralph Vaughan Williams* (Amherst, Massachusetts, 1964)
Vaughan Williams, Ralph   *National Music* (New York, 1964)
Vaughan Williams, Ursula   *R.V.W.* (New York, 1964)
Walker, Ernest   *A History of Music in England* (London, 1952)

14

Abraham, Gerald, and Calvocoressi, M. D.   *Masters of Russian Music* (New York, 1936)
Bertensson, Sergei, and Leyda, Jay   *Sergei Rachmaninoff* (New York, 1956)
Bowers, Faubion   *Scriabin: A Biography of the Russian Composer.* 2 vols. (Palo Alto, California, 1969)
Culshaw, John   *Rachmaninov: The Man and His Music* (New York, 1950)
Seroff, Victor   *Rachmaninoff* (New York, 1950)

15

Duke, Vernon   *Passport to Paris* (Boston, 1955)
Hanson, Lawrence and Elizabeth   *Prokofiev: A Biography in Three Movements* (New York, 1964)

Martynev, Ivan   *Shostakovich* (New York, 1947)

Nabokov, Nicolas   *Old Friends and New Music* (Boston, 1951)

Nestyev, Israel V.   *Prokofiev* (Palo Alto, California, 1960)

Slonimsky, Nicolas   *Music Since 1900* (New York, 1949). See pp. 684–712 for documentation of 1948 Zhdanov Decree.

16

Austin, William W.   *Music in the 20th Century from Debussy Through Stravinsky* (New York, 1966). See pp. 396–416 for essay on Hindemith.

Busoni, Ferruccio   *The Essence of Music* (New York, 1957)

  A Sketch of a New Esthetic of Music, in *Three Classics in the Aesthetic of Music* (New York, n.d.)

Busoni, Ferruccio   *Letters to His Wife* (London, 1938)

Dent, Edward J.   *Ferruccio Busoni: A Biography* (London, 1933)

Hindemith, Paul   *A Composer's World* (New York, 1961)

17

Broder, Nathan   *Samuel Barber* (New York, 1954)

Chase, Gilbert   *America's Music* (New York, 1966)

Copland, Aaron   *Copland on Music* (New York, 1963)

  The New Music (New York, 1968)

Cowell, Henry (ed.)   *American Composers on American Music* (Stanford, California, 1933)

Cowell, Henry and Sidney   *Charles Ives and His Music* (New York, 1955)

Gilman, Lawrence   *Edward MacDowell: A Study* (New York, 1909)

Gottschalk, Louis Moreau   *Notes of a Pianist* (New York, 1964)

Hoffman, Richard   *Some Musical Recollections of Fifty Years* (London, 1910)

Howard, John Tasker   *Our American Music* (New York, 1954)

Ives, Charles   *Essays Before a Sonata and Other Writings* (New York, 1962)

Lang, Paul Henry (ed.)   *One Hundred Years of Music in America* (New York, 1961)

Loggins, Vernon   *Where the Word Ends: The Life of Louis Moreau Gottschalk* (Baton Rouge, Louisiana, 1958)

Lowens, Irving   *Music and Musicians in Early America* (New York, 1954)

MacDowell, Edward   *Critical and Historical Essays* (Boston, 1912)

Mathews, W. S. B.   *A Hundred Years of Music in America* (Chicago, 1889)

Reis, Claire R.   *Composers, Conductors and Critics* (New York, 1955)

Smith, Julia   *Aaron Copland* (New York, 1955)

Thomson, Virgil   *Virgil Thomson* (New York, 1966)

18

Austin, William W.   *Music in the 20th Century from Bach Through Stravinsky* (New York, 1966). See pp. 223–242, 319–329.

Fassett, Agatha   *The Naked Face of Genius: Béla Bartók's American Years* (Boston, 1958)

Hodeir, André   *Since Debussy* (New York, 1961). See pp. 83–96.

Stevens, Halsey   *The Life and Music of Béla Bartók* (New York, 1964)

19

Boulez, Pierre *Notes of an Apprenticeship* (New York, 1958)

Leibowitz, René *Schoenberg and His School* (New York, 1949)

Moldenhauer, Hans *The Death of Anton Webern* (New York, 1961)

Newlin, Dika *Bruckner, Mahler, Schoenberg* (New York, 1947)

Perle, George *Serial Composition and Atonality* (Los Angeles, 1963)

Redlich, H. F. *Alban Berg: The Man and His Music* (New York, 1957)

Reich, Willi *Alban Berg* (New York, 1965)

Rufer, Josef *The Works of Arnold Schoenberg* (New York, 1963)

Schoenberg, Arnold *Style and Idea* (New York, 1950)

Stein, Erwin (ed.) *Arnold Schoenberg Letters* (New York, 1965)

Stuckenschmidt, H. H. *Arnold Schoenberg* (New York, 1959)

Wörmer, Karl H. *Schoenberg's 'Moses and Aaron'* (New York, 1963)

20

Cage, John *Silence* (Middletown, Connecticut, 1961)

Hodeir, André *Since Debussy* (New York, 1961)

Lang, Paul Henry (ed.) *Problems of Modern Music* (New York, 1960)

Mitchell, Donald *The Language of Modern Music* (New York, 1963)

Pleasants, Henry *The Agony of Modern Music* (New York, 1955)

Salzman, Eric *Twentieth Century Music: An Introduction* (Englewood Cliffs, New Jersey, 1967)

Yates, Peter *Twentieth Century Music* (New York, 1967)

Index